Reason in Madness

An Existential Approach
to Psychiatric Disorders

Reason in Madness

An Existential Approach to Psychiatric Disorders

by

M. D. Niv, M.D.

Edited by Declan Joyce

EVER Publishing, New York

First printing 1996

ISBN 0-9634433-0-5

LCCN 95-60784

ATTENTION UNIVERSITIES, COLLEGES, CORPORATIONS, AND PROFESSIONAL ORGANIZATIONS: Quantity discounts are available on bulk purchases of this book for educational purposes or fund raising. Special books or book excerpts can also be created to fit specific needs. For information, please contact EVER Publishing, 900 West 190th Street, New York, NY 10040.

To the Glory of the Lord

Acknowledgments

Acknowledgment and gratitude are here extended to:

Marc E. Romano, for editorial assistance
Kenneth R. Kirshbaum, Ph.D. for critical reading of the manuscript
Ada Niculescu, M.D. for criticism
Nava Niv-Vogel, M.S.W.
Ora Gilligan, for editorial assistance
Gideon Rubin
David Vogel, M. Psych.
Lorna McDonald
Magnus Sternlicht
Nancy Freedom, A.S.I. indexing consultant

To all who have entrusted this author with their confidences

And last but not least, to faithful Prince Clyde from the Kingdom of the Canines for inspirational walks in the park; and to tiny Lucy for her enormous patience.

Preface

Where is the wisdom we have lost in knowledge?
Where is the knowledge we have lost in information?
—T. S. Eliot, *The Rock*

In a series of articles devoted to the "puzzle" of schizophrenia, P. M. Boffey (*New York Times,* March 16, 1986) stated that, "more people are suffering from schizophrenia than ever before." And indeed, in spite of considerable gains in knowledge, advances in the biological and psychological sciences, and an almost exponential increase in the amount of data produced by scientific research, the incidence and prevalence of schizophrenia as well as other psychiatric disorders have shown a consistently rising trend. According to Belgian psychoanalyst Pierre Daco (1973), the number of alienated has doubled in the last century, with France, Sweden, and the United States taking the lead.

An increase in the incidence of schizophrenia, approaching 28 percent for the United States in the year 1985, was predicted by epidemiologist M. Kramer (1976).[*] Dr. Kramer made a point in stressing that the rise in prevalence of mental illnesses exceeds by far the expected rate of population growth for the same time period. Noting an "alarming rate in the prevalence of disabling mental disturbances," M. Kramer (1983) wrote seven years later that the world is in the midst of a pandemic of mental disorders, which he

---

[*] Then with the National Institute for Mental Health.

ix

believes will continue, unless "effective methods are discovered to prevent these disorders from occurring and means found for their application."

According to Epidemiological Catchment Area (ECA) prevalence studies (L. N. Robins et al. 1984), from 29 percent to 38 percent of the populations studied had experienced at least one psychiatric disorder in their lifetime. Ten years later, R. C. Kessler (1994), who headed a survey on the lifetime prevalence of mental disorders, reported that one in two Americans—actually 48 percent—had experienced a mental disorder at some time in their lives, and 14 percent of the sample studied had been affected by three or more psychiatric disorders at the same time, accounting for 90 percent of the most severe cases.

Dr. Kramer's prediction that the prevalence of schizophrenia would increase has, unfortunately, come to pass. Dr. Kramer also wrote: "It cannot be too strongly emphasized that the number of schizophrenia-affected persons will continue to increase until research produces the knowledge needed to prevent its occurrence."

Skeptical of the realization of hopes such as these, Dr. Manfred Bleuler (1979), son of Eugen Bleuler, known for his work in the dark fields of insanity, stressed by repeating, during a plenary session of the 131st Annual Psychiatric Convention that "hereditary predisposition to schizophrenia and schizophrenia itself go on in *highly human, highly spiritual spheres, to which biology has no access as yet*" [emphasis added]. Despite his emphasis on the "highly human, highly spiritual spheres," Dr. Bleuler failed to strike a chord of understanding among the thousands of his audience. Carried away perhaps by scientific adventures promising some solid, numerically validated tangible results, or intoxicated by the newest discoveries in neuroanatomy and psychopharmacology, very few could be persuaded to part from their own projects and statistical tabulations.

The conviction that the problem of mental disturbances can eventually be solved through chemical manipulations and neurosurgical procedures is, indeed, steadily gaining ground, and many millions in research funds are currently invested in an effort to achieve this goal. But it appears that the feverish race now engaging researchers allows them little opportunity to consult the past, and insufficient time to consolidate existing data, so that findings could be plotted along the axes of wisdom and logic. And as new discoveries in the biological as well as the behavioral sciences continue to accumulate, they tend to create confusion with respect to their meaning, and not infrequently, their significance is questionable. "Like adding yet another number behind the 0.9 . . . " to borrow Jean-Paul Sartre's expression. Initially shining with promise, many of these findings soon suffer extinction, and a good number become but specks of dust with respect to all that remains unknown. The question also arises as to the validity of our modern conceptions about the workings of the "mind" as opposed to the views of past generations—concerned as they were with the stirrings of the soul, the "psyche."

In reviewing the status of schizophrenia and updating it in the light of current research, Bleuler (1979) asked: "Is there a specific psychological stressor in the life-history of the schizophrenic person, a stress which is different from that in the life-histories of many neurotic and healthy people? If we cannot find a specific schizo-phrenogenic stressor, we must look for another factor in the pathogenesis." Tirelessly, researchers have sought to correlate specific events, conditions, and various psychic traumata with later schizophrenic developments, but in vain. Man certainly does not merely react to given external circumstances and does not necessarily follow hereditary or childhood-determined scripts. Man, in other words, is not reactor only, but proactor also—initiator of action. *What one does or fails to do, moreover, affects one's inner life more powerfully than any outside event,* even traumatic external circumstances.

The best proof to negate the "trauma" theories of schizophrenia has been provided by the utterly horrendous occurrence of the Nazi extermination camps, whose inmates—counted in millions—did not lose their reason in spite of extremely stressful and life-threatening circumstances. The tragic consequences of the Vietnam War on its combatants can also serve as an example. Many of those servicemen, who had engaged in senseless acts of violence—by choice and not by order, some "wild with the desire to kill" (R. Rosenheck 1985)—did succumb to the insanity now termed the **Malignant Post Vietnam Stress Syndrome,** whereas those who merely followed the call of duty did not. What needs to be urgently considered, therefore, is whether these unnatural "natural experiments" can provide the key for unlocking the mystery of insanity. They certainly offer a clue worthy of further exploration.

With respect to those motivations that dictate proaction, the biological model adopted by contemporary psychiatry would fail to explain them all, pertaining as they do to the living soul, not the "mind." Why does suffering when borne with courage, for example, tend to induce expansion, growth of the soul, and strengthening of the character? Why do intercurrent illnesses and common disasters so frequently cause improvement and even cure of existing mental diseases? And why does the presence of another psychiatric disorder, namely depression, augur a better prognosis for schizophrenia than otherwise? The biological frame of reference, moreover, cannot sufficiently account for acts of courage, transcendence, and ultimate self-sacrifice, which, dictated by man's spirit, run contrary to biological need. That certain endogenously manufactured substances play a major role in psychiatric disturbances does not confirm them yet as responsible for causing those disorders. Every emotion has its own biological counterpart and vice versa: certain chemical substances have the capacity of altering emotional states.

The psychosexual theories advanced by the psychoanalytic school of thought, so heavily stressing the Oedipus complex as a milestone in maturation, appear, by sheer common sense, unduly reductionistic. This complex may not be the only one upon whose resolution future developments depend. And from any vantage point one wishes to examine the Oedipus complex, it reveals itself as nothing more than a complex of sin and guilt, containing also the delusional fear/belief of possible castration as punishment. There is no good reason to regard the Oedipus complex more seriously than other, similar complexes. Further exploration in this direction may be the most fruitful field for future scientific investigation.

Whereas science has no access to the "highly human, highly spiritual spheres" alluded to by Dr. Bleuler, a glimpse of those realms is available to those scientists who are willing to explore the contents of subjective experiences—not only such phenomena as dreams, fears, and nightmares—but delusions, hallucinations, misperceptions, and various "twilight states" as well.

It is at this juncture that existential psychiatry enters to fulfill its task. Its scope of interest and healing approaches certainly extend far and above the biological existence—lived within the limits of time and space. This approach attempts to understand many intangibles and imponderables that enter into one's motivations. Existential psychiatry seeks to emphasize the individual's responsibility for making choices, and focuses mostly on actions and behaviors, rather than on feeling states. This approach, moreover, attempts to bridge the gap between past perceptions of mental illnesses and those of the present; to emphasize the sharp distinction between suffering induced by external traumata and that contingent upon mental disease; and to underscore the responsibility one has for making choices and how these choices affect psychological well-being and even one's destiny. Existentialists offer a new and different approach to the problem of mental disease that answers many questions regarding etiology, as it also offers new insights and effective treatment strategies. They also perceive the urgent need for the unification of biological with psychological theories, in confirmation of man's irreducible oneness. And last but not least, existential psychiatry calls contemporary psychiatry with all its streams of thought to recognize and heed man's most central, most fundamental striving: his spiritual quest.

Although existential psychiatry evolved principally as a reaction to the narrow, reductionistic theories elaborated by psychoanalysis and biologically based psychologies, its groundwork was laid down long before. It is to be understood, nevertheless, that existential psychiatry bases itself upon existential philosophy not as a new philosophy, but as a distillate of prior trends of thought, adapted to the modern world. Unfortunately for all concerned, the terms "existential" and "existentialism" have come to mean different things to different people, and even to existentialists within the psychiatric community. And in spite of all the power of Victor Frankl's Logotherapy, Rollo May's empathic understanding of the patient's world, and Irving Yalom's principles for psychotherapy, existential psychiatry has remained only a current—mostly misunderstood, and, therefore, lacking vigor—in the mainstream of contemporary psychiatry.

Perhaps more than anything else, the intention to dispel much of the ambiguity and misunderstanding surrounding existential philosophy and its application to psychiatry has stood as compelling reason to produce the work presented in these pages. Existential psychiatry has much to offer, and many of its insights might resolve at least some problems of etiology. Many mental illnesses may thus be rendered comprehensible, cancelling the need to list them among "functional disorders of unknown etiology," as they are classified in the DSM-III disease classification.

*   *   *

This work began with a study intended to investigate the religious dilemmas and philosophical quandaries with which the insane become obsessed. But with the progression of the study, it soon became apparent that the 144 schizophrenic patients investigated (M. Niv 1980) were actually suffering from unduly intense dread and an array of dysphorias related to feelings of guilt, which they sought to assuage by a variety of means. In their manifest behavior, these patients often resorted to tirades of self-justificatory statements, undertook acts of atonement, or engaged in semi-religious rituals. Withdrawal, defensive outbursts of rage, and self-inflicted punishments were also commonly observed. Far from representing artifacts of "craziness," the guilty dysphorias of these patients could be traced back to one or more crucial moral violations—an act or acts, not mere fantasies—for which these patients felt prosecuted and condemned. When asked to give their opinion regarding the cause(s) for their sickness, a substantial majority among them gave sin and guilt as reason(s) for their illness.

While the patients' assessment of the reasons for their illness may be understood as a product of their madness, the testimony of many leading psychiatrists has only tended to confirm the veracity of these patients' interpretations. Daring to shake off the dust from forgotten volumes of recorded wisdom as well as from a host of scientific documents, O. Hobart Mowrer (1961, 1974) came once again to identify the pathogens of many mental illnesses as complexes of sin and guilt. Probing into his personal experiences, in addition, Mowrer came to the conclusion that psychosis represents an "explosion of conscience" consequent to one or more serious moral violations. It is this breach in the moral code of the conscience that becomes responsible for shattering the Ego and weakening the personality. Anton T. Boisen (1936), founder of the Pastoral Counseling movement, assessed the function of psychoses more positively, by understanding them as events intended to "make or to break" those who became so affected. Boisen considered the insane to be "self-condemned"—seeking justification for themselves and/or courting punishment.

Early in the century, impressed by the psychological dynamism of schizophrenia, Carl Gustav Jung (1907) described what he termed the "schizophrenic complex." This complex, he believed, comes to assume preeminence and dominates thenceforth the mental processes of the schizophrenic patient. Jung intuitively perceived the existence of an affect in insanity, which he thought becomes eventually "toxic," even to the point of damaging the central nervous system. As it now appears, much of the toxic effects of guilt-related dysphorias may be correlated to increases in the chemical substance and neurotransmitter dopamine (characteristic of acute schizophrenias) whose metabolites have proven damaging to the central nervous system at specific locations (amygdala, hippocampi, and prefrontal cortex, among others).

The reality of sin and guilt, and its role in bringing about a schizophrenic development, may best be appraised from the signs and symptoms of distress engendered, as well as from the repercussions of the latter on the patient's biological and psychological existence. The schizophrenic complex of sin and guilt becomes even more evident when the symptoms of insanity—namely, nightmares, delusions, and hallucinations—are explored with respect to their contents. Not only dread-filled anticipations and awesome subjective experiences, but also the most bizarre behaviors and nonsensical utterances of the schizophrenic, become intelligible and acquire meaning when interpreted in terms of the schizophrenic complexes. Of high pathogenicity, these complexes of sin and guilt, when of undue magnitude and excessive number, may begin a destructive process: the disease, now designated schizophrenia. It is remarkable, indeed, that in all of the manifestations of insanity an intrinsic logic may be found—Reason in the chaos of Madness, and Reason for the Madness, revealed through complexes of sin and guilt.

$$* \quad * \quad *$$

The work presented in these pages makes no claim to originality. From the beginnings of recorded history, insanity has been considered the consequence of moral failures and transgressions. And as much as one may wish to dismiss this interpretation as "dated"—and in spite of the current "psychologization" of every existing evil and the advancement of "psychiatric alibis"—it is a perception of insanity that has nonetheless stood its ground throughout the ages. Subjectively and objectively validated, the veracity of this perception is responsible for much of the stigmatization of the mentally disturbed to this day.

Science has always built upon the foundations of existing knowledge, and the question as to whether this knowledge can just be declared obsolete and so discarded remains ever pertinent. In the case of mental illnesses, one may further ask the question: Do we believe that the human soul, aspirations, and states of disease have significantly changed with the passing tides of time? Or merely our apperception?

A reconfirmation of the moral conscience as the ruler supreme in the inner domain of the emotions might be one of the most important messages this work attempts to convey. Neither in the brain, nor in the "mind," but in the very center of the personality—its spiritual center and wellspring of the emotions—is the drama of every mental illness played out. The invasion of consciousness by spiritually meaningful symbols—mostly threatening in diseased states—immediately brings up the question concerning the role of the moral conscience in determining the contents of consciousness, in general. But the appearance of spiritual symbols highlights also the centrality of the Self, its identity, its spiritual nature, and essence of the soul.

How do faulty attitudes, moral failures, and frank violations of the moral law lead to the development of psychiatric illness? What moral violations are more serious and what symptoms more pathological? Common denominators have been sought and a rough systematization of psychiatric disorders attempted. Much of the material presented here has been gleaned from the timeless wisdom and knowledge of others, from data produced by scientific research, and from clinical observation. Logical deductions have been attempted in order to bind them all into a coherent whole. Much has also been gained from understanding the individual patient's world by the method of phenomenology, which not only describes, but searches out meanings as well. It is remarkable, indeed, that one can read from subjective experience, as though from an open book, all that is given to know about the depth, riches, wisdom, and justice that reign in the life of the living soul.

*   *   *

This book addresses itself primarily to those engaged in the mental health professions. A plea is here reiterated, calling for the recognition of sin and guilt as psychological realities, not symptoms of disease or delusions. More frequently than not, complexes of sin and guilt will be found directly responsible for the outbreak of a psychiatric illness, often a psychosis. Attention is thus repeatedly drawn to the central role of the moral conscience in determining the climate of the inner domain of the emotions. This work, moreover, urges researchers to venture into the vast underexplored territories of subjective phenomena such as delusions, nightmares, and hallucinations. These experiences, heavily charged with meaning, may also be the best available tools to benefit the process of psychotherapy.

It may well be time for psychiatry to veer in a new direction: one that regards biological factors as secondary; that can separate developmental issues from psychopathological manifestations; that can integrate intangible transcendental strivings that motivate behaviors; and finally, that can distinguish behaviors from feeling states—causes from effects. A revision of the prevailing predeterministic approaches, which hold psychiatric disorders to be the results of heredity and/or early childhood experiences to the exclusion of free choice and will, might now be due. The time has also come for expanding our appreciation of subjective experiences in general. These very personal, very creative constructs address consciousness with a message frequently spiritual in nature. "Man sees the sun by the light of the sun and he sees the Spirit by the light of his own spirit," wrote Juan

Mascaro (1978) in his preface to a translation of the Bhagavad Gita. How has it been possible to deny the *spiritual nature* of so many psychiatric disorders, while their symptomatology clearly and loudly speaks in the language of spiritual symbols?

Hopefully, this treatise on existential psychiatry will contribute to the understanding of subjective experiences as well as to the recognition of man's need for transcendence and his essentially spiritual nature. It may stimulate research in a new, perhaps much more rewarding direction. The clues provided by the Oedipus complex of sin and guilt (to be taken in a broader sense, with attention given to other such complexes)—as well as the unnatural "natural experiments" already mentioned, certainly deserve the investment of effort and further exploration.

Some passages from this book may prove of help to those already in the throes of an emotional disturbance or mental illness. Tormented by fears, nightmares, visions, and "voices," some of these unfortunates may find here a measure of solace in being understood, and in having their terrifying experiences explained. They may even follow some of the advice given here. I am confident that it can be instrumental in releasing them from their prisons of alienation, self-inflicted penalties, fears, and despair.

Those who have entrusted the writer of these pages with their confidences may be reassured that their identities have been carefully disguised.

Hopefully, the use of the male gender throughout this book will offend no one; it has been maintained for the sole purpose of grammatical simplicity.

To the families of mental patients, this work might bring some hope and consolation, for in the long-term studies it examines, proof can be found that late recoveries remain an ever-present possibility.

To the generations of our time, this book hopes to convey the message left by philosopher and prophet Sören Kierkegaard, who, standing at the gates of the Industrial Revolution, warned that only sin is man's perdition—a spiritual and psychological truth now conveniently forgotten. Yet a failure to heed this message might have contributed to the present tide of emptiness, psychological decline, and existential despair.

A debt of gratitude is due, and here expressed, to all those men and women who have entrusted me with their confidences. Above all else, this patient population, numbering above a thousand, has taught me to seek and find a ray of human spirit in even the most "deteriorated" among them. The tragedies of the insane have much to teach

Table of Contents

Introduction

During the many years I was engaged in teaching, I had the opportunity to poll consecutive groups of medical students and residents before their exposure to psychology and psychiatry. When asked to give their opinion on what they thought had a greater impact on them and had been more stressful on their inner life, outside events or their own actions and inactions, the majority, nearly 90 percent, responded that their actions and their failure to act affected their emotional life to a greater extent than outside factors. To the question of what they experienced as more painful, the hurt they had caused to another/others or being hurt by others, the majority of students thought that hurting others left them with a residue of inner distress far deeper and more pervasive than the experience of being hurt themselves.

Similar responses can, in general, be obtained from one's family as well as from friends, and even from oneself—which would, in effect, make Existentialists out of most of us. These responses also tend to indicate that we feel ourselves to be largely responsible for much of our failures and miseries and, conversely, for our achievements and the states of elation these tend to engender. When the same groups of students were asked whether they believed in the existence of the soul, and if so, where they thought it to be located, the majority pointed to their heart, believing the soul to reside in the center of the body. A few could not decide, and the remainder, pointing to their head, thought their soul to be identical with their brain.

These responses were obtained from healthy, ordinary people. To the same questions, mental patients may be heard responding somewhat differently: some bemoan the loss of some part of their soul; others lament a sense of solidification of their soul, as if it were transformed into matter. A few among psychopaths and deteriorated schizophrenics express with certitude the belief that the soul has left their body altogether.

Regardless of the various beliefs concerning the soul, its essence, and its location, a consensus seems to exist about our tendency to feel with the heart and in the heart. When sincere, emotions are said to be "heartfelt." Powerful emotions have long been known to have the capacity to alter cardiac function, to cause arrhythmias, to precipitate heart attacks, and even bring on sudden death.

In a study intended to investigate the effects of various "stressors" on the hearts of patients with coronary heart disease, A. Rozanski et al. (1988) found that what was most stressful to them—paralleling vigorous physical exercise—was the task of "talking specifically and honestly about personal faults and undesirable habits, with which the patients were dissatisfied." The stress of being asked and of speaking about one's failures induced cardiac ischemia, which occurred at low heart rates, as compared with that induced by physical exercise. The investigators linked the observed changes with the outpouring of catecholamines: substances produced by the body and released in times of stress.

This study is valuable because it serves to demonstrate that:

- a thought or thoughts can produce powerful emotions
- emotions can produce changes in physiological function and even cause damage—in this case to the heart by ischemia
- thoughts and emotions can induce an outpouring of certain chemicals—in this case, catecholamines
- it is stressful to be confronted with one's faults and failures

We pause and consider the pain of being confronted by our defects, failures, and past wrongdoings. The stressfulness of this confrontation may have little to do with our pride, narcissism, and fear of social rejection. We also begin to understand why we erect such defenses as avoidance, dissociation, projection, and denials; why we need to deceive others as well as ourselves.

Although the existence of body-mind connections has never been disputed, these relationships have been brought from a hypothetical position to one grounded in solid evidence by a technique, namely polygraph investigation, that has by now acquired the status of a science. We are thus brought to the problem of deception in general, and why it can be so easily detected. The truth about deception is that a lie produces physiological changes not only in the heart's function (where the changes are most prominent), but in the whole organism. The emotion that seems to trigger these physiological changes is experienced as one akin to fear. But the body reacts not only to an accomplished lie; it produces detectable physiological changes even by a thought—by the *intention* to deceive. More compelling perhaps is our tendency to betray ourselves somehow in outward behavior; and when we lie with our mouth, we must confess with the body, as if the laws of reality demand that we conform to them (p. 173).

Yet this may not be the correct explanation for the polygraph's capacity to detect deception (cf. Chapter III). In one of its latest refinements, the Silent Answer Test (SAT), the subject is asked to answer silently, to himself, whether he is guilty of the offense under investigation. Here neither deception nor the fear of detection play a role, since the subject answers only to himself. Yet when guilty of the offense investigated, the tracing of the level of the subject's guilty anxiety will mount even higher than if he were defending himself with a lie. During the SAT, guilt becomes a traceable, measurable emotion. And the question immediately arises of whether deception creates anxiety for being a moral violation.

We also learn from the polygraph that anxiety, guilt, and fear have much in common. Polygraphers John Reid and Fred Inbau (1977) have defined guilt as representing *fear of the unknown*—a comprehensive term that encompasses all guilt-related dysphorias. More interesting than the tracing of guilt without deception is the finding that even an intention to deceive creates anxiety, albeit to a lesser degree than outright deception. This intention-generated anxiety may well parallel the neurotic's fears, his phobias, his panic states—struggling as he is with a tempting but morally forbidden possibility. Even though the warnings issued by conscience are experienced as extremely dysphoric, in no way do they compare to the dread that follows the actual commission of a transgression. While the neurotic individual frequently fears he might lose his sanity, his mind, even his soul, and senses a threat to his very existence, the psychotic laments that he has lost his soul already, that he is dead and whatever is left of his life has lost all purpose and meaning.

As much as modern psychologies have attempted to explain guilty feelings in biological terms—as representing nothing but remorse, fear of the father, or fear of social ostracism—none of these interpretations addresses or does justice to the experiences of the insane, whom Anton T. Boisen regards as the "self-condemned." So pervasive are their feelings of guilt and their sense of being on trial that even Sigmund Freud (1933) was brought to wonder: "How would it be if these insane people were right: if in each one of us there is present in the Ego an agency like this, which observes and threatens to punish?"

What if the insane are right and their laments of having sinned true and valid? But then, who judges, condemns, and threatens to punish them? The question returns to the nature of the moral conscience, whether or not it is a private enterprise—every individual following his or her own specific moral code—or an innate characteristic of man. Cruel, self-punishing behaviors and suicide cannot be explained on the basis of the moral conscience alone, however, and this brings up the possibility that we are all subject to universal moral-spiritual laws that hold us to obedience and to which the conscience is sensitive. It may well be that our whole psychological life is actually governed by such laws, and these cannot be transgressed with impunity, just as certain physiological laws—those of homeostasis, for example—cannot be violated without detriment to the physical body. And just as the body resorts to remedial measures to correct imbalances so as to curtail damage, it is conceivable that the moral conscience issues warnings and admonitions in order to safeguard the integrity of the soul. In the case of the Oedipus complex, for example, the conscience speaks with fears of castration to those intent upon incest.

Such an interpretation of the dynamics of conscience may well satisfy biologically inclined psychiatrists and even those Existentialists with a rather positivistic philosophy. Yet, when one considers the contents of such subjective experiences as dreams, visions, hallucinations, and delusions—always heavily charged with spiritually meaningful symbols—one is brought to wonder. In times of crisis, of nearness to death, as well as in the precarious state of insanity, when consciousness becomes invaded by light and darkness, angels, and the devil, one is compelled to search out the meaning of these experiences. To those among Existentialists who hold a theistic worldview, spiritually charged experiences suggest the existence of a larger, albeit intangible Reality, which reveals itself to certain individuals in specific circumstances.

Be that as it may, the study of the dynamics of conscience and its impact upon consciousness offers fascinating possibilities for interpretation as well as for healing. We may follow the medical model by seeking to trace back to their origins the patient's presenting symptoms of distress. In the case of guilt, this would mean an exploration of the reasons for these feelings. Such an approach permits the systematization of certain moral failures and transgressions, as well as the specific symptoms of distress they would tend to engender. A follow-up of certain transgressions and their eventual transformation into mental diseases may then become possible, allowing for the classification of psychiatric disorders according to etiology, not symptoms. Further investigation into the dynamics of conscience may lead psychiatry in a new direction, where etiological considerations and effective healing go hand in hand. To myself, the existential approach has been a source of perpetual wonder as well as a gold mine of therapeutic success. It has compelled me to seek to share it with others.

But before all else, we must turn back several pages in the history of psychiatry in order to consult the wisdom of ages past, and, then turn the pages forward, to the present time. We may find that past and present perceptions *can* be reconciled.

Chapter I

Historical Perspectives

Hold fast to the ways of antiquity in order to keep the realm of today.
—Lao Tzu, *Tao Te Ching*

In philosophy, being new speaks against being true.
—Karl Jaspers

It is a natural tendency of scientific endeavors to pull and entrap researchers into black holes of detail, from which they can extricate themselves only with much difficulty. For this reason, among others, many modern scientists have tended to lose sight of the entirety of the problems they have sought to resolve, and as a result have rendered meaningless and inconsequential their partial solutions. This may explain the reductionism and oversimplification of the prevailing psychological theories, which often fall into the error of taking a part for the whole, *pars pro totalita*. This trend, for obvious reasons, is more evident in the behavioral than in the exact sciences.

Yet science has always built upon the foundations of existing knowledge, and if it is to take the immutability of the human soul as a given, this knowledge cannot just be declared obsolete and so discarded. With due respect to the validity of some of our modern theories, a good number among them appear to be rather mechanistic and deterministic. They obviously fail to take into account the wide range of variety in human behavior, and are at a loss when attempting to explain self-defeating motivations. What needs to be considered, nonetheless, is that within the "tails" (t distribution areas measure areas of deviance from the normal) of statistical analyses of human behavior, many degrees of freedom exist as choices; and these choices may be impervious to psychological interpretation, as they frequently transcend temporal-biological determinants. How is envy or covetousness, for example, related to biological need, learning theories, and cybernetics?

In a time of deterministic science, it is hardly surprising that the focus of attention in psychiatry has become centered around biochemical aberrations, not as secondary effects but as primary causes. It is not by chance, thus, that the dopamine theory of schizophrenia came to dominate the landscape of psychiatric research; and this may have less to do with the success of neuroleptics in blocking dopamine transmission, than with the hopes of investigators to find, eventually, a chemical solution to the problem of illnesses affecting the "psyche."

Yet, in order to understand the psychology of man in health and in disease, the heights of perspective and a clear vision—unobstructed by theories—would be essential prerequisites. The fact that man is a creature of desire rather than need, as stressed by Gaston Bachelard (1949), renders a good number of psychological explanations rather simplistic. Many of our modern psychological theories, moreover, have drawn their conclusions from animal experiments. The question then arises: How can the life of the soul—its plunges into abysmal depths through limitless greed, hate, lust, and revengeful strivings, and its ascents to heavenly realms through selfless, sacrificial love—be objectively investigated? Biology has no access to the intangible attributes of the soul and cannot explain man's compelling urge to transcend his biological existence, limited by time and space. Whether risking himself for power or glory, spending himself for lust or revenge, or offering himself in living sacrifice for faith, love, an idea, or a cause—for being in possession of a soul—man often emerges free from the burdens of heredity, blows of fate, adversity, and even his own instinctual urges, in order to become himself. But "you could not find the ends of the soul, if you traveled everywhere, so deep is its Logos . . . " cried Heraclitus, perceiving the soul as infinite and eternal. Not by coincidence was the study of the soul—in health and in disease—relegated to the domains of philosophy and religion in ages past. Even Immanuel Kant insisted that psychology remain the province of philosophy.

From ancient India to Greek philosophers, on to the writings of Emanuel Swedenborg and the poetry of John Keats and William

Blake, man's mental functioning has been compared to that of a chariot:

> The chariot is man's body, driven, however, by orders of the master, which is none other but man's spirit or soul. The master commands his charioteer, who is man's intelligence, to whatever direction is intended by the master's will. It is the charioteer or man's intelligence [the Ego of modern times] who holds the reins of the horses of passion [for Good and Evil, according to Plato and paralleling Freud's instincts of Eros and Thanatos].The chariot is reeled, nonetheless, on the wheels of the master's feelings. *(Condensed from the authors mentioned above)*

Not unlike the chariot, the psycho-biological system, according to L. Von Bertalanffy, who introduced cybernetics to psychiatry, is an open system, for it provides freedom to the spirit or soul.

With a definition of the essence of the soul and its function, we try to understand the whole psycho-biological system in health and in disease. As for the insanities: each of the passing generations has tended to perceive their pleomorphic manifestations in its own peculiar manner, every historical era casting its own light on one or another of their multiple facets. Yet, resisting the tides of time, the conception of insanity as consequence of some crucial moral failure or violation has persisted to this day. It has been, and is still responsible for much of the "stigmatization" of those affected. And even if rejected as nonscientific by modern psychologists and psychiatrists, this view of insanity prevails with remarkable consistency in many different cultures around the world. In the treasuries of literature, a profusion of works that express this same view can be found. Shakespeare's *Macbeth*, Dostoyevsky's *Crime and Punishment,* Mauriac's *Thérèse Desqueyroux,* and Maupassant's *Horlà* stand out as powerful examples. The story of Dr. Jekyll and Mr. Hyde, describing the developing madness of its protagonist, may speak perhaps more eloquently to the younger generations, as it addresses itself to the split (schism) of the personality, characteristic of insanity and to which it owes its new name: schizophrenia. Here is a poignant analysis of the split between Good and Evil in a personality, cleaved by the lie and shielded by pretense, where evil comes to predominate.

*   *   *

Unlike other diseases—with epidemics waxing and waning—the plague of insanity has remained a constant affliction of mankind.

Turning back 3,400 years in the pages of history, we find the following passage in the Bhagavad Gita:

> When a man dwells on the pleasures of the senses, attraction for them arises in him. From attraction arises desire, the lust of possession, and this leads to anger. From passion comes confusion of mind, then loss of remembrance, then forgetting of duty. From this loss comes the ruin of reason, and the ruin of reason leads a man to destruction (2:62-64).

In the oldest classification of mental illnesses, that of the Ayur-Veda (from the wisdom and tradition of ancient India, 2,500 B.C.) diseases were grouped according to various types of demon-possession (K. Menninger 1963). Mental disorders could thus be caused by the wrath of enraged spirits, demons, giants, gods, and the spirits of the dead entering the living. Perceptions such as these might appear anachronistic today, were it not for the fact that patients persist in complaining of being possessed by evil spirits and of being controlled by powerful outside forces of evil, monsters, and the devil. So consistent is this complaint among the modern-day insane that it has become one of the "first rank" criteria by which schizophrenia is currently diagnosed (K. Schneider 1959). Subjectively, the *experience* of insanity differs little from that described in the Ayur-Veda. Logically following their beliefs and perceptions of insanity, the treatment approaches applied to the mentally ill in ancient India included physical and mental shocks, expiatory rites, fastings, chanting, purifications, and medicines, among others.* Patients were also exposed to the benevolent influence of nature: sunshine, water, and fresh air.

The perceptions of insanity by peoples of Eastern cultural background are closely interwoven with their traditions and religious beliefs. Ancestor worship, filial piety, and the preservation of face (*Lien*) represent the most essential ingredients of Chinese tradition. Moral behavior is thought to be governed by universal cosmic forces that seek to safeguard the Common Good. Deviations from accepted rules of behavior, such as lack of reverence for elders and disgrace leading to the loss of honor, are regarded as important contributory factors in the causation of acute psychotic illnesses. Belief in the invasion of the mind by noxious spirits is accepted to this day.

---

* Worthy of note is their use of the plant *Rauwolfia serpentina*, still in use today for tranquilization as well as for the reduction of high blood pressure.

Similar perceptions of mental illness can be found throughout the cultures of the East, dating from antiquity.

The rich legacy left us by the ancient Greek civilization, its mythology, philosophy, and clinical observations, contains a wealth of ideas and concepts that are strikingly relevant even today. Hippocrates (460–377 B.C.), considered to be the father of medicine, and by whose oath novice physicians are still being sworn, is credited for some valid clinical observations concerning hysteria, paranoia, and phobias, as well as for his theory of the "humors" related to temperament. In mental illnesses, the humors of the body were believed to be both causes and effects. In depression, for example, the bile was noted to be black, hence the term "melancholia" (*melan* = black, and *chole* = bile). Greek mythology is permeated with the belief that transgressions of the moral code are liable to be punished by the gods with the curse of insanity. The wrath of the gods could also be incurred by excesses of passion, riches, and arrogance. Mania, the goddess of Fury, and Lyssa, the goddess of Dread, were believed to cause their victims to be invaded by a host of evil spirits. For drinking wine without moderation, Dionysus was stricken with madness by the goddess Hera. Orestes succumbed to insanity after murdering his mother and her lover.

In the philosophical writings of the ancient Greeks, at the height of their civilization and dating from that time, we also find that sin and moral transgression were perceived as acts of provocation, punished by their gods. Here and elsewhere, loss of mind is found associated with transgression of a moral law and not with any external blows of fate or personal disaster. The ancient Greeks, moreover, did not focus their attention on the various kinds of losses of reason, nor on the functions of the Ego, but on the evil by which the insane appeared possessed. Music, sleep, purification rites, introspection, and analysis of dreams and visions were all made use of in the healing procedures at Epidaurus center of spiritual healing.

Several accounts of mental illness and insanity can be found in the Holy Scriptures of the Judeo-Christian religion. For his rebellion against divine injunctions—"rebellion is as the sin of witchcraft and stubbornness as iniquity and idolatry" (1 Samuel 15:23)—the spirit of the Lord departs from King Saul, who begins to be troubled by an evil spirit. Only through the music played to him by innocent David does the evil spirit depart from the king, who then recovers (1 Samuel 16:23). The madman of Gadara, described in the gospel of St. Mark (5:1-15), lives in tombs, walks naked, frightens others, and cuts himself with stones. He is said to be inhabited by a "legion" of evil spirits, which depart from him, nonetheless, after a miraculous exorcism. He is then found "sitting and clothed and in his right mind."

Paranoid fears are frequently mentioned in the Bible. Of the wicked it is said that "they flee when none pursueth" (Proverbs 28:1). With respect to delusions, we find in the book of Isaiah (66:3-4):

> Yea, they have chosen their own ways and their soul delighted in their abominations. I will also choose their delusion and will bring their fears upon them, because when I called, none did answer; when I spake, they did not hear; but they did evil before mine eyes, and chose that in which I delighted not.

In the treatment of the mentally ill during the Middle Ages, superstition prevailed over charity and brotherly love.* Possession of the mind by evil spirits came to be accepted as the common cause for all mental illnesses and aberrations of the mind, with no distinction being made between organically determined and functional disorders; all were lumped together and treated by means less than charitable. More than a few among the mentally diseased were persecuted and even executed at the stake, in conformity with the belief that their souls could be saved through destruction of their bodies. Skull trepanation was also frequently performed as a means for providing an outlet for the emergence of evil spirits.** It is superstition that seems to have inspired the well-known "witch hunts," aimed at those believed to be possessed. The *Malleus Maleficarum* proposed the torture and extermination of the mentally ill.

As the forces of superstition that overtook the Western world during the dark Middle Ages progressively dispersed, a light of

---

* Although a great majority of peoples in the Western world embraced the Christian faith, many were sidetracked onto the paths of superstition. A short pause is here due for distinction to be made between the psychological forces of faith and those of superstition, for they are so divergent from each other. In the visible world, these diametrically opposed beliefs produce quite different effects. While the forces of faith engender love, hope, charity, and virtue in view of promoting the Common Good, the world becomes also changed for the better. Faith as a psychological force, furthermore, expects reward for the good and believes that evil will eventually be punished. Born of fear, superstition has no roots in any moral system and simply attempts to assuage the forces of evil through rituals, worship of idols, fire, inanimate objects, etc. Superstition seeks to master the future through divination and astrology. Fears are abolished through worship of evil or the devil. The fear of death is neutralized through worship of the dead.

** This procedure can be compared to leukotomy. Skull trepanation, nonetheless, may well have provided a sound treatment for disorders caused by an increase in intracranial pressure.

compassion and understanding began to shine over the lot of the mentally diseased, as the first mental hospital was founded in Valencia by Father Gilabert Joffré in 1409. With the monastic serenity of this hospital and the benevolent attitude of its caretakers, it is likely that many of the mentally deranged were enabled to recover, for Joffré was successful in convincing the authorities of the efficacy of his approaches. Five more hospitals were subsequently built in various cities in Spain and Mexico during the decade following.

In 1492—the *annus mirabilis* that saw the Spanish victory over the Moors, the expulsion of the Jews from Spain, and the discovery of America—the forerunner of an empirical approach to mental illness, Juan Luis Vives, was born in Valencia. Vives urged discrimination between functional disorders and those organically determined. He recommended compassion toward the insane for "so great a disaster to the health of the human mind" and advocated that these unfortunates be treated kindly, so that "like wild animals, they grow gentle" (G. Mora 1975).

Physician Johann Weyer (1515–88) came to be considered the first psychiatrist, as his main efforts were directed toward the treatment of psychiatric illnesses. His book *De Praestigiis Daemonium* is considered a landmark in the history of psychiatry. Weyer thought that benevolent attitudes, rooted in scientific principles, were the most essential ingredients to successful treatment. He believed in the participation of supernatural forces in mental illnesses, however, and foresaw the need for collaboration between clergy and physicians in treating psychiatric patients. A belief that the mentally diseased could be cured through intercession of the saints also came to be accepted; it was applied in the treatment provided by the famous Renaissance St. Bartholomew Hospital in London.

It has been said that mental patients who were witnesses to the decapitation of Irish princess Dymphna—which was ordered by her jealous father for her refusal to give up the Christian faith—suddenly recovered their sanity at the sight of the execution. From the time of St. Dymphna's decapitation, the Belgian town of Gheel, site of that event, has housed a religious order active since 1850, which, with the participation of the community, still continues to care for the mentally diseased.

Progressively, and paralleling the forces of the Enlightenment in the Western world, attitudes toward the mentally ill became more tolerant and their treatment more charitable. In 1795, Paul Pinel literally liberated the insane from the chains that had bound them with criminals in the dungeons of Paris. Pinel became superintendent of the famous Salpêtrière hospital, renowned throughout the world as a psychiatric center and which remained active for more than a century. At the same time, the "moral treatment" was instituted by William Tuke, who founded the famous York Retreat in England. In Italy, V. Chiarugi (1759–1820) served as director of the asylum Bonifacio, whose regulations stated: "it is a supreme moral duty and medical obligation to respect the insane individual as a person."

In the United States, Benjamin Rush (1745–1813) came to be recognized as the father of American psychiatry. Rush believed in the psychological origins of mental disorders, some of which he attributed to moral failures. His somatic treatments, some of which were more punitive than charitable, stirred much controversy. In the first general hospital in America—the Pennsylvania Hospital, established in 1756—a wing in the basement was allocated for the treatment of "lunaticks." Work was given here a central role in the treatment of the insane. In the hospital, the physician was urged to listen sympathetically to his patients so as to allow relief of feelings and unburdening of conscience. An opportunity to start afresh was offered to those disadvantaged by heredity, environment, excessive passion, and lack of self-discipline; and an occasion was provided for patients to repudiate deviant sexual appetites. Personal integrity was required of physicians in charge of treating the mentally ill. Clergy participation, group discussions, music, and reading were appropriately applied in this "moral treatment" regime. This approach, however, began to lose ground due to controversies regarding its effectiveness. In terms of sheer numbers, the moral treatment proved disappointing and, failing to fulfill the inflated expectations of its enthusiastic followers, was eventually abandoned.

The founder of phrenology, Franz Joseph Gall (1758–1828), considered mental faculties to be innate and to have specific topographical representation in the brain. In a similar vein, Wilhelm Griesinger (1817–68) associated all varieties of mental illnesses with organic causes. Despite the existence of two separate disciplines, namely psychiatry and neurology—separating psychiatric disturbances from illnesses affecting the brain—the temptation to grasp for organic causes as responsible for psychiatric disorders has persisted to this day.

Adamantly resisting organic interpretations of psychiatric disorders, Johann Christian Heinroth (1773–1843) flatly stated that "there is no mental illness except where there is complete defection from God. The etiology of madness is sin. Repentance and a return to faith are the means to cure." Heinroth believed that, "an evil spirit abides in the mentally deranged: they are the truly possessed" (1818). (*vide infra*)

But hereditary factors have also been recognized to play a role in the etiology of mental illnesses. Observations on the hereditary transmission of personality traits, criminality, and other psychological aberrations led Benedict-Augustin Morel (1809–73) to regard degenerative "stigmata" as becoming progressively more severe with each succeeding generation until their extinction three to four generations later (cf. Chapter IX).

The history of psychiatry will not be complete without mention of Sören Kierkegaard (1813–55), who, in his many writings, preceded Freud with his analysis of "objective dread" as fear of sin. Whereas objective anxiety parallels Freud's "signal anxiety," "subjective dread," according to Kierkegaard, follows the commission of sin (1844). (*vide infra*)

Meticulous research and keen observation led German psychiatrist Emil Kraepelin (1856–1926) to reach a new synthesis in psychiatric nosology. Kraepelin also introduced the sharp distinction between psychoses with mood disturbances, or manic-depressive psychoses, and illnesses involving other mental functions such as conation (will), cognition, and affect (emotions). He described "dementia praecox" (dementia occurring early in life) as insanity that affects individuals of young age, frequently leading to losses in cognitive as well as other mental faculties prior to the senium.[*]

The term "schizophrenia" was coined by Swiss psychiatrist Eugen Bleuler (1857–1939). It takes cognizance of several "splits" in the personality of individuals so affected, but Bleuler was apparently most strongly impressed by the split between emotion and cognition that is so obvious in this disorder. Schizophrenia became defined by Bleuler's four "A's" accepted as diagnostic markers: Affective disturbances, namely flatness and/or inappropriateness of affect; Ambivalence, or love-hate, in relationships; disturbances in Associative thought; and Autism, which stands for extreme egocentricity. Contemporary French psychiatrist Henry Ey added yet another letter to Bleuler's four A's: the letter "P," standing for Paranoia—never lacking in the symptomatology of schizophrenia.

---

[*] In Kraepelin's original case descriptions, one finds his patients lamenting about masturbation, hate, sin, and guilt, but these were not considered by him as relevant.

*   *   *

This brings us to present-day psychiatry, beset by controversial theories and an immense wealth of research findings whose integration into a cohesive structure remains, nonetheless, pending.

The question whether insanity, madness, or schizophrenia have changed in essence or only in name, begs now for an answer. Have the passing tides of man's evolution also wrought changes in the various manifestations of this state of being? A survey of the patient population in the most modern of psychiatric wards, where the newest and most "scientifically sound" treatments for insanity are being applied, convincingly disproves the notion that any change in the experience or course of schizophrenia has taken place since ages past. If the delusions of these patients have changed somewhat, it is in appearance only. Instead of Napoleonic visions, they may contain references to Adolf Hitler. Persecutions may now be undertaken by the KGB or its equivalents, by the Mafia, or by the FBI or CIA in the United States. Messages are now transmitted through radios and television screens, while schizophrenic patients feel "bugged" and watched by various electronic devices. Notwithstanding, the ever-watching eye, perceived by the paranoiac, has persisted in observing those determined on hiding secret misdeeds. And the snakes, the rats, the cockroaches, and the vampires, have they vanished from the schizophrenic's experience? They have not. And what of the claims we hear every day from affected patients, that they have lost their souls and became possessed by evil spirits, or that their souls have turned into solid matter? Are these experiences merely echoed from an archaic past, or just the products of imagination? With remarkable consistency these patients insist that for them, their experiences are more pressing, more awesome, and more real than any reality perceived by their senses.

As for the devil, his appearance in the subjective experience of so many schizophrenic patients can hardly be considered coincidental. The devil? He has not allowed himself to be deleted from the delusional world of the insane, in spite of the various measures taken against him and the application of scientifically validated treatment approaches. Whether he is named Archetype, Archangel of Darkness, or Absolute Evil has made no difference, for he has remained all too present, all too terrible in the infernal world of the insane. Enlightenment, and scientific progress, and even the emotion-bleaching powers exerted by Thorazine, have failed to force him into extinction. Dismissal of this fact and disposal of subjective experiences (where he makes his appearance) as representing but "primary process," regressive phenomena, might have some tranquilizing effects on psychologists and psychiatrists. Yet failure to deal with such material cannot be otherwise considered than as massive defensive denial—a refusal to acknowledge and grapple with the spiritual problems central to insanity. While ignoring their patients' desperate cries that they have sinned, feel condemned, and are heading toward Hell, the healers of the soul feel now more relief for themselves from the Prolixin they prescribe, and from interpretations according to the psychoanalytic gospel, than from measures intended to rescue these patients from their tormenting guilt and sense of condemnation.

Has schizophrenia changed any of its ugly faces? It has not. In a publication by B. L. McKinnon (1977), we find a description of what it feels like to experience a psychotic decompensation:

> My visual hallucinations filled me with wonder and awe, as well as scaring me more than any horror movie ever could have done. When I turned the Bible to the first page and found that the wording had all changed, it sent shivers down my spine. The first hallucination I had was really frightening. My brother-in-law was smiling at me when suddenly his features blurred and I saw the devil staring at me.

In an article assessing the perception of mental illness in various countries around the world, S. De Grazia (1967) finds that:

> Wherever on the world's continents, the life of the ruder communities is explored, the belief in the relation of mental disturbance to moral transgression is to be found. The persons who come to psychotherapy are all fired in the same crucible. They have thought bad things or done bad deeds, and so they suffer, ground and baked in a hot oven, cooked, no less in their own galled conscience. This is the history and ethnography of what is revealed in psychotherapy.

In a description of mental illnesses in rural Laos by J. Westermeyer and R. Wintrob (1979), the subtitle reads: *On Being Insane in Sane Places.* In Laos, insanity is known as *Baa,* and an individual so afflicted suffers moral stigma, as does also his family. In Laotian cosmology, such misfortune as Baa is explained as punishment for malfeasance. In Laos, as well as elsewhere in the world today, the common explanation of mental disease is spirit possession, loss of soul, and divine punishment.

Clearly, time and distance have not been able to change the *experience* of schizophrenia. What has changed is merely our perception of it: otherwise, we are where we began, and this in spite of the "revolution" created by Freud's psychoanalytical movement and the modern psychological theories that followed in its wake. Paradoxically, in attempting to explain the psychology of man on the basis of biological determinants, modern psychiatric trends have tended to exclude the "psyche" (Self or soul) from most of their considerations. Focusing attention on the workings of the "mind," the mental apparatus, developmental issues, and various stressors and functions of the central nervous system, contemporary psychiatry has been forced to concede in its introduction to the Diagnostic and Statistical Manual of Mental Disorders-III (DSM-III) that the etiology of most mental disorders is unknown. This might be the reason for modern psychiatry's need to extend itself over several other fields of scientific endeavor, such as sociology, anthropology, biochemistry, and neuroanatomy, among others. Beset by an abundance of theories and a diversity of treatment approaches, modern psychiatry clearly lacks cohesion, and the two major streams of thought that have come to dominate it—psychoanalysis and neurobiochemistry—run in diametrically opposite directions.

Clustered around psychoanalysis as one of the most convincing doctrines, the majority of modern theories—but not all—interpret the psychology of man in terms of biological determinants. Representing the most influential among modern trends, the following theoretical constructs will need to be given attention:

- psychoanalysis
- ego-psychology
- analytical psychology
- learning theories
- existential school of thought
- self-psychology
- general systems theory
- self-help groups

In attempting to bring scientific objectivity into psychiatry, Freud made efforts in his formulations to uproot existing psychological theories from philosophy and separate them from religion. Essentially, **psychoanalysis** sought to explain psychopathology on the basis of early childhood events, physiological functions, and biological urges—the "drives" of sexuality (Eros) and aggression (Thanatos, god of death and destruction). The theory rests on several assumptions related to early childhood traumata and milestones of development. Freud's tripartite "mental apparatus" comprises:

1. The Ego: an aggregate of mental faculties coherently organized (but by whom?), which reasons, mediates adaptation to the outside world, and, in normal circumstances, masters the world within, holding in check the internal forces of desire.

2. The Id: a seething cauldron of sexual urges and aggressive drives that press for gratification.

3. The Superego: the moral conscience—presumably derived from an *Anlage* (or remnant from an atavistic past and related to a fear of the father), from parental introjects whose injunctions remain engraved in the mind, and from a self-chosen Ego-ideal.

Most weighty in Freud's construct of the conscience is the Oedipus complex, in which he saw the beginnings of religion, morality, social life, and art. Based upon a distorted interpretation of a myth, the Oedipus complex contains, nonetheless, a solid grain of truth. In family life some relationships do indeed become sexually tinged (such as father-daughter, son-mother, brother-sister) and give rise to neurotic fears of enacting such urges in reality (fear of the Id), as well as of deserved punishment for infringement of a taboo—in this case, of castration. Incestual strivings represent, nevertheless, only one of many sinful attitudes to hold us culpable, and the fear of castration is not the only one to which we might become subject.

The problem of guilt and anxiety remained Freud's major preoccupation, as he recognized the central role of these dysphorias in the majority of mental illnesses. He believed feelings of guilt to have their origins in a conscience atavistically transmitted from generation to generation—derived from the "killing of the father" (because of his sexual monopoly over the women of the tribe)—and onto which parental injunctions are later added (1913).

In stark opposition to his predecessors, Freud sought the causes of mental illnesses in frustration, thwarted desire, and undue repression, especially of sexual desires. Thus, in order to forestall the occurrence of neuroses in adulthood, he advocated that children be allowed "free play in sexuality, as happens among primitive people" (1940). Even holding back aggression was regarded by Freud (1940) as "unhealthy, leading to illness, to mortification." He believed that many neurotics actually suffer from an "over-scrupulous conscience" that turns at times "sadistic." And since Freud held a hedonistic worldview and his moral valuations were clouded in ambiguity, he tended to regard guilt mostly as a neurotic phenomenon. "Where Id was Ego shall be," was the way Freud defined the goal of psychoanalytic treatment, as well as his hopes for humanity.

Freud's biological interpretations of psychological phenomena appeared highly attractive to the scientific world, for they offered a new "liberation," this time from traditional values and moral constraints. It is therefore hardly surprising that a whole set of propositions regarding human psychology, growth, development, and mental health, based upon myths and unproven hypotheses, came to be accepted.

Close to the tenets of psychoanalytic theory and developed by its followers, **Ego-psychology** places emphasis on the Ego and its various functions and faculties such as intelligence, reason, control over instinctual urges, and "object relations," among others. According to Ego-psychologists, most prominent among whom are H. Hartmann, E. Kris, R. Loewenstein, E. Fromm, E. Erikson, and K. Menninger, mental illnesses are predicated upon failings of the Ego— its deficits and/or weaknesses. These theories would certainly address such failures of the Ego as perception of reality and control over instinctual urges, for example—failings that are all too evident in the behaviors of the insane. Ego-psychologies, nevertheless, fail to account for the rather "hypertrophied" Ego in certain psychopathological states, such as the borderline condition, antisocial personality, criminality, etc., in which the Ego supplies all the necessary realities for the commission of a crime or moral transgression, as well as justifications and cover-up operations following its perpetration. In **Anorexia Nervosa** the Ego is also hypertrophic as it exercises inordinate control over instinctual urges—in this case the craving for food. In Anorexia, the Ego disregards biological need and overrules physiological laws. Consistent with their theories, the therapeutic approaches of Ego-psychologists, which attempt to strengthen the Ego by way of "reality orientation" and to increase relatedness through the sharpening of "social skills," have proved vain in the treatment of most psychiatric disorders.

Initially a follower of Freud's psychoanalytical movement, Carl Gustav Jung (1875–1961) eventually developed his own **analytical psychology.** Rejecting Freud's notion that every neurosis stems from thwarted sexuality, and aware of the spiritual nature of his patients' difficulties, he parted with psychoanalysis altogether. Jung's contributions to psychiatry are too numerous for even a summary account. He sought to derive common denominators from shared subjective experiences, and attempted to decode the meaning of universal symbols, which he termed "archetypes." He is frequently quoted as saying that every one of his adult patients suffered essentially from a spiritual problem. He also observed that many of his patients underwent experiences of rebirth as their Self emerged victorious over the shadow within them. Striving initially in reality for the sake of Self, the Self eventually emerges as a wholeness, directed toward goals that benefit others. Jung interpreted dreams and symbols in existential terms, perceiving that these phenomena serve a vital advisory function and frequently convey messages of a spiritual nature. Jung's analytical psychology has been regarded as a link, bridging psychoanalysis with existential psychiatry.

Jung had the opportunity to work under the guidance of Eugen Bleuler in the famous Burghölzli Hospital, where he was able to study the manifestations of schizophrenia. He became famous for his "word-association test," his understanding of schizophrenia, and his integration into analytical psychology a variety of subjective experiences whose message is spiritual. Jung described the "schizophrenic complex" and keenly perceived that in this diseased state, an affect becomes predominant and eventually "toxic" on several levels.

Several leading **theories based on learned behavior** emerged following I. P. Pavlov's observations on animal behavior at the beginning of this century. Early learning was found to be capable of dictating specific persistent behaviors, as shown by K. Lorenz's "imprinting" experiments on animals. Conditioned reflexes could be either reinforced or extinguished according to certain "operant conditioning," as demonstrated by B. F. Skinner. The behavioristic approach of rewards and punishments is naturally applied by parents and educators.

In an effort to explain and treat anxiety conditions, J. Wolpe (1982) developed the method of "reciprocal inhibition" as well as various anxiety-diversion tactics that find application in the treatment of anxiety disorders, panic states, and phobias. Wolpe's method of "counter-phobic desensitization," which requires repetitive exposure to the anxiety-provoking stimulus, has been found useful in the treatment of these disorders.

Among the major premises of the **existential school of thought** is the stress on the supremacy of the will over the intellect. A teacher of Freud as well as of Edmund Husserl, Franz Brentano believed that mental activity is directed toward objects, and this represents an expression of an *intentional existence* within consciousness. Phenomena are thus understood as products of selective attention. Jean Piaget's observations on child development led him to conclude that children construct their experience along given as well as chosen schemata.

Among **Self-psychologists,** Gordon Allport's concept of the Self (1955, 1961) most closely approaches the philosophical and religious concepts of "soul." Allport stated that, "A psychology which does not include religion as intrinsic to it, can hardly be considered psychology at all . . . ." He comes close to the existential perspective when he perceives the individual as continually evolving in the process of "becoming," and of choosing him-Self.

The **general systems theory,** developed by J. G. Miller in the 1960s, attempts to interrelate the individual within his social nexus in a system that presumes actions and transactions to be most relevant to the individual, as well as to those moving in his orbit, whether in health or in disease. The systems theory approach has found application mainly in the treatment of the family as a system.

Independent from modern psychological and psychiatric institutions, the self-help organization Alcoholics Anonymous has demonstrated an astounding success in effecting permanent abstinence for the majority of its participants. The results from the therapeutic approaches of A.A. have been so outstanding that similar programs have mushroomed all over the world, and are now available for other "addictions" as well. Organized according to the model of Alcoholics Anonymous, **self-help groups** are available for narcotic addicts (NA), overeaters (OA), gamblers (GA), overspenders (SA), and also for the emotionally troubled (EA) *(vide infra).* An international network offers its services to individuals in local chapters the world over. It may seem paradoxical that the record of permanent cures and remissions achieved in these self-help groups is better by far than that of conventionally administered mental health care, but the paradox is easily resolved by taking into account that in Anonymous groups, the spiritual needs of the participants are acknowledged and also met, whereas in conventional "therapies" they are largely ignored. Furthermore, whereas the "Twelve Steps and Twelve Traditions" promulgated by A.A. are grounded in spiritual principles common to all of the major religions, conventional therapies rely on such theories as are chosen by the particular mental health center or individual therapist.

*   *   *

Contemporary psychiatry saw a new dawn with the discovery of chemical substances that have the capacity to affect the emotions. Thanks to rapidly progressing research, a wide array of chemicals have become available for the treatment of various psychiatric disorders, ranging from anxiety to depression, and effective for some of the symptoms of schizophrenia as well. However, thirty years of medical treatment of psychologically determined disorders with "neuroleptics" (drugs that influence the nervous system) have proven disappointing. While the neuroleptic drugs in current use are quite effective in providing symptomatic relief, their beneficial effects end there. Neuroleptics may actually be redefined as *psychoactive aspirins,* for such a term accurately describes their action as well as limitations. Psychopharmacologists have recently reviewed the status of neuroleptic medications from a long-term perspective, as the ability of these chemicals to effect a cure has been seriously challenged. In assessing the effectiveness of neuroleptic medication, R. J. Baldessarini (*Psychiatric News,* Vol. 5, No. 1, January, 1988) came to the conclusion that these drugs are "neither curative nor prophylactic."

Notwithstanding, no one would dispute the benefits that have ensued from the fortunate discovery of neuroleptics, which by providing symptomatic relief, have allowed a substantial number of patients to walk away from mental hospitals and state institutions for the chronically disabled, where they were kept for years on end. To many, chemotherapy has opened the possibility of life outside and freedom. Yet, braced in their "chemical straitjackets," many patients have succumbed to what in colloquial language came to be known as the "zombie syndrome." The emotional dulling and clouding of consciousness caused by neuroleptics have, unfortunately, prevented many patients from mobilizing the motivation and will necessary to lift them out of their spiritual and psychological fall, and have deprived them of the courage to begin anew. The noncompliance with prescribed medication, so frequent among this patient population, is easily explained, however, on the basis of the side effects these drugs produce, as well as by their tendency to accentuate already existing *anhedonia,* i.e., the inability to experience pleasure.

Subtly, pharmacotherapy has also introduced the deceptive notion that schizophrenia is the result of a chemical aberration of some sort, and therefore is curable by chemical means. The symptomatic relief provided by the use of chemical substances may even have served to tranquilize into indolence some among mental health professionals. The improvements observed in certain cases and some spontaneous recoveries—attributed to the effects of neuroleptics—have frequently been utilized as justification for shirking the responsibility of difficult and lengthy psychotherapy, so sorely needed by most of these patients. Yet, while a good majority of contemporary psychiatrists believe in finding eventually a chemical solution to the problem of psychiatric disturbances, in general, an influential minority stands by the doctrine and method of psychoanalysis. However, neither the doctrine nor the method of psychoanalysis are relevant in any way to the most serious of psychiatric disorders that is schizophrenia.

The dualism of modern psychiatry is mirrored in its literature, where representation is given mostly to one or the other of its major trends: the neurosciences on the one hand, and psychoanalysis on the other. Obviously, these systems of thought have little to say to each other. And by reason of its narrow, mostly biological perspective, modern psychiatry has failed to understand and succor the truly psychiatrically disabled: sociopaths, narcissists, borderlines, gamblers, drug addicts, alcoholics, sexual deviants, and the millions consumed by the spiritual cancer now termed schizophrenia. Hence, for those neither wealthy enough to afford the cost of psychoanalysis, nor sufficiently healthy to benefit from it, modern psychiatry has but a limited supply of help to offer. It is thus hardly surprising that chemical substances came to displace other therapeutic measures. But modern psychiatry is addressed by its failures.

In the psychological realm, external stressors have been tirelessly sought to explain psychopathological developments, but in vain. Much effort has also been invested in the shuffling and reshuffling of diagnostic categories that would permit some measure of "standard-ization." It may well be, however, that as long as the community of mental health professionals refuses to acknowledge the reality of sin and guilt as major psychological stressors, the etiology of schizophre-nia will remain hidden behind numerical data, statistical analyses, and redefinitions, its horror attenuated by chemicals. The mystery of schizophrenia will most certainly continue to exact millions in research monies, yet will persist in eluding the wisdom of biologically grounded scientific investigations.

Chapter II

Existential Psychiatry

Only sin is man's perdition . . . .

—Sören Kierkegaard

Basing itself on existential philosophy and bearing the same name, existential psychiatry evolved as a reaction to the reductionistic tendencies of psychoanalysis, and to the narrow scope of the behavioral sciences, both of which have attempted to interpret the psychology of man in biological terms. In a historical sense, existential psychiatry may be considered a return to philosophy and religion, for it is in these realms that a solution to the fundamental problems concerning the "psyche" can be found. It ought to be understood, however, that existential philosophy, upon which existential psychiatry was founded, does not advance a new philosophy, but represents rather a distillate of prior trends of thought, adapted to the modern world. The majority, but not all, of the adherents of existential philosophy hold a theistic worldview. Notwithstanding, the basic principles of Existentialism are intrinsic to all of the major religions in the world.

Existential philosophy may be regarded as a product of the historical crisis that overtook the Western world at the end of the Middle Ages and beginning of the Industrial Revolution. With rising hopes in the progress of science and success of the movements for social justice, it appeared as though man could make it on his own, without recourse to the Higher Powers. It also seemed as if the notion of the soul could be explained away by biological theories such as child development, family constellations, early conditioning and "imprinting," for example, that would provide hard data to square much of what is unknown about manifest behavior in health and in disease. In the process of this "biologization" of psychological phenomena, the concept of the "mind"—identified with the brain and its functioning—came to replace what has hitherto been thought as constituting the "psyche." Man thus became little more than a conditioned stimulus-response automaton, a biological unit—driven mostly by instinctual urges and restrained by reality, at best.

The horizons of Existentialists extend much wider. In their perspective, man is a unity of spirit, heart, mind, and body. If regarded as a system, it is, nonetheless, not a closed one, for it provides some freedom to its functional parts, and allows the spirit to soar far and beyond. To exist (*existere*), is to dynamically participate in the molding of oneself, as well as in forging one's destiny. Existentialists insist also that this being—man—has a need for transcendence and meaning that surpasses the need for satisfaction of his biological urges. Thus, according to existential philosophy, man not only exists, but gives substance, i.e., essence to his life (*essere*) through his transcendental pursuits.

But instead of generalities, the cause of existential psychiatry will better be served by exploring its origins and evolution through a study of the work and lives of its major proponents. An outline of the main principles of this branch of psychiatry and a concluding condensation may clarify much that has, unfortunately, been misunderstood about this field of endeavor.

*   *   *

Sören Kierkegaard (1813–1855)

At a time when organized religion was progressively losing ground on account of past uses and abuses on the part of its institutions, the lonely and introspective Dane, Sören Kierkegaard, began preaching in his writings that authentic faith is possible outside of organized religion.

Kierkegaard perceived a great deal of hypocrisy in church officials as well as in his fellow Christians. With cutting sarcasm, he attacked those who professed the Christian faith but failed to manifest it in reality. He called for a Christianity based on truth, such as is produced in action and commitment, not in words. He also insisted that it is man who gives *essence* to his *existence*. In other words, existence precedes essence, but man has to *existere*, to "emerge" first, in order to *become* later what he *chooses* to become. Thus, man chooses himself. Kierkegaard appealed to his own as well as to future generations to change their lives and fulfill their respective "life-missions." He attempted to define the scope of sin and described its various ramifications. "Only sin is man's ruin," he insisted, and quoting from Socrates, found logical proof of the immortality of the soul, "as only sin has the capacity to corrupt it."

Kierkegaard also stressed that man can never become an end unto himself, and that happiness can be achieved only by leaving open the door to divine Providence. The more one intends happiness, the more one actually shuts the door, which opens only from outside, from the side of God. Kierkegaard enunciated the truth-as-relationship principle, by which he meant that truth is related to its seeker. This principle has been regarded as foreshadowing the Theory of Relativity. The concept of truth as related to its seeker has opened the way to the investigation of subjective experiences, which may seem to contradict observable facts. Dreams, visions, delusions, and hallucinations all fall into this category. But in the context of Kierkegaard's work, truth is also related to the Eternal: "By truth I mean eternal truth . . . . " One of these truths Kierkegaard enunciated in the following statement: "And to honour every man, absolutely every man, is the truth, and this is what it is to fear God and love one's neighbor . . . ." Although elusive and relative to the seeker, absolute Truth is indeed with the Eternal. For Kierkegaard, religion was not mere consolation but a *demand*.

Early in his rather short life, Kierkegaard suffered from what would today be diagnosed as a major depression. It followed certain events, which he described as "stormy." He wrote about this personal catastrophe at length in *The Sickness unto Death*; a sickness he overcame, however, through repentance and a "leap" into faith. The lonely "individual" (one of his favorite characterizations of man) Kierkegaard, confidently committed to the cause of Christianity, lived what he preached, and dying, he could say: "I stand fast and my works with me . . . ."

Out of the depths of his sadness and from the many volumes he has written, Kierkegaard emerges as the founder of existential philosophy as well as one of the prophets of our time. Not fully recognized as yet, his contributions to psychiatry loom enormous. He described ontological guilt, the anxiety of the neurotic, the dread of the psychotic, the torments of guilt, and much more. His philosophy is one of responsibility, commitment, freedom of choice, actions instead of words, and an "inwardness" that requires self-examination and scrupulous honesty.

Fyodor Mikhailovich Dostoyevsky
(1821–1881)

Living in the troubled times of prerevolutionary Russia, Dostoyevsky, a giant in the world of literature, is frequently numbered with Existentialists, for his ideas closely parallel those of other proponents of this philosophy. Long before the advent of psychoanalysis, Dostoyevsky foresaw how psychic determinism would invade the behavioral sciences. "Science has succeeded in so far analyzing, that we know already that choice," and "what is called freedom of will is nothing else but . . . " the ellipsis to be filled by an array of psychological explanations. Adamantly, Dostoyevsky defended the freedom of the will, and, with Kierkegaard and Nietzsche, he perceived man's supreme individuality as well as his subjectivity. He contradicted psychoanalytic theories: "Reason is defeated and consciousness of our deepest wishes does not help us to change anything in human nature," he wrote, believing that man does not always act in order to secure his own advantage. The glimmers of Existentialism shine through here: man's most basic need is to transcend his biological determinants. Science and knowledge, Dostoyevsky believed, will prove powerless to free man from his weaknesses, for his choices frequently run against his own best interests, and quite often, he acts just so as to assert his individuality.

Fyodor Mikhailovich Dostoyevsky began his life as the son of a brutal, ruthless, alcoholic landowner who was eventually murdered by his own serfs. Dostoyevsky's rather stormy life included participation in a revolutionary movement, a near-execution experience, imprisonment, exile, hard labor in Siberia, and two marriages. Well acquainted with debauchery, sexual orgies, and drunkenness, Dostoyevsky was a compulsive gambler as well. He had fits of epilepsy and suffered from deep depressions. He knew, however, experiences of happiness and states of elation. Bitter failures and some successes alternated in the eventful life of this passionate, larger-than-life psychologist, philosopher, and writer.

Summing up his life experiences, Dostoyevsky came to the realization that the quality of man's soul is more important than endured humiliation. For him, suffering, redemption, and rebirth of the soul were inseparable from and incomprehensible without religion. The last fourteen years of his life were spent in the bliss of a happy marriage and freedom from vice. During these final years he wrote, among others, his two great novels: *The Brothers Karamazov* and *Crime and Punishment.* Dostoyevsky thus brought a living confirmation to the possibility of a true rebirth of the soul. He died a Russian hero.

Even more than the writings of Kierkegaard, Dostoyevsky's visions of the future may be considered prophetic. He foresaw the failure of Communism and Socialism to resolve the real problems of humanity and perceived the threat to individuality those movements imposed (*The Possessed*). In spite of learning and knowledge, men may still choose that which runs against their best interest for the sake of power, dominance, and self-expression: "No one will ever submit himself to become a piano, played upon by another," he wrote. As for the progress of civilization: "The only gain of civilization for mankind is the greater capacity for a variety of sensations, and nothing more." Science and political systems, for that matter, will remain powerless to effect a change in the human heart: "If God is dead, all will be permitted . . ." predicted Dostoyevsky long before Nietzsche had taken the opportunity to make his awesome declaration: "God is dead . . . ." Since then, all has indeed become permitted . . . .

Dostoyevsky's psychological insights have yet to be given the recognition they deserve, for example: his description of depression, which pervades all of his writings; his insights into the borderline condition, described in his *Notes from the Underground*; his perception of the association of guilt and loathing; and his recognition of the duality of man's nature, elaborated in *The Brothers Karamazov.* Dostoyevsky's description of the evolution of a paranoid schizophrenia and its eventual dissolution, depicted in *Crime and Punishment,* may be considered a historical document. For psychiatrists, it can serve as a classical textbook case example.

The following psychological insight cuts straight through the heart of existential philosophy: "Without a pure heart there can be no complete, pure consciousness." Clarity of consciousness, according to Dostoyevsky, is related to the purity of heart, i.e., to the heart's motivations (impure when tainted by ulterior motives or clouded by pretense). In psychological terms, this means that the liar is incapable of seeing the truth (reality); that the malevolent can see only malevolence and fear it; and that none is more jealous than the adulterer. Dostoyevsky associated the functions of the Ego with the intentions of the heart, as did Swedenborg before him. His views on the clarity of consciousness come close to Kierkegaard's principle of truth-as-related-to-its-seeker.

Karl Jaspers (1883–1969)

Doctor of medicine, specialist in psychiatry, and later professor of philosophy, Jaspers wrote extensively on various psychological as well as philosophical subjects. He is the author of the well-known textbook *Psychopathology.* Deeply influenced by the writings of Kierkegaard, Jaspers embraced many of the essential principles of existential philosophy: "In every form of his being, man is related to something other than himself . . . " he wrote in *Existentzphilosophie.*

Man relates thus as a being to this world, as consciousness to objects, and as spirit to the idea of whatever constitutes Totality—as *Existenz* to *Transcendenz* (Deity). But man becomes man only by devoting himself to an "Other." Only through his absorption in the world of Being does he become real to himself. If he makes himself the immediate object of his efforts, he is on his last and perilous path. Strictly a theist, Jaspers wrote: "That Deity *is* suffices . . . to be certain is the only thing that matters. Everything follows from that . . . ." In Deity there is peace as well as the origin and aim of man, who by himself is nothing, and what he is, is only in relation to Deity. Truth can be found, according to Jaspers, through dialogue with an Other.

To psychiatrists Jaspers is known by his description of the preschizophrenic state, a condition he defined by the term "trema." This is an experience of dread, in which every object in the external world becomes endowed with ominous significance, portending inescapable doom. Jaspers differentiated between reducible delusions, namely delusional *ideas*, on the one hand, and irreducible delusions, *experiences* no one can change, on the other. He believed that at some point in life (usually in middle age), man suffers a "shipwreck," and this crisis, known as an existential crisis, often leads to new insights and a more authentic existence.

Martin Buber (1878–1965)

Martin Buber was born in Vienna, where he studied and lived until his emigration to the land he contributed to reclaim for the Jewish people. He became interested in the Chassidic sect of Judaism, whose way of worship is an expressive affirmation of faith, more in the spirit than the letter of the Law.

The philosophy of Buber is directly entwined with his theology. His small but epoch-making monograph, *I and Thou* (1970), which appeared first in 1937, became a cornerstone in the development of existential psychiatry. Buber attempted to avoid such concepts as "essence" and "existence." Essential is what is here and now. Man becomes man only through a "You," he wrote. "As soon as we touch a You we are touched by the breath of eternal life." Buber asked the same questions as those from his generation who no longer believed, but he answered in the affirmative: God *is*. He sought to grasp the central questions of meaning, suffering, and death, in both religious and philosophical terms. "God is present when I confront a You, but if I look away from You, I ignore him. As long as I merely experience a You or use a You—I deny God. But when I encounter You, I encounter Him." This You, however, may become the *means* to something, an object to be used and abused. The You becomes in this case reduced to an "it."

For Buber, encounter is when the You is met in reciprocity, "as every means is an obstacle to encounter. "In love there is the responsibility of an I for a You: "In this consists what cannot consist in any feeling . . . . " Buber saw man's need for meaning as most central to his being. From an encounter with the divine Thou, man acquires "the inexpressible confirmation of meaning. One cannot in any way define that meaning, yet it is more certain for you than the sensations of your senses . . . ." Like Kierkegaard, Buber stressed the immediacy of the I-Thou relationship, and like him he saw the "oughts" of religion as possible obstacles in this relationship.

Buber saw Good and Evil as alternate paths that confront man and from which he stands to choose. Evil cannot be done with the whole soul, he wrote, only good can be done with the whole soul. Evil leads to chaos, good to unification of the soul. Buber believed that every ethos has its origin in revelation (whether man is aware of and obedient to it or not), but every revelation is actually a calling for a mission. It is usually some human service to the goal of creation by which man is able to authenticate himself.

Friedrich Nietzsche (1844–1900)

Nietzsche was born in Germany, where he lived and died. Within the existential movement (in which he was placed by historians) he stands out as a prophet, but mostly of doom. Like Kierkegaard, Nietzsche challenged the religious practices of his fellow men, but went somewhat further in reaching a paradox, as was his style: "Faith means not wanting to know what is true . . . ." He went on to challenge "our great values and ideas"—morality in general—and accused Socrates of first "inoculating scientific work with the disease of morality." Nietzsche stretched man's capacity to will and accomplish what he wills to a paradoxical hyperbole. He considered the superior man—as he believed himself to be—as one endowed with the right and power to dominate inferior ones, setting him above morality, above Good and Evil.

As if hearing Dostoyevsky's fearful cry from faraway Russia, Nietzsche defiantly responded by declaring God to be dead. He foresaw the advent of Nihilism and predicted "a two-hundred-act horror play, to be witnessed by the world, were morality to be overthrown."[*] Nietzsche's philosophy has been frequently assailed as fueling the ideology of Nazism. An anti-Semite, Nietzsche hated women also: "Take a whip when you go to a woman . . . ," he recommended. His was a lonely, isolated existence. He succumbed eventually to madness and died in an asylum for the insane.

Like other Existentialists, Nietzsche believed in man's power to create himself anew, provided he could conquer his own weaknesses. The following statement contains a remarkably existential idea as well as psychological insight: "For one thing is needful, that a human being attain satisfaction with himself—only then is a human being tolerable to behold. Whosoever is dissatisfied with himself, is always ready to revenge himself, therefore . . . ." Along with other Existentialists Nietzsche was keenly aware of the need for meaning: "If one only knew where one was going, the 'how' would become unimportant . . . ."

Albert Camus (1913–1960)

Writer and philosopher, Camus sought to explain life in terms of accepting its futility and vain investment of effort. The worth of life? Living it, concluded Camus. In his book *The Myth of Sisyphus,* he describes the tragic mythological hero who, spurned by the gods, is condemned to carry stones to the peak of a mountain, fully aware that

---

[*]   A play presented before our very eyes (cf. Chapter IX).

the stones he brings up will invariably roll back down to the plain—
an absurd task, indeed. Camus died prematurely as a consequence of
a car accident, which the Paris newspapers proclaimed with the
headline "ABSURDE!" Like other Existentialists, he was well aware
of the necessity for a committed involvement in the struggles of life,
whose challenges he considered sufficient for giving it meaning.

Yet, Camus' philosophy lacks conviction. His novel *The Stranger*
subtly conveys a sense of tragedy as it describes the consequences of
unrelatedness. The hero's inauthentic existence slowly unravels: a
dark foil against which Camus sought to flash the brightness of a life
populated by others or an Other, and committed to someone, perhaps
to a cause. He was himself committed to the French Resistance
movement and various liberal causes.

Franz Kafka (1883–1924)

A brilliant writer, Kafka came to fame through his slow-moving,
dread-filled, and wrapped-in-a-cloud-of-ambiguity short novels. He
asked the same heavy-laden questions as those of his generation who
sought answers by way of reason and away from religious faith. In
The Castle, Kafka described an empty and meaningless universe
following the death of the Emperor (God). Kafka's novel *The
Metamorphosis* has been interpreted as an autobiographical account
of his slow descent into insanity. The main character of this story
suddenly perceives himself as a huge insect, loathsome and repugnant,
criticized and condemned by his fellow men. Why? In his *Diaries,*
Kafka admits to having taken a position at a railroad station because
it gave him an opportunity to kill animals, an activity in which he
delighted. Can his metamorphosis into an insect be interpreted as
punishment for this rather sadistic "sport?" Did he feel similarly
toward his fellow men? In *The Trial*, Kafka saw himself judged and
condemned by a court and judge he did not recognize, as he slowly
descended into the underworlds of madness.

Kafka is included among existentialist thinkers because he so
poignantly described the forlornness of modern man, whose life he
perceives as devoid of meaning; who feels prosecuted by an unrecognized judge in an unknown court (his conscience?); and who no
longer can appeal to a higher authority, for he has denied its existence
altogether. Kafka's world is our world also. His existential condition
of emptiness and despair is shared by all those who have ceased to
believe, by all those who have denied the existence of a Higher

Authority—and who have lost the privilege of appealing their respective sentences, because they have refused to accept the authority that has handed them down. Among Existentialists, Kafka may be considered a prophet of doom; it could have been his own.

Emanuel Swedenborg (1688–1772)

An overview of existential philosophy would not be complete without the inclusion of Swedenborg and his voluminous work. Long before existential philosophy came into being, the theologian, philosopher, scientist, and psychologist Swedenborg brought stress to bear on *deeds* and *truth* in religious expression rather than the often abused claim to a nebulous "faith." Most relevant to existential psychiatry are Swedenborg's formulations on the personality and its inner motivations: "What a man wills inwardly, he loves and what he loves he wills, and the will's love flows into the understanding where it makes its pleasure felt, and thereupon enters the thoughts and intentions . . . "(*Divine Providence*). One's world-design as well as secret inner motivations thus constitute one's loves, flowing into the understanding and directing the will. This would make our "loves" the rulers of our behavior, and not the Ego-mind-reason, which simply acts in the service of their pursuit. We are defined by what we inwardly love. "Intention is a person's nature . . . the actual person or bent," wrote Swedenborg in *Heaven and Hell*—a statement that cuts right to the heart of existential philosophy. In *Existentialism and the New Christianity*, H. W. Barnitz (1969) draws several significant parallels. He also finds most Existentialists and Swedenborg unified in their affirmation of the supremacy of the will over the understanding.

Jean-Paul Sartre (1905–1981)

The name of Sartre has become closely associated, if not almost synonymous with, Existentialism, which he made popular through most of his writings. For Sartre, Existentialism represented a doctrine "which renders life possible" (*Existentialism Is a Humanism*). Unlike Nietzsche and Kafka, who emphatically denied the existence of Higher Powers, Sartre considered himself an atheist; but, as he stated, he would not exhaust himself in order to defend his atheistic position. He recognized, nonetheless, that without a goal outside of himself, man's existence has no meaning. Sartre saw no guiding light for men and put all responsibility for the human condition upon man's shoulders. His philosophy is an ethical one, nonetheless: "I am obliged at every instant to perform actions which are examples," he wrote. And, "If God did not exist, there is at least one being whose existence comes before its essence, and that being is man." First existing, man encounters himself later and surges up in the world, to define himself: "Man is nothing else but what he makes of himself. This is the first principle of Existentialism." The first effect of Existentialism is that it puts every man in possession of himself as he is, and places all the responsibility upon his own shoulders. In his youth, Sartre suffered from a painful inner void, an existential despair he described in one of his early books, *La Nausée*. This crisis, it seems, prompted him to join the cause of the French Resistance against the occupying forces of Nazi Germany. The benefits he seems to have derived from this commitment might have been instrumental in his espousal of the existential movement as *causa sui*.

Existential psychiatry owes much to Sartre the philosopher, who called to debate some of our modern psychological theories. Giving due merit to the psychoanalytical technique, he took issue, however, with the major part of its doctrine.

A central and most pivotal issue in existential psychiatry, namely that "feelings are formed by the deeds one does," was dear to Sartre's heart. He proposed a new theory of the emotions (*Existentialism and Human Emotions*). This important insight, namely that actions generate emotions, is slowly gaining acceptance among psychologists and psychiatrists, who have begun to apply it in their treatment strategies for the mentally diseased. Yet mainstream psychiatry still lags considerably behind in recognizing the effects of behaviors on feeling states, as well as in separating the former from the latter—as causes from effects. As if we were but "driven" by emotions; as if our actions or inactions had but little influence on our system of self-rewards or punishments and on our feeling states. "There is no other reality than in man's actions," stressed Sartre, and "when Existentialists condemn a coward, they do so on the basis of the coward's deeds, not his feelings of fear."

Sartre successfully exposed some of the fallacies inherent in the psychoanalytic doctrine. By sheer power of logic, he defeated the notion of the "unconscious," showing the "subconscious" and "unconscious" to be less unconscious, after all. According to Sartre, when one submerges any truth or reality, for that matter, into levels less conscious, one is well aware of that reality, the need to "defend" it (by forgetting or denying it), and the act of repression itself.

As for the lie, it needs to be defended also. The problem becomes further complicated by the fact that, aware of his deception, the deceiver may either become cynical about it, or hide the truth even from himself. By admitting a driving "subconscious" Id into the life of the "psyche," psychoanalysis, according to Sartre, has substituted the notion of self-deception with the idea of a "lie without a liar": "The ideal description of the liar would be a cynical consciousness, affirming the truth in himself, denying it in words and denying the negation as such (*L'Etre et le Néant*). This creates, of course, an ontological duality: "Myself and myself in the eyes of others."

Resistances emerging in the process of psychoanalysis cannot be explained as emanating from a "complex" the psychoanalyst attempts to bring to light, for the patient's "censor" well knows what it is he is repressing. Self-deception is chosen, thus, by those who prefer to avoid and/or escape encountering their inner Selves. Contrary to psychoanalytic doctrine, Existentialists deny the powers of passion, and insist that *man is responsible for his passion also*.

Sartre advocated commitment and action in the strongest possible terms, even when the goal appears to be far off. As for love, he wrote: "There is no love apart from the deeds of love; no potentiality of love other than that which is manifested in loving . . . . "

Due to his atheistic worldview, Sartre's most eloquent moral exhortations lose some of their poignancy, nonetheless. By reason of its detachment from religion, his philosophy is weakened, as is also its persuasive clout. What benefit, indeed, does one derive from being moral, truthful, generous, courageous? Does one not extract more from this world by way of flattery, manipulations, exploitation, disguise, and cunning devices? And for what reason is one to be committed to causes beyond oneself? Just so as to follow existential philosophy? Or maintain perhaps one's mental health? What if the cause one becomes committed to serves actually a subversive goal—genocide, for example?

Dostoyevsky's statement, "If God did not exist all would be permitted," was regarded by Sartre as representing the beginning of Existentialism " . . . and quite burdensome at that, for it means that man is condemned to be free . . . "(*Les Chemins de la Liberté*). Did Sartre himself feel condemned? Simone de Beauvoir, his lifelong companion, describes Sartre in her book *L'Age de Raison*, as intermittently suffering from a "hallucinatory psychosis," during which he felt pursued by lobsters, crabs, and other insects.

*   *   *

While all major religions of the world contain an essentially existential philosophy, not all Existentialists adhere to a theistic worldview, as becomes evident from the summary description of their ideas. The question then arises as to whether existential philosophy can sustain its vitality—and this applies perhaps to any other philosophy—without recourse to religion. The tragic destinies of some atheist existentialists may be speaking louder than all of their writings. Kafka's denial of God, for example, brought him to a trial whose judge he did not recognize. This gifted writer eventually came to experience himself as a repugnant, giant insect. While still young, he plunged into an abyss of madness, out of which he was unable to extricate himself. The deicide proclaimed by Nietzsche, his repudiation of morality, and his grandiose presumptions of superiority, led him to spend the last years of his life in the company of demented and imbeciles with whom he would be sharing his paradoxes. The life of Albert Camus, who extolled the absurdity of human endeavors, ended abruptly through an absurd car accident. Intellectual Existentialism, it would appear, could not sustain them. By contrast, the lives of Swedenborg, Kierkegaard, Buber, and Dostoyevsky, inspired by faith, proclaim victory over their destinies, and the reality of their actions speaks more eloquently even than their writings.

*   *   *

It has frequently been said that existential psychiatry evolved out of the need for expansion from the narrow confines of the behavioral sciences, especially psychoanalysis. And indeed, if one is to take seriously the laments of the mentally anguished and diseased, the scope of their concerns would surely be found to extend far and beyond matters of pleasure, sexual gratification, past traumatic events, various conflicts, and difficulties imposed by the demands of reality.

As with the history of existential philosophy, the history of existential psychiatry evolved and became interwoven with the thought of its major theorists.

Ludwig Binswanger (1881–1966)

A considerably younger friend of Freud and his collaborator in the psychoanalytic movement, Binswanger is considered the founder of existential psychiatry. His field of endeavor, defined as "phenomenological anthropology," encompasses not only the study of phenomena or subjective experiences, but also integration of the latter into the

totality of the experiencer's world. Jasper's descriptive phenomenology has been considered the first step toward a more accurate
investigation of subjective phenomena. But Sartre, the philosopher,
went even further in assigning to phenomenology the task of decoding
the meaning of phenomena. For Binswanger, *existential analysis*
represented a synthesis of psychoanalysis and phenomenology. Hence,
the patient undergoing existential analysis is asked not only to give
an account of his past, but also to elaborate on his deeds and
misdeeds. Binswanger was influenced to a large extent—as were
many other Existentialists—by Martin Heidegger (1899–1976), and
especially by his *Analysis of Being.*

Not unlike psychoanalysis, existential analysis plots its data on a
horizontal axis: setting life-events in their sequence along the
longitudinal axis of existence, limited by space and time. However,
it does not content itself with probing into the past and present, as
does psychoanalysis, but considers aspirations and projections into the
future—plotted along a vertical axis—as more relevant by far.
Although frequently invisible and also intangible, our goals and
strivings have a stronger influence over us—what we are, and what
we intend to achieve—than our biological drives. Much of our
behavior, indeed, is motivated by the compelling pull exerted by our
inner wishes and strivings. We may turn our gaze upward in search
of the Sublime; we may seek the bliss of love; we may toil to obtain
the satisfaction from duty fulfilled or the elation that follows
achievement. But we may also be blinded by ambition, consumed by
hate, greed, and revenge, or driven to power. "The vertical axis is the
basic axis to which our most vital experiences are related," wrote
Binswanger. *The vertical axis is the axis of transcendence.* Language,
metaphors, literature, folklore, popular belief, and subjective experiences all relate to this vertical axis, as shown by French philosopher
Gaston Bachelard (*La Vie Ascentionelle*). For existential psychiatrists,
transcendence represents a basic human need.

Daseinanalyse and Existential Analysis

Contemporary psychiatrist Meddard Boss, a pupil of Freud and
influenced by Heidegger, advanced his own *Daseinanalyse,* which is
considered a branch of existential psychiatry. His is an empathic, but
rather passive, understanding of the patient's world. It is an analysis
of his *Dasein,* i.e., of his ways of "being here," in the world.

With other Existentialists, Binswanger holds a conception of man as relationship. Man thus relates to the world around him, his *Umwelt*; to the world of others, his *Mitwelt,* comprised of the "Yous" he encounters; and finally, to himself in his *Eigenwelt*, the subjective inner world of Self. But the Self *transcends* its world through the goals toward which it strives. It may seek to encounter the divine Thou.

Hence, in addition to past life-events, existential analysis attempts to determine the subject's world-design, his ways of being-in-the-world, and also his attitude toward the beyond-of-this-world—his transcendental and spiritual aspirations. The psychopath, for example, uses and abuses others, the world. He attempts to evade his inner Self, his *Eigenwelt*, and frequently resorts to drugs and alcohol. He may become emotionally hardened in the process, however, as he gravitates toward the material. Through destructive intentions, hostility, and compulsion for domination, the schizophrenic is brought sooner or later to sever his relationships with others and the divine Thou, remaining alone at the end, with only "its" (inanimate objects) left to be exploited. It is not a condition of loneliness that he ultimately comes to suffer, but a state of alienation from himself, from others, and from the divine Thou, as his world progressively condenses into matter. It is shrouded by an atmosphere of dread and populated by dark shadows and invisible "voices."

In existential analysis, symptoms of distress are traced back to their source, whether external or internal. Guilt is explored with respect to its derivation, and the moral failures or offenses responsible for its surge are further investigated. Existentialists do not recognize guilt as "irrational," nor do they accept the notion of "unconscious" guilt. Basic attitudes and repetitive behaviors are identified, as well as their true motivations. Exploration extends further into the individual's beliefs and "beyond-the-world" aspirations, life-philosophy, and worldview. All relationships are brought to scrutiny, and this includes the way one relates to oneself as well as the way one relates to the divine Thou.

Phenomenology

Psychologist Franz Brentano (1838–1917), who taught both Freud and Husserl, believed that mental phenomena are directed toward objects and are thus expressions of an intentional existence within consciousness.

Edmund Husserl (1859–1938) attempted to establish phenomenology on a sound scientific basis. The difficulties inherent in such a task became immediately obvious to him, however. Given the unique individuality of human beings, their specific circumstances, different worlds, and variability in inner experience, phenomenological data would, clearly, fail to satisfy the rigorous criteria of scientific research that demand reliability and validity.

Gestalt Psychology

Considered a branch of existential psychiatry, Gestalt psychology has been recognized for its provision of valuable insights, a treatment method, and also a compendium of definitions for the variety of modes of being-in-the-world. Developed by Frederick S. Perls (1893–1970) in the early 1930s, Gestalt psychotherapy was defined by its focus on the "here and now" and "I and Thou." The term "life-script" is often used by Gestalt psychotherapists to define one's goals and the specific manner of obtaining them. For Gestaltists, self-realization is the ultimate human goal. "Gestalt" means constellation, and in the context of Gestalt psychology, the figure-ground is completed by self-realization. By engendering excitement, interest, and desire for change, Perls confronted his patients (mostly in groups) with their "toxic" ways of living, and made use of a medical-sounding terminology: "approvalitis" for a compulsive search for approval; "failuritis" for a phobia that prevents the enjoyment of life; "rebellionitis" to describe the "hippie" syndrome; "emotional constipation" for the fear of crying; and the "dumping syndrome" for the tendency to dump on others—wife, therapist, or husband—all that is unpleasant in life.

Victor Frankl and Logotherapy

Popular the world over for his prolific writings on existential themes as well as for his Logotherapy, contemporary psychiatrist Victor Frankl has been most influential in initiating a new school of thought within the mainstream of modern psychiatry. A prisoner of the Nazis and inmate of a concentration camp, Frankl became aware of man's need for meaning (*logos* = meaning, and also spirit). During the years of suffering he endured, Frankl perceived that under very similar circumstances certain individuals became "beasts," while others were able to transcend themselves and their terrible predicament, attaining saintliness instead. More than the need for power (Nietzsche's *élan vital*), or gratification of the craving for pleasure (Freud's pleasure principle), man needs to find meaning in his life, his efforts, and even his extinction. But meaning, according to Frankl, can be found only by the individual himself, for no one else can "read the signs" of another's destiny. Meaning, by the same token, can never be too far removed from the duties imposed by one's circumstances, by one's predicament.

Along with existentialist writer and philosopher Gabriel Marcel (1889–1973), Frankl sought to emphasize man's responsibility to "read" the signs of his destiny as well as to respond. To whom? To what? For Marcel, the Self is a response, an aspiration, a creative engagement in something other than oneself. Frequently man senses a compelling call. By whom? To whom is the Self answerable? This brings up the question of the origins of the conscience, to which, according to Frankl, there can be no psychological answer, only an ontological one. For Frankl, "conscience not only refers to transcendence; it also *originates* in transcendence. This fact accounts for its irreducible quality" (*The Unconscious God*). Frankl also takes issue with Freud's concepts of the Ego and the Superego. The Self cannot be responsible merely to itself, nor can the conscience issue categorical imperatives, be its own lawgiver. "Just as freedom means little or nothing," writes Frankl, "likewise, responsibleness means little without a 'to what?' 'to whom?'" Frankl's Logotherapy is rooted in religion, but in his therapeutic approach he gives full respect to the beliefs of those who seek his help. He directs the patient toward the particular meaning that would contribute to his self-realization. For Frankl self-realization is achieved through the fulfillment of one's specific life-mission(s), usually a task that serves others in the plan of creation.

*   *   *

A full appraisal of the contribution of existential philosophy to psychiatry is still pending, and hardly by chance. Veering in a direction opposite to philosophy, contemporary psychologies have tended to avoid "metaphysical" questions and challenges to their neatly structured biological schemata. They have tended rather to promote individual self-realization through the attainment of self-serving goals and worldly rewards. Guided by a much larger view of man and the universe he is part of, Existentialists recommend self-detachment and the fulfillment of one's specific life-mission(s). An authentic existence is lived, according to this philosophy, in close proximity to one's Self, but this requires frequent and oftentimes painful self-examination. To the "others," the "Yous" of one's world, one is to relate in honesty and reciprocity. Regardless of the consequences in reality, this philosophy requires that one be truly truthful in all of one's communications, and truly benevolent to others in thought as well as deed.

For reasons to be considered elsewhere (Chapter IX), contemporary psychiatry—at least in North America—has allocated to existential psychiatry but a peripheral position. This attitude seems quite astonishing in view of the fact that according to the survey of I. Yalom (1975), the majority of patients present difficulties existential in nature. Yet, with neurobiology falling from glory, genetic research lacking in accuracy, and the ever increasing vacuum in the soul of modern man, the day may not be so far off when existential psychiatry will command—as it has in the past—a dominant position.

In health and in disease, man is nothing in isolation; he is always related to him-Self as well as to something, someone *other*. People's ways of relatedness may vary, nonetheless. They may be abusive, neglectful, hateful, manipulative, extortionistic, and dominating, but they may also be loving, caring, giving, and sacrificing. And for their stress on the ways of one's being-in-the-world, their seeking out secret inner motivations, their attempts to identify "toxic" ways-of-being, their recognition of man's transcendental strivings, and their confirmation of sin and guilt as powerful psychological realities, existentially oriented psychiatrists have much to offer to the understanding of psychiatric disturbances and diseases. Additionally, existential psychiatrists attempt to separate causes from effects, feeling states from behaviors. They also recognize that behaviors may be motivated by feeling states and conversely, that feeling states may be the consequences of behaviors.

Beyond heredity and childhood "traumata," the existential approach seeks to identify factors of transcendence, in recognition of the psyche's essentially spiritual nature. In the process of Logotherapy, the patient is assisted in his search for meaning; encouraged to unburden his guilty conscience; and aided in coming to terms with bereavement, suffering, and death. Existential psychiatry has thus much more to offer to those in the throes of a mental disturbance or disease than conventional psychological approaches. In Logotherapy the patient is directed toward self-detachment, not self-involvement. This may be achieved through humor, love, and engagement in causes that benefit others. Existential psychiatry insists, moreover, that one can engender feelings of elation even in the midst of disaster: for actions have the capacity to engender feelings. Endowed with an ethical instinct, man can find relief from tension, guilt, and despair by filling the ever passing minute with an action that would gratify this instinct.

Of major concern to existential psychiatry is the moral conscience, considered central to the life of the psyche. The judgments of the conscience are deemed inscrutable and also inviolable. Existential psychiatry may be defined thus by its adherence to an essentially Superego psychology. Feelings of guilt are thus heeded and their source investigated. Let no one dare to assist a patient in repressing, suppressing, denying, or demolishing his or her conscience. Let the pain of guilt and remorse be relieved by tranquilizers, but never anaesthetized to the point of indolence. Just as physical pain is a symptom of inner distress or sickness calling for attention, mental anguish and distress point to a deeper disturbance and call for remedial action. The laws of physiology cannot be violated without detriment to the physical body. Likewise, the spiritual laws that govern the life of the soul cannot be violated without causing damage or sickness to the psyche, the soul. Let, therefore, no one tamper with the operations of the living conscience, that "wired-in existential monitor," to borrow Frankl's expression. This metaphor, which describes the essence and function of the moral conscience, may best serve to guide and direct the healing efforts of those involved in the care of psychiatric patients. It also summarizes much of what has filled the preceding pages.

Chapter III

Neurobiological Correlates to Psychiatric Disorders

The organically damaged can't, the emotionally disturbed won't.
—H. J. Schulman

There can be no mistake about the tendency of mainstream psychiatry to move in a direction away from "psychological intangibles" and toward the acceptance of biological determinants in the causation of mental disturbances and diseases. From the profusion of research data in the neurobiochemical and neuroanatomical sciences as well as the growing interest in psychopharmacology—which overwhelmingly outnumber other subjects in the current psychiatric literature—one may be justified in concluding that contemporary psychiatry hopes to solve the mysteries of mental illness through research in the biological sciences. Not by chance, the latest Diagnostic and Statistical Manuals of Mental Disorders (DSM-III-R and DSM-IV) classify mental disorders according to the symptoms they produce, without consideration given to their underlying causes. In its efforts to retain an "atheoretical" perspective, as well as for practical purposes of research and treatment, the American Psychiatric Association has tended to focus its attention on the signs and symptoms of disease, clustered into syndromes, rather than on their source, in accordance with the prevailing belief that most psychiatric disorders are of "unknown etiology."

And then, with the growing use of chemical substances among the general public—whether for recreational purposes or the relief of tension—and with the widespread use of medicines by physicians in general and by psychiatrists in particular, there is little wonder the man on the street has come to the conclusion that "it's all in your chemistry." Even more so for mental patients, who are frequently told that, like the diabetic who needs insulin for the rest of his life, they will have to take their medicines indefinitely or else risk a relapse of their disease. And while it is true that the symptoms of a mental disease may become attenuated by chemical compounds, medicines in no way provide a solution to the problem of diseases that affect the psyche.

Moreover, a good number of research data—and this is especially true for psychiatry and the psychological sciences—lend themselves to several different interpretations, some of which are liable to be misleading. With all due respect to the reliability and validity of psychiatric research findings, they are mostly static with respect to time; do not take into account the sequential order of psychological and biological phenomena; and fail to recognize the psychophysiological remedial system of the body, operative in the living individual. For these reasons, among others, research data may not tell us much about causes and effects; about what is stimulus and what response; or answer the question of whether repeated physiological changes and insults may be harmful over time and cause anatomical damage to an organ, in this case to brain structures. The debate over whether psychological factors produce biological changes and even disease, or conversely, whether biological-organic factors are to be held responsible for the causation of mental illnesses, is evidently not so easily resolved.

It may not be our chemistry, after all. We may not just be the pawns of our biochemical reactions, mere victims of the whims of our molecules. Anatomical abnormalities and lesions in the brain may not by necessity produce psychiatric disturbances or diseases. We may be affected by many more events and circumstances than those stemming from our heredity and traumatic childhood experiences. For all of these reasons, and before undertaking the conceptual burial of what we have known as the soul or psyche, we may wish to pause and reconsider.

Physiological Changes in Neurotic Illnesses— Anxiety Disorders

There may not be a better point of departure for solving the controversy regarding the assumed biological causation of mental disorders and diseases than by focusing attention on the physiological changes observed in the various **Anxiety Disorders,** previously known as the **Neuroses.** And there may not be a better example whereby the issues related to the body-mind (soma-psyche) dilemma are brought to a point, than the recent studies on the increased concentration of lactic acid (with its attendant changes in pH toward acidosis) found in the plasma of phobic and panic-stricken patients. Does this increase in lactic acid cause phobias and panic attacks? Or is it the effect of these patients' anxious state? The infusion of sodium lactate was found inducive to panic attacks in patients so predisposed, but not in others. The infusion of sodium bicarbonate (known for its capacity to increase pH and induce alkalosis) was also found capable of provoking panic attacks in patients with this disorder, but not in others. Similarly, the inhalation of 5.5 percent carbon dioxide was found to be anxiety and/or panic inducing. In a study by E. Hollander et al. (1989), who also measured cortisol levels in the plasma, these researchers found that lactic acid infusion produced panic attacks in agoraphobics and panickers only, but not in normal controls, and did not activate those mechanisms responsible for the release of cortisol as occurs during generalized or anticipatory anxiety states in normal subjects exposed to real stress.

These data may be interpreted to mean that along with other physiological changes that take place during anxiety states (cf. section on polygraph investigation, Chapter V)—including inefficient respiratory gas exchange and an increased demand for glucose by the brain that is created by the anxiety-provoking stimulus (the brain can metabolize only glucose)—an increased anaerobic breakdown of glucose (producing lactic acid) also takes place, just as happens during various medical conditions, such as diabetes, cardiogenic and hypovolemic shock, and septicemia. The common denominators to all of these conditions are an increased demand for glucose, needed during the stressful situation, and a relative decrease in available oxygen, necessary for the normal, aerobic metabolism of glucose.

Yet without taking into consideration that lactic acid increases occur *because* of the inefficient hyperventilatory activity, characteristic of anxiety states, and the increased demand for glucose by the brain, the net result of the physiological adjustments that occur in anxiety states cannot be understood. The time-sequence of events also shows that the mere presence of increased levels of lactic acid produces panic only in those with an already high level of basic anxiety, and not in others. This phenomenon may be understood to mean that the anxious become more so when the body signals danger with a rapid heart rate, anoxia, as well as an accumulation of lactic acid. It also explains the relatively normal anxiety levels of diabetics whose lactic acid elevation is due to their illness, and not to psychological factors. As for the fact that increased baseline anxiety states produce so many changes in the body, these findings underscore the marvelously efficient operations of the body's physiology, sounding an alarm for disturbed homeostasis and taking remedial action. Yet, without taking into consideration the element of time and determination as to cause and effect, as well as the physiological adjustments and readjustments continually taking place in the body, many of the biological concomitants and manifestations of anxiety states would still be considered as they are now: an enigma.

Organic Syndromes and Schizophrenia

Any theory of schizophrenia which claims that the etiology of this diseased state is determined by organic factors—such as cerebral defects, injuries, neurocellular abnormalities, or metabolic aberrations—would need first to integrate into its structure the character traits of the premorbid personality, so heavily implicated in every aspect of insanity. Any such theory, moreover, must also account for certain distinct clinical manifestations which separate the schizophrenias from known organic brain syndromes.

Little strength is added to organic theories of schizophrenia by the recent findings of shrinkage in brain size and ventricular enlargement frequently encountered in chronic cases. Functional disturbances of prolonged duration are known to produce anatomical-pathological changes in the organs so involved. Even glucose, the most "metabolizable" of all metabolites, when in excess, produces disturbances in function that may eventually cause anatomical changes in many parts of the body. Yet this does not implicate glucose as the pathogenic factor in diabetes, which is actually caused by a deficiency of insulin secreted by the pancreas. Thus, excesses in dopamine at certain cerebral sites may well be damaging, but do not necessarily incriminate this substance as responsible for the causation of a schizophrenic illness.

Nothing of substance is said, furthermore, when the various signs and symptoms of schizophrenia are explained on the basis of a "faulty chemistry." The same holds true for **Manic-Depressive Illnesses.** The physical body being made of matter, it is only natural that its smallest particles, namely the molecules, enter into various reactions and transactions, due to the constant change and flux in the state of the living organism. Thus, biological functions, as well as thought processes and emotions, have by necessity their counterpart in cellular metabolism, which involves changes on the molecular level. It thus logically follows that emotional changes and turbulence will have repercussions in the molecular world of the living organism.

When I decide to deceive, for example, the ensuing pause in my respiration and the temporary anoxia thus created produce a whole chain of chemical reactions by which all the organs of my body are affected. When I receive a message announcing to me the loss of a loved one, and I begin to cry in sorrow, my whole body participates in this sorrow. "This is the characteristic of emotion, that it is transmitted to the whole organism . . . " wrote J. A. Larson (1969). Within 15 seconds of a deceptive communication, the whole organism undergoes a change, thanks to the remarkably efficient system of transmission along the neurons of the nervous system. This system of relays functions in a way quite similar to the transmission of an electrical current, with the neural impulse travelling along neuronal tracts by a process of depolarization and repolarization of neuronal cells (the Na+/K+ pump system). In addition to neuronal impulse transmission, the central nervous system can release specific substances known as "neurotransmitters" which relay coded messages to specific brain cells via certain neuronal pathways. Neurotransmitters may also command the release of certain hormones which cause target glands to release substances that will affect every system of the body—all effected with remarkable speed.

I can decide to tell the truth, nevertheless, rather than deny it, and by so doing keep my nervous system in relative tranquility and my hormones in balance. I do not have control over the sorrow the sad message of the loss of a loved one has set in motion, however, and cannot alter the ensuing chemical processes.

Yet it is I, my Self, who have the final and decisive vote on the course of my actions, and for this reason I am, to a certain degree, responsible for my emotions and physiological state. Even in the case of the suddenly produced sadness, I still have the choice to mourn and cry or else deny such emotional responses. Whatever my decision, my chemistry will change accordingly.

Nothing is added to biological interpretations of mental disorders by the claim that certain chemical compounds, when introduced into the body, have the capacity to modify emotions or change their pitch and intensity. Every alcohol and drug abuser will readily confirm this fact. That chemical substances can alter the quality and strength of some emotions does not mean that chemicals by themselves normally produce emotions; they, certainly, cannot induce states of passion. As for the reversal or transformation of the constructs of inner reality, no chemical substance is known to have this capacity—inner states being contingent upon life experiences past and present. Neither is any chemical known to duplicate the deep sense of satisfaction ensuing from the fulfillment of some difficult task or duty, or the thrills from love reciprocated. If and when mind-altering substances on the order of LSD, cocaine, amphetamines, and alcohol are capable of producing a "high," or of transforming a given emotion, their effect is evanescent at best. The net result of substance use is always negative, because the states of "hangover," depression, and "rebound" they leave in their wake are far worse than the initial emotional condition. Experienced as more dysphoric than the initial feeling state, the plunge into depression or "hangover" compels the user of substances to avail himself of yet another glass, another sniff, another "fix," in order to allay the pain of withdrawal.

Nor can the capacity of certain chemical compounds to produce psychoses be accepted as sufficient evidence to support an organic etiology of schizophrenic illnesses. The psychotogenic effects of amphetamine, d-dexedrine, benzedrine, Ritalin, etc., have long been known to be associated with their chemical structure, which is very similar to that of the catecholamines dopamine and norepinephrine—both endogenously manufactured and heavily implicated in schizophrenic illnesses. For the heavy amphetamine abuser, it is the dopamine effect that predominates over that of norepinephrine. In both amphetamine-induced psychosis and authentic schizophrenia, excesses in available dopamine intensify existing states of fear and dread. In schizophrenia, these states are rooted in guilt; in amphetamine-induced psychoses, fear-filled dysphorias are projected out onto the environment which becomes threateningly transformed.

The claim that every thought and emotion has its chemical counterpart is merely to say that we are in constant flux on every level of existence. When even the whitest of lies produces changes in oxygen consumption, it is clear these changes do not just happen, but represent the consequences of an action, in this case the morally forbidden act of deception, to which we all show remarkable sensitivity. In the absence of deception, when valid guilt is being elicited by a polygraph investigation with the Silent Answer Test (SAT), this guilt produces ripples of disturbance (Chapter V) in which the whole organism participates. Even when not outwardly communicated, the conscious awareness of wrongdoing creates a turbulence in mind and body, experienced as a fearful anticipation. The fact that widespread changes occur in the body within 15 seconds of the elicitation of guilt or deceptive communication, unambiguously attests to the sensitivity of conscience in general, and also demonstrates its major role in creating emotional states. Yet this does not implicate either the process of transmission or neurotransmitters as responsible for the disturbance.

Little is said also by the claim that specific chemical transactions have the capacity to create distinct emotional states. The serious condition of hypoglycemia (low blood glucose), for example, is perceived as dangerous and may produce feelings of anxiety that may mount to the point of panic. But the contrary has also been observed: in states of fear, anxiety, and panic, blood glucose tends to be rapidly metabolized and may reach hypoglycemic levels as well as lead to lactic acid accumulation. The physiologic systems of the body are ever ready for changing contingencies, executed through various reactions and transactions on the molecular level. Not only do feelings have the capacity to evoke certain thoughts, and even to color thinking, certain thoughts have the capacity to *create* feelings, and both thoughts and emotions may cause changes in biochemical reactions. Mind and body: both have the capacity to produce emotional states, and these in turn can dictate behaviors.

*   *   *

The problem of organic determinants in schizophrenia needs to be examined from the vantage point of two possibilities: either organic factors engender psychological disturbances and behaviors (as neurobiologists tend to believe), or psychological disturbances produce neurobiological changes which eventually damage the nervous system. But before naming or blaming any one factor as responsible for the causation of mental illnesses in general and schizophrenia in particular, a closer scrutiny of their clinical manifestations would immediately separate organic brain syndromes from purely psychiatric disorders.

Much can be learned from the manifest behaviors of patients. Not infrequently, behaviors alone allow for the separation of organic brain syndromes from psychiatric disturbances and diseases. For example, when examined in the emergency room, the patient who is organically damaged usually lies spastic or limp, and if he moves, does so in an aimless manner. The catatonic, seemingly paralyzed schizophrenic, on the other hand, lies rigid, motionless, guarded, and extremely frightened; he may evoke fright in others. In states of agitation, the organic patient usually shows no purpose or skill in his motor activity. The schizophrenic, on the contrary, may show amazing agility in jumping over windowsills, or hitting his target, and his agitation most commonly derives from aggressive urges, acted out against himself or others. As a general rule, the patient who is organically impaired cooperates in the process of his examination; the schizophrenic usually resists and may even attack his examiner. A simple clinical test to distinguish the organic from the mentally disturbed patient has been suggested by M. Stern (1982): it consists in offering a handshake as greeting to the patient in question. The patient who is organically damaged readily accepts the physician's outstretched hand as a sign of friendship, whereas the emotionally disturbed patient—whether hostile, negativistic, or paranoid—will refuse, more frequently than not, the hand offered him as a token of good will. H. J. Schulman, director of the Institute for Rehabilitation of Retarded Children in New York City, introduces the new guard of trainees with the following definition:

> The mentally retarded or cerebrally damaged can be distin-
> guished from the emotionally disturbed child by their general
> attitude: the child who is organically impaired *cannot* perform
> demanded tasks, whereas the child who is emotionally disturbed
> *will not*, refuses to cooperate.

Organic lesions of the brain stand in no relationship to hate, malevolence, and oppositional, defiant attitudes such as characterize the schizophrenic. A thorough search of the literature and textbooks of neurology for an organic illness that would produce hate and defiance has failed to identify any such syndrome.

Even in states of mental confusion or clouding of consciousness, certain diagnostic clues are usually provided by the contents of the patient's delirium. In postoperative and posttraumatic conditions, toxic and anoxic states, cerebrovascular accidents, etc., the content of the delirium—whether producing misperceptions, visions, delusions, or hallucinations—usually tells the tale, as it also distinguishes organic from functional disorders. As a general rule, whatever the effect of the toxin or metabolite that disturbs cerebral function and causes the "psychosis," its manifestations can only reflect the *contents of that inner reality* that prevailed at the time of the "delirium," and nothing else. Among the patients examined by this author, all those who suffered from organic brain syndromes reported benign experiences during their "deliria." One reported seeing castles amid beautiful landscapes; another saw her dead cat; one saw peas flying out of her plate; another, a strawberry shortcake. G. Berrios (1990) reports on the frequent occurrence of musical hallucinations, especially in elderly women affected by deafness, who had no history of prior psychiatric illness. The visions of schizophrenic patients, are mostly malignant. Infernal symbols are invariably present and external realities are perceived as threatening.

The concreteness of thinking observed in organically impaired patients merely reflects the limits of possibilities produced by the neurological damage. Living in terms of "I" and "my Self" and not "we," the concreteness of thought in schizophrenia reflects but these patients' egocentricity. In children, egocentricity may assume extreme proportions and manifest itself as **Autism,** a disorder with multiple manifestations in the psychological as well as biological and neurological realms.

It is of interest to note that no linear correlation is known to exist between the extent of cerebral damage and losses of personal attributes. As much as 40 percent of functional cortical tissue (containing centers of higher integration) may be destroyed before any clinical defect becomes manifest (contrasted with the cortical loss of schizophrenic patients, which is neither constant nor very pronounced). "By and large," wrote M. Stern (1982), "behavioral abnormalities, when existing in organic patients, are, as a rule, the product of bilateral brain dysfunction." Stern found also that organic patients distinguish themselves from those functionally impaired by their orientation to Self. Whereas losses in orientation with respect to time, location, and person are almost typical in the organically damaged, *their orientation to Self is rarely lost.* The neurologically impaired patient usually asks: "Where am I?" The hysterical patient, having dissociated from his Self some unacceptable "selves," usually wonders: "Who am I?" The organically impaired patient, obviously, has not sustained losses in the integrity of his Self, his soul. Hysterical patients (as well as patients belonging to other psychiatric categories) frequently complain of having lost the integrity of them-

Selves, their personality. But what defines the personality? The Self? The soul? It is not unusual to hear schizophrenic patients lament that they are lost, and their identity dissolved.

Characteristically, in the **Organic Personality Syndrome,** changes appear in the individual's habits as well as in his general adaptability. In this syndrome, rigidity and concreteness of thought reflect the impaired capacity and constriction of the patient's world—mostly due to losses of possibility caused by the disability—whereas in schizophrenia, the patient's world is not only constricted, but also malignantly transformed. In long-duration schizophrenias, the effects of age become added to functional impairment as well as to deficiencies contingent upon organic damage caused by the effects of schizophrenia on the brain. In the neurologically impaired, emotions remain relatively unchanged in their essence, although their pitch and expression may become distorted or exaggerated in some cases. Emotional lability and incontinence are characteristic of many organic syndromes, such as pseudobulbar palsy and multiple sclerosis, for example.

A "**Catastrophic reaction**" to the loss of functional capacity has been observed and described by K. Goldstein (1952). This is a reaction of rage and anger for the loss of function and is not due to the injury *per se*. Usually, only left hemispheric damage produces such reactions, as the right hemisphere is indifferent to matters concerning the body. Organic lesions cannot convert love into hate, however, or vice versa. In presenile dementias such as Alzheimer's disease, the patient may become slovenly in personal habits and even slacker in observing the moral code of his conscience, but he will not become hateful, amoral, defiant, or hostile if he has not been so before.

While neurological damage or disease may bring about states of depression, indifference, or elation (as frequently occurs in the case of frontal lobe involvement), it may also lead to the expression of aggression (as is frequently observed in diseases located in the temporal lobes). Hypothalamic lesions have been frequently observed to cause hyper or hyposexuality. No organic lesion, however, is known to exist that can change the "loves" or "hates" of a given personality. Swedenborg defines the personality by its "loves" and its "wills": "Intention is the actual person, not thought, except as it is derived from intention. Intention is a person's nature or bent." (*Heaven and Hell*)

And elsewhere:

> For what man wills inwardly he loves, what he loves he wills, and the will's love flows into the understanding where it makes its pleasure felt and thereupon enters the thoughts and intentions. *(Divine Providence)*

It is these loves and hates that endure all disasters, even those that involve damage to the central nervous system. Whereas the powers of cognition, judgment, orientation, and control over the emotions may become impaired or lost following organic lesions in the brain, the question regarding what is preserved in the personality in such cases remains ever pertinent.

In comparison to the organically impaired patient, the schizophrenic stands out by his multiple (or global) hostilities, selfishness, pride, and defiance. He lusts for power, glory, domination, and revenge. He loves mostly perverse ways of sexual gratification. Essentially, he loves nothing but his needs. Eventually, his real sickness will deprive him of his will also, even of the capacity to obtain the objects of his needs.

In the realm of cognition, a most distinctive feature separates brain syndromes from functional mental disorders in general, and from schizophrenia in particular. While the organic patient may try to fill— perhaps unsuccessfully—the gaps in his failing memory with fantasies and confabulations, the schizophrenic patient skillfully covers the intrusive remembrance of his past misdeeds and adeptly defends himself with projections, justifications, and various deceptive operations. This is precisely what the neurologically impaired patient is not capable of doing, for he suffers from what P. Hoch (1972) has termed as "operational deficit." This means that he loses the ability to perform complex mental operations and to devise foresight planning. As for the schizophrenic, before he becomes mentally deteriorated or demented, he shows himself to be a master in the craft of adulterating truth. His mental acrobatics in deception, mind-twisting, and misleading strategies have long been recognized. "The cunningness of a madman can never be overestimated," holds popular opinion. The sharpness of mind of borderline and schizophrenic patients needs, therefore, to be explained by those who rely on theories that interpret schizophrenia in terms of organically determined disturbances and damage. M. Bleuler (1979) refutes theories that attempt to regard schizophrenic illnesses in terms of organic lesions of the brain, giving the following arguments:

Nearly a third of schizophrenics recover for good. In general, the psychosis does not progress after five years but rather improves. Very late improvements are frequent and very late recoveries do happen. These and other factors concerning the course and outcome of schizophrenic psychoses are certainly not characteristic of organic and metabolic disease.

Relevant Anatomical Sites in the Brain

Whereas no direct correlation has been found to exist between the extent of cerebral injury and losses in personal attributes and functioning, the location of a lesion in the central nervous system makes an enormous difference in determining symptomatology. Concerned with the inner world of the emotions, certain areas of the brain manifest symptoms related to specific feeling states, and certain sites are associated with distinct behaviors. Most relevant to the system of emotions and to the subject matter here discussed are changes that occur as a consequence of lesions in the limbic system, temporal lobes, frontal lobes, diencephalon, corpus callosum, and right cerebral hemisphere.

a. The Limbic System

The limbic system comprises a centrally located chain of masses of neurons arranged in a manner suggesting a circle, the so-called circle of Papez. This anatomical arrangement within the subcortical areas of the brain may well provide an explanation for the apparent circularity of emotional states. Feelings, indeed, are frequently experienced as if running out their course, almost beyond the control of volition. It is within this semi-closed circle of neurons that the whole drama of the emotions seems to be played out in psychophysiological terms. The limbic system receives numerous connections from lower as well as higher centers of integration. In this manner, the limbic system of the emotions both influences the thought processes of higher centers and becomes subject to their influence in turn. It has an input in various involuntary neurological and physiological processes as well. Coded messages are relayed from one center to another by way of special substances, the neurotransmitters, whose activity seems of great import and influence in determining the climate of the "inner world of the emotions." Here, as elsewhere in the central nervous system, neural impulses are transmitted through the Na^+/K^+ pump depolarization and repolarization mechanisms.

Coded messages and neural impulses can thus be relayed to every part of the body with remarkable rapidity. The limbic system is also known as the "visceral brain," for its influence on physiological processes in the organs of the body, mediated through the sympathetic and vagal nervous systems respectively (P. McLean 1969). The mesolimbic system of the temporal lobes, which comprises the paired amygdala, hippocampi, and parahippocampal gyri have repeatedly been found heavily implicated in schizophrenic illnesses. The mesolimbic system is strategically located alongside the hypothalamus (terminal station of a multiplicity of neuronal tracks) believed to be associated with the release of defensive behaviors determined by threats, danger, and feelings of fright. Functionally, *the amygdala are thought to be repositories of negative emotions such as fear, anxiety, anger, and hate, as well as feelings of guilt.*

The question immediately arises as to the possibility of emotions being "stored." Current theories on the biological correlates of depression, schizophrenia, and related disorders tend to suggest the existence of such a possibility. What seems almost certain is that specific areas of the brain "secrete" certain substances, which, when released or relayed to other centers, produce widespread changes in the body and are experienced as emotions. Norepinephrine, 70 percent of which is secreted in the locus ceruleus, is such a substance. Available norepinephrine has been found linked to general arousal and feelings of elation, whereas its depletion has been associated with depression. An increased availability of dopamine, secreted at crucial structures of the ventral tegmental area, substantia nigra and in proximity of the basal ganglia, has been established as characteristic of the acute stages of schizophrenic illnesses. According to H. Morrison (1982), tumors of the temporal lobes involving mainly the amygdala are often unrecognized and receive the diagnosis of schizophrenia, because their symptomatology is so similar.

In the amygdala, especially the left, an increase in the concentration of the neurotransmitter dopamine has been repeatedly confirmed. "An asymmetric increase of dopamine in the left hemispheric amygdala is specific to the schizophrenic group," according to G. P. Reynolds (1983). Histological examinations of the amygdala of patients suffering from schizophrenia of lengthy duration, obtained postmortem (B. Bogerts et al. 1985) have shown structural abnormalities and "degenerative shrinkage of unknown etiology." These findings have been reported by other investigators as well. The changes observed involved not only the amygdala, but various components of the circle of Papez as well. Atrophic changes of the amygdaloid-hippocampal structures were present in the brains of chronically ill schizophrenics, but not in normal controls.

Experimental ablation of the amygdala in animals results in passive behaviors, fearlessness, loss of rage reactions, and the relinquishment of retaliatory behaviors, as demonstrated in 1939 by the studies of H. Kluver and P. C. Bucy. Amygdalectomized monkeys, moreover, have been observed to play with and ingest snakes, of which they are utterly terrified by nature (H. I. Kaplan et al. 1975). Stimulation of cats' amygdala, on the other hand, produces states of anger, which are inversely proportional to lowered brain norepinephrine. The localization of centers in the brain that either secrete, produce, or store substances that determine emotions of a negative nature ought to be of great interest to psychiatrists, for mental patients frequently complain of feeling inexplicable anger, hostility, depression, and similar dysphorias. It may well be that stimuli originating in sin-guilt complexes (possibly located in the hippocampal-amygdaloid structures), by generating guilty dysphorias, trigger also the secretion or release of other substances, whose transmission to specific centers is experienced as hostility, anger, and depression, as the case may be.

The hippocampi, tiny structures believed to carry out the difficult task of storing affect-laden memories, are found located in close proximity to the amygdala. In addition to their interconnectedness, both the amygdala and the hippocampi are associated with higher cortical centers that seem to determine whether certain memories will be permanently stored or else erased. It is generally accepted that memories bound by emotions become permanently engraved. For this reason, in evocative psychotherapies, painful emotions can be released through the memories to which they are bound. Such memories, if traumatic to the experiencer, may, when brought back into awareness and relived, become reintegrated into the mental life—losing in this manner much of their affective sting.

But the functional association between the hippocampi and the amygdala does not seem to end here. According to the findings of neurophysiologist H. L. Morrison (1982), the hippocampi exert an inhibitory function as well:

> Since 1927 to these days, the hippocampus is considered central among the psycho-physiological mechanisms governing the processes of internal inhibition.

That some stored memories, may, when bound to an affect, exert an inhibitory effect in the psychological realm, needs to be considered of utmost relevance. Such a mechanism of internal inhibition may well explain the function of guilt as educator and inhibitor as well as deterrent to further transgression of the moral code. When confronted by a tempting but morally forbidden possibility, one's memory may bring back to awareness all the dysphorias pertaining to guilt, such as shame, remorse, anxiety, fear, and depression, that had followed the commission of a moral offense in the past. Nothing, it seems, but these painful experiences can teach their subjects to avoid their reoccurrence.

b. The Temporal Lobes

There is no controversy among pathophysiologists that amidst the principal brain masses, the temporal lobes, containing key limbic structures, are most heavily implicated in schizophrenic illnesses. According to B. Bogerts et al. (1985), "most clinical symptoms of schizophrenia can be related to the pathophysiology of key limbic structures." This is hardly surprising in view of the temporal lobes' function of registering memories and their containment of the amygdaloid complexes, sources of negative emotions and aggressive urges. During "uncinate fits"—epileptic discharges originating from foci proximal to both the hippocampi and amygdaloid nuclei—several interesting phenomena have been observed to occur. These patients may report a sense of *déjà vu*; they may also engage in behaviors quite similar to those observed in schizophrenia. Fear, rage, and depression may be "discharged" during such a "psychomotor" seizure, and thought, taste, or smell hallucinations experienced.

Temporal Lobe Epilepsy (TLE) has recently become the subject of considerable interest because of its frequent coexistence, overlap, and similarity in clinical manifestations with schizophrenia, and also because of clinical observations indicating that the drug carbamezapine can be of benefit to both of these disorders. TLE has long been associated with acts of violence. In 1980, an international committee was given the task of investigating whether murder could be committed during a TLE "psychomotor seizure equivalent." Aggression, the panel agreed, is different from violence, the former being diffusely expressed, while the latter requires a target, a person. The panel also came to the conclusion that it is nearly impossible to murder during a "psycho-motor seizure attack" (A.V. Delgado-Escueta et al. 1981). Amygdalectomies carried out in human subjects, intended to relieve intractable TLE, left those individuals with diminished aggressiveness, flat affect, and a decrease in social interaction (H. Terzian et al. 1955). Most relevant to the problem of cause and effect is the observation that in some cases of unilaterally amygdalectomized humans (extirpation of one amygdaloid complex), a "mirror" focus of epileptic discharge develops on the other side.

These observations bring up the question of whether repeated emotional stimuli of a negative nature, such as have their substrate in the amygdala, can eventually create foci of irritability and epileptic discharge. According to recent findings, repeated subthreshold stimulation by electrical current or pharmacological means can "kindle" foci of irritability, which might lead to seizures. Seizure activity was found most easily kindled in the limbic system, and raises the possibility that the biochemical correlates of certain affects may be toxic, and have the capacity to trigger an epileptic discharge.

The problem of TLE and its relationship to schizophrenic psychoses appears to be rather complex in nature. With respect to timing, psychoses may appear before, during, and after seizures (preictal, ictal, and postictal psychoses). Researchers have long been puzzled by the seemingly antagonistic relationship between **Epilepsy** and psychotic illnesses. The fact that psychosis occurs much more frequently with TLE than with general epilepsy (12 percent and 1 percent respectively), and more frequently with TLE than in the general population, has rendered the belief that convulsions and psychosis antagonize one another somewhat paradoxical. In a review article on the subject, *Psychotic Syndromes in Epilepsy*, P. J. McKenna et al. (1985) came to the conclusion that "when psychoses occur in epilepsy, they are selectively associated with TLE."

The presence of bilateral or multiple foci seems to "especially increase the likelihood of psychosis," which may appear after 10 to 14 years of TLE (J. S. Stevens 1982). Seizures originating in the temporal lobes have previously been considered to represent "psycho-motor equivalents," but the term is unspecified—equivalent to what? It is tempting to consider the antagonism of convulsive seizures and psychoses on the basis of strong inhibitory activity, such as is exercised by the temporal lobes. Inhibition would explain the interplay between seizures as products of strongly inhibited aggressive urges, preventing the individual from acting them out, but producing an epileptic "equivalent" instead. The later evolution of TLE into schizophrenic psychosis—the outcome of which was found to be mostly unfavorable—may be explained on the basis of an eventual failure and/or exhaustion of inhibitory mechanisms. Aggressive, hateful, and revengeful urges may, by being eventually carried out, create complexes of sin and guilt whose accretion, after reaching a critical level, may lead to disease—much like the development of schizophrenia.

This author has treated for several years a patient with TLE and residual schizophrenia who recovered from both disorders following the conscious decision to renounce prior hateful and malevolent tendencies.

The **Epileptic Personality,** characterized by rigidity, stubbornness, and religiosity, would tend to underscore the presence of mostly inhibitory trends as outstanding in this character disorder.

The anatomical-functional substrata of feelings are believed to reside in the limbic system of the temporal lobes. Here emotional components are sorted out and, by decision derived from higher cortical centers, become either, "just felt," dismissed, inhibited, integrated, or else expressed. Although the limbic system has been held responsible for certain behaviors, its connections to higher centers belie the psychoanalytical conception of an alleged supremacy of feelings over thought in dictating manifest behavior.

Several other behavior-determining centers have been identified within the temporal lobes. Stimulation of the lateral hypothalamus, for example, typically, produces "sham rage" and acted out aggression. Deviant sexual behavior has been found associated with activity in the temporal limbic system. A center of self-punishment has been identified in the mesodiencephalic paraventricular fiber system, whose stimulation gives rise to unpleasant sensations and is believed to dictate self-punishing behaviors.

c. The Hypothalamus

Shaped like a funnel and so functioning, the hypothalamus is one of the most central and protected areas of the brain, as is the hypophysis, to which it is intimately connected. Various neuronal pathways converge in the hypothalamus, relaying to it decisions made by higher centers. Through its connections to both autonomous nervous systems, namely, the sympathetic and the vagal, the hypothalamus is the chief executive of directives received from higher centers as the organism prepares for various contingencies. The hypothalamus secretes certain substances, such as vasopressin, for example, whose release is associated with an elevation of blood pressure. It also stimulates the master gland, the hypophysis, to secrete hormones that activate other endocrine glands to secrete their own hormones as needed. B. J. Betz (1979) described the functions of the amygdala and hypothalamus as follows:

Each amygdala serves as a sentinel that transmits to the hypothalamic keyboard. The defensive responses are turned off, down or on. The hypothalamus, a target organ of the limbic process, exerts the ultimate elaboration of neural, neuroendocrine or behavioral responses, and its activities can be observed in the organism's behavior.

d. The Frontal Lobes

According to neurophysiologist A. R. Luria (1973), the frontal lobes "constitute an apparatus with the function of forming stable plans and intentions, capable of controlling the subject's subsequent behavior." Patients affected with extensive frontal lobe lesions lie passively, as a rule, and seem to have neither wishes nor desires. Terming this state the **Apathico-Akinetico-Abulic Syndrome,** Luria stresses the fact that massive lesions of the frontal lobes disturb only the most complex forms of regulated conscious activity, while simple and more basic forms of behavior remain unimpaired. In order to elucidate the reciprocal relationship between the limbic system and the frontal cortex, D. R. Kelly et al. (1973) undertook the interruption of connecting fibers by surgical means, destroying in this manner a significant part of the limbic system. Of the 40 patients thus treated, all of whom were considered suffering from intractable psychiatric illnesses—anxious, obsessional, depressive, and schizophrenic—67 percent showed considerable improvement six weeks following the procedure. They were left, nevertheless, bereft of feelings, slovenly in appearance, and slack in moral constraints. The "success" of this operation is hardly surprising in view of the concern of the frontal lobes with affective tone, imagination, future planning, foresight, and apperception of Self, all of which tend to be colored by emotions (W. Russel Brain 1975).

For his development of the "frontal leukotomy" procedure, Egas Moniz received the Nobel Prize in 1939. The leukotomy "treatment" has now been largely abandoned, however, in favor of psychopharmacotherapy. Although most patients "responded" to leukotomy, they became disabled for life. No longer could they appreciate their sad state of being, nor could they use affective channels to exercise their will. Abulic and indifferent, such patients may still be seen on the back wards of mental institutions for the chronically disabled. Although patients suffering from damage to the frontal lobes (and this applies to other areas of the brain as well) may show personality changes, these are only accentuations of premorbid characteristics—

the organic patient becoming a caricature of his basic personality, the major traits of which become exaggerated.

e. The Basal Ganglia

Lesions in these structures and in the extra-pyramidal motor system to which they are related, give rise to various disturbances in the emotions as well as in behaviors and motor activity, both voluntary and involuntary. The extra-pyramidal system serves several important functions. Most studied has been its role in the synergistic action of muscular groups, muscular tonus, modulation of voluntary movement, and facial expression. In **Parkinson's Syndrome,** slowness of mentation and movement, a vacuous facial expression, muscular rigidity, and disturbances in autonomic functions, such as drooling, may be present in various constellations. In the agitated form of Parkinsonism, akathisia, restless leg movements, "pill-rolling" with the fingers, tremors, and grimacing, may be present. An iatrogenic Parkinson's Syndrome can be produced by means of neuroleptic medications, which have the capacity of blocking dopamine receptors.

Of great interest is the existence of a direct dopaminergic neuronal connection between the amygdala and the basal ganglia through the nucleus accumbens of the latter. Negative emotions such as hate, revenge, rage, and aggressive urges may thus become outwardly expressed by way of grimaces and tics: involuntary movements that had somehow "escaped" the control by higher centers, exercised over them in normal circumstances. Tics and grimaces are frequently observed during polygraph investigation when the subject is deceiving. They are also frequently noted in schizophrenic patients, whether treated with neuroleptic medications or not. Tics and grimaces (if not organically determined as in **Sydenham's Chorea,** for example) usually betray thoughts, feelings, and attitudes these patients try desperately to conceal: hostility, contempt, anger, defiance, and mistrust, among others. Tics and grimaces are also characteristic of **Gilles de La Tourette Syndrome** (TS), but those so affected may shout obscenities and curses, in addition. According to D. L. Pauls et al. (1986), TS has been found to be genetically associated with **Obsessive-Compulsive Disorder.** As many as 35 percent to 60 percent of patients with TS eventually develop obsessive-compulsive disorder later in life. Among obsessive-compulsive disordered patients, about 12 percent are liable to experience a schizophrenia, usually of the catatonic variety (p. 165). Schizophrenia, TS, and obsessive-compulsive disorders can actually be clustered as a single nosological entity, for their similar genesis. And, in spite of some differences in symptomatology, the designation **"hate and malevolence syndrome"** would appropriately explain their etiology, natural history, as well as some of their manifestations.

f. The Right and Left Cerebral Hemispheres

Of the various investigations intended to localize specific psychological functions in the brain, the study of the right and left cerebral hemispheres has produced the most interesting and thought-provoking information. After an extensive review of the literature on the subject, D. Galin (1974) wrote as follows:

> In man the hemispheres are not only separate minds, but because of their specialization, they are different, but not duplicate minds.

Commenting on the work of R. W. Sperry with subjects who had suffered from a disconnection between their two cerebral hemispheres, Galin wrote further:

> The most remarkable effect of sectioning the cerebral commissures continues to be an apparent lack of change with respect to ordinary behavior. The subjects who suffered from the **"Hemispheric Disconnection Syndrome"** exhibited no gross alterations in their personality, intellect or overt behavior even two years after their operation.

In spite of the operation that left these patients with "two separate brains in one head," their sense of personal unity remained intact. They did not become "split" personalities, nor did they experience a schizophrenic psychosis. They were not unduly conflicted, either. Strikingly, the personality of these individuals preserved its unity.

Considered to be the dominant hemisphere in right-handed individuals, the left cerebral hemisphere is mainly concerned with the concrete and practical tasks of daily living. The left hemisphere thinks by way of words and is the major organ for verbal communication, reading, writing, arithmetic, complex mathematics, etc. The left hemisphere uses causal, linear logic for the solution of problems.

Aside from exercising control over the motor functions of the left side of the body, the right cerebral hemisphere is distinguished by several highly specialized functions and attributes, such as solving problems through multiple convergent determinants, grasping nonverbal cues, distinguishing physiognomies rather than faces, and perceiving and being attuned to music and other aesthetic productions. It is relatively unconcerned with matters of the body (denial of the body). The right cerebral hemisphere is superior to the left in seizing wholeness, i.e., the entire Gestalt or configuration of a situation (D. Galin 1974 and A. R. Luria 1973).

Clinical observations and investigations carried out on "split-brain" monkeys indicate that the two hemispheres can sustain emotional responses and goals that are divergent from each other. In normal conditions, when the commissures connecting the two hemispheres are intact, their harmonious functioning is achieved through reciprocal inhibition, a system characteristic of the activities of the central nervous system in general, and clearly evident in the sensory-motor realm. On the basis of research on "split-brain" monkeys, it has been postulated that the hemisphere that cares more about *outcome* preempts the output and ultimately gains control. The manner of the right hemisphere's nonverbal cognition is reminiscent of what Freud termed "primary process" thinking. Its logic and judgments, nevertheless, show themselves to be superior, and not "regressive" or "primitive." The judgments of the right hemisphere—determined as they are by multiple converging factors which are holistically grasped—would certainly be superior to those of the left, for their concern with outcome. It is tempting to postulate, in view of these findings, that the right (non-dominant) cerebral hemisphere—relatively unconcerned as it is with time, the body, and matters of practical nature—is the organ that processes material relevant to the higher levels of existence.

The right hemisphere is adept at art and music appreciation; it perceives the meaning of novel and complex situations; it judges through multiple given determinants; it perceives in a split second the physiognomy of a face, and comprehends the meaning of nonverbal cues. All these attributes establish the right hemisphere as a "super-computer" whose apperception comprises perception, conception, judgment in the light of past experience, and perhaps much more.

Due to its mode of cognition, namely by way of images, feeling states, and sensations, the right hemisphere has been thought to be the repository of the "unconscious" (D. Galin 1974). But this "unconscious" means different things to various interpreters (cf. Chapter VII). Speaking by way of images, inner feelings, and sensations, the right cerebral hemisphere may well be the seat of judgment in matters concerning the moral conscience, for its warnings and admonitions enter consciousness in this manner (cf. Chapter V).

With the capacity to perceive loosely defined intuition, inspiration, and enthusiasm, the right hemisphere may well be the window that opens onto an invisible, spiritual world. This is a tempting speculation. If true, this theory may clarify such phenomena as automatic writing, premonitory knowledge, and extrasensory perception (ESP). There might, indeed, be a reality "out there" whose subliminal components are perceived only in extraordinary circumstances, through a sharpening of all the senses. This possibility immediately explains such phenomena as hallucinations and lends credence to claims made by schizophrenic patients that they are controlled by outside forces, that their thoughts are read aloud and also broadcast, that voices are commenting on them, and so on. These delusional/ hallucinatory experiences, also known as "first rank" symptoms, unite schizophrenics from the remotest corners of the world.

The question then arises as to how the right hemisphere gathers its data. It would be logical to assume that it does so through the senses. Yet, as a more perfect organ of apperception, the right hemisphere may well have the capacity to integrate data from past experiences and be more directly connected to the "inner domain of the emotions" as well as to the spiritual center of the personality. This would explain the sharpening of the senses that occurs in states of danger, to which the state of schizophrenia certainly belongs. The hyperacusia, hypervigilance, and hyperosmia observed in schizophrenia may well be due to a lowering of the threshold for the perception of stimuli arising from an invisible, spiritual world. Dostoyevsky came close to such an interpretation in *Crime and Punishment* (cf. Chapter VII). All of these explanations leave out, however, one of the most puzzling phenomena, namely, the perception of nonimaginary visions (not recollections) while the eyes are closed, such as hypnagogic hallucinations.

Be that as it may, on a functional basis alone, the right hemisphere would be expected to be more active in schizophrenia than the left. In this state of being, it seems as if the left hemisphere abdicates some of its functions in favor of the right, as the schizophrenic patient shows disability in the performance of the common, practical tasks of daily living. He becomes slovenly in appearance, and, if he was previously scholarly inclined, loses even the capacity for reading and comprehension as his consciousness becomes flooded with images, strange perceptions, and experiences perfused with dread.

Measuring the biochemical activity of brain locations with the Positron Emission Transaxial Tomography (PETT) technique, T. Farkas and A. Wolf (1980) were able to demonstrate that in the uptake of a tracer for glucose metabolism, the right hemisphere— mainly its temporal lobe—is asymmetrically favored over the left in schizophrenic as well as in manic illnesses. The problem of hemispheric preponderance seems to be more complex, however. In recent studies on schizophrenic patients, the left hemisphere has been found more active than the right, raising questions about duration, timing, and acuteness of the disease.

From studies on motor laterality and eye dominance, N. Piran et al. (1982) came to the conclusion that right-handedness and left-eye dominance were much more frequent in schizophrenics of late adolescent age. Early-onset schizophrenics also showed a pattern of left-eye dominance. This preference is visible and represents quite a reliable clinical sign by which schizophrenia can be recognized. It is manifested by an increase in the palpebral fissure of the left eye, which appears to be protruding, as well as by the eye's slight shift to the left, which gives the impression of "cross-eyedness." The layman recognizes the madman by this asymmetry of gaze, often interpreted as the "evil eye" (p. 68).

The thick band of neural fibers that connects the two cerebral hemispheres, known as the corpus callosum, represents their major tract of functional association. In early-onset schizophrenia, the corpus callosum has been found "markedly thickened," as compared to that of other diagnostic categories and late-onset schizophrenias (H. A. Nasrallah et al. 1979). This thickening may well be the consequence of excessive use, as "the callosal code transmits a higher order of information" (H. L. Morrison 1982).

Cerebral Atrophy: Cause or Effect?

A general shrinkage of the brain with a compensatory increase of cerebrospinal fluid has been known to occur with advancing age. Certain cortical areas of the brain, concerned as they are with highly specialized and complex tasks, may show areas of thinning as well as widening of their sulci (furrows between the convolutions). To some measure, these changes explain the cognitive deficits characteristic of the elderly. But patients with a long-standing schizophrenic illness have also been found to have smaller brains and significantly larger ventricles than normal controls, as demonstrated by postmortem studies, utilization of the Computerized Tomography (CT) technique, and Magnetic Resonance Imaging (MRI) scans. Studies with CT scans (D. Weinberger 1979) show that over two-thirds of chronic schizophrenics have some structural brain abnormality, and of these 32 percent evidence cortical atrophy. In 53 percent, ventricular size exceeded two standard deviations of the control mean. Since the first report of ventricular enlargement in schizophrenia was published by

Peculiarity of the Madman's Gaze

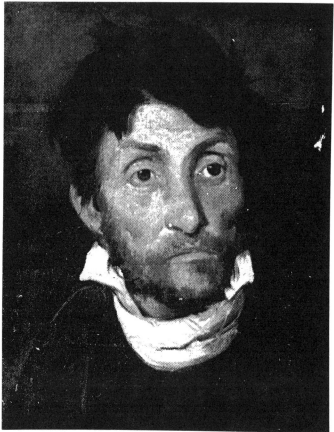

MONOMANIAC du VOL (KLEPTOMANIAC)
Painting by Théodore Géricault
(The *Louvre* Museum).

The left eye is bulging and asymmetrically turned to the left. Popular opinion holds these peculiarities as indicative of the "evil eye."

E. C. Johnstone in 1976, 90 more CT studies of brain structure in schizophrenia have appeared in the literature. Enlargement of the lateral and third ventricles, atrophy of the frontal lobes, atrophy of the cerebellar vermis, abnormalities in brain density, and reversed cerebral asymmetry have been reported by various investigators using this technique.

According to the more recent studies with MRI scans, the area of the third ventricle was found to be increased by 73 percent and the lateral ventricles by 62 percent in schizophrenic subjects, as compared to controls (J. R. Kelsoe et al. 1988). The question as to whether the structural abnormalities preceded, occurred simultaneously with, or followed the schizophrenic illness is answered by research data from various studies. N. C. Andreasen, S. A. Olsen et al. (1982) and N. C. Andreasen, M. R. Smith et al. (1982) compared patients who showed the largest ventricles (and smallest brains) to patients who had the smallest ventricles (and largest brains), using the measuring ratio, ventricular size/brain size, and came to the conclusion that the patients with small ventricles had a significantly younger age of onset and a shorter duration of illness. The patients with the large ventricles were significantly older and their illness of longer duration.

According to B. T. Woods et al. (1983), "There is a direct relationship between the size of ventricles and duration of schizo-phrenic illness." On these findings alone, one may be justified in assuming that since chronicity, advanced age, and duration of schizophrenia tend to correlate with brain atrophy and ventricular enlargement, it is the illness that somehow causes damage to the brains of schizophrenics and that their "dementia"—progressively developing over time—parallels the atrophy.

In light of the CT findings described, a correlation between symptoms of schizophrenia and structural abnormalities in the brain was sought by several investigators. Focusing his attention on symptomatology, T. J. Crow (1980) suggested the existence of two types of schizophrenic illnesses: Type I, acute syndrome with florid symptomatology, contingent upon increased dopaminergic activity, responsive to neuroleptics, and a reversible outcome; and Type II, with a "defect" symptomatology, unresponsive to neuroleptics, with cognitive deficits and a deteriorative outcome. According to studies by N. C. Andreasen et al. (1982) on 52 schizophrenic subjects, those patients who had small ventricles demonstrated a florid symptomatol-ogy (delusions, hallucinations, agitation, etc.) were younger, and their illnesses of shorter duration; whereas those with a "defect" symptom-atology (such as flattened affect, loss of conation, lack of spontaneity, and cognitive capacities) were significantly older and their disease of longer duration.

The factor of time may be crucial in separating acutely ill patients, mostly young, who complain of hearing "voices;" who see monsters and the devil; who fear impending punishment and doom; and who struggle with intense feelings of guilt. What is usually lost in descriptions of their "florid" symptomatology—although eminently predominant in their mental processes—are the complexes of sin and guilt and the invasion of their consciousness by spiritually meaningful symbols. As for the existence of a Type II illness, it is certainly not well delineated, because acute exacerbations do punctuate the course of one-third of all schizophrenics, and acute symptoms may then reappear. As for that third of schizophrenics who "deteriorate," i.e., who suffer losses in cognitive capacities, feel deprived of the joy of life, and become divested of all moral constraints, their frequently expressed complaint of having lost their souls may well be true and may explain their "defect" symptomatology and irreversible outcome. Chronic schizophrenics do hear voices, nonetheless. They also entertain delusions and experience dread, although to the observer these symptoms may appear less dramatic, less "florid." Dementia "praecox" is a multi-symptom disorder: it does not specify exactly the age of its occurrence; and there seems to exist a wide latitude with respect to all its variables.

Neurotransmitters

Neurotransmitters are endogenously manufactured substances that relay coded messages along specialized tracks in the central nervous system. The message is transmitted across the synapse from one neuron to another, where a specific receptor "accepts" the message as a stimulus. From here, it may be relayed to yet another neuron. The messenger substance is either "re-uptaken" by the primary neuron or degraded by a specialized enzyme, present in the synaptic relay station(s) as well as in the fluids of the body. Most remarkable is the capacity of neurotransmitters to effect enormous changes in emotional states as well as in behaviors, through minute changes in their concentration. Recent advances in histochemical techniques employing radioactive ligands were instrumental in demonstrating the fixation of certain substances along tracks and receptors at specific sites in the nervous system. Opiates and naturally manufactured endorphins, for example, were found to be maximally concentrated in the limbic system, while Valium, a benzodiazepine, tended to concentrate maximally in the hippocampi and olfactory tracts, where it probably exerts its anxiolytic action.

Of the neurotransmitters, the most extensively studied have been the catecholamines, belonging to the category of "biologic amines." They contain a basic "catechol" ring and only one amine radical, hence the term "monoamines." Acetylcholine is the longest-known neurotransmitter, and it is recognized as mediator in the vagal autonomic nervous system, whose function is believed to be mostly anabolic (building up), associated with experiences of pleasure and subserving gratification. The sympathetic nervous system, on the other hand, is thought to be associated with various "stressful" contingencies, its function being mostly catabolic (of degradation). It mobilizes and uses all available resources in order to prepare the organism to meet danger with either fright, flight, or fight. The activities of the sympathetic nervous system have been thoroughly investigated. The "stress-hormone" epinephrine (adrenaline) and norepinephrine have been recognized for their capacity to effect extensive physiological changes in the organism. Excess of adrenaline release has been found associated with elevation of blood pressure, increased cardiac output, increased oxygen consumption, and rapid glucose utilization, among others. Both the vagal and the sympathetic nervous systems have widespread connections throughout the body, and their activities are believed to be governed by the limbic system (the "visceral brain" of McLean). Neither autonomic nervous system is subject to the control of volition. The limbic system, however, receives and sends messages to higher cortical centers. Of the neurotransmitters, dopamine and norepinephrine have been found most heavily implicated in various mental illnesses, especially in schizophrenia. Most recently, serotonin has taken center stage, attracting the attention of neurobiologists and psychopharmacologists.

The majority of depressive states have been found associated with diminished availability of norepinephrine at important functional sites, while a functional hyperactivity in the dopamine system has been repeatedly demonstrated in schizophrenic illnesses. The dopamine theory of schizophrenia rests on a wealth of research data, the majority of which have tended to strengthen its major premises. The dopamine system originates in cell bodies in the ventral tegmental area and substantia nigra and projects in two principal tracts: the mesocortical system which projects to the limbic regions and to the prefrontal cortex, and the nigrostriatum which projects to the caudate, putamen, and globus pallidus. It is of interest to mention here that in postmortem studies of the brain, a highly significant increase of dopamine in the amygdala—centers of hate, anger, guilt, and various other negative emotions—was found in the schizophrenic group of patients studied by G. P. Reynolds (p. 57). Dopamine is a metabolite of the amino-acid tyrosine, which is first converted into dopa and then to dopamine. Under normal circumstances, dopamine is converted into norepinephrine through the activity of an enzyme, namely dopamine-beta-hydroxylase.

In the living organism, increased dopaminergic activity may be produced by the administration of L-dopa (a precursor of dopamine). L-dopa is used in the treatment of Parkinson's disease, believed to result from a deficiency of dopamine in the basal ganglia and corpus callosum of the brain. But L-dopa is also known to have the capacity of producing psychiatric complications in a certain number of patients treated for Parkinsonism. According to a study by G. Sathananthan et al. (1973), 20 percent of patients treated with L-dopa developed some of the following symptoms: paranoid ideation, agitation, confusion, depression, delusions, hallucinations, increased anxiety levels, lethargy, insomnia, and vividness of dreams.

Exploring the effects of L-dopa on nonpsychotic[*] patients, the same authors reported the following rather heterogenous responses: one alcoholic showed no response to the drug; another alcoholic entered into a toxic confusional state; an amphetamine abuser became hyperactive, experienced a "speeding" of his thought processes, became panicky, hypervigilant, and developed ideas of reference; a homosexual patient became overly sexually aroused and needed to masturbate compulsively; two subjects became insomniac; and three subjects developed dystonic movements. One patient with no prior psychiatric history suddenly developed paranoid ideas, started to ramble, manifested a thought disorder, became extremely fearful, and developed delusions betraying past involvement with the Mafia, dealing in narcotics, and secrets involving his lawyer and brother-in-law. This rather wide array of responses to increases in available L-dopa suggests that more than the substance acting as a neurotransmitter is here involved, both in the induction of symptoms (i.e., ideas of reference), and in the production of the whole schizophrenic syndrome itself, as in the case of the last patient. Premorbid personality factors, undoubtedly, come into play, but even more so, premorbid deviant behaviors (i.e., homosexual practices) and the dysphorias

---

[*] Although the term "psychosis" is mostly used for acute schizophrenic illnesses, it may refer to toxic as well as to manic-depressive psychoses.

generated as a result. The authors of this study seek to emphasize that the effects from L-dopa administration surpass mere increments in alertness. Caffeine, for example, despite its capacity for increasing alertness, does not produce the same effects as those observed following L-dopa administration. The antidepressant imipramine (Tofranil) causes only 20 percent of schizophrenics to develop an exacerbation of their symptoms. Citing a study by B. Angrist, S. H. Snyder (1973) noted that 70 percent of the schizophrenics to whom L-dopa was administered showed "marked deterioration in clinical status with either worsening of the original symptoms or emergence of *de novo* symptomatology." Indirect evidence in support of the dopamine theory of schizophrenia has been supplied by studies exploring the effects of neuroleptic medications, i.e., drugs that have the capacity of reducing psychotic symptomatology. The first researchers to suggest that antipsychotic drugs act through a "dopamine receptor blockade," A. Carlsson and M. Lindquist (1963), were able to demonstrate an increase in dopamine metabolites following treatment with chlorpromazine (Thorazine) and haloperidol (Haldol).

A proliferation of dopamine receptors at strategic sites in the brains of schizophrenics has been documented by several studies. In animals, long-term treatment with neuroleptic agents has been found to produce an increase in the number of receptors. An increase in the density of dopamine receptors has also been demonstrated by postmortem examinations of brains from chronic schizophrenic patients. This finding has been interpreted as representing the consequence from treatment with neuroleptics but it may well represent a compensatory phenomenon: reaction on the part of the "blocked" receptor neurons, intended to circumvent the blockade. An increase in brain dopamine content has also been demonstrated by A.V. P. McKay et al. (1982), especially in the nucleus accumbens and caudate, in the brains of young schizophrenics with onset of illness before age 25.

In the biochemical analyses of W. Pollin (1971), excesses of urinary catecholamines were found excreted in both members of a monozygotic pair of twins. Although both demonstrated this increase, the twin who later became schizophrenic showed an increased turnover of catecholamines in addition. Reduced activity of the enzyme monoamine-oxidase (MAO) was found with consistency in the platelets of both acute and chronic schizophrenic patients. According to T. A. Ban (1977), low monoamine-oxidase activity could be "responsible for the functional excess of dopamine, which is in keeping with the finding that dopamine-receptor blocking agents produce improvement and remission, whereas MAO-inhibitors produce aggravation or exacerbation in patients suffering from schizophrenia." Several substances other than L-dopa and MAO-inhibitors have been found to have a dopamine-agonistic activity, important among which are the amphetamines, methylphenidate (Ritalin), cocaine, "crack," and apomorphine. These chemical substances are believed to enhance dopaminergic activity through their capacity to block dopamine re-uptake by the primary messenger neuron (S. H. Snyder 1970). Their capacity to produce schizophrenia *de novo* in individuals so predisposed, as well as to exacerbate existing latent illnesses, is now well recognized.

A good case for a "chemical substance" theory of schizophrenia can be made from the "model" schizophrenias produced by ingestion of amphetamines in high doses, as reported by S. H. Snyder (1973). The powerful psychopharmacological effects of these substances are now believed to be related to their chemical structure, very similar to that of dopamine as well as to norepinephrine, both heavily implicated in schizophrenic illnesses.

Until recently, amphetamines were used for their capacity to lift the "spirits," enhance arousal, and produce a general sense of well-being. Named "black beauties" on the streets, amphetamines have now been largely replaced by the more potent as well as more addictive cocaine and "crack." Yet it is not the chemical composition of a mood-elevating substance that really counts, but the delusional idea it induces: "it's all in your chemistry." This false belief insinuates also to the user that there are shortcuts on the road to felicity and no real need to follow those "straight" paths where normal, ordinary pedestrians obtain their "highs" and inner satisfactions. Whether using marijuana, amphetamines, or cocaine, the drug addict commits yet another error when he mistakes excitement for happiness. It is an error he shares with every gambler, overspender, sexual pervert, and individual immersed in vice and crime.

In an attempt to differentiate **Amphetamine-Induced Psychoses** from authentic schizophrenia, S. H. Snyder (1976) found disorders of thinking to be mostly absent in the former. This finding, however, is hardly surprising, considering that formal thought disorder is predicated upon deceptions, justifications, and various cover-up operations, of which the amphetamine abuser is not so much in need. According to Snyder, the key feature of amphetamine psychoses is the occurrence of these illnesses in a "clear setting," i.e., in the absence of obtundation or confusion. During amphetamine psychoses, the subject experiences an increased awareness of his surroundings, enhanced capacity for recall, and a sense of exciting novelty. This is quite contrary to what happens in paranoid schizophrenia, where dread and fears of various sorts prevail, as well as a general *neophobia,* which dictates the shunning of every new experience. A biphasic response to increments in amphetamine dosage has been observed and described by E. H. Ellinwood, Jr. (1967). Initially providing enhanced self-confidence and relief in awkward social situations, increments in dosage have the potential for whipping up aggressive urges, which may lead to violent behaviors. In terms of milligrams, the distance between amphetamine-induced euphoria and states of overwhelming dread—reaching psychotic dimensions for some abusers—appears to be rather short. Some patients erroneously resort to higher doses of amphetamines to combat their fearful state. In Ellinwood's study, the minority of patients who did not become psychotic (30 percent), and the majority who did experience a psychotic state (70 percent), both reported overwhelming fear and terror as part of their state of intoxication. Most ubiquitous for all amphetamine abusers was their sense of being watched. The majority of those who did not become psychotic reported a decrease in sexual desire. An increase in libido with marked tendencies toward sexual excesses and polymorphous perversions were noted among those who did became psychotic. Yet Ellinwood made a point by emphasizing that "polymorphous sexual activities preceded the psychosis."

The psychotogenic effects of amphetamines are believed to be due to their inhibitory effects on dopamine and norepinephrine re-uptake by the primary neuron as well as by release of these substances into the synaptic cleft (S. H. Snyder 1976). Nevertheless, amphetamine-induced psychoses fail to represent an ideal model of schizophrenia in Snyder's conception, because of the contaminating effect of norepinephrine, released into the synaptic cleft along with excesses of dopamine. On a clinical level also, the similarity between amphetamine-induced psychoses and authentic schizophrenia ends precisely there. Whereas the amphetamine abuser may be able to squeeze some euphoriant effects from this stimulant, even in the worst of fearful states, the patient who suffers schizophrenia, tormented as he is by visions, delusions, nightmares, and hallucinations, hardly overcomes his cynical indifference and anhedonia (the inability to experience pleasure). Instead of reaching a state of euphoria, amphetamines might provide him with some unusual sense of excitement as substitute, nonetheless.[*]

*   *   *

Available knowledge concerning the function of the various catecholamines singles out norepinephrine as the substance of self-rewards and states of felicity. The euphoriant effects of amphetamines are believed to be due to their ability to enhance the release of norepinephrine into the synaptic cleft as well as to inhibit its re-uptake by the primary neuron. In animals, amphetamines produce a general arousal, exploratory activities, appetitive behaviors, sexual stimulation, and increased motor activity. When norepinephrine is directly injected into the brains of rats at low but constant concentrations, similar behaviors can be observed. Depressions are associated with absolute or relative deficiencies of norepinephrine at crucial sites in the brain. The manic phase of manic-depressive illnesses is associated with increases in norepinephrine, depressive phases with depletion of this substance. Drugs that deplete norepinephrine from crucial cerebral sites (such as Reserpine) may bring about severe depression.

According to researchers C. D. Wise and L. Stein (1973), norepinephrine and its pathways are associated with "pleasure and rewards, hence with organization and control of goal-directed behavior." A failure of the conversion of dopamine into norepinephrine (believed to occur normally) at crucial cerebral sites has been postulated to exist in schizophrenia, and is clinically confirmed by a central feature of the illness: the inability to experience pleasure (anhedonia). But schizophrenics also suffer from a low self-esteem, and consequently, from a lack of feelings of self-rewards. Wise and Stein (1973) undertook the examination of postmortem brains from 18 schizophrenics and compared them with those of 12 control subjects. A marked reduction in the activity of the enzyme dopamine-beta-hydroxylase (DBH) was demonstrated in the brains of the schizophrenic patients, most accentuated in the hippocampi and diencephalic regions. Theoretically, an interference with this enzyme's activity, namely with DBH—which normally converts dopamine into norepinephrine—would be capable of precipitating a psychosis. Clinically, the substance known as "Antabuse" or disulfiram, used in the aversive treatment of alcoholics due to its interference with the

---

[*] A more detailed description of the effects of amphetamines is given in Chapter IX.

activity of DBH, has been recognized as capable of precipitating psychoses in predisposed individuals. Nevertheless, no linear correlation could be found between brain content of DBH and severity of schizophrenia, as subsequent studies have demonstrated. A low DBH activity in the cerebro-spinal fluid has been found in patients with a better prognosis, however, often resembling "reactive" schizophrenias, and also in patients with a depressive symptomatology (D. E. Sternberg 1983).

These research findings notwithstanding, most investigators of the neurobiological aspects of schizophrenia would tend to agree that the enzyme DBH plays a major role in the tragedy of schizophrenia. This little enzyme, enormously influential in the physiology of the organism, seems to wield a powerful double-edged sword. By preventing dopamine from being converted into norepinephrine, self-esteem, self-rewards, sense of well-being, and the experience of felicity are all undermined. At the same time, by allowing the build-up of excesses of dopamine, consciousness becomes flooded with feelings of dread, fears, and rage—promoting aggressive acting out and self-punishing behaviors. How is it possible that the horror-filled experiences of schizophrenics and the self-satisfactions and inner rewards of "normals" hinge but on one hydroxyl (OH) radical—the difference between dopamine and norepinephrine? Obviously, much more is involved in the biochemistry of schizophrenia than has been hitherto discovered. Moreover, the similarity of the "stress hormone" molecule, namely epinephrine (adrenaline) to that of norepinephrine cannot be ignored from both their biochemical and psychophysiological aspects.

The effects of norepinephrine in the brain have been investigated by S. H. Snyder (1970), who came to the conclusion that "maps of reward centers tend to coincide with norepinephrine tracts." The principal reward center was found in the lateral hypothalamus, where the highest concentration of noradrenergic nerve endings are located. The majority of noradrenergic axons are believed to emanate from the median forebrain bundle, associated with self-rewarding, pleasurable feelings. The major site for the release of norepinephrine is believed to be located in the locus ceruleus of the septal nuclei. Stimulation of the septal nuclei—at least in rats—induces such intensely gratifying sensations that the animals are ready to forego all other available satisfactions. Even when deprived of food and water, under experimental conditions, animals consistently chose stimulation of this center over satisfying their hunger and thirst. They were observed to stimulate their self-reward center at the rate of 7,000 times per hour, but died eventually from exhaustion. Whether certain activities can stimulate the self-rewarding center and produce states of ecstasy in humans, to the extent they would be willing to forego satisfaction of their biological needs, is perhaps best answered by those who have so tried.

Norepinephrine deficiencies in target sites of the brain fail also in telling the whole story of schizophrenia in biochemical terms. Although a schizophrenic illness may well begin with symptoms of depression, the majority of patients present florid symptoms of acute upheaval, agitation, confusion, hypervigilance, delusions, and a sense of dread. In biological terms alone, acute schizophrenic psychoses manifest all the signs and symptoms of an *acute emergency, a state of danger*, that dictates fright, flight, or fight. In spite of the exper-iencer's recognition of the irrationality of his fears, the danger perceived is no less frightening.

As for the existence in schizophrenia of an "affect-toxin," postulated by C. G. Jung, available data tend to converge in support of this being the substance dopamine or perhaps its metabolites.[*] Persistent "stimulation" by dopamine or its metabolites at specific locations in the brain may well be responsible for causing organic changes and eventual damage. This would be an attractive hypothesis, but not entirely conforming to *all* of the existing research findings. As substance-messenger, dopamine means different things to different neurons in different locations. To the caudate nucleus, an excess of dopamine means synergistic involuntary movement; to some neurons in the lateral hypothalamus, perverse sexual appetites; while to others, emotions pertaining to rage.

Regardless, the fact that large doses of "minor" anxiolytic agents, such as Valium, can produce a clearing of schizophrenic symptoms and sustain remission (J. N. Nestoros 1982), serves to demonstrate the central role of *fear and dread* in this diseased state. The substance dopamine, however, does not appear determinative of all the symp-toms present in these states, as indicated by the studies of G. Sathananthan et al. (1973) cited above. The administration of L-dopa produced sexual arousal and compulsive masturbation in the homo-sexual only; one alcoholic and not another entered into a confusional

---

[*]   It has been recently demonstrated that a metabolite of dopamine, namely 6-OH-dopamine, is extremely toxic and can destroy cells (R.O. Rieder, 1988 — Symposium on the Biology of Schizophrenia). This may well be the "toxin" of schizophrenia, whose presence at specific sites in the brain eventually causes permanent damage to and/or loss of neuronal bodies.

state; only the secret narcotics dealer was suddenly brought to experience a paranoid schizophrenia. The symptoms, which made their appearance at lower doses, were merely intensified by an increase in dosage.

The neurons of dopaminergic tracts connect to relay stations, among which the most important have been found in the corpus striatum, the nucleus accumbens, and the amygdala, with projections to the diencephalon, hypothalamus, and olfactory bulbs. In an attempt to locate the "anatomical site" of schizophrenia, J. R. Stevens (1982) undertook to examine by histological techniques certain structures mapped out by psychopharmacological research. Stevens made use of the newest methods for exploring brain structures. She compared the brains of 28 schizophrenic subjects with those of non-schizophrenics matched for age. Focusing her attention mainly on the basal forebrain, limbic structures, and basal ganglia, Stevens found a patchy fibrillary gliosis (scarring in the nervous system) that affected primarily the paraventricular regions of the diencephalon, subependymal horns of the lateral ventricles, amygdala, and substantia innominata. No acute inflammatory process could be identified, however, to account for the gliotic scarring. The postmortem pathological findings of Stevens were unaffected by prior treatment with Electro-Convulsive Therapy (ECT) and/or neuroleptics. Stevens commented that the changes she observed "evidenced past injury, but did not disclose cause." The subependymal gliotic scarring (scarring produces shrinkage) in the diencephalon and hypothalamus were consistent with the results of CT and MRI scan studies (see above) whereby an enlargement of the third and lateral ventricles in schizophrenic patients was found. According to Stevens, the hypothalamus was involved in the highest percentage of cases, followed by the amygdala, midbrain tegmentum, bed nucleus, stria terminalis, and hippocampi. From these findings, as well as those mentioned above, one cannot avoid the conclusion that increases of dopamine and dopaminergic hyperactivity are somehow "toxic" and may have produced the damage and scarring observed. Stevens attempted to correlate antemortem clinical manifestations with the histopathological findings of the patients she investigated. The most frequent symptoms reported by the 28 schizophrenic patients were: auditory hallucinations, paranoia, and assault. Seclusiveness, flat affect, speech disturbances, signs of catatonia, and "religiosity" were less commonly reported.

The postmortem findings from investigations on the brains of schizophrenic patients are open to various interpretations, nonetheless.

Especially those involving the amygdala (centers of negative emotions) and their connections with the hippocampi (where memories are stored and selected) would command attention. Complexes of sin and guilt, which persistently encroach upon the thought processes of every schizophrenic patient, may well have their anatomical substrate in these highly active, highly vulnerable nerve centers. Dopamine-coded messages might well proceed from the nucleus accumbens toward the lateral hypothalamus, where they can produce reactions of rage. Other dopamine-coded messages may proceed toward centers of aversion and into the diencephalic center of self-punishment. The compulsive, self-inflicted penalties of those obsessed with hate would tend to confirm the existence of some active psychological reflexes in the subcortical regions of the brain. Such a possibility is reinforced by the manifestations of **Gilles de La Tourette Syndrome** (TS), whose psychopathological substratum is known to reside in the basal ganglia. Clinically, the syndrome is evidenced by tics and grimaces which, reflexively activated, betray the subject's hateful thoughts (p. 63). Through its own specific tracks, norepinephrine may reflexively stimulate the median forebrain bundle, causing enhancement of self-esteem, and contingent to it, feelings of elation.

Of great relevance to psychopathology as well as to neurobiology would be the study of stimuli that provoke one or another reflex activity within the central nervous system at any given time. Past stored experiences, among other factors, must by necessity be contributive and condition somehow the operations of the human "supercomputer," the brain. Certain receptors seem, indeed, to be primed by internal reality, so that even a "happy" event might act as stimulus and trigger reflex (involuntary) responses that, paradoxically, engender dysphorias and compulsions to self-punishment. The following case illustrates the role of internal reality in setting certain reflexes in motion after a specific event-stimulus:

> An office clerk was suddenly advised of his winning a long-standing case in court, which entailed a huge sum of money. He had already made preparations for a cruise around the world, in advance. Instead of generating feelings of elation, however, the good news suddenly gave rise to a florid paranoid psychosis, for the case had rested on false evidence.

This case can demonstrate the *power of a thought* to modify emotions, and also to bring about changes in chemical reactions and transactions that involve the whole organism. Eloquently, this case affirms also the importance of internal reality and its receptiveness to certain specific stimuli. It further demonstrates the power of guilt and the central role of the moral conscience in producing dysphorias which are liable to set in motion reflex responses and self-punishing behaviors. But why is one thought and not another privileged to enter the inner domain of the emotions? And what specific stimulus ignites the spark that brings about an "explosion of conscience," a psychosis? With regard to the biological counterparts of emotional transactions, more remains unknown than has already been discovered.

The areas of devastation—mentioned before—in certain locations in the brains of chronic schizophrenic patients, as described by Stevens (1982), can only demonstrate the existence of specific sites, where, presumably, the emotional drama (in neuro-biochemical terms) had taken place and not much more. The areas of gliosis, where scarring and brain shrinkage have been found, indicate damage, but do not identify the damaging agent. It may well represent the consequences of psychologically determined biological exhaustion. Someday, the "toxic" effects of emotions such as hate, anger, envy, and aggressive urges—"secreted" by the amygdala and transmitted through dopaminergic tracks and relay stations—may well be found commensurate with the intensity of these feelings and their duration, as well as with their biochemical counterparts.

Notwithstanding, it would be erroneous to consider the catecholamines solely responsible for the symptoms and manifestations of depressive as well as schizophrenic illnesses, for other neurotransmitters have been found to be implicated as well. The indole-amine serotonin, for example, has recently captured the attention of a host of researchers as well as psychopharmacologists. This substance, derived from the metabolism of tryptophan, has long been known to function as a "damper," attenuating the pitch of all emotions, be they euphoric, depressive, or aggressive in nature. In criminals, the metabolite of serotonin 5-hydroxy-indole-acetic-acid has been found to be decreased. A decrease of this metabolite has also been observed in psychopaths and individuals with a history of aggressive behaviors. A number of psychopharmacological agents, such as clomipramine and fluoxetine (Prozac), believed to function as inhibitors to the degradation of serotonin, have been found beneficial in the treatment of obsessive-compulsive disorders as well as in depressions. Another neurotransmitter, gamma-amino-butyric acid (GABA), has also received a great deal of attention, for it is believed to act as the most important inhibitory transmitter. GABA inhibits the "firing" of neural impulses in general; it also prevents dopamine-coded messages from being transmitted further. For its powerful inhibitory activity, GABA has been compared to Valium and termed, for this reason, "endogenous Valium."

*   *   *

Although many of the operations of the brain have become better understood thanks to data provided by current research, the reason (the"why?") and manner (the "how?") of mental processes remain, for the most part, a mystery. And while much has been clarified with respect to the messengers, codes, relay stations, specific tracks, terminals, and various centers of behavior in the brain, the question as to who it is that "feeds" the brain-computer still looms enormous. Who is it that screens incoming stimuli? Who determines whether they will be granted entry into the inner domain of the emotions, and into consciousness? Who pushes the buttons in the center of euphoria? Who presses the levers of self-rewards? What emotion, so intense, has the capacity of kindling a focus of activity in the brain? And who decides whether to allow the outward expression of feelings, or to push the brakes of inhibition? The brain, after all, is but an organ, an organ of mentation.

I use the brain to serve me in the pursuit of my "loves," to fulfill my will, to realize my intentions, but it is me, my-Self, who presses on the keyboard of this organ, my brain. It may produce sweet melodies of love or ugly sounds of hate, all depending upon my intentions. I have no direct access to my center of felicity and self-rewards in the median forebrain bundle, whose stimulation would suffuse me with euphoria and a sense of inner satisfaction. Nor do I have the capacity of eliciting "melodies" that would sing praises to me, unless I have deserved them in reality.

I have no access to the center of dysphoria in the paraventricular mesodiencephalic system, whose stimulation produces negative feelings of aversion and compulsions to self-punishment. Nor do I have control over my complexes of sin and guilt; I cannot prevent guilty feelings from entering my consciousness if and when I transgress the moral code of my conscience. Nevertheless, having learned from past experiences how certain thoughts and behaviors give rise to anguish, fear, shame, remorse, and guilt, I am also free to choose to avoid their repetition.

Whereas I have little control over the feelings that well up in the center of my being, *I am free to act*, and by my actions modify and even create new feelings. This is the freedom and responsibility about which Existentialists shout loud. It is the essence of Existentialism. It is also common sense and basic wisdom. That "even feelings are formed by the deeds one does," to quote from Sartre (*Existentialism Is a Humanism*), represents a universal truth to which we all resort at one time or another.

The major doctrines accepted by contemporary psychiatry, exhorting the individual to follow his "feelings," are subtly misleading. We cannot be guided, nor guide others, merely by "feelings." Much of the evil that has descended upon our modern world has been the result of "feelings," which, instead of being repressed, are allowed "free expression." Most unreliable as guides, feelings can be followed, but on the condition that they are aligned with reason and conform to the moral dictates of the conscience.

The Christian dictum "love thy enemies" is psychologically sound. A loving action that advances the welfare of an enemy immediately cancels out feelings of hate, revenge, jealousy, resentment, and anger. Such an act (or even intention) of the will instantly presses on the keyboard, and by a psychological reflex mechanism, produces melodies of praise and enhancement of self-esteem in the inner domain of the emotions. It might even transform an enemy into a friend. Psychiatric interventions need, for this reason, to be action-oriented, for actions have the capacity to modify feelings, and these in turn may change the internal climate of the organism.

I cannot change my genetic propensities and defaults in upbringing, nor can I cancel hurt and rejection. I cannot prevent blows, hurts, offenses, or the pain of injustice. I cannot change the disappointments, humiliations, bereavements, and various other traumatic events I encounter on my path. The sadness and suffering are there. But I am free to direct my thoughts away and set them upon things more edifying. I am also free, to some degree, to change the realities of my world, which by necessity will create changes in the private domain of my emotions. I am also free to contribute something *to* the world in view of cancelling injustices; to improve the lot of the less fortunate; and to bring about changes that will benefit the Common Good. A release of norepinephrine might then occur, relaying through specific tracks to the forebrain bundle a message of merit, resulting in inner satisfaction, enhanced self-esteem, and feelings of elation.

My brain is but an organ. It is I, nevertheless, who decides on the choice of the musical script I am going to play, and how I am going to play it. When I decide to make my goal revenge, and push on the keyboard of my brain to execute such intentions, I can expect not melody, but threatening visions and so many "voices" that will then accuse me. But it is I who play on the organ of my emotions and not any of my molecules. I can take amphetamines and reach some unusual high, but I will have no control over the crash that will invariably ensue. I can decide to fail in the fulfillment of my obligations, or refuse to honor my contract with an Other or others, but this will lead me into a state of depression, perfused with anger directed at myself for failing. I can, on the other hand, decide to raise my self-esteem through an act of love, courage, or self-sacrifice, and feel then a blissful state, perhaps even ecstasy. I am the captain of my fate and orchestrator of my emotions.

Chapter IV

Heredity and Childhood

. . . visiting the iniquity of the fathers upon the children, unto the third and fourth generation of them that hate me; and showing mercy unto thousands of them that love me, and keep my commandments.
—Exodus 20:5-6

Always in pursuit of biological solutions to the problem of psychopathological developments, the behavioral sciences have, naturally, extended their search beyond neuro-anatomical-biochemical aberrations and into factors of heredity, childhood experiences, and family constellations.

Whereas no one would now dispute the genetic derivation of an individual's physical characteristics, the role of heredity in personality traits—being less visible and clear-cut—has produced a prodigious amount of research data. Certain personality attributes and idiosyncrasies as well as psychopathological trends are, indeed, clearly discernible in one's progenitors. The same is true for mental illnesses and criminality, which have always been recognized to "run in families." "Bad seeds," may skip one generation, however, and appear in the next.

Not many would also stand to dispute the "imprinting" effects of early childhood experiences and their influence on the development of the mature personality. The debate, however, as to whether nature (heredity) or nurture (environment) is responsible for molding the personality—and when deviant, for the eruption of a psychiatric illness—is practically dying out, for these determinants are no longer held to be mutually exclusive. Much has also happened in the last decade to devalue the deterministic psychoanalytic theories of child development, as well as to undermine to some extent the position held by geneticists with regard to psychopathology.

Indeed, so much more enters into the structure of the personality, into the individual's world. In the course of our life-journey, we also contribute a great deal in the building of our character as well as our environment. And because we tend to construct our experiences along a vector—the vector of intentionality—we become eventually much of what we strive to be.

The Child

In the search for hereditary factors responsible for the causation of psychiatric disorders, other contributory trends need to be sorted out first, and agreement reached on what exactly is inherited; what is the impact of childhood experiences and external traumata. Thus, in evaluating the antecedents of psychiatric disorders, it stands to reason to assume that the earlier mental disturbances make their appearance, the higher the probability of their being inherited; and conversely, the later these disturbances become manifest, the more likely the possibility that environmental influences and personal choices have been contributory or causative.

Unquestionably, some children arrive in the world already blighted by physical and/or mental defect and disability. In a comprehensive description of the *Neurobiological Antecedents of Schizophrenia in Children*, B. Fish (1977) underscores the fact that **Childhood Schizophrenia** needs to be regarded as a "pandevelopmental disorder" (PDD), for it encompasses physical as well as psychological growth processes. Achieved by leaps and bounds, as well as multiple regressions, the development of preschizophrenic children seems to be lacking a directing *central regulator*. Children so affected may manifest defects in motor, cognitive, and linguistic capacities as well as social relatedness. Considered a subvariant of childhood schizophrenia, **Childhood Autism** is evidenced by emotional coldness and egocentricity of an extreme degree. According to various investigators, when these "emotionally refrigerated" children also manifested motor and cognitive disorders, their disability proved most severe. The distinction between PDD and schizophrenia has remained unclear, but what unifies them is their evolution into psychiatric disorders of one kind or another in adult life. Genetic studies tend to indicate that childhood schizophrenia is continuous with adult schizophrenia; the childhood form, however, progresses to become the most severe of all such illnesses. Regarding this to be a biologic disorder of the total organism, Fish writes:

> We will not unlock the riddle of schizophrenia until we understand how the biologic disorder disrupts the total integrative functioning at all levels of central nervous system functioning, from physical and motor growth and development up to the perception of abstract reasoning.

The riddle of schizophrenia may well be unlocked by considering it predicated upon defects of that *integrating principle*, the center of the personality, known otherwise as the soul, and recently conceptualized as the Self. It ought to be of great interest to psychologists and psychiatrists that one of the chief and most painful symptoms lamented by many schizophrenics is their sense of having lost their souls. We may want to dismiss this "symptom" as being but a product of their "craziness," but we might also do well to ponder and reflect on the weight of this awesome complaint. We might also try to understand the child whose *central regulator* has been blighted by heredity and compare him with the individual who believes he has lost his soul. Whereas the child is unaware of his inner disorganization and wonders what exactly is required of him, the schizophrenic, who laments the loss of his soul, has been aware of its progressive dissolution. Knowingly and willingly he has acted in violation of the counsel of his conscience, and consistently he has broken the laws that organize and govern his being.

French psychiatrist Benedict-Agustin Morel (1809–73), who studied and described many psychiatric disorders—then subsumed under the common designation of "psychopathic degeneration," which included psychopathy, criminality, and *démence precoce,* now termed schizophrenia—found these disorders to worsen for three to four successive generations, at which point they are brought to a halt.

Much can also be learned from another set of disturbances, already noticeable at an early age and believed to be biologically determined. This is a multi-symptom disorder whose various designations reflect a shifting focus of interest and prevailing trends of thought, rather than the essence of the syndrome itself. Initially, children who appeared restless, fidgety, and *hyperactive* were thought to be suffering from Minimal Brain Damage (MBD), but since "soft" neurological signs were not demonstrable in all such cases, MBD was broadened to include every type of dysfunction (Minimal Brain Dysfunction). More recently, the poor learning capacity of these *hyperkinetic* children became focal to their diagnosis. They are now grouped under the category of **Attention Deficit with Hyperactivity Disorder** (ADHD). In a study by J. H. Satterfield et al. (1982), 36 symptoms and behaviors were found characteristic of this disorder: fidgeting, being easily distracted, talking a lot, bothering other children, disrupting the class, leaving projects unfinished, clowning around, being hard to discipline, fighting, being irresponsible, being easily upset, and more. The investigators in this study, which followed 110 ADHD boys until adulthood (17.3 years average range) and compared them to 88 normal adolescents, found a delinquency rate (at least one arrest for a serious offense) for the ADHD boys of 58 percent, as compared to 11 percent for the control group. Of the ADHD boys, 25 percent were institutionalized, either in jails, juvenile halls, group home residences, or psychiatric hospitals. According to another investigation by M. Menkes et al. (1967), the prognosis for these children ought to be considered as guarded. The authors drew this conclusion from their 25-year follow-up (average 14 to 17 years) of 14 ADHD children. At the conclusion of the study, four were still in institutions for psychosis; two proved to be mentally retarded. Only eight were found to be self-supporting, but four out of these had spent some time in institutions: two in a home for delinquent boys, one in jail, and one in a hospital. No correlation between home environment and present social adjustment could be established, nor was eventual outcome related to psychiatric treatment. In another study, also with a 25-year follow-up, B. L. Borland and H. K. Heckman (1976) found their subjects to be "overactive, distractable and impulsive; to have had long histories of difficulties with parents, teachers and peers; and to have become sociopathic in a substantial minority of 20 percent." The authors advanced the suggestion that childhood hyperactivity is etiologically related to sociopathy, alcoholism, and hysteria in adulthood. Here also, home environments did not appear to have had adverse effects on these children.

A deficit in the capacity for integration of stimuli has been frequently invoked to explain the psychopathology of hyperkinetic children. Their widely divergent life-destinies, as well as the excellent adjustment achieved by some, tend to suggest that hyperkinesis represents a rather heterogeneous group of disorders. The variety in outcomes may reflect also the fluidity of psychiatric diagnoses in general. Whether some children arrive into the world with some lacunae in their consciences (their Superego)—as has been postulated to explain antisocial behaviors—or these defects are progressively acquired, remains open for further investigation. Certainly, the "driven-ness" of these children represents an effort on their part to avoid deeper inner experiences and encountering themselves. When coached into stillness by this author, some children became very serious and sad. Deficient perhaps in some crucial attribute of the soul, such as the capacity for love, interest, and achievement, these children suffer from a chronic sense of failure, depression, and low self-esteem. Those who in adolescence, by some important choices and decisions made themselves anew—as so frequently happens—had, in all likelihood, the capacity to overcome their congenitally determined lack of integrity, and became well adjusted as adults. Those who preferred to follow the pull of their lower inclinations— "progressing" further in this direction—became antisocial as adults, falling eventually into one or another category of psychiatric disability.

Differences in temperament and behavior are discernible even in the newborn, and not infrequently, nursery staff can spot the child who will become "difficult" to manage. In an anterospective, long-term study of infants who were examined shortly after birth and followed up to 12 years later, A. Thomas et al. (1968) compiled evidence to show that certain abnormalities and a cluster of symptoms, discernible early in infancy, can be predictive of future psychopathology. Of a population of 133 children, carefully studied— and their parents' observation records taken into account—42 eventually became "clinical cases," i.e., in need of professional help. Of those identified early as "difficult" children, 70 percent developed behavioral problems, and among them, some became what the authors bluntly termed "mother killers." The authors of this anterospective research project made efforts to standardize the sample of parents as well as the environments they would tend to create. The following cluster of temperamental attributes was found to be predictive of future psychopathology: irregularity in biological function, a predominance of negative moods, negative responses to novel stimuli, and intense reactions. While sideline observers and researchers in the field of child development tended to regard the child's difficulties in terms of "adaptation" and "adjustment," the parents considered them *deliberate attempts at thwarting their purpose* and disturbing the routine of family living. The child's oppositional tendencies and overall indiscriminate negativism were interpreted by the parents as *defiance*.

In a retrospective longitudinal study of 54 hospitalized adult schizophrenic patients, N. F. Watt (1978) examined the past records and the school teachers' comments about these individuals, and compared them to the records of 143 controls. The preschizophrenic boys distinguished themselves by oppositional behaviors that were more pronounced than those of the controls, and progressively worsened until they culminated in the index hospitalization. *Negativism, unsocialized aggression, and defiance of authority were the outstanding characteristics of those children who later became schizophrenic.* The authors made a point of underscoring the fact that these behaviors anteceded psychotic disorganization and disturbances in thinking. Both boys and girls manifested excessive egocentricity; the girls, who appeared initially shy and withdrawn, later became rather "aloof." Examination of the high school records of these children and their teachers' comments revealed that preschizophrenic children, as contrasted to controls, flouted and rejected authority more than their peers. Preschizophrenic girls showed the lowest level of social participation; boys, on the other hand, gave the appearance of "oversocializing." The manner of their interaction with others, however, consisted in fighting, quarrelling, bullying, and similar activities. According to the observations of Watt et al. (1970):

> Unsocialized aggression is the most prominent pattern of behavior in the pre-schizophrenic boys. They were rude and defiant towards persons in authority. The pre-schizophrenic boy will deceive others and refuses to accept the blame for his behavior. He will destroy the property of others as well as attack their person, with little feeling and remorse.

The central characteristics of these preschizophrenic children thus emerge as *defiance of authority, uninhibited hostility, cruelty, opposition, and deliberate intention to hurt.*

From a study of 150 children followed into adulthood after their initial referral to a child guidance clinic, P. O'Neal and L. N. Robins (1957) reported that the children who later became schizophrenic distinguished themselves by their *incorrigibility, fighting, and truancy. Acted out aggressive urges and pathological lying* were also singled out as characteristic (O'Neal and Robins 1958). In a later study, which involved 524 children and 100 controls, Robins (1966) found preschizophrenic children to have manifested antisocial behaviors more numerous and more serious than those of children who later became sociopathic adults. More than 50 percent of the preschizophrenic children had run away, were incorrigible, and manifested severe antisocial behaviors as well as sexual acting out. As adults, the schizophrenics continued to show antisocial behaviors, and 50 percent of them met more than five of the criteria for antisocial personality disorder. Two-thirds were arrested at some point in time. It is worthy of mention that aggression in preschizophrenic children was more frequently directed toward kin or children they knew, than otherwise. The majority of these children (74 percent) were referred to the child guidance clinic not for disordered thinking, autism, or florid psychotic symptomatology, but for antisocial behaviors that *anteceded* their psychosis. The studies of O'Neal and Robins (1957) ought to reassure those who fear the prognosis of neurotic children, for the highest proportion of healthy adults came from their midst. As for the children who later became schizophrenic, most outstanding was their acting out behavior, in defiance of the demands made by school, family, and the laws established by society.

In a syndrome closely related to schizophrenia, namely **Clérambault's Syndrome,** also known as **Erotomania,** willfulness, narcissism, pride, and defiance combine to produce a most intractable insanity. The erotomaniac, characteristically, persists in demanding reciprocity from the object of his amorous pursuits, in spite of clear and unambiguous rejection. In defiance of the wishes of the object of his "love," such an individual refuses to renounce his own desire, and will delusionally entertain the belief that he is actually loved. In the famous case of the daughter of French writer Victor Hugo, Adèle H. persisted in pursuing the object of her love, in spite of repeated clear-cut rejection. Following her beloved from continent to continent, this unfortunate ended her years in an insane asylum. The case of John Hinkley, Jr. is well known: rejected by film star Jodie Foster, he made an attempt on President Reagan's life, in order to draw her attention to himself. His sad story serves to demonstrate to what lengths such individuals may go, in the face of obvious rejection and in defiance of reality—just for the sake of satisfying their own desire.

In the defiance of individuals who persistently engage in antisocial activities and in the intransigence of the erotomaniac, a major common dynamism can be identified: the compulsion *to assert their will no matter what.* Defiance and negativism need for this reason to be distinguished from poor adjustment capacity, such as is characteristic of the elderly, for example, and present in certain neurotic conditions. In defiance and negativism, a force of opposition is *exerted against* another which demands compliance. Flouting of authority, disobedience, and incorrigibility appear to be the primary and basic traits of the schizophrenic premorbid personality. In view of these characteristics and the strength of his power of opposition, the schizophrenic may no longer be considered the helpless victim of external circumstances. Excessive willfulness, stubbornness, and defiant attitudes that become manifest early in life, might well be located on that "major gene of high penetrance," referred to by geneticists, which, when passed on to the offspring, is liable to bring the latter into conflict with parents, educators, and representatives of the law. In willfulness and defiance, such an individual may disregard the demands of his conscience and dismiss its corrective measures. Another gene of high penetrance may account for the propensity for "unsocialized aggression," or hostility, which has always been recognized as the *sine qua non* dynamic force behind every schizophrenia. "Stubbornness is as iniquity and idolatry" in the Holy Scriptures (I Samuel 15:23). Hostility violates the most fundamental spiritual law enunciated by all religions around the world—the law that demands that one love one's neighbor as oneself.

The Child's Heredity

Although the hereditary transmission of psychopathological traits and mental illnesses, including schizophrenia, has been repeatedly investigated, there is no consensus as to *what* exactly is transmitted to successive generations, and *how* this actually occurs. Of all mental illnesses, **Manic-Depressive Psychoses** have shown most clearly a hereditary pattern of transmission. The gene or genes for this disorder are thought to be located on the X chromosome. This is clinically demonstrated by the following findings: manic-depressive illnesses more commonly affect females; affected fathers rarely produce manic-depressive sons, but may have manic-depressive daughters; manic-depressive mothers have sons and daughters with this condition in equal distribution (J. E. Jeffress 1975). Concordance rates given as 100 percent for monozygotic twins and 25.5 percent for dizygotic twins establish manic-depressive illness as a disorder of very strong hereditary derivation. According to F. J. Kallman (1953), when one sibling is affected, the risk for other full siblings is 22.7 percent, and 16.7 percent for half siblings.

The genetic pattern as well as recent research findings tend to support Kraepelin's original separation of manic-depressive illnesses from schizophrenia as mutually exclusive disorders. The life-histories, premorbid personality, and clinical picture of these two major psychoses distinguish them, indeed, as separate nosological entities. The premorbid personality of the manic-depressive is socially well integrated and achievement-oriented, whereas the premorbid schizophrenic is hostile, withdrawn, and prone to failure. The manic-depressive, furthermore, completely recovers from a psychotic episode, whereas the schizophrenic characteristically suffers a scarring of his personality, steps down on the socioeconomic ladder, and is liable to deteriorate.

Clinically, the symptomatology of manic-depressive patients can be regarded as due to an emotional incontinence, which allows for excessive elation during the manic phase and unduly deep sadness during depression. Being exceptionally endowed, as a rule, the manic-depressive individual turns his gifts into achievement. Neither weakness nor defect are apparent in the premorbid personality of the manic-depressive, except for an exaggerated sense of self-importance and excesses of *hubris*, pride. But unlike the grandiose, omnipotent paranoid schizophrenic, the manic-depressive individual has good reason to value himself highly, for he knows himself to be loving— even excessively at times. He is also well aware of his achievements, which are frequently superior to those of his fellow men. Successes and achievements, however, might send the manic-depressive on what patients bluntly designate as "Ego-trips," which land their victims in the realms of unreality and into psychosis. Minor pricks of criticism, or a trivial slight, may, on the other hand, cast them into the depths of depression. Bouts of depression, nevertheless, may spur new heights of creativity, as the cycle of this illness tends to be repeated. In biochemical terms, manic-depressive psychoses have been found associated with excesses (in mania) or depletion (in depression) of norepinephrine and aberrations in the metabolism of serotonin (modulator of emotions). **Hypomania** is a disorder similar to manic-depressive illness, differing from it, however, by its somewhat milder manifestations. Not unlike the manic, the hypomanic relates to others by demanding their respect, which he needs to fuel his own sense of Self, as well as his excessive pride. There is an exaggerated overbearing and intrusiveness in the "loving" of these individuals and a desire for domination. Those "others," however, may not tolerate so well the subtle enslavement of the hypomaniac and may reject him—giving him, then, cause to sink into depression.

Standing between schizophrenic psychoses, on the one hand, and manic-depressive illnesses on the other, **"Atypical" Psychoses,** which include schizophreniform, schizo-affective, hysterical, and cyclic psychoses, have been investigated by W. Procci (1976), who found strong homopathic tendencies in the manner of their hereditary transmission: "In effect," wrote Procci, "bipolar affectives, schizophrenics and atypical schizophrenics have a strong proclivity for each to 'breed true.'"

This proclivity does not apply to schizophrenia, however, as Procci made a point in stating, for "schizophrenia cannot be regarded as a unitary entity, but rather as a wide spectrum of disorders." The study of the genetic transmission of schizophrenia is complicated not only by virtue of the multiplicity of disorders included in this spectrum, but also by the existence of a rich terminology that is periodically changed with the reshuffling of diagnostic categories and new disease classifications. Of major import to the exploration of the hereditary pattern of schizophrenic illnesses has been the inclusion within its spectrum of such characterological syndromes as the borderline, schizoid, schyzotypal, and inadequate personality disorders (S. S. Kety et al. 1968), psychopathic personalities (L. L. Heston 1966), schizoid psychopathy (F. Kallmann 1938), and paraphrenia, among others. Genetic studies on the transmission of schizophrenia reveal, moreover, that criminality, alcoholism, drug addiction, sexual perversion, and schizophrenia are strongly interlocked conditions.

Since hereditary characteristics tend to become manifest early in life, observations of children have served as a basis for the derivation of common denominators to later schizophrenic developments. According to the studies of P. O'Neal and L. N. Robins (1957), preschizophrenic children not only engaged in antisocial behaviors prior to their psychosis, but their behaviors were more seriously deviant and frequent than those of children who later became antisocial adults. The preschizophrenic children, moreover, tended to carry their antisocial activities far into adulthood. The fathers of preschizophrenic children were found to be antisocial almost as often as were the fathers of psychopaths (L.N. Robins 1966).

In a long-term study designed to disentangle hereditary from environmental influences, L. L. Heston (1966) undertook the investigation of 47 children born to schizophrenic mothers from whom they were separated at birth (or shortly thereafter), and compared them with 50 well-matched "controls." Born between 1915 and 1945, these children were interviewed by Heston in 1964. Information about them was gathered from various sources such as school, armed forces records, police files, and local newspapers. Nearly 50 percent of the experimental sample (adoptees born to schizophrenic mothers) were found to be affected by either schizophrenia or "schizoid psychopathy." Of the 47 children, five became schizophrenic, while none in the control group became so affected. This age-corrected rate of 16.6 percent is consistent with Kallman's (1938) 16.7 percent rate of schizophrenia, when one parent is so affected. Eight subjects from Heston's experimental group became psychopathic personalities, two became homosexuals, and one a narcotics addict. Seven from this group were convicted felons. The children of schizophrenic mothers, from whom they were separated at birth, spent eight times as many years in penal and/or psychiatric institutions compared to their matched controls (112 years vs. 15 years for the controls). The lifestyles of some of these individuals were consistent with Kallmann's diagnostic entity of "schizoid psychopathy," a state suggestive of schizophrenia but not revealed during the interview. They had multiple arrests, lived in hotel rooms, and, if they worked, engaged mostly in menial, casual, or temporary occupations. Another group of adoptees born to schizophrenic mothers manifested high levels of anxiety, paranoid fears of people, phobias, panic attacks, etc.—disturbances that would qualify for the diagnosis of "pseudo-neurotic schizophrenia" as described by S. Dunaif and P. Hoch (1955). A relatively high percentage of mental retardates with low IQs were also found among the offspring of schizophrenic mothers—almost 10 percent of the 47. This relatively high percentage confirms the findings of other investigators, including those of F. J. Kallmann (1938), whose data indicate a prevalence of 5–10 percent of mental retardates among the relatives of schizophrenics, compared to 3 percent in the general population. Heston's data show the genetic heirs of schizophrenic mothers to be a heterogenous group of individuals that includes mental retardates, criminals, psychopaths, inadequate and borderline persons, as well as the frankly schizophrenic. Heston interpreted his data as confirming the validity of the genetic transmission of schizophrenia as well as related disabilities, "nearly as malignant."

In another study of adopted-away schizophrenic individuals, Heston (1971) found a concentration of psychopathology, significantly in excess, among their first-degree relatives. Along with Kallman, Heston came to recognize that "schizoidia" and "schizoid psychopathy" define individuals who exhibit impulsive behaviors, engage in senseless crimes, arson, assaults, rape, etc., abuse alcohol and drugs, and/or prefer perverse sexual activities. Both Kallmann and Heston regarded schizoid psychopathy as a single disease entity, manifested in different degrees of severity. The genetic pattern and distribution in the general population of this disorder would lend support to such a hypothesis. Nearly 50 percent of the offspring of one schizophrenic parent became affected by "schizoid psychopathy" in one form or another, and monozygotic twins showed a tendency to be concordant with respect to its severity. Kallmann's and Heston's genetic studies thus tend to validate Morel's concept of "psychopathic inferiority"and its familial transmission. Whether a worsening of these disorders occurs for three to four succeeding generations, and whether they are brought to a halt thereafter, needs to be further explored.

The problem concerning a hierarchy of severity of "psychopathic inferiority"—now included within the "schizophrenic spectrum" but previously diagnosed as "schizoid psychopathy"—has remained largely unsolved. One reason for the difficulty may be found in the static, one-time diagnoses given to those suffering from a "mental disorder." A better perspective of psychiatric disturbances, in general, would necessitate their exploration as *dynamic processes evolving over time*. The sociopath, for example, may become an alcoholic and also a drug abuser. A narcotics addict by necessity becomes a sociopath, for the high cost of his vice leads him to commit various crimes. S. Guze (1976) defines the sociopath by the rate of the criminal's recidivism. C. R. Cloninger (1975) believes that "most convicted felons and nearly all recidivists are sociopathic," but fails to distinguish between the born, true psychopath and the sociopath (cf. Chapter IX). Be that as it may, clear demarcation lines between psychopathy, sociopathy, and criminality—if they existed—would be difficult to draw, due to their contiguity to other disorders and their evolution over time. In another study, C. R. Cloninger and S. Guze (1973) found the risk of recidivism to be associated with such unrelated disorders as drug dependency, alcoholism, and homosexuality. But as will be shown later, antisocial behaviors may lead to psychotic outbreaks, to schizophrenia, and even to schizophrenic deterioration.

In a recent study by the National Institute of Mental Health, involving several catchment areas (Epidemiologic Catchment Areas, ECA studies), the finding that one mental disorder increases the odds for the occurrence of even an unrelated disorder, was found to be "intriguing" (D. X. Freedman 1984). From the existential perspective, however, which regards complexes of sin and guilt to be pathogenic stressors and etiologic of a good number of psychiatric disorders, this findings does not appear quite so enigmatic. Even if inherited, once a sinful propensity becomes enacted in reality (not just in fantasy), this act will tend to be repeated as long as the "repetition compulsion" (p. 149) remains operative. Every *unrepented* moral transgression, moreover, will tend to be compounded by yet another, even unrelated offense, as the moral forces of the conscience become weakened and the powers of the Ego-reason lose the capacity for control.

The natural course of psychiatric disorders thus shows a trend toward worsening over time. Unless jolted into change through an "explosion of conscience," an existential crisis, a "hitting bottom" experience, or a physical illness, the psychopathic schizoid (engaged in antisocial activities directed against either society or individuals revolving in his social circle) will tend to slide further. The narcissistic individual might become borderline, the borderline frankly schizophrenic, the criminal "hardened." Eventually, with the loss of the capacity for feeling guilt, the born psychopath, hardened criminal, and deteriorated schizophrenic become—by their own admission—spiritless "robots" who can feel neither joy nor pain, only some undifferentiated excitement.

Diagnostic differences, moreover, tend to level off in the course of the lives of severely affected individuals. Progressively, they dry out emotionally, and are liable to become spiritless, loveless, and guiltless—their existence losing all meaning. In terms of severity, the one-time schizophrenic who, having heeded the warning imparted to him by his psychotic ordeal, repents and changes his life-orientation, has a much better prognosis than otherwise. He might be able to leave the list of psychiatric casualties altogether. As for the schizophrenic who experiences fears, delusions, and various dysphorias pertaining to guilt, he must be considered "healthier" than the hardened criminal and unrepented sociopath, for his conscience is still alive, even as it is condemning. Given these considerations, it would appear that the most severe of all psychiatric conditions is true psychopathy, for the individuals so affected seem to be devoid of a soul.[*] But as has been said before, when criminals, borderlines, and schizophrenics fail to remedy their ways, they are liable to lose their souls and die while living—reaching the same state of being as that of authentic psychopaths.

The gap in understanding the genetic transmission of psychiatric disorders is widened further by research indicating that some children, although born of schizophrenic mothers, did *not* become affected by any disease belonging to the "schizophrenic spectrum." According to Heston (1966), nearly 50 percent of the children born to schizophrenic mothers and reared by adoptive parents were not only free of

---

[*] The moral conscience is central to the Self, the soul.

psychiatric disorders and psychosocial disability, but grew up to become successful adults. These children, moreover, appeared more spontaneous and better endowed with musical, intellectual, and artistic talents than were the "control" children born to normal mothers. What makes for the excesses in endowment of children born to schizophrenic mothers, vis-à-vis their siblings and matched "controls," remains to be explained.[*]

The investigations of P. Wender et al. (1977) on adopted-away offspring of schizophrenic parents lend support to the findings produced by Heston. Commenting on their research data, Wender et al. explain the markedly increased prevalence of psychopathology among biological parents of schizophrenics as "compatible with a genetic, not psychological transmission." Employing a systematic sampling, their studies attempted to take into account offspring-induced psychopathology in the parent.

The Child's Family

In order to assess the genetic pattern of schizophrenia, its familial incidence was compared to that of the general population. According to various statistics, the incidence of schizophrenia (new cases per annum) around the world ranges from 0.35 percent to 2.85 percent, with a mean approximating 0.85 percent (S. Kessler 1980). The overall picture of the hereditary distribution of schizophrenia among the relatives of an index case shows that the risk for the disease is decidedly greater, being from 2 to 46 times higher than the average for schizophrenia in the general population. The wide scatter of risk rate for schizophrenia has been regarded as evidence that many more variables are actually needed for the schizophrenic predisposition to become manifest (N. F. Watt 1978).

As has been mentioned before, the highest concentration of schizophrenia-spectrum diseases was found among the first-degree relatives of frankly schizophrenic patients; with second-degree relatives showing a lesser concentration; and third-degree even a lesser concentration, but still higher than that in the general population. When cases of schizophrenia were added to cases of "schizoidity," 45 percent of the first-degree relatives of schizophrenics were

---

[*]   Socrates' view on madness adds a new dimension to the current, scientifically derived hypotheses: madness has a divine purpose.

found to be affected. With one parent schizophrenic, the risk for the offspring is 16.7 percent for schizophrenia and 32.5 percent for schizoidity (F. J. Kallmann 1938). When one sibling is schizophrenic, the risk for another is 14.3 percent for schizophrenia and 31 percent for schizoidity, provided only one parent is schizophrenic. When both parents are so affected, 66.1 percent of their children will, in all probability, be also affected. The genetic burden, nevertheless, seems to fall heavier on the children, for they are affected to a greater degree than are their parents. This finding has been subsequently confirmed with remarkable consistency by several independent investigations.

Whereas the weight of evidence overwhelmingly implicates genetic factors in the etiology of schizophrenia, the fact that so many children born of schizophrenics do not become affected, are not mentally retarded, and do not become sociopaths or criminals tends to suggest that more than hereditarily transmitted tendencies are here involved. The difference among siblings who are schizophrenic, schizoid, or normal is too great to be accounted for by hereditary tendencies (some following Mendelian laws) and factors of upbringing alone. Siblings, after all, carry similar hereditary propensities and are subjected to quite similar conditions when raised in the same family. Whence the difference in their personalities, their mental health? The mystery of this "functional disorder of unknown etiology," named schizophrenia, looms even larger considering the fact, stressed by Heston, that 90 percent of schizophrenics do not have schizophrenic parents.

The study of twins brings more supporting evidence to the participation of genetic factors in schizophrenia and allied disorders. In his review of *The Genetics of Schizophrenia*, S. Kessler (1980) attempted to summarize the research findings of several investigations. Estimated "probandwise" (meaning independently counted affected twins), the concordance rate for monozygotic twins for schizophrenia was found to range from 35 percent to 58 percent, dropping to 26 percent and 9 percent for dizygotic twins. In a study of 17 pairs of twins raised apart (thus eliminating environmental factors), E. Slater and V. Cowie (1971) found 11 of the pairs to be concordant for schizophrenia, representing an actual rate of 65 percent. The most compelling evidence, however, in favor of a strong genetic input for the development of schizophrenia, according to Kessler, has been provided by a series of sophisticated and elegantly designed studies of children adopted away since birth. This "cross-fostering" method of investigation can separate, to a great extent, hereditary from environmentally induced psychopathology. Availing themselves of the Danish Adoption Register, D. Rosenthal et al. (1968, 1971) investigated the records of approximately 5,500 children who were given to nonfamilial adoption soon after birth. The children born to schizophrenic mothers were selected to serve as "index" cases. A total of 76 such cases was compared to a total of 67 control adoptees. Among the "index" adoptees, 30 percent were diagnosed as belonging to the "schizophrenic spectrum," whereas only 17.8 percent among the control group could be so considered. When the study narrowed its focus on adoptees who had been admitted to psychiatric facilities (S. S. Kety et al. 1968), it was found that their biological relatives had a considerably higher concentration of individuals with schizophrenia-spectrum disorders than the control group. No such difference was found among the adopting relatives, indicating that their influence was of lesser import than the genetic transmission of factors favoring a schizophrenic development.

Genotypes (genetic makeup) for schizophrenia may, however, remain unexpressed, as studies on twins' offspring seem to indicate. If one looks at the concordance rate among monozygotic twins (ranging between 60 percent and 70 percent in studies prior to 1965, and employing different criteria), the contribution of factors other than genetic to the development of schizophrenia becomes more obvious. The rate of schizophrenia among the offspring of discordant (only one twin is affected) for schizophrenia monozygotic (who have the same genetic makeup) twins, has been studied by E. Kringlen and G. Cramer (1989). Although the children of the schizophrenic twin parent were found to fall more frequently within the "schizophrenic spectrum" than the children of the discordant for schizophrenia twin, the difference was not significant at the 5 percent level, indicating that other than genetic determinants need to be present in order to activate the hereditary predisposition to these disorders.

Several cases of twins reared apart have come to the attention of the news media because of the striking discovery that these twins— some of whom grew up in completely different circumstances and cultures—exhibited similar tastes, made similar choices in vocation and marriage, and chose even the same names for their children. The similarity of their choices and preferences not only affirms the strength of hereditary loading, but serves also to cement Swedenborg's conceptions regarding the personality, which he defines by its "loves", affections, choices, and strivings (p. 54).

Although the role of genetic factors in schizophrenia-spectrum disorders has now been solidly established by a variety of strategic investigative approaches, the question as to *what* exactly is being inherited remains largely unanswered. That a deletion of genetic material may occur is well known in the world of metabolic disturbances. Defects or lacunae in the conscience have long been held responsible for the apparent lack of guilty dysphorias, characteristic of the true psychopath. The existence of a genetic defect in schizophrenia would lend support to those theories that attribute this diseased state to weaknesses of the Ego. Such defects may, indeed, account for certain personality traits as incontinence of anger, deficient impulse control, poor work performance, and these individuals' lags and lacks of achievement, in general. Weaknesses of the Ego, however, cannot explain *excesses* of willfulness, nor account for the defiance so characteristic of the schizophrenic personality. Neither can they account for the pervasive hostility of the schizophrenic—the smoldering passion that fills to the brim the domain of his emotions, and that needs to be differentiated from aggression. Nor does the schizophrenic's allegedly deficient capacity for perceiving reality hold true in every instance. It is rather Ego-psychology that fails to perceive that these individuals' cunning devices and sharpened capacity for distortion of certain truths cannot be attributed to any weakness of the Ego. Misperceptions, yes, and a world filled with ghosts and uncanny creatures—these are definitely present in the experiences of every schizophrenic—but they do not detract from the skillfulness with which he may bind half-truths and execute various deceptive operations. Without his rather "hypertrophic" sense of reality, the "slick" psychopath would not be able to succeed in executing complex and not infrequently dangerous exploits.

The Hereditary Load

What exactly is transmitted in disorders of personality and overt psychiatric disturbances? Kallmann regarded schizophrenia to be the same disease as schizoidity but more severe in degree, a view he shares with Kety and Heston. Indeed, a longitudinal view of the life-course of character-disordered "schizoid" persons shows that such precursory states do not necessarily lead to a schizophrenic development. Yet, some widely divergent disturbances such as obsessive-compulsive disorders, borderline states, sexual perversions, and antisocial activities may develop further, and culminate eventually into outright schizophrenia. Were the outbreak of schizophrenia to represent a sudden illness—an unheralded catastrophe—its roots would not reach deep into the substance of the premorbid personality, as has been repeatedly confirmed (cf. Chapter VII). If "craziness" were to represent mere "irrationality" and be inherited as such, the florid symptoms of psychosis as well as disordered thinking would not make their appearance after a time-lag, and always succeeding antisocial activities, practiced sexual perversions, aggressive behaviors, and various acts of malevolence, as they actually do.

Were, however, irrationality to mean inherited evil propensities turned into conscious undertakings, and choices of evil considered "irrational," this formula would reconcile current theories on the genetic transmission of insanity with the premises of Existentialism, and cancel the need for further debate. Irrationality, however, is not synonymous with the "unconscious" (onto which psychoanalysts have projected all the evils humans are capable of devising). Nor can the unconscious be held responsible for fantasies, which do not just assail the conscious mind, but are conjured up as an act of the will. In certain choices of evil, the Ego-mind-reason fully participates. The abandonment of children, spouse, or old parents, for example, or perverse sexual activities, defraudations, abuses, exploitations, deceptions, and premeditated crimes would obviously fall into this category.

In attempting to unravel the complex pattern of heredity in schizophrenia and related disorders, Heston (1971) suggested the operation of several genes whose action is cumulative. A polygenic manner of transmission has also been postulated by K. K. Kidd and L. L. Cavalli-Sforza (1973), whereby "in the right constellation, a particular number of genes whose action is cumulative" produce propensities that lead to a schizophrenic development. A Mendelian type of inheritance has also been suggested, whereby "one trait, one gene" is transmitted to the offspring, or perhaps a combination of several traits-genes which is critical in shaping the personality structure of the future "schizoid psychopath." Heston advanced yet another possibility, namely, that a "main gene of large penetrance, and modified by multiple factors may be here involved, which when present in the hereditary load of an individual would make for a 'schizophrenic diathesis.'" A vulnerability to schizophrenia is, in fact, believed to exist (N. F. Watt 1978), but many more variables seem to be needed in order to activate it.

The following personality characteristics have been observed to distinguish the future schizophrenic and schizoid psychopath: unsocialized aggression, defiance of authority, incorrigibility, and persistent lying (O'Neal, Robins, and Watt et al., quoted in this section). As common denominators of the psychiatric disorders considered to belong to the "schizophrenic spectrum," hate and defiance—never lacking in the personality structure of the individuals affected—might well be those crucial traits-genes of high penetrance, whose presence in the genetic makeup of an individual predisposes him to a schizophrenic illness. Needless to say, hostility and acted out aggressive urges carry wide-ranging consequences, especially in interpersonal relationships, which they will tend to preclude. Defiance may well be cementing all the negative traits within the structure of the schizoid psychopath's personality, described as "incorrigible."

Defiant attitudes create difficulties at every step in an individual's adjustment to his environment and also to his predicament. Thus, for *refusing* to submit to the rules and regulations established by family, school, workplace, and society—so necessary for their harmonious functioning—the defiant individual is perpetually brought into conflict with the world outside; and for his refusal to abide by the laws of love and morality which bind the human family together, he is eventually extruded from its midst. In his relationship to himself, the defiant individual is liable to disregard the counsel of his conscience: warning signals, admonitions, and corrective measures; but by so doing, he only enhances for himself a career of psychiatric disability, the outcome of which will depend on his willingness to give up the defiant stance.

Childhood Experiences

It goes without saying that hate and defiance create their own specific environments. It would be appropriate, for this reason, to begin the exploration of environmental factors with the study of defiant children and how they grow up. Far from representing Ego-weaknesses, the defiance, persistence, and demandingness of some children may, nonetheless, be explained by their excessive need for instant gratification of their every whim and wish. Yet, more frequently than not, these children's stubbornness serves no other purpose than the assertion of their will. Thus, the child born with a hereditarily transmitted *willfulness* begins to shape his own environment. Reacting to a child such as this, a nervous, anxious, and resentful mother might give in to her child's wishes, just for the sake of peace.

Whereas a child born with autistic tendencies may greatly sadden the heart of his parents for failing to respond to their loving ministrations, the child who is defiant and negativistic engenders anger and frustration. Before long, the patience of the child's caretakers may wear thin, and they may attempt to correct him through various punitive measures, often unjust and even excessive. As for the effect on siblings and other family members, a child who constantly disobeys, of necessity disrupts the harmony of family living and creates tension and dissension. A fencing match between the parents is liable to ensue, each parent insisting on one or another method of correction. A negativistic, defiant, and incorrigible child thus creates a double bind for his caretakers, who become divided with regard to the best method of his upbringing—vacillating between a permissive, "laissez-faire" attitude and various punitive measures. Notwithstanding, for an incorrigible child no limit-setting will avail: permissiveness increases acted out behavior, while punishment increases resistance and rebellion. Indeed, there seems no single, no correct way that will work in the rearing of a child such as this. A closer analysis of any specific conflict frequently reveals that neither this nor that issue was actually at stake, but the child's stubbornness and willfulness. Marital discord and even rifts have been observed to occur from the hardship imposed on the family by unmanageable children.

Before the current tide of permissiveness, the customary handling of disobedient, obstinate children was to first "break their will." This rather conservative method of child-rearing may appear shocking to modern Western societies, yet it can boast of having produced fewer individuals belonging to the narcissistic, borderline, self-indulgent, overeating, alcoholic, and drug-addict categories than its liberal counterpart.

With an inherited load of hatefulness and defiance, choices of evil become natural. A child so stamped by heredity frequently feels compelled to execute these choices, despite the family's efforts to restrain him. As has been pointed out by several researchers, it is very difficult to separate the negative characteristics of the parents, which may have been passed on to the child, from the climate such characteristics would create for their offspring. According to D. Rosenthal et al. (1975), both genetic predisposition and the quality of child-rearing may affect the development of psychopathology; the amount of variance accounted for by rearing practices tends, however, to be low. With their "cross-fostering" method of investigation, P. H. Wender et al. (1974) compared children adopted-away at birth whose parents had no psychiatric history with children reared by a disturbed parent, and found that for the children who had one adoptive parent with a schizophrenia-spectrum diagnosis, the *experience* of being reared by a family with such a member does not increase the risk for schizophrenia unless a predisposition to the disorder already exists. In a study investigating the adoptive parents of schizophrenic and normal children, Wender et al. (1977) found "clear-cut" evidence that the biological parents of schizophrenics show a markedly increased prevalence of psychopathology, confirming the findings of Rosenthal (mentioned above). Of particular interest was the finding that the normal adoptive parents of schizophrenic children were affected by their adopted child's inherited psychopathology, and gave the appearance of being anxious, depressed, and guilty.

After reconsidering his own views in one of his last publications, S. Arieti (1977) sought to dispel the "half-truth which had become myth" regarding the existence of a "schizophrenogenic" mother, whose presumably "perverse sense of mothering" produces the disease in her offspring. According to Arieti, the patient is not merely a passive recipient of his genes and environment, but acts and integrates his experience as he also shapes his destiny. Arieti wrote: "We believed what our patients have told us . . . . Yet the patient makes his contributions to his own psychopathology. He picks up the negatives in his family and transforms and deforms them."

Fixated upon the notion that the "formative years" irreversibly mold children for life—as psychoanalytic theories have sought to impress—behavioral scientists have tended to place undue emphasis on early childhood experiences to the exclusion of other influences and circumstances. Yet children are not only *reactors* to various externally determined circumstances, but *proactors* also—contributing to their environment and taking stock of the consequences of their actions. Although attractive to biologically oriented psychologists, the theories of psychoanalysis—which base later psychopathological developments on alleged "traumatic" experiences in the first years of life—have stood neither the test of scientific reliability nor the validation of their data. Erected upon retrograde hypothetic observations involving not more than a *few* subjects, the theories of psychoanalysis have frequently been challenged with respect to their veracity. Scientific proof does not seem to be forthcoming either, as the experiences of preverbal children will, in all likelihood, persist in resisting the curiosity of scientific exploration. According to these theories, it appears as if traumatic experiences lurk at every turn on the road of the child's "psychosexual" development. Allegedly beginning their life-journey with the "trauma of birth" (Otto Rank), children need, then, to confront the "bad breast" of mother, which they must fuse with the "good" one, in order to avoid later "splitting" the good from the evil in human relationships (Melanie Klein). And before becoming truly civilized and independent, children need also to put up a struggle against implacable Mom, so as to ensure their individuation (Margaret Mahler). And many more power struggles need to be won, before children can convince their "controlling" mothers to "let go." They also need to overcome their incestual strivings for fear of being castrated by their fathers. Yet once their Oedipus complex is resolved, according to psychoanalytical theories, they become aware of having acquired a conscience as well as a sense of morality.

Be that as it may, of all of the psychosexual developmental theories conceived by psychoanalysts none is applicable or relevant to serious psychiatric disturbances, schizophrenia in particular. It can be said that schizophrenia has steadfastly refused to follow any of the available modern scripts. It certainly bears no relationship to the trauma of birth, breasts of the mother, toilet training, or the Oedipus complex, except in cases of incest acted out. Nor is schizophrenia contingent upon depression, the presence of which actually augurs a better prognosis than otherwise (Chapter VII). Early childhood deprivations have not been found associated with later schizophrenic developments. Insanity has never resulted from repression *per se.* Quite the contrary: it bears a direct relationship to the expression of hateful fantasies, perverse sexual appetites, revengeful intentions, or aggressive urges. Insanity tends to follow intentionally committed felonies, be these crimes against one individual or the larger group of society.

If modern scientists respect the data derived from large-scale investigations and are versed in the language of statistics, the findings of a national study on Swedish adoptees, conducted by A. Von Knorring et al. (1982), may be accepted with more credibility. In this study of 2,215 adoptees, a correlation was hypothesized to exist between negative experiences in early infancy and the development of psychiatric disorders later in life. However, after repeated statistical univariate and discriminate function analyses, no such correlation could be demonstrated, with the sole exception of **Reactive Neurotic Depression** (RND):

> Except for the risk of separation from the mother during the period 6 to 11 months of life, for the later development of Reactive Neurotic Depression (RND), early negative experiences did not explain the manifestations of psychiatric disorders in general.

This study, impressive for the large number of cases investigated, lends support to earlier observations made by R. Spitz (1946), who saw that the very young do poorly in a climate deficient of love, as the knowledge of being loved and the need to love are most fundamental to the living process. The emotional impact on infants separated from their mothers did not go beyond states of depression, however, which Spitz called *anaclitic* (*anaclitic* = leaning, in Greek) depressions. Whereas the deprivation of loving supports led many infants to experience sadness and depression—their dependency needs remaining unmet—it remains questionable whether these experiences could remain active and motivate gratuitous acts of arson, sadism, violence, and perverse sexual acts later in life.

Persisting, nonetheless, in their search for adverse environmental influences early in life, researchers have attempted to solve the riddle of later schizophrenic developments by invoking faulty parental child-rearing practices as well as pathological family communications and transactions in general. According to the "double bind" theory proposed by G. Bateson et al. (1956), the parents of the preschizophrenic child relate to him by way of conflicting injunctions: "When a person is caught in a double bind situation, he will respond defensively, similar to the schizophrenic." The "double bind" theory also holds that a "breakdown will occur in the individual's ability to discriminate between logical types." According to Bateson, the child is not only trapped by being the recipient of hostility simulated as love, but suffers also confusion from his parents' mostly negative injunctions and various contradictory attitudes. Persistently threatened with punishment, the child, according to this theory, may begin to hallucinate (as if one can choose to hallucinate): "The pattern of conflicting injunctions issued by the parent may even be taken over by hallucinatory voices," wrote Bateson.

Following similar lines of reasoning and attempting to explain the evolution of schizophrenia in terms of family constellations that would *make* the child schizophrenic, M. T. Singer and L. C. Wynne (1965) have sought to ascribe thought disorder to parental defects and deviance in communication. Concentrating their efforts on the study of the transactional styles of family members, these authors have regarded parental styles as codeterminants—along with other experiential and genetic factors—of the thinking-communication defect seen in the schizophrenic offspring. The family relationships of schizophrenics have been variously described as "pseudo-mutual," "pseudo-hostile," and masking emptiness and meaninglessness. Ideas of reasoning were allegedly conveyed "piecemeal, blurred and in deviant ways which revealed the parents' own 'attentional deficit.'"

The theories proposed by Bateson, Singer, and Wynne could gain considerable clarity and precision, were the terms "pseudo-mutuality," "double-bind," and "pseudo-hostility" replaced by deceptive communications and hypocritical attitudes in general. Needless to say, deception and hypocrisy always provoke feelings of anger. Being exquisitely attuned to truth and to reality, children can perceive parental deception and hypocrisy even by nonverbal cues. But what deception and hypocrisy attempt to hide might be even more malignant: rejection, impatience, disinterest, and resentment of the child's very existence.

Nevertheless, parental attitudes may represent but *reactions* on their part to the child's willfulness, stubbornness, and frankly defiant attitude. The parents of such a child would, for this reason, tend to resort to various artificial attitudes and communications in order to hide their sorrow and disappointment—being themselves caught in a "double-bind" situation. While striving to love a preschizophrenic child, the parents may not be able to ward off the angry feelings and frustration such a child provokes. But then, hate and defiance may well be those crucial traits-genes transmitted to the child by one parent, or perhaps by both. *The circle closes when the child who is hateful and defiant because of his genetic makeup becomes the recipient of parental hostility and punitive attitudes caused by the parents' own psychopathology, to which the child reacts in kind.*

Although drawn with considerable sophistication and following the laws of logic, the systems theory is not applicable to families with a schizophrenic member. The schizophrenic truly demolishes systems theory approaches by his unwillingness to submit to the rules and regulations established by the family, and by his refusal to accept the limits set on his behavior. Attempts at coercing him into submission frequently evoke retaliatory behavior of which none other than the members of his family become recipients.

Adverse environments, undoubtedly, adversely affect the growing child and may cause deformities in the structure of his personality. Hostile environments, needless to say, create anxious and resentful children. Keenly sensitive to truth, children are well aware of its distortion or denial, and when deceived by their parents, may lose respect for them altogether. Deprivations *per se* have not been found causative of later psychiatric disorders, with the exception of the previously mentioned reactive neurotic depression (RND). Deprived of deprivations, the "spoiled child" might, in fact, be at a greater risk for later psychiatric disorders, as he may demand from others and the world more than is possible to grant him. More often than not, the frustrations engendered by the denial of his wishes kindle in him resentment and anger.

The two-dimensional frame of reference employed for the study of etiological factors conducive to the development of psychiatric disorders, namely factors of nature (heredity) and nurture (environment), has proven unsatisfactory, as it does not allow for the extrapolation of a tenable solution to this difficult problem. In his article *Behavior Genetics: Nature and Nurture,* R. Plomin (1990) does not minimize the importance of family experiences, but stresses that environmental influences affecting development are specific to every child even when reared in the same family. The nature (heredity) of the child contributes much to determine his environment and experiences. Behavioral geneticists have begun to tackle genotype interactions (GE) and correlations. Multivariate analyses have been applied to longitudinal data (life-history) in order to determine the extent to which genetic and environmental factors affecting a trait change from one age to another. While genetic effects on the IQ have been found to be remarkably stable from childhood through to adulthood, data on personality have suggested more change than continuity, and, according to Plomin, "No longitudinal behavioral genetic data have been reported for psychopathology." The focus of interest remains to be that "rich but relatively unexplored territory, namely the hyphen between the nature-nurture dimensions," Plomin points out.

The hyphen between nature and nurture allows for a certain measure of freedom, such as is known to exist in the world of molecules, where in spite of being subject to the natural laws of physics, these particles still enjoy a certain degree of random movement. How many degrees of freedom from the stigmata of genetics and bounds of the environment do humans enjoy? And how many alternatives present themselves to them for choice?

In all of the formulae conceived by behavioral scientists and geneticists in their search for factors to explain the genesis of schizophrenia-spectrum disorders, glaringly missing is a very important factor, perhaps of greater significance than all of the others—*the factor of transcendental strivings.* With transcendental strivings such as the acquisition of power, domination of others, greed for material possessions, insatiable sexual desire, passion for revenge, and destructive urges—all unrelated to biological need—the dynamic forces motivating deviant behavior become more obvious. But an equation that takes into account only factors of heredity plus environments plus degrees of freedom plus transcendental strivings, still fails to resolve the problem of schizophrenic developments, for all of the factors this side of the equation may become invalidated by yet another one: the coefficient of *will*. Carrying either a positive or a negative charge, the multiplying factor of will may render personality traits as well as externally determined circumstances either valid or invalid, depending upon the intention and its strength. The debate regarding the relative importance of the various determinants that lead to a schizophrenic development loses its relevance once the factor of will is introduced into the equation, for it may cancel the others altogether.

Sören Kierkegaard's analysis of the predicament imposed by one's heredity reads as follows:

> What the Scripture teaches, that God visits the sins of the fathers upon the children, unto the third and fourth generation, life itself proclaims in a loud enough voice. To want to chatter oneself away from this terrible fact, that this saying is a Jewish doctrine, is of no avail. Christianity has never subscribed to the notion that every particular individual is in an outward sense privileged to begin from scratch. Every individual begins in a historical nexus, and the consequences of natural law are still valid as ever. The difference now consists in this, that Christianity teaches us to lift ourselves above the "more" [which has been inherited] and condemns him who does not so do, as not willing to do so. (*The Concept of Dread*)

Along with the curse of iniquity, which passes on to the children and children of those who dare to hate God and His commandments, there is also given the promise of:

> . . . showing mercy unto thousands of them who love me and keep my commandments. (Exodus 20:6)

Chapter V

Guilt

And the Lord said unto Cain Why art thou wroth?
And why is thy countenance fallen? If thou doest well shalt thou not
be accepted? And if thou doest not well, sin lieth at the door.

—Genesis 4:6-7

Every guilty man is his own hangman.

—Seneca

The Source of Guilt and Its Nature

a. Psychoanalytical Interpretations

The psychology of guilt has given cause to much debate, numerous interpretations, and heated controversy. Most divisive, however, among the various related issues, continue to be those concerning the derivation of the moral conscience and its function.

According to psychoanalytical theory, the moral conscience represents nothing more than a vestige from an atavistic past onto which parental introjects and their injunctions are added later. For those exclusively grounded in a biological conception of man, therefore, the only consequence to be feared from the violation of a moral law is an *adverse reality* in the future that may entail losses of honor, prestige, power, love, friendship, career, and material possessions. The dysphorias associated with guilt are understood by psychoanalysts to be closely related to realistic shame and remorse. Psychoanalytical theories have posited, thus, the "reality principle" against the "pleasure principle" (which disregards reality by providing mostly short-term gratifications). Accordingly, one of the major functions of the Ego-mind-reason is to test this reality and, whenever the need arises, to issue warnings by way of "signal anxieties." Freud regarded these warning anxieties as important in preventing an individual from acting out forbidden wishes, unacceptable to the moral conscience and carrying untoward repercussions in reality. That the "reality principle" can of itself deter the acting out of forbidden-by-conscience wishes and desires dictated by the "pleasure principle," might, nevertheless, be an overestimation of this "reality principle" and a poor estimation of reality itself.

For Freud (1924) the consciousness of guilt represented but a "tension between the Ego and the Superego." Freud regarded Kant's categorical imperatives as merely an "inheritance of the Oedipus complex," from which allegedly "the origin of morality in each of us" derives. The truth about the Oedipus complex, however, is that it is based on the distorted interpretation of a myth, as presented in Sophocles' original play. Upon this distorted interpretation Freud built most of his theories regarding the "psychosexual" development of children, the origins of conscience, and the causation of neurotic illnesses in general. What Freud actually discovered in the Oedipus complex is nothing more than a *complex of sin and guilt*, such as forms the nucleus around which a good number of psychiatric disturbances and diseases may become crystallized. The Oedipus complex contains an intention and a warning. Some sin-and-guilt complexes contain actual transgression (not just intention), and instead of mere anxiety produce a sense of dread and a fear of impending punishment.

In a sense, Freud was justified in modelling the neuroses around the Oedipus complex, nonetheless, for in neurotic states the conscience issues warnings by way of various fears and threats of punishment—purposing to prevent the morally forbidden wish from becoming enacted in reality. Freud failed to perceive, however, the cardinal difference between intention and action, between *the anxieties of the neurotic for what he might do in the future, and the dread of the psychotic for what he has already done*. The problem of guilt remained one of Freud's main preoccupations, as he recognized its central role in the majority of mental illnesses. Yet he attributed feelings of guilt to the "original transgression," namely, "the killing of the father for his sexual monopoly over the women of the tribe," atavistically transmitted from generation to generation. The father, allegedly, was also eaten by the sons (S. Freud 1913). At the same time, Freud was well aware of the supremacy of the moral conscience and its capacity to override the judgments of the Ego—designating it "Superego" for this reason. He also astutely observed that an ever-watching and all-knowing conscience pronounces judgment and punishes even forbidden thoughts and intentions.

Aware that conscience's sensitivity varies among individuals, and in derision of Kant's statement that through the workings of conscience one finds proof of the existence of God, Freud (1933) mockingly remarked:

> As regarding conscience, God has done an uneven and careless piece of work, for a large majority of men have brought with them only a modest amount of it, or scarcely enough worth mentioning . . .

Freud (1940) sought the causes of mental illnesses in frustration, thwarted desire, and undue repression of instinctual urges. He believed that many neurotics suffer, actually, from an "overscrupulous" conscience that at times becomes "sadistic." Recognizing, however, the central role of guilt, anxiety, and fear in mental diseases, he sought with his treatment strategies to "oppose the Superego, lower its demands," and even to bring about "its demolition" (*An Outline of Psychoanalysis*).

Freud went even so far as to blame feelings of guilt for being the *motivators* of crime. In an intellectual somersault over the lines of logic, Freud (1924) set forth "the indisputable fact" that exacerbation of unconscious guilt could turn people into criminals. And further: "In many criminals, especially youthful ones, it is possible to detect a very powerful sense of guilt, which existed before the crime and is not its result, but its motive . . . ."

In a punishing Superego, Freud (1924) saw a "heightened sadism to which the Ego submits itself," calling this phenomenon "moral masochism" (1924).* What he failed to perceive, however, is that the

---

* In another monograph (1930), Freud wrote: "The need for punishment is an instinctual manifestation on the part of the Ego, which has become masochistic under the influence of a sadistic Super-ego; it is a portion that is to say, of the instinct toward internal destruction present in the Ego, employed for forming an erotic attachment to the Super-ego."

"sadistic" Superego has its reasons, which, to paraphrase French philosopher Blaise Pascal, reason may not know.

Nevertheless, Freud apparently never so much as thought of investigating whether the claims of conscience were valid and its punishments just. A thorough exploration of his patients' past histories would have revealed that the alleged "sadism" of the Superego had in no way exceeded the seriousness of the moral violation(s) it had set out to punish. As observed by one of the pioneers of the psychoanalytic movement, W. Stekel (1929), the laws of conscience follow the laws of talion: "An eye for an eye, a tooth for a tooth . . . ." The operation of this law is clearly evident in the mental processes and outward behaviors of psychiatric patients, criminals, antisocial persons, drug abusers, and especially in schizophrenics. An impressive assortment of cruel self-mutilating acts— mostly through the insertion of foreign bodies into the urethra— among a high-security prison population is described by R. T. Rada and W. James (1982). Self-cutting, hand-smashing, setting one's cell on fire, and swallowing knives and razor blades are common occurrences in incarceration settings. They hardly come as a surprise to jail authorities, who believe that self-mutilating behaviors are frequently undertaken as a manipulative operation intended to sway the authorities to effect a transfer, to grant a particular demand, or just to attract attention. But a deeper exploration of these senseless and unduly cruel acts of self-mutilation frequently reveals a compulsive need for self-punishment intended to assuage guilt. The psychiatric community has frequently regarded self-injurious behaviors as simply the product of the patient's "craziness," dictated by delusions. Yet, delusions always contain both the source of guilt—be that sin or crime—and its justly deserved punishment *(vide infra)*. As a general rule, the part of the body these patients assault had participated in some way in the particular crime or offense. The answer to masochism is not just pleasure derived from suffering.

b. *The Existential Perspective*

On the derivation of conscience and sources of guilt, Existentialists hold quite a different and even contrary opinion to that of psychoanalysts. Existentialists begin with the premise that man owes something to the world, and that he is basically well aware of guilt as an "inevitable being-in-debt," when he senses the never-ending call of his conscience from the depths of his being. F. Perls (1959), one of the founders of Gestalt psychotherapy, challenged Freud's views on the moral conscience:

> In ancient times conscience was thought to be God-given. Even Immanuel Kant thought that conscience was equivalent to the eternal star, as one of the two absolutes. Then came Freud and shocked us, stating that conscience is nothing but a fantasy, an introjection, a continuation of what he believed was the parents. I believe it is a projection onto the parents . . . .
> (*Gestalt Therapy Verbatim*)

According to Swiss psychiatrist Meddard Boss (1963), proponent of Daseinanalysis, man's existential guilt consists in his failing to carry out the mandate to fulfill all of his potentialities. This definition has often been interpreted as meaning that it is man's duty to realize himself by unfolding all of his potentialities in the pursuit of self-serving goals. But this is not what Kierkegaard, Buber, Marcel, and Frankl believe, and have also sought to convey. Man's sense of existential guilt derives not from omitting to develop his potentialities, but from failing to fulfill those life-tasks and missions imposed on him by the realities of his destiny. In this sense, self-actualization is achieved through self-transcendence, which frequently entails suffering, pain, and self-sacrifice. In their writings, both Buber and G. Marcel (1946) stressed man's responsibility to read the "signs" of his destiny, for self-realization is achieved through response to their call.

Undeniably, the sensitivity of the moral conscience varies among individuals, but this attribute of the soul is not fixed and static: it changes with the progression of life. The character-disordered individual as well as the criminal often "succeed" in hardening their consciences with the passage of time. True maturity and saintliness, on the other hand, tend to increase the sensitivity of the conscience. According to Swiss psychoanalyst Paul Tournier (1962), "The spiritual life and ministry, far from alleviating the burden of guilt, increases rather its weight." This means that higher spiritual levels impose more difficult tasks and challenges on the mature conscience.

The never-ending pull exerted by the conscience is described by French philosopher Gaston Bachelard (1943), whose perspective encompasses folklore, mythology, metaphorical elaborations, world literature, philosophy, and psychology. The "primordial reality of the moral forces" active in man's emotional life remains remarkably evident throughout Bachelard's work, as he perceives the existence of a powerful drive for ascendance and a compelling need for self-transcendence. The striving toward Eternal Bliss and the Path Supreme is sustained by the upward-aiming forces of morality, nonetheless. Citing C. de Saint-Martin, Bachelard writes: "The movement of the spirit is like that of fire, accomplished in ascendance."

Bachelard's observations are supported by the results of a recent study whose data, derived from computer analysis of the verbal productions of "normal" subjects, demonstrated that their conversations centered mostly around concerns for family, friends, pleasures, and themes of *ascendance* (S. Rosenberg et al. 1979).

The never-ending indebtedness of the conscience, perceived by Existentialists, adds a positive dimension to the concept of "Superego," quite distinct from the notion of Ego-ideal, which is subject to changes at will. But we may wish to leave the grounds of biological urges, self-gratification, and "moral masochism" and venture into transcendental realms instead, where we are liable to hear praises sung by the spirit, and perceive perhaps some glimmers from the brilliant Light.

The problem of the severity of conscience presses for yet another answer, namely, to what extent can the demands of conscience become oppressive and even tyrannical. As in some of the cases of vain sanctity described by William James in his *Varieties of Religious Experience*, a "good conscience" may be swayed by self-presumptive righteousness, often conjoined to pride. But it is the sin of pride and presumption, then, which become oppressive and tyrannical, not conscience *per se*. Existentialists have rightfully drawn attention to the fallacy inherent in the pursuit of a "good conscience for its own sake," for it is motivated by pride. In "the struggles of the soul," to borrow Buber's expression, one must not only "read the signs" of one's predicament, but follow their guidance as well. All major religions around the world hold the believer to obedience to the Higher Power, before all else.

Existential analysis undertakes the task of disentangling the various forces that move the soul, and strives to uncover its real motivations. Neurotic trends such as the overscrupulous performance of rituals would need, thus, to be separated from demands issued by the conscience. The case of the obsessive-compulsive neurotic, whose compulsive behaviors represent nothing more than little bribes offered to conscience in order to silence its reproaches, may serve as an example of such neurotic tendencies. Perfectionism may also, in some cases, serve as a smokescreen behind which a multitude of sinful attitudes and acts can be hidden. In all of these neurotic conditions, the seeds of madness become perceptible through the illusion they create: as if conscience can be bribed or covered by a screen!

Freud (1930) gave a rather complex interpretation of what he designated as the "aggressiveness" of conscience. According to his views, when a child renounces his aggressive urges, "a considerable amount of aggressiveness must be developed in the child against the authority which prevents him from having his first, but nonetheless, most important satisfaction . . . ." And further:

> The effect of instinctual renunciation on the conscience, then, is that every piece of aggression whose satisfaction the subject gives up is taken over by the Super-ego and increases the latter's aggressiveness [against the Ego]. (*Civilization and Its Discontents*)

* * *

Regrettably, the majority of existing psychological theories have tended to accept the psychoanalytical conceptions regarding the derivation of conscience and the function of guilt. When depressed, narcissistic, borderline, and schizophrenic patients lament that they feel guilty because they have sinned, these complaints are usually considered delusional, products of the patients' "craziness"—irrational manifestations in need of eradication. That "normals" are relatively free of guilt because they attempt to avoid transgressing the moral law, has hardly been given even minimal consideration. Instead of attempting to trace guilt to its source, namely to a moral offense, the notion of "unconscious" guilt came to be accepted. Who has buried guilt into subconscious or unconscious levels? Does it not stand to reason and conform to the laws of logic to assume that the more an individual transgresses the moral law the guiltier he is liable to feel; and the guiltier he feels, the more he would be predisposed to become "disturbed," i.e., sick? Who has declared guilt a morbid manifestation, and who has thrown blame for morbidity upon the forces of conscience? The reasons behind a strict, aggressive, and sadistic conscience would need to be investigated first. And as appealing and comforting as the theories of psychoanalysis may appear, in no way are they applicable to those who suffer from a mental sickness. Under the "unconsciousness" of guilt a multitude of moral violations can be hidden.

The Manifestations of Guilt

The first indicator of a guilty state may be a sudden surge of unexplained anger and hate. Frequently, the subjects of these feelings have great difficulties in identifying the source of their unprovoked anger. Yet upon further analysis, the guilty individual finds that his hatefulness and anger have been directed primarily to himself, because of his failure to fulfill a mandate of the moral conscience. Self-directed anger has been regarded characteristic of depressive states, but it is also found in schizophrenia, where anger may escalate into rage and contain elements of defensiveness in addition. The outward expression of anger by the guilty has long been recognized by psychiatrists as "defensive rage." Dostoyevsky was struck by the surge of anger and hate in the guilty: "The guiltier a man, the more he hates," he wrote in *The Brothers Karamazov*. But the reverse also holds true: the more one hates, the guiltier one is liable to become, and angrier. Here is the tragedy of the obsessional neurotic, and he finds no exit from the circularity of his dilemma.

Global hatred and anger, which have no specific target, are commonly, if not invariably, present in schizophrenic patients, and their "defensive rage" greatly contributes to the precariousness and volatility of their emotional state. "Guilty anxiety," wrote H. B. Lewis (1971), "is associated with hostility directed outwards." Anger may be the first indication of a guilty inner state, betraying drug abuse, adulterous affairs, fraud, deception, or sexual indiscretions, among others.

The Function of Guilt

Even before parental prohibitions have become absorbed into memory and presumed threats of castration have prompted resolution of the Oedipus complex, an awareness exists in children—at a very early age—of a living conscience that frequently issues troublesome feelings. Containing various elements of fear, shame, depression, and remorse, guilt feelings are experienced as painfully real, and the growing child attempts to avoid their resurgence. The enormous pedagogic capacity of conscience and the impact of its "lessons" are well known to parents as well as educators, who utilize them as deterrents to the child's deviant inclinations. Even child psychiatrists avail themselves of the impact produced on the child by experiences of guilt. Allowing the child to "play it out," so to speak, in play therapy—which may involve violent piercings, stranglings, dismemberment, etc., of dolls or stuffed animals, that symbolically represent the child's mother, father, siblings, and significant others of his world—produces, as a rule, feelings of guilt of such unendurable intensity that some children forsake altogether their "jocular aggression," in both play and real life.

In the maze of ever new events and situations, parental "introjects" and their injunctions tend to recede and fade into the past, as they become powerless in providing a solution to ever new moral quandaries and dilemmas. For this reason, resolution of the Oedipus complex and parental introjects may not be very helpful in deciding, for instance, whether one is to join a mob of cowards or an army of fighters—the latter choice entailing, nonetheless, the possibility of breaching the commandment: "Thou shall not kill." Or when confronted with the suffering of a loved one, how can parental introjects be of assistance to the struggling soul in reaching a decision: whether to allow a painful agony to take its course, or to incur the guilt for a "mercy killing?"

With respect to deviancy, the "reality principle" of psychoanalysis shows itself a weaker instructor and deterrent, compared to the emotional forces at the disposal of conscience—its guilty feelings and torments. Are any of the bleak realities in store for the gambler, alcoholic, sexual deviant, and drug abuser of sufficient clout as to deter these vice-enslaved individuals from acting against their self-defeating inclinations? Have punishments, even severe, prevented sex offenders and criminals from repeating their offenses? Much more is needed. From the histories of alcoholics, one can learn what a conspiracy of life-circumstances is necessary to jolt them into reform. Compared to the moral conscience, the Ego and its "reality principle" appear significantly inferior as reformers and exorcisers of passion, vice, and waywardness.

Consider the case of the homosexual, who continues to follow his deviant inclination in spite of warnings and signalling anxieties. Do the bleak realities of a lonely old age, emptiness, childlessness, and their attendant despair, have the power to impose upon him their vision, and to convince him to return to the "straight" path? But, as has been said before, the Ego may become the servant of desire and the "reality principle" thrown overboard. Even before the grip of reality has taken hold of an individual, his guilt for a moral offense has spoken loud and in a language quite convincing. As paradoxical as this might appear, the insane can teach the sane: how much more tormenting are the reproaches of the conscience compared to the suffering that ensues from adverse external circumstances.

Guilt and Suffering

In spite of the accumulation of sufficient evidence to show that serious mental disturbances are unrelated to sustained "stress," blows of fate, adverse circumstances, or various "psychic traumata," the search for a specific stressor, etiologic to psychiatric disorders and schizophrenia in particular, continues to preoccupy the scientific community. Schizophrenia has already exacted millions of dollars in research grants and other financial resources, not to mention the enormous drain it has tolled in human effort and energy. Yet the fund of possible "stressors" to be held responsible for bringing about a schizophrenic development has by now become all but exhausted.

In a study designed to investigate whether prolonged stress leads to **Major Depression** (MD), N. Breslau et al. (1986) reported that no such correlation could be established. Several studies, intended to explore whether the extreme conditions existing in the German concentration camps during World War II had led to an increase in the incidence of schizophrenia, found only 14 individuals to be so affected—this among a population of 19,000 displaced persons returned from the camps (L. Eitinger 1967, L. Eitinger and A. Stroem 1973). The prevalence rate for schizophrenia among Norwegian survivors of concentration camps, investigated later, proved identical to that found in the control group of the Norwegian population. Intensely stressful circumstances, such as existed in the German concentration camps, did not increase the incidence of schizophrenia among this highly traumatized population. Extremes of suffering and persistent threats to life—such as were experienced by the Jewish inmates of the Nazi death camps—not only failed to destroy these unfortunates psychologically, but created within their majority a new spirit that infused them with much enthusiasm—enabling them to reclaim the desert and fight for the freedom of their new homeland. Even though their horrible ordeal carried "flashbacks" into their new lives and reminded them of their suffering, it seldom penetrated so deeply into their personality as to shatter its bearings (p. 199). Very few among them became cynical, and a *relatively* small number committed suicide. When interviewed many years later, concentration camp survivors were found more vulnerable to suffering, nonetheless, manifested symptoms of "nervousness," and had a relatively high incidence of a variety of *physical* illnesses (L. Eitinger and A. Stroem, 1973).

Another most unfortunate and unnatural "natural" experiment, that provided by the Vietnam war, confirms that indeed, veterans who were subjected to the atrocities of combat suffered for various lengths of time from frightening flashbacks—reminding them of their horrifying experiences. Nevertheless, those who had followed orders and the requirements of duty, rather than their own aggressive urges, eventually recovered from their **Post-traumatic Stress Syndrome** (PTS)—with or without treatment. The outcome for those combatants who had followed their own murderous inclinations—killing and maiming for no reason at all—was found to be less favorable, as they became afflicted by the insanity termed **Malignant Post-Vietnam Stress Syndrome** (p. 207). The impact on the emotional life of blows of fate, bereavement, oppression, adversity, natural disasters, and losses, compared to the effects of intrinsically determined events, is represented graphically in Diagram # 1 (p. 139). Whereas adverse external circumstances can cause physical illnesses, emotional turbulence, and disturbances in mentation due to preoccupation, they do not by themselves produce "splits" within the personality, nor do they cause disturbances in thinking, or obliteration of emotional outflow. In spite of anguish and suffering, the personality remains intact and does not suffer losses of self-esteem.

Only rarely do externally determined calamities reach such proportions as to deform the personality and invert its value system. Rarely do events such as these bring about a global rebellion against Providence and produce attitudes of negativism, hostility, and cynicism. Several such cases have come to the attention of this author, all involving young adults who had lost a parent, most commonly the father. This loss, they thought, "entitled" them to act out their rebellion through various antisocial activities, which led some among them to experience the outbreak of a psychosis.

Physical illnesses may impair Ego-functioning on a temporary basis, but these "regressions" involve, as a rule, only the periphery of the personality. Even as suffering caused by physical illness may bring about depression, bitterness, and despair, these feeling states do not disrupt the harmony of being, do not cause losses in self-esteem, and do not lead to alienation from one's Self.* Suffering, in fact, when borne with courage, may bring about an enhanced state of being. "Naught but suffering raises thee beyond thyself," wrote German philosopher Artur Schopenhauer.

Suffering needs always to be separated from moral corruption, however, as repeatedly stressed by Kierkegaard (1848):

---

* Commenting on a study of cancer patients, S. B. Guze (1982) thought it of great interest and significance that so few commit suicide.

Sin is man's destruction. Only the rust of sin can consume
the soul—or eternally destroy it. For here, indeed, is the
remarkable thing from which already that simple wise man of
olden times [Socrates] derived a proof of the immortality of the
soul. Sin is not like bodily illness which kills the body . . . .
There is also a yawning distinction between suffering and sin.
(*Christian Discourses*)

*   *   *

Propelling the individual ever higher in his spiritual quest,
existential guilt needs to be differentiated from guilt that results
directly from the commission of a moral transgression. Kierkegaard
(1844) attempted to differentiate "objective dread"—the result of
man's basic sinfulness, transmitted by heredity from past generations
as fear of possibility of a moral offense—and "subjective dread,"
which follows the commission of transgression. Leaving existential
guilt behind as a "normal" phenomenon and objective dread to be
resolved by the healthy-minded, it is subjective dread that needs to
be further explored for its relevance to psychopathology. Subjective
dread may be experienced as **Depression;** it is often admixed with
various degrees of anxiety. Although many cases of depression result
from losses, bereavement, injury, and disillusionment, a good majority
is contingent on personal failures and omissions. Increasing in
intensity and paralleling the degree of existing psychopathology,
subjective dread progressively intensifies in schizophrenia-spectrum
illnesses and culminates as overwhelming dread at the pole of
schizophrenia.

In a study published by M. Prosen et al. (1983), 93 depressed, 29
schizophrenic, and 43 normal subjects were scored for the extent of
their feelings of guilt by various parameters, including self-esteem,
self-report of conscience, etc. The highest scores for guilt feelings
were obtained from schizophrenics, followed by depressives.
"Normal" subjects showed surprisingly little guilt. In this study,
however, feelings of guilt were regarded as a "feature of depression"
and correlated to the "severity of conscience." Nowhere in the study
was there mention of the possibility that guilt had been the direct
consequence of transgression; nor were attempts made to trace guilt
to its source, namely to a moral offense. And surprisingly, nowhere
has the possibility been entertained that schizophrenics score high on
guilt because they have broken the moral law. Nowhere are depressive states correlated to the failings of their subjects, and nowhere is
the possibility raised that "normals" are relatively free of guilt,

because they tend to avoid transgressing the moral law, and this may be the reason for their "normalcy," their mental health.

Strangely enough, the much sought documentation to prove the authenticity of guilt as consequent to transgression—rather than representing remorse or fear of social persecution—has come from polygraph investigations and not from medicine or the behavioral sciences. That the judicial system in many states refuses to admit the results from polygraph investigation as evidence in court—for its lack of absolute accuracy (given as 90 percent only, but this failure is attributed to the unresponsiveness of psychopaths, who lack the capacity for experiencing guilt)—in no way invalidates the data produced by polygraph investigation and research. More than other sciences, in behavioral sciences curvilinear rather than linear correlations can be accepted.

Moral Transgression, Guilt, and the Polygraph

Conceived by the criminal justice system as means for achieving a measure of objectivity and accuracy, the polygraph method of investigation represents a most remarkable scientific achievement, whose implications reach far into the domains of psychology, psychiatry, and psychosomatic medicine. The technique allows for the graphic recording of the emotional impact of a thought through its effects on the body. Physiological changes are recorded within 15 seconds of a thought that causes emotional disturbance. The polygraph does not detect the content of thoughts, unless these give rise to emotions of sufficient intensity to produce measurable behavioral and physiological changes. The polygraph can detect an intention to deceive (intention of moral transgression), the consciousness of deception (for it is sinful), and guilt when valid (guilt for the particular offense under investigation), where no deception is involved. Detection of emotional arousal is possible because guilt and deception produce a state of danger arising from within, which activates the central as well as peripheral sympathetic nervous systems.

One of the latest developments of polygraph investigation has been the Silent Answer Test (SAT), which requires that the subject answer silently, to himself, whether or not he has committed the offense under investigation (J. E. Reid and F. I. Inbau 1977). Whether the subject lies to himself or not is of little consequence, for if he is indeed guilty of the offense investigated, his recorded graph will mount higher than were he defending himself with a lie. The SAT is one of the most sensitive tests for guilt detection where no deception is involved. For the subject who is innocent, confronting his innocence within himself will cause the polygraph recording to return to a baseline of calm, even if previous records have shown some fear and anxiety associated with the procedure of the investigation.

Even more striking an achievement is the accuracy with which the polygraph technique, known as the "Guilty Knowledge Test," can identify sums of money, dates, locations, etc. The exactness of these data brings confirmation to Sartre's postulates (p. 172) and demonstrates how well one is aware of any truth that one attempts to alter.

Leading polygraph investigators and innovators J. E. Reid and F. I. Inbau (1977) have attributed the pronounced responses obtained during the SAT—where no deception is involved (and where the real danger of being found out is averted by silence)—as being due to guilt. According to these investigators' definition, guilt represents a *fear of the unknown.* This rather broad yet succinct definition of guilt encompasses feelings of shame, fear, remorse, and anxiety, as well as dread over an uncertain future. But this fear also brings to awareness a gnawing certainty of the existence of a higher, infallible, and inevitable Justice. The definition of guilt as a fear, charged with the dread of impending punishment—so frequently expressed with these same words by schizophrenic patients—opens wider the doors to understanding one of the most central symptoms of insanity. As subjective dread, guilt eventually assumes a dominant position in the inner domain of the emotions of every schizophrenic patient, and may well be the affect that eventually becomes toxic—the "affect-toxin"of schizophrenia postulated by Jung.

The Denial of Guilt

Hardly by chance has the central role of the moral conscience in the life of the soul been omitted from the schemata of modern psychologies, for the concept of the "soul" itself has now been discarded as anachronistic. In Freud's psychoanalysis—unswervingly dominated by a materialistic, Helmholtzian Weltanschauung—as well as in the hedonistic life-philosophy of modern Western societies, the judgments of conscience frequently come under attack; the validity of its decrees are questioned; and the justice of its verdicts pulverized by a myriad of arguments. As if the moral conscience were subject to the whims of cultural changes, advances in science, and tides of "modernization," and the authenticity of guilt could be denied and even dismissed as a symptom of neurosis. This is in the best of cases, for some among theorists consider guilty feelings delusional and even *causative* of certain illnesses, such as delusional depression and antisocial deviancy, as examples. To the mental health profession, the denial of the validity of guilt has proven costly, for it has led to the acceptance of various precariously constructed theories as, for example, those involving preverbal children (whose mental processes are inaccessible to study), or those related to the existence of a nebulous "unconscious," onto which all of the manifestations of psychopathology can be projected. And aside from the financial expenditures incurred by costly research projects, the denial of the centrality of conscience in the life of the soul has led psychologists and psychiatrists to venture into various and ever more remote fields of science such as ecology, ethology, anthropology, sociology, and biochemistry, among others. How far away—even into the domain of cosmology—have psychiatrists veered from the sin-sick soul is reflected in *several* recent studies, which have found an excess of 8 percent in winter-births for schizophrenics.

As for the individual who dares to suppress, repress, or deny his feelings of guilt, such an enterprise proves also costly, for it drains considerable quantities of mental energy and may even lead to psychological bankruptcy. The defense mechanism "isolation of affect" so designated by psychoanalysts describes the various mental operations undertaken to prevent certain painful feelings from entering awareness. Tormenting and threatening, feelings of guilt may thus, by an act of the will, be warded off from entering consciousness. A dissociation between thought and affect—such as is characteristically present in schizophrenia—is effected in this manner. The dissociation may result in alienation from the Self, which, needless to say, is a rather sad state of being. Instead of being denied, guilty dysphorias may become displaced onto lesser offenses, onto "misdemeanors," to borrow Jung's expression. Even so, the guilt generated by moral "felonies" remains dynamically active. It may motivate the use of projections of various kinds, by which blame is thrown onto others, circumstances, or the past. Feelings of guilt may also dictate a general tendency for justification, as is evident in patients who manifest a "formal thought disorder." A good number of criminals and individuals involved in antisocial behaviors dilute their guilty feelings with alcohol or anesthetize them with drugs.

Whereas the truly psychopathic individual (a very rare condition) lacks the capacity for experiencing guilt, the majority of criminals and individuals engaged in antisocial behaviors learn how to evade, deny, ignore, displace, or project their feelings of guilt, and these defense operations may become habitual—persisting as character traits. Many actively antisocial individuals eventually become truly "psychopathic," for in the process of denying the reproaches of their guilty conscience they lose the capacity for experiencing guilt altogether. That repeated offenses and deceptions cease to produce anxiety is confirmed by polygraphers Reid and Inbau. Whether this lack of responsiveness is the product of a voluntary "learning process," or represents the involuntary outcome of repeated and consistent disregard for the dictates of conscience, may need to be further explored. As for compulsive liars, it is of interest to note that in many cases, they begin eventually to believe their own lies. Nowhere is this phenomenon more evident than in the delusional-justificatory constructs of those who deny their guilt. A last-ditch defense, *delusional-justificatory ideas* may be so well construed that they often carry more conviction than even truth itself. The road from sociopathy to hardcore criminality and psychopathy may stretch long, nonetheless. During polygraph investigations, many individuals engaged in antisocial activities were found to show "large and indiscriminate reactivity" (S. Abrams 1974). Whether this pronounced reactivity presages an imminent psychotic "explosion of conscience" would also need to be further investigated.

The folly of the criminal and sociopath begins with the false belief that the voice of the conscience can so easily be stilled. But this same delusion they share with other character-disordered individuals: narcissistic, borderline, schizotypal, and antisocial. Needless to say, the denial of guilt forces these individuals to exist on the periphery of themselves, distanced from the wellspring of their emotions and not too far removed from the borders of sanity.

Unlike the neurotic, who puts up a fight against morally forbidden wishes and temptations, and who usually emerges victorious from the struggle, the individual who disregards the warnings of conscience, who learns to juggle his guilt or attempts to sweep it under the rugs of consciousness, so to speak, this individual already labors under delusion, for the conscience is not so easily stilled.

a. Dissociation and Conversion Syndromes

The most obvious of dissociations is observed in the syndrome known as **Multiple Personality Disorder.** Individuals so affected no longer can bear to "live with themselves," for what they had done or what they had been, and enter for this reason into the role of another person they create by imagination. A small dose of Sodium Amytal—the "truth serum"—frequently brings these patients to admit their deceptive and self-deceptive maneuvers, nonetheless. And as is true of every other confession, it affords considerable relief. The judicial system is often confused with respect to a defendant who claims to have multiple personalities, as if he were suffering from a mysterious "sickness." Would not justice better be served by prosecuting the various personalities' offenses separately, but judge the defendant's offenses collectively?

The syndrome known as **Psychogenic Fugue** aptly describes these patients' escapades, as well as their fugitive ways of being. Taking leave from themselves, these individuals may plunge into various morally forbidden activities, most commonly: gambling, sexual indiscretions, and stealing exploits—skillfully blotting the memory of their escapades with a cloud of "amnesia" afterward. But by becoming refugees from their own past, they also negate part of themselves. It goes without saying that the self-negation of these patients brings them precariously close to insanity and to a sense of existential perdition.

As is true for other syndromes in psychiatry, **Hysteria** has undergone several metamorphoses during the past few decades. Initially it covered a rather broad spectrum of disorders, which were studied by French neurologist and hypnotist J. M. Charcot (1825–93). Sharp demarcation lines between the various nosological entities associated with Hysteria have not been established to this date, however, but the ambiguity has more to do with the considerable overlap of these syndromes than with the skills of the diagnostician. **Briquet's Syndrome**—where hypochondriacal symptoms predominate—may be regarded as a split-off from the syndrome; **Conversion Reactions** may be similarly considered. The **Hysterical Personality,** which affects mostly females, is characterized by excitability, emotional instability, immaturity, seductiveness, self-centeredness, and self-dramatization. But hysteria has also been found closely related to **Sociopathy** by C. R. Cloninger (1975), S. B. Guze (1976), and B. I. Liskow et al. (1977).

Briquet's Syndrome occurs, as a rule, before the age of 35 and is characterized by a "minimum" of 25 out of 59 medically unexplained symptoms, which have interfered with the patient's ability to function (R. A. Woodruff et al. 1971), and for which no organic causes can be found. When patients diagnosed as hysterical personalities and patients with Briquet's syndrome were subjected to the Minnesota Multiphasic Personality Inventory (MMPI) test, many of their scores were consistent with psychopathic deviation and schizophrenia.

Conversion Reactions with neurological symptoms, for which no organic causes can be demonstrated, were also found to be associated with sociopathy (R. A. Woodruff et al. 1971). And indeed, the various symptoms of distress, complained of by the sociopath, reveal themselves upon closer scrutiny as nothing more than guilt converted into somatic equivalents. Instead of anguish of the soul, guilty dysphorias become transformed into aches, pains, and various physiological dysfunctions. It is of great interest as well as of significance for psychotherapy that the areas affected had, in some way, participated in the condemned act/s, and it is in these organs that punishment is now expected. Castration threatens the child who entertains Oedipal strivings. Sexual excesses, deviations, and exploitations characteristically give rise to symptoms that involve the genitalia (or the rectum of homosexuals). Stealing produces painful sensations in the right upper extremity. Visual disturbances may follow the acting out of lustful preoccupations. This author has come across a case of attempted eye enucleation following a complicated adulterous entanglement. The symbolic significance of symptoms in hysteria has already been recognized by the pioneers of psychoanalysis, and especially by Sandor Ferenczi (1873–1933).

From studies on female criminals, S. B. Guze (1976) found that hysterics were much more likely to report complete innocence (67 percent), in spite of being actually guilty. Here again, guilt denied became guilt converted.

Whether converted into bodily pain or dysfunction or experienced as fears of various kinds, guilt remains an active dynamic force even when buried into less conscious levels of awareness. A blunting of affect may signify that emotional outflow has been obliterated by repeated suppression and repression, but these mental operations are more the craft of the sociopath than viable possibilities for "normal" or neurotic individuals. Emotions may, nonetheless, become extinguished altogether, as observed in hardened sociopaths and deteriorated schizophrenics.

When, many years ago, this author was assigned to work on a ward with drug addicts and hardened criminals in Metropolitan Hospital, it was striking to observe how frightened many became of any emotional stirring. While the sweet voice of a singer, soft melody of a violin, or gripping message of a "spiritual" during sessions of music therapy, brought a few of these hardened individuals to a blissful state of tearfulness, the majority was literally "scared away." Their fears of "breaking down" were fully justified, indeed, for their avoidance spared them much pain and feelings of guilt, which they correctly perceived could lead them to an "explosion of conscience"— and to madness.

b. Dreams, Nightmares, and Delusions

Whatever defensive operation is employed to ward off feelings of guilt from entering consciousness, when the evader or denier of such dysphorias attempts to burrow into the comforts of sleep, various dreams and visions may bring to his awareness all that he fears and tries to avoid. The images perceived during the hypnagogic state (just before the onset of sleep) or during sleep may appear grossly exaggerated, frightful, threatening, unreal, and grotesque. They are described by patients as "more terrifying than anything experienced in reality or seen in a horror show" (Chapter VII). The terrifying visions of the dreaming state define the nightmare, whose function is, precisely, to frighten. In a study investigating the relationship between the nightmare and personality patterns, A. Kales et al. (1980) found the nightmare to be associated with global psychopathology: with psychopathic deviancy taking the lead over schizophrenia, leading in turn over hysterical conditions. The horrifying contents of the nightmare cause spontaneous awakening and a state of intense fear. It is followed by prolonged wakefulness, during which the vivid details of the dream are relived as they become engraved in the memory. Not infrequently, the same nightmare is repeated several times in one night and some patients dare not go back to sleep, for fear of its return. The nightmare has fulfilled its function when it has frightened the dreamer with punishments to come and convinced him to remember and reflect (M. Niv 1981).

The dreams of muggers, robbers, and killers convey to their awareness, in this manner, the realistic possibilities of bloodshed, police persecution, arrests, jail, and bodily injury. But their nightmares also assail them with some very specific, very personal, spiritually meaningful symbols, quite similar to those that pervade the dreams of schizophrenics: wild beasts, darkness, monsters, vampires, spiders, and, of course, the devil. Both the sociopath and the schizophrenic dread forthcoming retribution. The punishments expected, whether for legal or moral violations, become thus projected at night on the dream-screens of these guilt-ridden offenders— threatening and disturbing.

During the quiet and stillness of night, when external distractions are by and large extinguished, internal stimuli take precedence and appear in the perceptual field of the dreamer—cancelling, then, all denials and dissociations. The real drama of the guilty is played out at night, when repression, suppression, diversionary tactics, and denials no longer avail. Whereas the neurotic sees himself enacting the morally forbidden wish-intention in the dream, and perceives its untoward consequences in reality, the criminal, sociopath, and schizophrenic are in the nightmare but passive recipients of attacks from animals, snakes, crowds, and monsters, which are perceived as punishment for what they have already done. It is of great interest that the punishments presented by the nightmare always fit the crime—following as they do the law of talion: "An eye for an eye, a tooth for a tooth."

c. The Penal System of Conscience in Prepsychotic States

The presence of consistently recurring nightmares has long been recognized as a good diagnostic sign, but for the ominous possibility of an impending psychosis. One may glean the precipitating causes of the psychosis from the contents of the nightmare, as they clearly reveal the major moral or legal offense which is punished in the dream. The formula to be applied for identifying the offense is very simple: the nightmare's punishment reflects the particular transgression.

> A 21-year-old unemployed male related having a recurrent nightmare in which he was pushed out of a window. When further questioned, he admitted that many years previously, he had thrown a "friend" out of a window, intending homicide. (From author's caseload)

The judicial system of the conscience functions in a gradual and systematic manner. With the accretion of moral failures and unrepented transgressions, as well as with persistent disregard for the warnings of conscience, self-esteem begins to sink low, and depression admixed with various elements of anxiety progressively sets in. Here begins the "continuum" of symptomatology, a continuum which parallels also the degree of psychopathology (schematically represented in Diagram # 2, p. 140). Gradually, free-floating anxieties become condensed, more focused, and transform, eventually into **Phobias.** In phobic disorders, anxiety is precipitated by a situation that symbolizes the morally forbidden wish/temptation, which the neurotic struggles to avoid. Failing in such efforts, however, phobias are liable to intensify and produce **Panic Attacks,** which may coalesce and give rise to prolonged **Panic States.**

Yet with all the wide array of anxiety disturbances, we are still in the realm of the neuroses, i.e., disturbances in which the moral forces engage in a struggle against the enactment of a forbidden wish/desire, and in which the conscience continues to issue warnings by way of "signalling" anxieties. Neurotic anxiety, however, never remains quiescent, unless the forbidden wish or intention is given up— renounced once and for all. Short of such a renunciation, anxiety tends to expand and intensify along a gradient, often reaching such global proportions as to virtually paralyze its subject. Anger and shame may suddenly surface, as well as aches and pains and a variety of bodily dysfunctions as the guilt generated by the pursuit of some forbidden wish becomes converted into a symptom.

With the accretion of moral failures and transgressions, guilty dysphorias eventually produce a state of alarm whereby everyone and everything seems to refer to the transgressor. In addition to these *ideas of reference,* the guilt-ridden individual begins to believe that he is being watched, commented upon, ridiculed, judged, and also persecuted. To the offender in this state of alarm, the unrepented moral violation becomes central to his life-experience and all his mental processes begin to revolve now around it. Secretly entertaining his malevolence, the hater begins to feel as if he is emitting odors; the sexual pervert senses himself to be filthy; the shady dealer deems himself ugly. And as is the rule for every delusion, those related to paranoid fears and ideation—ubiquitous among mental patients— contain within themselves an important truth: were the offender to be unmasked, he would need to suffer rejection, ostracism, persecution, and condemnation by others, by society. The delusions of the paranoiac, however, contain much more than fears of detection and social condemnation, for they carry spiritually meaningful threats in addition. So constant are ideas of reference, feelings of being judged, and paranoid fears and ideation, that in their absence a prepsychotic state may be safely ruled out.

It has become tradition to regard paranoid feelings and ideas of persecution as representing "projections" of one's hostilities, anger, jealousy, and similar emotions, onto others, the outside world. Presumably, projections serve to attenuate the threat arising from within. Hatred, revenge, anger, and rage, it is argued, are better tolerated when perceived as coming from without than from within oneself. Such an interpretation of paranoia, however, fails to account for the patients' feelings of persecution and condemnation. In order to explain delusions of persecution, some theorists have attributed them to the grandiose self-perception of these patients, who believe they have enemies wishing to destroy them by reason of their superiority. Nevertheless, delusions of persecution are also entertained by individuals who do not hate, experience anger, or feel superior, but are involved in adultery, fraud, lies, sexual abuses, or other activities committed in violation of the moral law. Paranoid fears and ideas are characteristically present even when no external danger threatens these persons. A good example is the following case:

> A prostitute began to fear the couch of her living room and preferred to spend most of her time in the bathroom, where she felt safe. She became convinced that, eventually, she would have to endure physical torture on the couch, whereon she used to dispense sensual pleasures—well aware that these activities were morally wrong. (From author's caseload)

From paranoid uneasiness to fears of retribution, the patient eventually becomes convinced of an inevitable judgment as well as forthcoming penalty. In the case of the prostitute, the feared punishment was to be physical torture.

*   *   *

When the flood of guilty dysphorias, ideas of reference, paranoid fears, panic states, and nightmares fail to convey their intended message, the voice of conscience begins to speak louder. Since the switchboard of perception—now fully lit up by messages signalling danger arising from within—can no longer accept incoming stimuli from the world outside, by reason of the overload, these stimuli suffer extinction. When the input of perception becomes "jammed" in this manner (not by reason of excesses of externally determined "pressures," as patients claim in justification, but due to internal overloading), attention becomes focused more and more inwardly, where the drama of the guilty begins to unfold. An attention deficit is thus created, and concentration on any given task becomes increasingly difficult. The spiritual center of the personality has asserted its preeminence, as it has gained dominance over conscious thought. But due to a persistent disregard for the warnings issued by conscience, the nightmare progressively invades the day and begins to merge with external occurrences. Reality slips away, and a state of *trema* sets in, whereby, according to K. Jaspers (1963), "a transformation in the total awareness of reality has taken place, and whose atmosphere of dread is charged with meaning." Jaspers described this state and gave it the designation of *trema*, considering it a prepsychotic delusional state that is psychologically irreducible, i.e., refractory to attempts at reorientation toward reality. Considered to be "the most outstanding and baffling symptom of mental illnesses," (A. Arthur 1964) delusional experiences and states of trema have given cause to much debate as well as to theories (some of which are untenable) and a good number of speculations. After an extensive review of the literature on the subject, Arthur fails to arrive at any definite conclusion regarding these phenomena.

Nevertheless, there is no reason to consider dreams, nightmares, and delusional experiences other than as phenomena that stand on a continuum and in parallel to existing psychopathology. These so-called "primary process" phenomena, certainly, have a common denominator, for they all convey to consciousness matters of concern to the soul or Self—spiritual center of the personality. Throughout the ages, visions, hallucinations, nightmares, and delusions have been considered to be individualized subjective experiences, *whose content is revelatory and whose function is instructive.*

In the Book of Job (Job 33:14–18) in the Holy Scriptures the following interpretation of dreams, visions, and similar phenomena can be found:

> For God speaketh once, yea, twice, yet man perceiveth it not. In a dream, in a vision of the night, when deep sleep falleth upon man, in slumbering upon the bed; then he opened the ears of men, and sealeth their instruction, that he may withdraw man from his purpose and hide pride from man. He keepeth back his soul from the pit, and his life from perishing by the sword.

Compared to the nightmare, delusional experiences are more concrete and their message more distinct. As in the nightmare, but more eloquently, delusional experiences define with striking exactitude the moral violations that gave them cause, as they also depict forthcoming punishment.

> The vision of the devil, suddenly appearing to a married mother of two, had such an impact, that it made her cry out in terror for several weeks following the event. More than all of the "therapies" she was then engaged in, this vision dissuaded her from continuing her involvements with men (the devil) in

adulterous romantic and not-so-romantic amorous affairs. (From author's caseload)

The most bizarre delusion can be understood, provided that account is taken of the patient's total life-experience as well as his ways of being-in-the-world:

> An attractive, well-groomed 25-year-old unemployed man began to suffer from the delusion that he was prey to a peacock, who relentlessly hammered on his head. In addition to this delusion, he had a recurrent nightmare in which he experienced a man falling on top of his body. This patient had never worked and secured his livelihood by means of prostitution. Habitually, he disrobed himself in a men's club, and lying on the billiard table, sought to attract homosexual clients. His delusion reflected simultaneously: his peacock existence, the practice of prostitution, the threat of hammering blows over his head by a peacock, and the possibility of bodily injuries. (From author's caseload)

It cannot be too strongly emphasized, at this juncture, that delusional states and states of trema are reversible conditions, binding the therapist, therefore, to attempt their resolution.

When a patient complains of seeing shadows, ghosts, snakes, devils, and their likes, and perceives darkness invading the light of day, paralyzing him with fear, he has entered a delusional state that requires active therapeutic intervention. Albeit irreducible—for it is impossible to dissuade the patient from believing in the falsity of his delusions—these states are, nonetheless, reversible. Recoveries from such states *can* be achieved, provided the experiences are grasped and interpreted by the patient himself. When interpretations are true to their meaning, and capable of inducing an admission of guilt with sorrowing over it, they may dissolve the delusional state and even induce in the patient a "change of heart." A reversal of the psychotic process is then liable to take place.

Unfortunately for all concerned, contemporary psychiatry perceives delusional experiences as nothing more than "primary process" regressive phenomena—products of these patients' "craziness" and undeserving of investigation and interpretation. But this attitude is, to say the least, grossly erroneous. Empathic understanding and a search for the meaning of the patient's delusional experiences are capable not only of dissolving delusions, but also of producing changes in the personality and in the individual's ways of being-in-the-world. Brushing away monstrous misperceptions as "imaginary" has never made them disappear. Chemical agents such as Thorazine, Mellaril, and Haldol, among others, have been shown to possess but scanty "bleaching" properties for the horrors conveyed through delusional experiences, and no capacity for modifying their contents. Even hikes in dosage of neuroleptic medicines have not been capable of erasing the image of the devil, for example, nor have they prevented the television set from broadcasting to the world the shameful deeds for which the patient feels guilty. Whereas defensive rage, dread, and over-vigilant anticipation may become attenuated by the use of medicines, and lead the frightening visions and "voices" to recede into the background of the patient's experience, drugs cannot abolish them altogether. Patients have made this very clear: they still see the same visions and hear the same voices while under the influence of neuroleptics, yet "pay them no mind . . . ."

With the appearance of delusions, the road to a final schizophrenic "break" or "fall" becomes even steeper and the distance to the underworlds of madness shorter. Things now appear as if endowed with a special, deeper meaning. A sense of meaning, which insinuates itself into the very core of existence, is also frequently experienced during periods of suffering, illness, shattering events, and the inevitable crises that occur with movement from one stage of life to another. Such conditions may impose different life-tasks and goals, often leading to new states of being. In the stages preceding a psychosis, even the commonplace and the ordinary become endowed with meaning, but they carry a threat:

> A 35-year-old housewife, given to violent outbursts and
> destructive behavior (involving the breaking of furniture),
> suddenly perceived the armrests of her chairs waving at her in
> a threatening manner. (From author's caseload)

The appearance of double vision, a very common symptom in prepsychotic states and which gives occasion for a round of medical and neurological examinations, represents in actuality but a functional phenomenon. It hallmarks the occurrence of a "split" on several levels of existence. Perceptual vision becomes divided into one that is inwardly directed and another that contemplates the external world. Deception also divides one's view into two separate perspectives: one false, the other true—two uncompromising perspectives. And then, there is the mask of the outer, false "me," which serves to defend against the real, true "me," creating a split in identity. Furthermore, since feelings of guilt are oftentimes too painful to endure, they may become suppressed along with other emotions and a dissociation between thought and affect established.

Eventually, the double realities of a prepsychotic state give way to the singular dread-filled experience of schizophrenia, which grants to its subjects a glimpse of some "other worlds" and of Hell, no less. Not infrequently—and this is especially true for the first psychotic episode(s)—the visions of Hell are interspersed with visions of Heaven. The message of these experiences is well understood by the psychotic, and frequently heeded. Such a fortunate outcome may result in complete recovery and may even occasion important changes in the personality through changes of its principal goals (Diagram # 7, p. 274). Interventions such as the "talking down" maneuver and "reality orientation" psychotherapy are of no avail in these serious conditions. The only light that can be shed on the darkness of these experiences is through understanding their *true meaning*. When it is grasped and also heeded, it may lead to recovery. With the therapist as catalyst and the patient as main interpreter, delusional experiences may lessen or disappear altogether, provided their meaning has been understood (M. Niv 1981). The "talking cure" of psychotherapy is otherwise of no effect.

If and when the delusional experience, its atmosphere of dread, *trema* and all, has failed to impart its intended message and jolted the wayward into reform, a further invasion of consciousness by spiritually charged symbols is bound to take place. The patient then enters into what has been termed psychosis, nervous breakdown, schizophrenia, or "decompensation," to name but a few of the designations given to this shattering event. Symbols, not only of personal relevance, but also of cosmic significance, progressively invade the conscious mind of the psychotic, gaining, eventually, preeminence. Matters of daily routine recede in the background, as if of secondary importance.

The absence of "primary process" imagery (imagery that contains symbols of spiritual significance, such as angels, the devil, the Judgment, etc.) from altered states of consciousness is most conspicuous in organically determined illnesses (unless terminal), and this absence may be of diagnostic significance. Psychiatric disturbances may thus be differentiated from organically determined disorders on the basis of the contents and imagery of subjective phenomena. Notwithstanding, spiritually significant experiences may accompany organic illnesses, especially when these illnesses pose a threat to physical existence.

Be that as it may, it is undeniable that delusional prepsychotic and psychotic states impose upon awareness matters of spiritual, not realistic import. Hardly by chance did those stricken with madness enjoy a special "awed" status in antiquity. Already then, the insane were recognized as possessing a greater awareness of certain spiritual realities. The term "mental disease" may be a misnomer. In most languages, such illnesses are termed "spiritual"—diseases of the soul, the spirit, the Self. Psychological disturbances may thus be understood as signifying the presence of turbulence, or damage, or loss of integrity of the soul as primary events, to which the losses of other mental functions (i.e., cognition, memory, orientation, etc.) are but consequences. Philosophical conceptions of the relationship between the soul, the mind, and the body concur with those of the major religions, whereby the "psyche" represents the soul; the heart is associated with the emotions; the functions of the mind are linked to the Ego; and all are contained in the body-soma. William James (1892) perceived a similar hierarchical order, as he described the bodily "me" at the bottom and the extracorporeal material "selves" in between.

> But the spiritual self is so supremely precious, that rather than lose it, a man ought to be willing to give up friends and good fame, property and life itself . . . . By the "spiritual me" I mean no one of my passing states of consciousness. Our capacities for sensation, for example, are less intimate posses-sions, so to speak, than our emotions and desires; our intellec-tual processes are less intimate than our volitional decisions. The more *active-feeling* states of consciousness are, thus, the more central portions of the spiritual Me. The very core and nucleus of our self, as we know it, the very sanctuary of our life, is the sense of activity which certain inner states possess. This sense of activity is often held to be a direct revelation of the living substance of our soul.

The appearance of spiritually charged symbols in mental disease cannot be explained by factors of acculturation alone. The proponents of the dopamine theory would thus need to explain why a syndrome such as Parkinson's, for example, in which an increased turnover of dopamine occurs at certain cerebral sites (in some of these cases), does not produce the spiritually charged visions we find in mental illnesses. The hierarchical order described by James has, unfortu-nately, become reversed in the concepts of modern psychologies: disorders of the "mind" are now explained as due to changes in the body (soma), and the mind (in terms of the brain) is held responsible for creating emotional disturbances. In the currently prevailing theories, neither the soul nor its life are given substance.

Notwithstanding, men of vision from all times have persisted in regarding the soul as the center of the personality. Contemporary writer Nikos Kazantzakis (1961) wrote not long ago:

> Every integral man has inside him, in his heart of hearts, a mystic center around which all else revolves . . . . Alas for the man who does not feel himself governed inside by an absolute monarch . . . that center which battles . . . to reach that summit we are ceaselessly about to attain and which ceaselessly jumps to its feet and climbs still higher . . . *(Report to Greco)*

A schematic representation of the "psyche," mind, and body, and position of the spiritual Me is given in Diagram # 3 (p. 141).

*   *   *

Contemporary psychiatry attributes psychopathological phenomena to heredity, factors of upbringing, childhood traumata, stressful events, various "pressures," blows of fate, bereavements, losses, socioeconomic conditions, and impairments in physical well-being. These adverse external circumstances are presumed to be causative of such dysphorias as anxiety, guilt, and depression. While, indeed, externally determined traumatic events may affect one's psychological state, impinge on mental processes as preoccupations and disturb the various streams of emotional outflow, the suffering caused by adversity remains, as a rule, at a distance from the soul, the center of the personality, the spiritual Me which retains its autonomy. The body-soma may react, however, by dysfunction or physical illness.

Pathological relatedness parallels the symptoms of distress it tends to generate. A gradient of hatefulness may be observed to intensify along the spectrum, becoming murderous at the pole of schizophrenia. Symptoms of distress also intensify along a continuum of severity, culminating at the pole of schizophrenia.

Diagram # 1

The Impact of Adversity
on the Psychic Life and Physical Well-being
Suffering as Distinct from Mental Illness

suffering may involve the body, the mind, and the emotions

adverse external circumstances may produce pre-occupations giving rise to disturbances in cognition

reaction to adversity may give rise to symptoms of distress, dysfunction, and even to psychosomatic illness

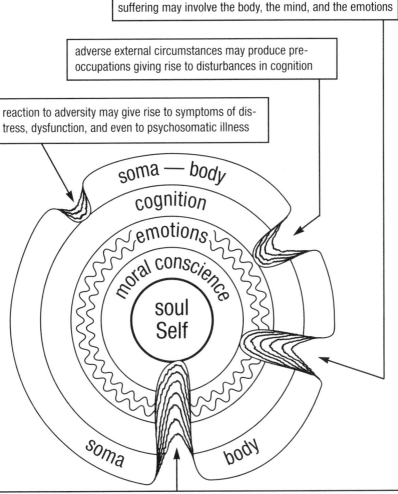

when associated with moral failure/s, external calamities may reach deep and near the borders of the soul, leading to depression, guilt, and self-recriminatory ruminations. A characteristic slow-down occurs in all vital processes.

Externally determined traumata do not penetrate or deform the soul, the Self, which, as a general rule, remains intact.

Diagram # 2

The Spectrum of Psychiatric Disorders:

Schematic representation of neurotic and schizophrenia-spectrum disorders. Pathological relatedness parallels the symptoms of distress it generates. A gradient of hostility intensified along the spectrum, becoming murderous at the pole of schizophrenia.

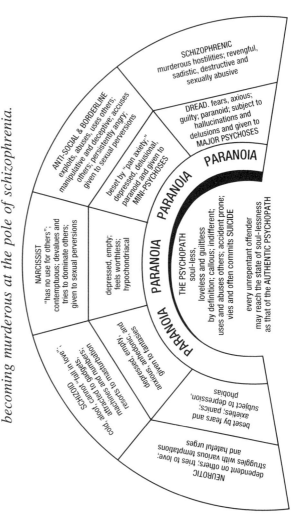

SCHIZOPHRENIC
murderous hostilities; revengful, sadistic, destructive and sexually abusive

DREAD. fears, axious; guilty; paranoid; subject to hallucinations and delusions and given to MAJOR PSYCHOSES

ANTI-SOCIAL & BORDERLINE
exploits, abuses, uses others; manipulative and deceptive; accuses others; persistently angry; given to sexual perversions

beset by "pan anxiety," depressed and given to paranoid, delusional. MINI-PSYCHOSES

PARANOIA

NARCISSIST
"has no use for others"; contemptuous; devalues and tries to dominate others; given to sexual perversions

depressed, empty; feels worthless; hypochondriacal

PARANOIA

THE PSYCHOPATH
soul-less,
loveless and guiltless
by definition; callous; indifferent; uses and abuses others; accident prone; vies and often commits SUICIDE

every unrepentant offender may reach the state of soul-lessness as that of the AUTHENTIC PSYCHOPATH

PARANOIA

depressed empty, anxious, anhedonic, and given to fantasies

SCHIZOID
cold, aloof, cannot "fall in love"; attracted to gadgets, machines and numbers; resorts to masturbation

beset by fears and anxieties, panics; subject to depression, phobias

NEUROTIC
dependent on others; tries to love; struggles with various temptations and hateful urges

140

Diagram # 3

The Central Position of the Spiritual Me, the Soul or Self

In conformity with the psychologies of W. James, W. McDougall, G. Allport and Existentialists

The spiritual Me, soul or Self sends emotional ripples to the mind and the body.

Here is the center of self-esteem: for approval, praise, and feelings of elation or else, for disapproval, condemnation and dysphorias of guilt.

From the spiritual center, core or "heart" of the personality proceed its "loves," aims, and intentions. It is here that transcendental strivings are determined: ascending for love, sacrifice, faith, and achievement, in sublimation of desire, or descending, through lusts, hate, and desire for power, domination and material possessions.

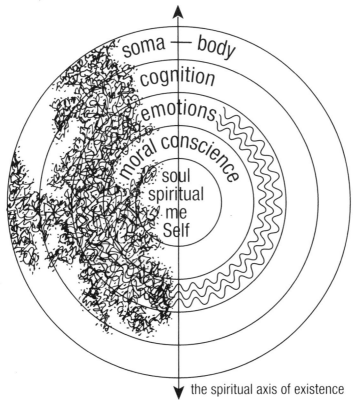

soma — body
cognition
emotions
moral conscience
soul
spiritual
me
Self

the spiritual axis of existence

From the center of the personality, spiritual Me, soul or Self may begin corruption, sickness, and eventual destruction of soul, mind, and body.

Chapter VI

Moral Transgression

. . . for the imagination of man's heart is evil from his youth . . .
— Genesis 8:21

The Great Way is easy, yet people prefer bypaths.

— Lao Tzu

The Nature of Sin and Its Attributes

If, indeed, the moral conscience holds a central position in determining psychological well-being and, conversely, in producing "emotional disturbances," this would mandate a more thorough exploration of its functioning than has hitherto been undertaken. While the impact of guilty dysphorias upon mental processes has been well recognized, the stimulus that evokes them, namely moral transgression, has remained outside the scope of interest of modern psychologists and psychiatrists. But this is hardly by omission, for scientists in these fields recognize neither moral transgression nor guilt as psychological realities. Yet these may turn out to be precisely those "psychopathogenic stressors" that modern researchers so eagerly strive to discover. The latest reclassifications of mental diseases, the DSM-III-R and DSM-IV, still regard sin and guilt to be delusional manifestations. This conclusion has been drawn without scientific investigation, however, and one may wonder why the psychiatric community has not taken the trouble to find out whether the patients' complaints of having sinned and being burdened by guilt represent but "symptoms" of their illness or have a basis in reality.

Sin is a heavily charged word. One may wish to approach the concept it stands for from a biological perspective first, and then proceed by regarding it as a psychosocial problem. But needless to say, the effects of sin on the individual can scarcely be separated from their impact on his family and society. And when one seeks to explore moral transgression not solely in terms of its repercussions on the individual's environment and important others, but also from the psychological effects on the perpetrator, a turning to philosophy, religion, and those sciences that deal with human experiences common to all of mankind, becomes unavoidable. The existence of certain spiritual-moral laws that govern the life of the soul—just as some physiological laws govern the life of the body—may thus be revealed.

There is hardly any controversy regarding the fact that man is first and foremost a social being. It also goes without saying that in the depths of themselves, all members of the human family find a kinship and a law of love by which they feel bound together. Realistically, man can scarcely survive in isolation; and he has many physical as well as psychological needs whose satisfaction depends on the presence of others, of a social nexus. Psychologically, loving relationships have long been recognized to be the source of our deepest satisfactions—our very happiness, maybe. To the explorers of man's psychology, therefore, it ought to be of great interest that one of the most outstanding functions of the conscience is to foster loving relationships and to condemn their absence. That loving relationships protect the physical as well as the psychological well-being of the individual has long been recognized, but they protect the welfare of society as well.

All major religions around the world require from believers to love their neighbor, stranger, and even enemy. This law is positively enunciated in the Judeo-Christian Scriptures by its essential commandment: "Thou shalt love thy neighbor as thyself" (Leviticus 19:18, Matthew 19:19). In the Moslem Holy Book, the An-Nawawi, it is written: "No one is a believer until he loves for his brother what he loves for himself." The compassionate Buddha teaches that to follow the Path of Enlightenment, one must "let his spirit of compassion display itself to the utmost degree . . . . " In the Tibetan doctrine, this law is negatively enunciated: "That which one desireth not for oneself, do not do unto others."

Whatever its reasons, a breach of this most fundamental law is strikingly evident in each and every psychiatric illness. Infinitesimal quantities of hate and even minute acts of malevolence immediately give rise to painful dysphorias—feelings related to guilt and fear. The quantity and quality of malevolence toward others stand in close parallel to "psychopathology" as well as to the intensity of symptoms and signs derived therefrom (Diagram # 2 , p. 140).

A further exploration into the nature of moral transgression reveals that, although perceived somewhat differently by the various peoples around the world, and colored by local culture and tradition, the essence of sin shows more invariability than difference. Psychoanalytic theories concur with most religions in perceiving that man is basically "evil" through his inherited propensities, which may show themselves already at an early age. All children are egocentric, narcissistic, jealous, and greedy, and their majority are envious of attributes they lack in themselves. Revenge appears to be an obligatory psychological reflex. Inherited seeds of evil can thus germinate—given certain circumstances of childhood—to become ingrained within the personality and determine its structure. Such a proposition would reconcile the tenets of religion (the sins of the fathers) with the findings of modern research, overwhelmingly implicating the hereditary transmission of psychopathological traits. Yet children are considered "innocent," and so they are, indeed. Still unaware of their inherited propensities and the consequences of their actions, they learn eventually the laws of morality from the approval or disapproval of their parents, as well as from the pangs of their own consciences. Constitutionally determined or structured within the personality, sinful attitudes may grow strong, provided they conform to the individual's choices as his "loves" and intentions. The sin of pride, for example, inherited as a propensity, may develop further and when unchecked, become vain conceit, which may grow into contempt. It may then lead the contemptuous individual to find satisfaction in humiliating others and, in more extreme cases, compel him to seek sexual satisfaction through denigration of the sexual partner.

As for the role of the Oedipus complex in child development, there is no good reason to consider it more seriously than other complexes of sin and guilt, or to value it above them in the genesis of psychopathology. We may be depending on the successful resolution (by following the dictates of conscience) of many sin-guilt complexes, not only for the development of our personality and maintenance of our mental health, but for our self-fulfillment and spiritual growth as well.

From the perspective of religion, moral transgression is sin, which is defined in Webster's dictionary as follows:

> Any voluntary transgression of a religious law or moral principle, moral depravity, wickedness, iniquity. Sin may consist in commission, when a known divine law or principle is violated, or in omission, when a positive divine command or a role of duty is voluntarily or willfully neglected.

The dictionary's formulation does not recognize unconscious drives as sinful, only consciously undertaken willful acts of commission and omission. Existentialists view moral transgression in a slightly different manner. M. Buber (1953) divides sin into two stages, as he writes in *Good and Evil*:

> In the first stage, man does not choose, he merely acts: in the second stage he chooses himself . . . . The first stage does not yet contain a "radical evil"; whatever misdeeds are committed, their commission is not doing the deed, but sliding into it. In the second stage evil grows radical because what a man finds in himself, is willed . . . .

When unrepented and unrenounced, in spite of the warnings of conscience, sin becomes a fixed attitude, *a position*. This is what sin really is; and according to Kierkegaard (1843): sin is sin when it becomes an entrenched position. Buber concurs with Kierkegaard's views of sin as position, and goes further by saying that whereas the sinner sins, the wicked *is* wicked.

More frequently than not, sinful acts and attitudes appear to be irrational, i.e., devoid of reason, for given sufficient time, they cause harm primarily to the sinner. This applies to such attitudes as presumption and arrogance, for example; to sinful goals such as dominance; and to such practices as drug abuse, gluttony, laziness, and sexual excesses, to mention but a few. And as much as the sinner is liable to compromise his health, career, social standing, love life, his whole future maybe, the penalties imposed on him by the courts of his moral conscience by far exceed those of any retributive reality. But moral transgressions are not only "irrational" for their damaging effects on the perpetrator, they are unnecessary as well. Rarely is transgression dictated by biological need such as hunger, thirst, or danger to life—it therefore represents, for the most part, but a *by-path preferred by people* (Lao Tzu).

The question immediately arises as to why people prefer bypaths, while the Great Way is easy. This question is answered in existential terms by the premise that man does not live by bread alone, and neither pleasure nor the reality principles are to him sufficient as guides. Some transgressions, undeniably, hold a strong attraction; they would not be otherwise committed. Many moral transgressions, moreover, promise some higher "highs" than ordinary life can offer. Some provide unusual excitement; others have the capacity to "tickle" the senses. The hater is rewarded by the acquisition of a sense of power; the avenger by feelings of omnipotence. But when linked to moral transgressions, absurd goals, strewn on the bypaths preferred by people, bring no lasting satisfaction. Goethe's Faust cries to Mephistopheles: "Thy bread it satisfies never . . . ."

The question as to why people prefer by-paths may best be answered by what Existentialists have insisted as being a most basic human need: the *need for transcendence*. A compelling force urges man to step forth, to extend himself, to live "ex-centrally"—as explained by M. Heidegger (1899–1976)—beyond the given biological confines of his existence. Man may thus transcend himself through love for an Other, or for others, as Socrates did. Man may devote all his life-energies to causes he deems just. Man is even capable of throwing away the gift of life for the sake of an idea, a principle. Man is a creature of desire, not of need, we are reminded by G. Bachelard (1949). Man may also risk his life for the sake of a trophy, or for some elusive satisfaction such as revenge, as did Melville's Captain Ahab. He may seek to achieve some sexual thrills through various acts of sadism and even murder.

In the teachings of the Buddha, lust and desire are equated with Hell. In the fourth chapter of the Holy Scriptures (Genesis 4:8), Cain receives a warning regarding the nature of sin: "And unto thee shall be his desire . . . ." Yet: "Thou shalt rule over him" (Genesis 4:7). Sin and desire elude the biological frame of reference into which the modern sciences have attempted to encase man. Who can define the reaches of imagination? The powers of fantasy have certainly carried men on their wings far and beyond biological need. Of greed, envy, jealousy, and revenge it is said that they enlarge themselves as *sheol* (the bottomless pit). The gap between biological need and desire yawns wide, indeed. *Sin does not serve biological need*, nor does it always have a cause. What biological need does gambling satisfy? Or vainglory? Or alcoholism? The first murder, namely the fratricide committed by Cain, had nothing to do with provoked, reactive anger—an emotion upon which psychology has hung most of the evils that beset the human heart. The murder of Cain's brother Abel—conceived in pride and rebellion—was motivated by envy. This gratuitous act of murder may be considered without a cause, nonetheless, for Cain had no *need* to be envious of Abel, and had before him other options besides the annihilation of the object of his jealousy. This sad occurrence may serve to demonstrate, nevertheless, that man is not merely *reactor* but frequently *proactor* also—initiator of action—and his actions may be entirely determined by factors of transcendence.

The Consequences of Transgression

The nature of sin and its attributes are most meaningfully explored from the effects they tend to produce. Curiously, in spite of the gratifications and satisfactions obtained from the commission of a moral violation—with the system of self-esteem immediately signalling a fall, and the various dysphorias pertaining to guilt, fear, shame and remorse flooding the conscious mind—the enjoyment of sin is considerably curtailed.

But the body reacts to moral transgressions as well—amply demonstrated by the polygraph. It is not any particular transgression that becomes transparent during polygraph examination, but the emotional turbulence it creates—measured by the magnitude of certain physiological changes.

Indeed, the most convincing evidence of the stressfulness of guilt for transgression of the moral law (inclusive of the sin of deception) has been provided by polygraph techniques and research. Within 15 seconds of a deceptive communication, a reaction is produced which involves all the organs of the body. The level of guilt, *when valid* (i.e., based on real transgression, not mere fantasy) may be recorded by the polygraph due to its effects on the physical body. The reality of sin becomes thus evident through the guilty dysphorias it provokes—the latter measurable through various disturbances they create in physiological function. One has no control over the physiological changes produced during polygraph investigation, when one is really guilty. And just as physical injury is followed by a series of reflex (automatically executed) responses—the withdrawal reaction, for example, which occurs automatically when any part of the body comes into contact with a noxious object—the commission of transgression, followed as it is by an inner sense of danger, immediately sets in motion various physiological and behavioral reactions.

One is thus justified in classifying these reactions as obligatory psychological reflexes: obligatory, since every transgression produces guilt (although its intensity might vary among individuals), and reflexes, because these responses are set in motion automatically—beyond the control of volition. Guilty feelings, nevertheless, may become suppressed, repressed, denied, or displaced at will. It goes without saying, however, that these voluntarily undertaken mental operations can be executed only *after the dysphorias pertaining to guilt have entered consciousness.* Subjectively, the commission of transgression and being confronted with it, is experienced as dangerous. And as in every situation of danger, the organism responds with an "all or none reaction"—preparing the subject for fright, fight, or flight. The enactment of a forbidden-by-conscience wish/desire produces physiological reactions as well as various dysphorias pertaining to guilt, with a pervasive *fear of the unknown.* Sin and guilt are bound thus by a reflex mechanism that is not unconscious, but automatic, and cannot be controlled by the will. Other psychological reflexes such as hurt-revenge, rejection-depression, and deception-anger, may also be universal and potentially active. Research in this direction is certainly warranted: it might enlarge the scope of the neurological as well as the psychological sciences.

But offenses, needless to say, may also cause disruption and even cancellation of relationships with the "Yous" of one's world and, strangely enough, with all other members of the human family as well. The sinner always feels judged and condemned by others, in spite of the fact that "others" are frequently unaware of his sin or crime. Serious moral violations change everything in the experience of life. Guilt and shame may compel the offender to shun the company of others—condemning him thus to isolation and alienation. Moral transgressions, furthermore, deeply cleave into the relationship one maintains with one's Self.

Whatever the particular nature of a moral transgression, the following characteristic is common to all: when *not repented and renounced, the same offense will tend to be repeated under compulsion.* Although aware of the existence of what he termed "repetition compulsion," Freud (1920) did not distinctly associate it with moral offenses. The repetition compulsion is operative, nonetheless, in criminal recidivism, prehospitalization behaviors of schizophrenic patients, and in certain human frailties now considered addictions: gambling, compulsive spending, overeating, drug abuse, and many more. The repetition compulsion explains the worsening of the mental condition of those so driven. And, as every addict would readily attest, because of its operation, a release from the grips of sin, vice, or crime becomes ever more difficult. In the repetition compulsion, learning theories, psychoanalysis, and the tenets of religion tend to converge. Yet religion offers a way out, whereas learning theories and even psychoanalytically derived insights provide none.

*   *   *

Existentialists recognize the legitimacy of guilt feelings and attempt to trace them to their source—to the particular moral offense that caused their emergence. On this point Existentialists stand in stark opposition to modern psychologists and especially to psychoanalysts, who consider feelings of guilt to be but neurotic artifacts—unnecessary impediments to the emotional life. But this is in the best of cases, for guilty dysphorias are often held responsible for *causing* psychiatric disorders and illnesses, while the source of guilt remains for psychoanalysts in the shadows, so to speak—acknowledged as being there, but ignored.

It is of great interest to observe that in pronouncing its "guilty" verdict, the conscience seems to take all factors into account: heredity, traumatic events, extenuating circumstances, secret motivations, and many other variables. In his writings, Kierkegaard persisted in his claim to the effect that "sin belongs to the category of the individual." From the judgments of the conscience—as observed clinically—it seems that sin is indeed an individual matter, and the sense of guilt dependent on variables that are unaccessible to us. For this reason, among others, we are all disqualified as judges. We need, therefore, to respect every individual as such, and accept the rulings of his conscience as just—based upon a reality we may not be able to comprehend. The moral conscience might well be subject to a higher judiciary authority, whose decrees we might not always be able to appreciate. But for those whose treasures have become invested in statistics, the many intangibles and imponderables that enter into the dynamics of conscience would be of little value; and researching the forces of conscience would hold for them but weak appeal. Notwithstanding, the psychological sciences are urgently called to incorporate the patients' complaints of sin and guilt into their schemata and interpretations. For it may well be that by failing to recognize moral transgression as a major psychopathological stressor, contemporary psychiatry will neither be able to succor nor contain the ever growing number of psychiatric casualties.

Fear of Transgression: The Neuroses

It is not by chance that neurotic illnesses have become deleted as such from the latest disease classifications, for these disorders are less commonly encountered than just a few decades past. In the present era of moral ambiguity and permissive attitudes, in general, neurotic conflicts and illnesses are rarely encountered. The latest classifications (DSM-III-R and IV), delete neurotic illnesses as such and categorize them according to the nature and intensity of their central symptom, namely anxiety. Freud, who first described the neuroses, was well aware of this symptom, which he saw as "central to the problem of the neuroses." He believed, nevertheless, neurotic anxiety to have its origins in the Ego-mind-reason, and saw its function as the signaling of danger. Freud believed that with "signal anxiety," the Ego-mind-reason forewarns of untoward consequences in reality, were the forbidden wish/desire to be acted out. Later in his writings, Freud (1940) explained "signal anxiety" on the basis of the existence of an unresolved conflict, but could not dismiss the possibility that the warning anxieties of the neuroses are actually issued by the moral conscience—the Superego. Yet, in spite of all the psychoanalytic theories that regard the anxieties of the neurotic to be valid for their warning of adverse repercussions in reality, to the neurotic they speak otherwise. For the neurotic is not so much as concerned with the repercussions of his morally forbidden actions in reality, as he entertains fears and forebodings more powerful by far. Actually, he dreads insanity, the loss of his soul, and even death—irrational as such fears might seem to be. *The fears of the neurotic are fully justified, nonetheless, for acting out the morally forbidden fantasy may indeed bring about a loss of soul, insanity, a "nervous break-down," or psychosis*, as one may wish to regard this cataclysmic occurrence.

What hides behind neurotic anxiety is another matter altogether. In his time, Freud was justified in identifying sexual urges and aggressive drives as the major components of conflict, for this is what he saw and treated in his private clinic in prewar Vienna. But these are not necessarily the only morally forbidden wishes neurotics entertain. Some hide secret intentions of misappropriation of monies; others may be angling a favorable drug deal; some struggle with the idea of abortion; and the list extends quite long with all the evil deeds man can imagine in his heart.

Neurotic disorders need not be considered as separate nosological entities, however, but as standing on a continuum, according to the intensity of the signs and symptoms they produce. But as is true of every psychiatric disorder, the symptoms of neurotic illnesses tend to overlap and merge, as shown below.

Anxiety Neuroses are characterized by vague feelings of anxiety for which the individual can find no explanation. One may be dealing with a case in which an existential forewarning is being conveyed that all is not well in the life of that particular individual. He may not be answering the call of his duties, his responsibilities, his destiny. Vague anxiety may also appear as the first symptom of a hidden intention, such as adultery, for instance. But this anxiety may progress and become fear, as happens particularly when the fulfillment of the forbidden wish draws near. Anxiety may then become transformed into a **Phobia,** i.e., a fear of an object or situation that symbolizes the forbidden-by-conscience wish/desire.

Social Phobia (see also Chapter X) must always be set and examined apart, for it may represent a paranoid uneasiness due to shame and guilt for either past or continuous moral misdemeanors or felonies. Social phobia must also be differentiated from the avoidance of people, which may be due to inner hate, envy, jealousy, contempt, and other unacceptable attitudes. Some cases of social phobia may actually hide neurotic struggles with secret wishes to be noticed, applauded, admired, etc., and with sexual exhibitionism as well.

Agoraphobia, (see also Chapter X) or the fear of open spaces—described and interpreted by Freud—represents the fear of a possibility (open spaces symbolizing possibilities): it may be a homosexual encounter, a shoplifting venture, or other such temptation.

Claustrophobia, or the fear of closed spaces, symbolizes a closed situation: marriage, a business contract, an inescapable responsibility.

Acrophobia is an irrational fear of heights. It is a frequently encountered phobia that usually symbolizes the possibility of a moral fall. This type of phobia is most commonly found in young adults, who often experience also a fall in their dreams—faced as they are with multiple temptations. Their fear of heights and dreams of falling serve as forewarning.

The fear of elevators has not been given a Greek name yet, although it is quite frequently encountered. This fear usually symbolizes a fear of "crashing," by which the individual is warned of a psychotic decompensation, were he to act on the particular temptation entertained. The fear of elevators may also contain a fear of heights as well as of closed spaces.

Phobias may generalize along a gradient, and become increasingly more paralyzing. They will not recede, however, until the forbidden wish is given up—renounced once and for all, *as an act of the will*. In the absence of such a resolve, anxieties and phobias will tend to increase and give rise, then, to attacks of panic.

Panic Attacks may lead to physical illnesses, most commonly to cardiac arrhythmias. "Homosexual panic" may precede or follow such an encounter. This author has witnessed the transformation of "homosexual panic" into a psychotic "breakdown."

As debilitating as anxieties, phobias, and panic states may be, in no way do they compare with the dread that ensues from the enactment of a forbidden-by-conscience wish/desire. The following reality has somehow eluded the psychoanalytic eye: it is a matter of utmost importance, whether a wish has been fulfilled in reality, or has remained in the domain of the neurotic's fantasy. For unclear reasons, psychoanalytic theories have failed to appreciate the enormous difference between their patients' fantasies and their enactment in reality, yet it is precisely this difference that separates neurotic illnesses from the psychoses. In neuroses, desire-propelled fantasies struggle against the moral forces of conscience, and this interplay between the various forces that enter into the conflict of the neurotic is dramatized in his dreams. Characteristically, the neurotic sees himself fulfilling the tempting wish, but it all ends with some horribly exaggerated (for stronger effect) punishment. Freud was well aware of the meaning of these dreams, designating them "punishment dreams." Dreams of neurotics distinguish themselves from dreams of psychotics by an essential difference: in psychoses there is no longer a struggle with the moral forces of conscience, as the choice against them has already materialized. What remains for the psychotic is not only to deal with the consequences of his actions in reality, but also and much worse: to bear the torments of his guilty conscience. Along with other symptoms of distress, the pangs of the psychotic's guilty conscience present themselves by way of nightmares, in which the psychotic might see himself transformed into an animal, plant, or inanimate object; he might also be attacked by wild beasts, vultures, monsters, and the devil.

With respect to neurotic disorders, it is worth repeating that *the polygraph is able to detect even mere intention to deceive, confirming the meaning of neurotic anxiety as fear of sin.*

In accordance with the psychoanalytic understanding of neurotic illnesses, these are currently treated by various doses of "reassurance," behavior modification techniques, Ego-building strategies, and desensitization procedures, as well as with various anxiolytic and antidepressant medicines. No longer does one bother to sit down with the neurotic and dissuade him from acting on the tempting but morally wrong possibility. Yet by this omission, and by targeting only the symptoms of distress afflicting the neurotic, modern psychotherapeutic strategies have tended, albeit indirectly—by removing the red signals of danger issued by conscience—to allow for the enactment of morally forbidden wishes/desires. Inadvertently, such "therapies" might have facilitated the conversion of neurotic illnesses into psychoses.

In the framework of existentially oriented psychotherapy, the warning anxieties that characterize the neuroses are also recognized as signs of danger, but they are believed to be issued by the moral conscience, and not by the Ego-reason. Instead of relief from his anxieties, the conflicted neurotic needs to be strengthened in his resolve to abstain from acting on the dangerous temptation. A complete cure is then attempted, by encouraging the neurotic to renounce definitively his pathogenic fantasies/wishes/desires, which need to be analyzed in depth and their roots exposed to the light of reason. On the wings of imagination, desire might lead its subjects not only away from reality, but from morality as well. Neurotic disorders do not engender anxieties on account of unresolved conflict, but because the morally forbidden intention is still active and the conscience continues, for this reason, to issue signals of danger. What appears irrational and frequently ridiculous in the phobias and panic states of the neurotic begins to make sense when regarded from the existential vantage point. Capitulation to the feared and at the same time tempting possibility may, indeed, be the crucial event to tip the balances of justice in the courts of conscience toward a verdict of "guilty." It may lead then to an "explosion of conscience," to psychosis. Everything will change thenceforth in the life-experience of the individual so condemned.

Depression: Failures and Omissions

Depression may be but a temporary state that mars one's life-experience; it may also be a component of other psychiatric disorders. We all suffer from depression at some time or another during the course of our life-journey. Depression, however, becomes a disease when it prevails in the inner domain of the emotions, colors all mental processes, causes disturbances in various physiological functions, and deprives the depressed of motivation and a zest for life. Depressed Spanish-speaking patients complain of a lack of *"animo"*—

meaning a lack of spirit, of animating spark. Helplessness and hopelessness pervade the depressed person's being. Depression exceeds the realm of sadness and is frequently admixed with elements of anxiety. As a rule, it causes a general slow-down of all activities, physical as well as mental. Various physiological functions are also affected, and the depressed may complain of somnolence or insomnia, digestive disturbances manifested by anorexia or excessive appetite, constipation, lack of sexual desire, and a loss of sexual potency. When anxiety prevails over depressive features, it acts as a stimulant and produces symptoms of agitation—a variety of depression known as **Agitated Depression.** Depressed patients often console themselves with alcohol and/or drugs. Alcohol abuse is frequently justified as being the depressed's "medicine" and drug abuse may begin with the vacuous depressions contingent on "boredom."

More than other psychiatric disorders, the *symptom* of depression has been responsible for justifying the tendency to equate emotional states with psychiatric illnesses as such. The symptom of depression, moreover, has fortified the belief that psychiatric disorders are actually due to some sort of biochemical aberration. Nevertheless, like every other symptom of a distressed "psyche," depression rings the bell of alert, signalling that all has not been well in the life of the depressed, and calling for remedial action.

Anxiety and depression are the starting points on the continuum of psychiatric symptomatology. Certain individuals, already stamped by heredity, manifest anxieties almost from the cradle; others show the symptoms of a depressed state very early in life. Still others enter into depressions that exceed a certain depth and limit of time. Depressions triggered by well-defined life-events are termed **Reactive Neurotic Depressions.** Among external factors capable of producing depression, the following have been observed more frequently than others: loss of health, bereavement, loss of opportunities, loss of physical attractiveness, defeat in career, and, paradoxically, loss of a goal through its achievement. Most keenly painful, however, seem to be losses involving loved ones, and the bereaved may lament that part of his soul has gone with the departed. It is of interest to note that these depressions appear quite similar to those involving losses of Self. But, if and when the depressed is a loving individual, and his bereavement relatively free from guilt and remorseful self-recrimination for failing the departed, he will eventually—with the passage of benevolent time—find some new "loves" or become invested in a worthwhile cause, lifting himself in this manner out of the depressed state.

As a general rule, sins of omission and failures to respond to the call of duty or to the voice of conscience produce low-grade anxieties as well as sadness, which may evolve into the clinical state of depression. Such depressions are contingent upon losses of self-esteem. In more severe cases, a sense of loss of Self may also be experienced as part of the depression. Among the sins of omission liable to produce depression, failure to fulfill obligations toward family, friends, society, and one's country are most frequently observed. Failure to use one's talents, to realize one's potentialities, and a lack in achievement over time may also induce a sense of self-devaluation and depression. Yet, of pain and anguish leading to depression, those caused by rejection rank highest on the list. But the agony is not so much related to the loss of love and self-esteem, as it is to the gnawing suspicion that the rejection had been somehow deserved.

A closer scrutiny of the subjects given to depression, their past histories, and ways of being-in-the-world, reveals that a great majority among them actually belong to one or another category of personality disorder. Narcissistic, borderline, schizoid, schizotypal and especially **Dependent Personalities** suffer from depressive states of various degrees, more often than do "normal" individuals. In addition to their marked dependency on others, depressed individuals, notably, lack in motivation and initiative. One may regard their dependency as "need," or else a fixation at certain stages of development. One may also regard their dependencies as products of their depression, but such interpretations would only bring back the question as to cause and effect. Is depression the cause or the result of excessive dependency? For Existentialists, the answer to this question is self-evident. Given the rather limited affectionate zeal and narrow scope of interests of depressed individuals outside of themselves, it is hardly surprising their world shows poverty and constriction. The shrinkage of their world is confirmed by projective tests. And for their entrenchment in a passive-dependent position, depressives forever suffer from disenchantment, rejection, and hurt. They also tend to harbor anger and resentment toward others for not fulfilling their inflated expecta-tions, as well as toward themselves for their sins of omission. Knowing themselves to be beggars for love instead of its dispensers; whiners instead of consolers; extortionists of pity rather than extenders of compassion, how can they love and respect themselves? Existentially, depressives may be considered as suffering mostly from their own ways of being-in-the-world. Their predicament is certainly related to their failure to unfold their wings, but this privilege seems to be granted only to those willing to spend themselves in giving, love, and sacrifice.

Distinct from temporary states of depression and characteristic of the personality-disordered, severe depression may overtake individuals who, on the surface, appear well-functioning and immersed in the battles of life. An existential analysis of their lives and ways of being-in-the-world reveals, however, that when they succumb in middle life to **Involutional Melancholia** or **Endogenous Depression,** this distressing condition serves to alert them that in their past they had pursued mostly self-serving goals, or else were involved in some rather abstract or general cause. "It is easier to love humanity than love one's neighbor," poignantly remarked Dostoyevsky, and this insight aptly applies to the sufferers of endogenous depression. In this psychiatrically impaired patient population, a good majority belongs to one or another personality disorder, as mentioned before, but with excess representation of the "schizoid," "borderline," and "dependent" categories. Cold, detached, and indifferent to others, the **Schizoid** person is usually attracted to scientific pursuits; tends to enjoy mechanical gadgets; and may become infatuated with numbers as symbols of money. The excessively dependent individual frequently brings forth claims to various entitlements and, obviously, enjoys the act of receiving more than that of giving. It would appear as if the felicity derived from satisfying human relationships, harmonious family living, and rewards ensuing from self-detachment, eludes somehow these self-absorbed and self-seeking individuals. The "task-masterish" housewife-mother, whose devoted ministrations actually covered a compulsion for orderliness and a drive for mastery and control, may be suddenly "struck" by a depression for which no external event can account. The "workaholic" husband-father, more absent (by his detached, indifferent presence) at home than outside of it, may become similarly affected. He may have deluded himself as to the purpose of his relentless pursuits: angling promotion, power, fame, and riches for his own gratification, and not for the benefit of others or his family. Despite diversions and distractions as well as self-deceptive rationalizations, these individuals are, nonetheless, keenly aware of having avoided the real tasks of their respective calling, that of caring and loving those near and close. Reaching the middle years of their lives—a time of crisis and reckoning—they might find themselves crying in outrage and despair; they might also persist in their attempts to convince themselves that all they had done was "for the sake of the family." Their vague and diffuse sense of guilt is usually manifested by depression and anxious agitation, hence the common designation of "agitated depression" given to these disorders.

The guilt and sense of failure lamented by the victims of endogenous depression have frequently been regarded as unfounded, even delusional. However, were the basic defect of these individuals, namely their incapacity for loving, to be uncovered, as well as so many little acts of neglect, disregard, insensitivity, and various other omissions, their "sickness" would have been better understood and their treatment more successful. Otherwise, with the years relentlessly advancing—and before it is too late—the finger of destiny might menacingly point toward them with the accusation: "Thou hast not loved!"

Although depression may appear at any time during the course of schizophrenia, it occurs more frequently in its initial stages. But if and when the schizophrenic is capable of sorrowing over his failures—suffer from depression—this could lead him to repentance and even to a permanent cure. It is now well recognized that at any stage of schizophrenia, the appearance of depression augurs a better prognosis than otherwise (pp. 282, 286, 410).

Pride and Rebellion

For disturbing the Heavens of Harmony—in disobedience to the divine decree and in pride desiring "to be as gods"—the first man and woman are said to have been expelled from their abode in Paradise, condemned thenceforth to sweat and toil. Pride or *hubris* has always been considered as the basic form of sin in Western culture; it is also prominent in the mythology of the ancient Greeks. Erasmus' Philautia (*phil* = love, *auto* = self), representing the madness of self-presumption, is the first figure Folly leads in her dance, "but that is because those two are linked by a privileged relation: self-attachment is the first sign of madness, because a man attached to himself accepts error as truth, lies as reality, violence and ugliness as beauty and justice" (M. Foucault 1973). Foucault's interpretation of insanity carries the notion that the judgments of the autistic, unless balanced by those of others, must by necessity be perverted, and his sense of truth, morality, and aesthetic values laden with ambiguity. Governed exclusively by the laws of self, and seeking mostly self-gratification and self-aggrandizement, egotistic and frankly autistic individuals exempt themselves from the obligation to subordinate their selfish interests to the demands imposed on them by society and morality.

But by so doing, they also exclude themselves from the bonds of love and kinship which bind all members of the human family together.

Autism is one of the cardinal manifestations of early-onset schizophrenias. It may be defined as egocentricity carried to the extreme. The child who is destined to become vulnerable to the various disturbances within the schizophrenic spectrum characteristically disrupts the harmony in the life of his family: first through willful disobedience, and later by frank adolescent rebellion. Willfulness, incorrigibility, defiance, and aggressive acts were found to mark preschizophrenic children (cf. Chapter IV) and not any lack in their capacity for adaptation. Thus, many of their sinful attitudes may, through pride, become entrenched position. Pride precludes self-examination; and pride prevents the sinner from admitting wrong. The majority of defined psychiatric disturbances are malignantly contaminated with excessive pride.

In psychiatric terms, excessive self-love is known as **Narcissism,** a designation derived from Greek mythology. The story of self-adoring Narcissus unfolds with his spurning of the nymph Ego, an act for which he incurs the curse of the gods. Soon thereafter, while admiring himself in the limpid waters of a pond, he suddenly falls therein and is lost forever. As a memorial to his tragic and untimely death, a flower, named narcissus after him, begins to grow at the edge of waters. Loving and admiring mostly himself, the narcissistic individual is cursed by a painful loneliness in reality. In subjective experience, this curse becomes compounded by a weighty emptiness and an "ugly," tearless depression. Equally malignant among the many subjective distresses of the narcissistic individual are his excessive preoccupations with bodily functions, namely, his hypochondriasis, which may take over much of the activities of his conscious mind.

By definition, **Hypochondriasis** means that the individual so affected suffers from aches, pains, and bodily distresses which do not have an organic basis. Always in abhorrence of a vacuum, nature fills the empty world of the self-lover with distresses and sensations arising from his own body. The narcissist thus tends to "overvalue" and "over-cathexe" his own material body.

Compelled to devalue others in view of self-aggrandizement, the narcissist is also brought to suffer that which he dreads most: *rejection.* And since life is close to impossible when devoid of loving relationships, these self-adoring antiheroes frequently exit the stage of life by committing suicide.

But before leaving the narcissist to his self-admiring and self-absorbing preoccupations, a distinction needs to be made between his psychiatric disturbance and that of the autistic individual. The difference is not just one of degree and quality of self-centeredness, but also of their relation to others, to the world. Whereas the autistic individual shows almost no interest in others or in the world, the narcissist seeks others for the admiration he can extract from them, and is eager to amass worldly possessions.

While the **Paranoid Personality** is viewed by others as secretive, defensive, devious, and scheming, existential logic binds these ways of being-in-the-world to the exaggerated mistrust and suspiciousness characteristic of these individuals. This means that the paranoid person expects to be mistreated the way he mistreats others. But the paranoid is also described as domineering, rigid, cold, and resentful of authority. Oversensitivity in matters that concern the egotistic strivings of these individuals, and an overvalued self-image, are central to their being. The paranoid person is also a collector of grievances and reacts excessively to the merest slight or prick to his inflated self-representation. It would seem as if psychological reflexes of hurt-revenge are unduly powerful and have a low threshold here, for these individuals continually seek to avenge themselves in order to satisfy the urges of their indomitable pride. A caricaturist would depict the paranoid person as a giant commanding a minuscule world. *Hubris* does not always have a cause, however, and the psychological explanations now advanced, that it represents compensation for feelings of inferiority, seldom hold true. As succinctly pointed out by Alfred Adler and elaborated by Ernest Becker in *The Denial of Death* (1973), our pride propels us all to try to "stick out" somehow above our fellow men.

Most psychiatric disorders contain elements of pride, and this is hardly by chance. For if psychiatric disorders are indeed predicated on the wrong one does and the right one does not, excessive pride would prevent these individuals from recognizing their faults and from attempts to correct them. The fall of the proud is predicted by wise King Solomon: "Pride goes before destruction, and a haughty spirit before a fall" (Proverbs 16:18). The defiant, hostile, and intransigent demeanor of the insane is all too obvious, but so is also their fall.

The sin of vainglory depicts yet another human caricature: that of the adolescent (usually female) or woman with **Anorexia Nervosa** and/or Bulimia. Obsessed with vanity-related concerns and the desire to be "the fairest of them all," some female adolescents engage in absurd acts of self-denial for the sake of their beauty. Other elements enter into this syndrome as well: rebellion and revenge against the parents, executed in a rather passive manner; jealousy of siblings and/ or friends whom the patient attempts to "out-do;" refusal to grow up and assume the female role; and in pride, desiring to be uniquely special. **Bulimia Nervosa** differs from Anorexia only by the poorer control these women have over their urge to eat. Some fall into bingeing compulsions and may resort, for that reason, to self-induced vomiting in order to cancel their periods of culinary indiscretion. It is of great interest, however, that Anorexia and Bulimia are extremely rare, if they exist at all, in countries with an insufficient supply of food, and that these disorders are practically nonexistent in men. On these observations alone, biochemical theories—which attempt to explain Anorexia and Bulimia on the basis of chemical aberrations— might trip and stumble.

Manic Psychoses (p. 92) affect, as a rule, individuals who are loving, achieving, and excel otherwise in their life-tasks—especially those in creative occupations. But their excellence might lift these individuals—in pride and exultation—above the base of reality and into the peaks of a manic psychosis. The delusion of being superior to their fellow men might even provide them with a sense of omnipotence and drive them into irresponsible ventures such as spending sprees, exhibitionistic acts, and romantic entanglements. Nonetheless, those among them who are capable of sorrowing over their madness may suffer a "crash" into depression soon afterward. Due to their generally good premorbid personalities, manic-depressives do not sustain losses of their Selves as a result from their psychotic ordeal (as occurs in schizophrenia), and do not suffer mental impairment as a consequence.

Anger, Hatred, and Hostility

Mad-angry or mad-insane? In Greek mythology, the gods first make mad those they intend to destroy. Anger transformed into hate frequently becomes destructive, known in psychiatric terms as "destructive rage." The Holy Scriptures warn against anger, for it can lead to transgression, and advise the angry, "Let not the sun go down upon your wrath" (Ephesians 4:26). That anger may transmute into passion hardly needs further proof, for almost everyone has experienced at one time or another a temporary "eclipse of reason" in the heat of anger. The temporary loss of reason, eclipsed by passion, has long been recognized, and the verdict of "innocence by reason of insanity" is allowed to rest in the courts for this reason. Externally provoked anger needs to be differentiated from hatred, with which it may, nonetheless, coexist or coalesce.

Although aggression has become almost synonymous with hatred and anger in the jargon of psychologists and psychiatrists, these emotions need to be sorted out and examined apart. Rather than an undesirable trait with destructive potential, aggression may in some cases be a desirable attribute. Individuals so endowed may have the ability to "take the bull by the horns," so to speak, and attack challenges and difficulties with courage, strength, and determination. Hatred is an altogether different feeling, and hatred belongs to the coward. When anger is not willingly forsaken or outwardly expressed, it may become transformed into a smoldering passion, into hatred. But hatred need not draw its substance from unexpressed anger alone; it may grow out of envy, passivity, revenge, or jealousy. According to W. Stekel (1929), "One cannot overestimate jealousy as the wellspring of hatred." Hatefulness may have no cause, however, yet become all the more malignant for this reason. From the spiritual vantage point, the sin of hate represents a breach of the most fundamental divinely ordained injunction, which requires that one love the neighbor as oneself, no less. Needless to say, hatred dictates behaviors that violate also the most basic social and legal laws, promulgated in order to safeguard the rights and welfare of others, the larger community.

On the spectrum of psychiatric disorders (Diagram # 2, p. 140), the neurotic's deficiency in loving capacity gradually merges with narcissism, becomes excessive dependency and exploitation in the borderline, and transforms into murderous hatred at the pole of schizophrenia. Due to their characteristic malevolence, schizophrenics have always been thought to be possessed by evil spirits, a view which prevails to this day among peoples deemed to be primitive. As much as one wishes to avoid it, spirit possession is, nonetheless, a *universally shared experience*, which every schizophrenic, whether scaling the trees in Papua or smoking cigars in a Paris drawing room, will attempt to explain and convey. This perception of insanity, clearly, has withstood the progress of civilization and the psychological enlightenment it has brought in its wake.

In his *Interpersonal Theory of Schizophrenia*, H. S. Sullivan (1953) noted that a "malevolent transformation" takes place in insanity, which, he believed, could be traced back to childhood. If by "spirit" an affect is meant only, whether of joy, sadness, anger, or hatred, a spirit of hate and malevolence, indeed, appears to obsess, possess, as well as consume the insane. Yet those so afflicted would not be satisfied with such an interpretation, and would persist in insisting they are possessed by an evil spirit, i.e., by a spirit of Evil.

The malevolence of the insane may contain various elements of anger, envy, destructive urges, and negativism, liable eventually to coalesce and become generalized, global hatred. Global hostility becomes, then, directed against all living creatures: plants, animals, men, and women. Cruelty to animals in childhood has long been recognized as an early sign of later schizophrenia. So characteristic is hostility in schizophrenia that in its absence this diagnosis can safely be ruled out.

S. Arieti (1974) wrote as follows:

> Hostility is to be found sooner or later in every schizophrenic patient, but it is disguised in several forms.

The malevolence that marks the insane ought perhaps to become that long-sought litmus test to differentiate emotional from organically determined disorders. Both Jung and M. Bleuler describe the difference in demeanor of the emotionally disturbed hostile schizophrenic, as compared to the subdued manner of the neurologically impaired. The hostility factor is used as a diagnostic marker for schizophrenia in various psychological tests and scales.

*   *   *

Most malignant among the neuroses, **Obsessive-Compulsive Disorder** (OCD) is firmly grounded in hatefulness and malevolent intention. According to psychoanalysts, these disorders are the results of alleged "arrests" or "fixations" during the anal-sadistic stage of development. Many character traits of the obsessive-compulsive individual may thus be explained: sadistic urges, compulsive withholding, malevolence, stinginess, negativism, willfulness, and stubbornness, among others. The debate regarding the origins of OCD does not end with such explanations, however. The child's behavior may be the result of hereditary propensities, which become manifest precisely at the time he begins to ambulate and exercise control over his bowel/urinary functions. Being also curious about the world around and unaware of certain dangers, the child is in need of utmost restraint at that time. But a child with inborn negativistic attitudes will not listen to his parents' admonitions and may also resist bowel control, or else withhold his excrements. Such a child will oppose parental demands in other areas of life as well, and engage in various power struggles, just so as to assert his will. Typically, such a child throws a "temper tantrum" and, in this manner, usually succeeds in having his wishes fulfilled. Harshness in bowel training from an affection-withholding mother—given by psychoanalysts as explanation for later sadism and malevolence, such as are observed in the obsessional-compulsive neurotic—needs to rest upon firmer grounds than provided by a patient's reconstructed past. How much can one remember of the early years of life? But, as has been said before, feelings of hate may draw their sap from other roots, such as sibling envy, for example; or revolt against Providence for some inborn defect or imperfection; or from the difficulties inherent in human relationships or other tasks of life the individual may not be able to master. Parental severity, harshness of upbringing, and even child abuse do not necessarily produce the hatefulness observed in OCD and schizophrenia. And if the conscience of the hate-obsessed neurotic appears to be harsh and oftentimes "sadistic," it is not on account of parental "introjects," but because conscience is sensitive to any thought or feeling of hostility.

Sooner or later, when sufficiently nourished by anger, envy, bitterness, or revenge, malevolent urges may grow strong and demand expression through action. This is a crucial moment for the hater, for he needs to decide whether to fight off his malevolent urges or yield to them by acting them out. Nothing prevents the hater from forsaking his hatefulness, however. By sheer decision as an act of the will, hate may at any moment be replaced by benevolence, perhaps even by love. But the hater may also choose to placate his feelings of guilt (which hate invariably engenders) by means of various rituals and acts of atonement, which eventually become compulsive.

Obsessive-compulsive disorders represent disturbances in which reflexes of sin and guilt are continually set in motion. The stimulus to these mental processes, however, is the sin of hate. Sooner or later, the hate-obsessed neurotic discovers that, in order to attenuate his feelings of guilt, he *must* yield to the demands of his "atoning" compulsions, but these, unfortunately, have a tendency to multiply and generalize. And since feelings of guilt are closely related to fear, the obsessive-compulsive seeks to dominate them not through religious faith, but its opposite: through superstition. In *The Psychopathology of Everyday Life*, Freud (1905) wrote as follows:

> Superstition derives from hostile and cruel impulses, and is in large part the expectation of trouble; and a person who has

> harbored frequently *evil wishes* against others, but has been brought up to be good . . . will be especially ready to expect punishment. [emphasis added]

Unwilling to renounce his hateful intentions and propelled by the pride engendered by his power over others, the obsessive-compulsive neurotic becomes engaged in the most bizarre and ridiculous acts of ritual and atonement: hand washing, avoidance of cracks on the pavement, crossing streets on even numbers only, and so on and on. He is willing to go to great lengths and is ready to endure all kinds of humiliations, yet he will persist in refusing to give up his malevolence. It is of great interest to note that in a recent review of OCD, this disorder was found to evolve into true schizophrenia in 1 percent to 12 percent of cases. According to Arieti (1974), many obsessional neurotics blend, actually, with schizophrenia.

As is true for every other neurotic, the fears of the hate-obsessed compulsive patient are fully justified. He may, indeed, lose control over his malevolent intentions and act them out, but with disastrous psychological consequences, as he is liable to succumb to a psychosis of the catatonic variety. It may be his first and last episode. **Catatonic Schizophrenia,** however, shows a strong proclivity for recurrence. During catatonic states the patient may either burst into a frenzied destructive, aggressive behavior, or become paralyzed by horror-filled hallucinations that forbid his every move. When the notion of "latent," "masked" schizophrenia was still in vogue, it contained the category of the obsessive-compulsive neurotic as well, due to the pervasive hostility that was perceived to be the common denominator of all of these disorders. The overlap between schizophrenia and obsessive-compulsive disorders stretches further, moreover, with the *ambivalence* that permeates much of the "loves" of both obsessive and schizophrenic individuals. One ought to use the word "love" with caution, nevertheless, for so many of these individuals' "loves" are possessive, destructive, degrading, clinging, and dependent. In the ambivalence of both the obsessive-compulsive neurotic and the schizophrenic, it is hate that comes to predominate.

Yet in the eyes of contemporary psychiatry it is not the *hatefulness* of the obsessive-compulsive that is considered his "sickness," but rather his strict, severe, and overscrupulous conscience. It is held responsible not only for dictating rituals and compulsive behaviors, but for *producing* this malignant disorder as well. In keeping with the theories that regard the conscience as nothing more than an aggregate of parental introjects, to which the resolution of the Oedipus complex is later added, modern therapeutic approaches have tended to target the compulsive symptoms of this neurosis rather than its source, namely hatefulness. Antidepressant medicines, tranquilizers, serotonin-uptake-blockers, precursors to certain endogenous substances (such as clomipramine and tryptophan, for example), and various other chemicals are now in vogue for the treatment of this severe disorder. Behavior-modification techniques such as aversive imagery, desensitization, and "flooding" strategies have all produced equivocal results at best. And psychotherapeutic approaches that aim at weakening the allegedly overscrupulous conscience, have, needless to say, proven useless. Ablation of certain tracts in the brain through surgical interventions has caused more harm than good. Clearly, the multiplicity of therapeutic approaches betrays their dubious effectiveness. In their overview of the literature on obsessive-compulsive disorders, from 1953 until 1978, L. Salzman and F. Thaler (1981) were forced to concede that, "It is not pessimistic to conclude that few significant changes in our views and treatment of this disorder have been made."

Obsessive-compulsive disorders represent disturbances in which sin-guilt reflexes become transformed into sin-guilt-expiation complexes. These disorders are much more malignant than other neurotic disorders, however, because the compulsive rituals and superstitious observances have served to placate existing guilt, without eliminating the sinfulness of hate. Similar to the reverberating circuits in chronic pain syndromes, obsessive-compulsive complexes stubbornly persist in their activity. Overwhelmed by their dilemma and desperate for a cure to their "sickness," obsessive-compulsive neurotics often end their life by suicide. According to statistics provided by E. Hollander (Symposium on Obsessive Compulsive and Related Disorders, May, 1994), the suicide rate for noncomplicated OCD is 3.6 percent and 7 percent for OCD complicated by other disorders, as compared with 0.9 percent for no psychiatric disorder.

Can actions produce emotional states? Following the trails of psychoanalytic theories that stress emotional vectors as major determinants to the course of action, psychologists have tended to overlook the fact that actions are quite powerful in determining emotional states. As much as wrongdoing immediately produces a lowering of self-esteem and engenders dysphorias pertaining to guilt, the reverse also holds true: acts of love and charity immediately cause a rise in self-esteem and bring forth feelings of benevolence as well as self-satisfaction. *That actions are more powerful in determining feeling states than thoughts and fantasies, represents one of the basic tenets of existential psychiatry.* Even when unrelated to a particular hateful obsession, acts of charity are recognized for their capacity to erase hostility, which becomes "detoxified" in this manner. Such is the therapeutic approach of eminent French psychiatrist Henrik Baruk (1976). Loving actions speak louder than obsessive thoughts to the harbingers of malevolence. Acts of charity not only cancel out the stimulus of sin-guilt complexes, but tend to produce an inner state of well-being of their own accord.

Obsessive-compulsive disorders have been allotted extended space and a relatively lengthy elaboration here, because they contain all the basic ingredients of insanity and can be used as its simplified model. In the madness of obsession with malevolent intentions, it is equally insane to presume that the sin of hate lends itself to expiation by absurd compulsive rituals, as it is to believe that it is curable by medicines. After the murder of Duncan, Lady Macbeth begins to wash her hands compulsively. Her physician, who sees that "Her eyes are open, but their sense is shut," candidly admits her disease to be beyond his practice.

Obsessive-compulsive disorders share yet another characteristic with schizophrenia, namely a basic negativism, which may be expressed by way of passive resistance, oppositional behaviors, obstructionism, argumentativeness, and antagonism, among others. Negativism may be noted early in infancy when the child refuses to eat, drink, sleep, smile, and refrains even from uttering signals of communication (mutism). A negativistic child may vomit its hostilities, choke them in an asthmatic wheeze, or proclaim them with incessant crying. Negativistic attitudes, needless to say, carry the seeds of self-defeat; frequently, they also bar the way toward meaningful human relationships, so vital in one's life-journey. Negativism opposes all those forces that make life possible, namely love, faith, and hope. Intellectual negativism can appear masked as cynicism. As destructive in its consequences as hostility, cynicism combines *hubris* (arrogant pride), self-centeredness, and—harder for others to endure—a chilling indifference.[*] Cynicism is the *Leitmotif* (leading tune) of schizophrenias that have no clear precipitants, among them **Nuclear** or **Process Schizophrenia,** which was identified by Langfeldt in 1939. Inexorably progressing toward early deteriora-

---

[*] It is of interest to note that the themes most characteristic of the verbal productions of schizophrenics were found by computer analysis to relate to *hostility, negativism*, body concerns, and *death* (S. Rosenberg et al. 1979).

tion, these illnesses lead to dementia at a young age. They affect mostly young adults whose choices of evil become confirmed by pride, negativism, cynicism, and hostility. The inner attitudes of these individuals become expressed in various subversive activities as well as in frank acts of malevolence.

Sin, Crime, and Insanity

The problem whether "bad" or "mad," frequently brought forth in the courts of justice as a crucial issue, is always resolved with much difficulty, for these two conditions share a large area of overlap.

According to the theories developed by Ego-psychologists, sin represents but a "symptom" of disease—it is not its cause. Sin is thus regarded as a sort of weakness or defect of the mature Ego, presumably failing to curb the urging forces of the Id, in conformity with the demands of reality. Yet sin and crime cannot be considered solely from the vantage point of the Ego and its failures, without taking account of possible increments in the powers of the subterranean, unconscious Id—a seething cauldron of lusts and desire. In the assessment of Id's evil forces, hereditary predisposition, environmental factors, early childhood experiences, as well as transcendental strivings such as greed, envy, revenge, and hate, would need to be included. Jung (1907) regarded Ego-weaknesses *as secondary* in psychotic illnesses:

> As a matter of fact, the insane person has always enjoyed the prerogative of being one who is possessed by spirits or haunted by a daemon. That is, by the way, a correct interpretation of the psychic condition. The primitive valuation of insanity, moreover, lays stress on a special characteristic which we should never overlook: it ascribes personality, initiative and willful intention to the unconscious, again a true interpretation of obvious facts. From the primitive standpoint, it is perfectly clear that the unconscious, of its own volition, has taken possession of the Ego . . . . It is not the Ego that is enfeebled; on the contrary, it is the unconscious that is strengthened by the presence of a daemon. The primitive, therefore, does not seek insanity in a primary weakness of consciousness, but rather in an inordinate strength of the "unconscious." *(On the Psychogenesis of Schizophrenia)*

The "command" hallucinations so frequently complained of by the insane never prompt them to benevolent action, but rather to destruction, murder, and suicide.

We are all aware of certain thoughts that fleetingly cross our minds. Nevertheless, if we find the contents of such thoughts repulsive, or Ego-alien, we do not begin to build a nest for these "flying temptations," to borrow Martin Luther's expression. Therefore, in order for an obsessive thought to settle in consciousness and begin its obsessive activity there, it needs to be first accepted, nourished, and to some extent, bound to the will. In the interim, the Ego-mind-reason may be bribed by rationalizations and the conflict grow fiercer. Clearly, the more the Ego yields to bribes and self-deception, the more corrupt it also becomes. One sin usually follows another, even more senseless than the first, and often unrelated. This is how the cancerous process of sin is liable to bring about destruction of soul, mind, and body.

It is said in Jewish tradition that sin appears first as a passer-by, then becomes a guest, and eventually takes over as master of the house. Some sins give rise to pleasure and excitement, at least initially. Were this not so, they would not have been committed. In due course, conflict may cease altogether and the Ego become an accomplice of the Id, supplying it with all the know-how and apperception of reality needed for the realization of complicated acts of embezzlement, for example, or fraud, or criminal sexual activities. Inordinate amounts of energy and creative effort are also frequently invested in the commission of sin and crime. It then appears as if the forces of the Id and the Ego have won victory over the moral conscience, temporarily silencing its warnings and appeals. In due time, however, the judiciary proceedings in the courts of conscience will reach a decree, pronounced with abundant clarity.

Raskolnikov, the tragic hero of Dostoyevsky's *Crime and Punishment*, rightfully wonders whether "The eclipse of reason and failure of willpower attacked a man like a disease, or perhaps crime from its own peculiar nature is always accompanied by something of the nature of disease." Unable to decide the issue, Raskolnikov proceeds to bribe his Ego-reason by convincing it that the murder he was contemplating "was not a crime," for he considered "useless" the old woman whose murder he was contemplating. Besides, he intended to distribute to the poor the loot he hoped to acquire from this deed. Raskolnikov's true "sickness" begins to unfold, however, only *after* his commission of what became a double murder. Assailed by feelings of guilt, thereafter, he becomes the subject of various horrifying "deliria" (now called delusions and hallucinations). In addition to the torments of his guilty conscience, Raskolnikov suddenly senses himself *painfully alienated* (p. 236), even from those he had loved most before, and who were caring for him still.

Can undue "pressures" on the Ego-mind and its failure to "cope" with external realities produce such drastic reactions as the commission of a crime, as Ego-psychologists would have us believe? While indeed, during a psychotic decompensation, the powers of the Ego become subjugated to the evil forces of the Id, and the patient enacts what he has long intended, it is not the psychotic state that releases the patient from his restraints, as has been frequently claimed, but his ever intensified compulsion, which acquires potency and finally becomes action. External circumstances, undoubtedly, play a role in the commission of a crime or moral offense, but it is a secondary role. Raskolnikov's murder was bred in an atmosphere of poverty, isolation, bitterness, and desire for revenge, as he came to understand later on. Thus, during a psychosis or its exacerbation, the patient may release his hatefulness and become violent; the sex offender may walk naked in the street, overcome by desire.

The legal system of justice weighs crime according to its severity, degree of premeditation, inner motivations, and various related circumstances. When a defendant is found "psychotic," confused, paranoid, and delusional, these symptoms of distress ought to be recognized as secondary—as consequences—and not as causes. The insanity defense in the courts of justice needs, for this reason, to first establish whether the defendant was psychotic before the crime or became so in its wake. That the examining psychiatrist finds the criminal confused, paranoid, anxious, and disorganized following a certain crime, means nothing by itself, except to indicate that the accused's conscience is active and condemning. The strength of the legal "M'Naghten Rule" is its stipulation regarding the state of mind of the defendant *at the time of his commission of the crime.*

Described in 1898 by German psychiatrist S. J. Ganser, the **Ganser Syndrome** is a short-lived psychosis which affects prisoners on their way to court. In addition to "deliria" of guilt, these patients, characteristically, give approximate answers (*Vorbeireden*) when interrogated. Ganser's psychosis is strategically located on the map of psychiatric disorders. It serves to demonstrate how feelings of guilt, compounded by anxieties related to the outcome of the forthcoming trial, can erupt into an "explosion of conscience"—into a psychosis. It also clarifies the function of *Vorbeireden* as a defensive operation, not far removed from the formal thought disorder considered characteristic of schizophrenia.

Incarceration Psychoses are rooted in similar factors, and have less to do with sensory deprivation, monotony, and other adverse prison conditions than with the reasons for the incarceration. In these cases, as in others, the various determinants of insanity need to be sorted out and appraised: severity of the crime, premeditation, heat of passion, as well as factors relating to the precriminal or premorbid personality.

It is important to mention again in this context that, as a general rule, every unrepented moral transgression tends to be repeated under compulsion. This rule applies to crime as well. In judiciary language, the repetition compulsion is known as recidivism; its frequency has been estimated by S. Guze (1976) to range between 75 percent and 85 percent. Similarly, examination of the serial hospitalization records of any single schizophrenic patient reveals that prehospitalization behavior was repeated over and over and over again. The same morally forbidden act that brought about the initial "explosion of conscience" had been repeated with remarkable monotony before every new "exacerbation."

Sin and crime share yet another common characteristic: they need the cover of deception as protection against social ostracism and legal prosecution. But the lie that protects sin and crime only serves to increase their sinfulness.

Deception: The Inauthentic Existence

a. Deception

Since man by his very nature is socially dependent, and because rejection and social ostracism are endured with much pain, suffering, and anguish of heart, most sinful attitudes and acts need to be shielded from the view of others. Deception frequently fulfills this function. It may be carried out by various maneuvers: flat denial, dissimulation, distortion of facts, diversion tactics, and many more. As a general rule, individuals endowed with creativity avail themselves of some half-truths, so as to enhance credibility. Distractions, evasions, vague statements, and dissimulations of various kinds are used by the less crafty with equal effectiveness. The simplest form of lying is accomplished by way of silences, perseverations (vain repetition of some words or sentences), and flat denials.

In addition to its use as defense, deception may be employed as an offensive weapon also. Its effects can be wide-ranging, nonetheless, and the harm therefrom often serious and of lasting consequences: a misrepresentation before marriage; a false witness in court; the swaying of an army through false intelligence; manipulation of statistical data; business fraud, and many more. But the damage from deception is not always measurable, for many intangibles enter into the equation. Interpersonally, the lie reaches into the realm of mental abuse and is often less tolerable even than violence. Deception leads to mistrust, suspicion, anger and may become responsible for rupture. As for the liar himself, the morally offensive act of deception may in some cases be of such a serious nature as to tip the judicial balance of the courts of conscience toward a verdict of "guilty." This decree may cause the mind to lose its reason.

> A 23-year-old housewife lied regarding the paternity of her child, who was the product of an adulterous relationship. The alleged father's family became responsible for the child's care. A full-blown psychosis, which ensued shortly thereafter, was interpreted by the patient as due to the deception, not the adulterous relationship. (From author's caseload)

A complicated, conscious mental operation, deception involves the following mental processes:

a. knowledge of a certain truth
b. decision to alter it
c. selection of an appropriate modality for the adulteration of this truth
d. verbal expression of the lie

Even if a truth is buried in the "unconscious," it has to be known first in order to be subsequently repressed (J.-P. Sartre 1969). There is no question regarding the impossibility of using deception with an organically damaged brain. A damaged tool for thinking (the brain) could not allow for the subtle and intricate operations needed in order for deception to be carried out, since organic brain lesions characteristically create what is known as an "operational deficit." And since deception represents the major defensive operation of the schizophrenic, this finding alone precludes the possibility that organic-metabolic factors can be held responsible for causing the disease. *Confabulation* can be easily distinguished from intentional deception;

and *misperception* of reality can be differentiated from its deliberate denial or distortion. But, oddly enough, as if different from *reality*—so highly esteemed by modern psychiatrists—*truth* has found no place in their evaluations, and thus the lie became excluded also.

The word "deception" can hardly be found indexed in psychiatric texts; not by neglect or omission, but because the subject of deception has received little or perhaps no attention in the psychiatric literature. In her classical monograph *The Ego and Its Defenses*, Anna Freud (1966) barely pauses to consider deception among the varieties of defensive operations she describes and classifies. She gives considerable space, however, to the various forms of denial: of feelings, of reality, of past events, etc. But like her father, Sigmund Freud, as well as most psychoanalysts, A. Freud regards defensive operations more as preventive measures against *future* acting out of forbidden wishes than as protective of what has already been enacted in the past. For psychoanalysts, what one has done in the past seems less important than the fears and fantasies of what one might do in the future (fear of transgression)—as the model of the neuroses dictates.

The detection of deception is possible because it causes a stir akin to fear, which like every other emotion involves all the organs of the body. Besides an unphysiological (i.e., not according to normal physiology) state of arousal, deception causes changes that are quite characteristic and involve, among others: voice, respiration, heartbeat, skin conductance, and glucose metabolism. It would appear, thus, that *while absolute truth may be elusive, we remain nonetheless responsible for intentionally altering any known-to-us truth.*

With respect to lying and its detection, neuropsychiatrist P. Schilder wrote the following in his preface to J. A. Larson's (1969) book, *Lying and Its Detection*:

> There is an inner drive in human beings to truth and to reality. This drive is probably a characteristic of life. The world of reality needs to be respected. When our conscious self deviates from the truth and denies it, the subconscious self and the body demand to be adapted to reality, to be truthful. We come to the paradoxical formulation, that *human beings lie with their consciousness, but are truthful with their unconscious*(!) and when they do not confess with their mouths, they confess with their body [emphasis added].

It is this confession by the body that allows for lie detection. In polygraph investigation, most characteristic of lying are: inhibition of respiration and/or irregularities, and increased Galvanic Skin Responses (GSR). During deception many other physiological changes are observed, involving heart rate, blood pressure, voice, eye movements, sweating, and more. The manifest behavior of deceivers strikingly resembles that of schizophrenic patients: restless motor activity, avoidance of eye contact, a shift of the left eye (popularly regarded as a sign of madness), pallor, sweating palms, outbursts of anger, and explosive rage. The verbal responses of deceivers are slow to come, since time is needed for the construction of a deceptive communication. The delay in responses observed in deceivers appears to be the same delay in associations, observed by Jung (1907), which takes place whenever the "schizophrenic complex" is being "hit." The Psychological Stress Evaluator detects emotional stress through a component in the human voice that changes during deception.

The questions immediately surge: Why is deception so stressful? What is the nature of this stress? Since the same responses—albeit more accentuated and intense—are obtained during the Silent Answer Test (SAT) where no deception is involved (p. 123), it would stand to reason to conclude that it is the *inner* knowledge of guilt that is experienced as stressful. The lie may well be alleviating the sense of guilt through a false sense of protection, however. Be that as it may, both deceptive communication and guilt from a moral transgression give rise to a subjective state sensed as dangerous. And just as in other states of danger, fear produces an increased reactivity of the central and peripheral sympathetic nervous systems. An increased reactivity of the sympathetic nervous system is characteristic of and has been repeatedly demonstrated in states of psychosis. Outwardly, just like the deceiver, the schizophrenic manifests unusual pallor, sweaty palms, and exhibits a fine tremor—"trembling from fear," so to speak. The danger perceived by the psychotic, however, is vague and unclear; his fear is actually a fear of the *unknown*. This fear, nonetheless, is experienced as more distressing by far than that provoked by threats derived from external circumstances.

It is of great interest to note that even when subjects examined by the polygraph were lying about matters of no consequence to them, or during laboratory experiments, the sin of deception immediately "turned on" signals of danger and produced an emotional upheaval.

b. *The Inauthentic Existence*

While Freud's psychoanalysis was built on the model of the neuroses—illnesses engendered by anxiety over the possibility of morally forbidden actions in the future—what the majority of humans compellingly defend concerns not what they might do in the future, but what moral offenses they have committed in the past. The overwhelming need to erase guilt for past wrongdoing leads some individuals to resort to various deceptive operations, which serve to diffuse the sense of inner danger as well as to protect them against social rejection and ostracism.

For the dread-stricken, guilt-ridden schizophrenic individual, deception becomes the most effective armor and means of social survival. A psychologist who chose to remain anonymous, and who himself had suffered from a schizophrenic illness, wrote as follows on this diseased state:

> What is a schizophrenic? A terrified, conscience-stricken crook, whose favorite commandment is the Eleventh: Thou shall not get caught! Motivated in the first place by Fear, the schizophrenic psychoses originate in a break with *sincerity*, and not in a classically assumed "break with reality." Schizophrenia is the cultivation of a lie. A lie is proven to be the truth. The real truth is that the schizophrenic is responsibly guilty for some crucial misdeeds . . . I take Lady Macbeth to typify schizophrenic psychoses; the motto of the schizophrenic might well be: "Out Damned Spot." (Anonymous 1958, condensed and abbreviated)

A simple truth is stated by S. Bok in her book *Lying* (1979): "Lying requires a reason, while truth-telling does not." Truth flows spontaneously, unless efforts are made to suppress it. The reason the schizophrenic avails himself of deception, simply stated, is that he has sinned. Many of his offenses, however, do not belong to the legal category of antisocial acts, but are committed in the interpersonal realm. How can a sexual pervert, hater, embezzler, adulterer, wife beater, or child abuser maintain even a tenuous social survival except by hiding behind the shield of deception? Yet, as J. M. Shlien (1967) has pointed out:

> The lie begun in self-defense slips into self-deception. This is the end of sanity because it leads to self-negation, which is the end of being and the ultimate anxiety.

Sin, guilt, and deception, moreover, bring about several "splits," not only in one's ways of being-in-the-world, but in one's personality as well. Deception cleaves the personality into an external, apparent, false personality and an internal true one. There is no question regarding the fact that everyone's external personality differs to some extent from the internal, *Eigenwelt* (inner world of the self) one, yet in schizophrenia the disparity is greater by far. Characteristically, the schizophrenic hides behind a thick defensive facade, which he maintains, nonetheless, at the cost of an enormous expenditure of mental energy. Needless to say, these efforts represent a considerable drain on his cognitive capacities, interfere with attention, and impair his powers of concentration. He may not be able to perform complex job assignments for this reason.

An even more disastrous split than that of divided attention is created when deception extends into the realm of the emotions—an operation recognized by psychoanalysts and designated "denial of feelings." In the case of guilt, shame, fear, anguish, and even despair, these feelings may become consciously denied and prevented from entering awareness; but the emotional blockade thus created deprives the denier of positive emotions also—cancelling, in this manner, joy, love, faith, and hope.

The affective state of many schizophrenics appears to be flat, dull, blunted, and even deadened. Yet this state of seeming indifference may be reversed in some cases. It is striking to observe the changes effected on the patient when he reaches a critical insight that is also associated with emotion—recognized by psychoanalysts as "emotional insight," and known to existentialists as repentance or sorrowing over one's failures and wrongdoing—when he bursts into tears or other emotional release. That such a reversal of affective blunting is possible at all would seem to indicate that emotional outflow had been voluntarily obstructed, or else had been blocked by other emotions such as anger, hate, contempt, and fear. A dissociation between affect and thinking has always been considered a characteristic sign of schizophrenia—defined as "incongruity of affect with the content of thought." And indeed, most painful events may be recounted, and most horrifying deeds accomplished by the schizophrenic, without so much as "a flicker of the eye." The schism between thought and emotional outflow, moreover, creates alienation from one's deeper, real Self, where the central regulator—soul, or spiritual Me—as well as the fountain of truth, emotions, meaning, and spontaneity are believed to reside. (Diagram # 4, p. 178). Cognitively, emotionally, and existentially, the patient loses his way, his goal, and his sense of meaning. False, affected, superficial, and devoid of meaning, the utterances of the alienated accurately reflect their inauthentic state of existence.

When deception is employed in the service of self-defense and justification, a formal thought disorder becomes apparent. It is a valuable diagnostic marker, although it carries an ominous prognosis. Thought disorder may be lacking altogether in schizophrenias with otherwise clear-cut symptomatology.[*]

For its toxic effects on soul, mind, and body, and for what it hides, deception is of major concern for existential psychiatrists. The lie begun in self-defense progressively slips into self-deception; before long it reaches the borders of delusion. The lie creates disturbances in one's relationships also, some of which it may preclude. It goes without saying that the lie mars the I-Thou dialogue, but it also angers the Yous of the deceiver's world—provoking rejection. More serious even than these: deception carves deep into the soul and becomes responsible for estrangement from one's true Self and center of being. Alienated from himself, his soul, and distanced from the wellspring of his emotions, the liar is forced to live on the periphery of his existence—mostly in the intellectual realm. His attraction to evil may no longer be hindered by anxieties and phobias. This is what is meant by an inauthentic existence.

The Paraphilias

The last classifications of mental diseases (DSM-III and IV) have given the designation **Paraphilias** (*para* = side, and *philia* = love) to deviant sexual proclivities, but this may be a misnomer. There is little or no love at all in aberrant sexual activities, which seem to belong rather to the bypaths preferred by some people—the majority of whom are deficient in the capacity for loving.

Such, at least, is the opinion of Freud and also of Wilhelm Stekel (1929), who wrote that inability of psychic love, or flight from it, is a characteristic symptom that seems to be wanting in no case of sexual perversion. Both Freud and Stekel were struck by the basic narcissism of homosexuals, which drives them to seek love objects among those who resemble them—of their own sex, that is, with whom it is easier for them to relate. Stekel believed that, "The solution to all paraphilias lies in narcissism, in morbid self-love." Contemporary expert on sexuality R. J. Stoller (Sixth Congress of Psychiatry 1977), goes even further when he states that sexual perversions contain in all cases hostility toward the sexual partner.

---

[*] Thought disorder is not a prerequisite for the diagnosis of schizophrenia.

Diagram # 4

The Various "Splits" of Schizophrenia

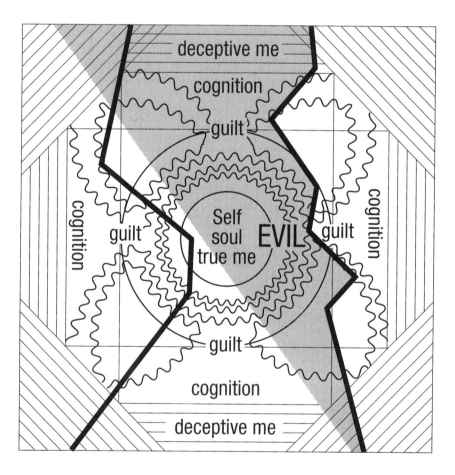

The personality in schizophrenia is fragmented on several levels. It is split along lines of Good — Evil; love — hate; faith — cynicism; truth — deception, and more.

Deception walls off the soul or Self and splits the personality into a true inner Me and a deceptive, facade Me.

Cognition becomes split off from the emotions, which are walled off in order to avoid the pain of guilt. To this schism between thought and feeling, insanity owes its new name: schizophrenia.

The soul, Self, true Me, and spiritual center become walled off from cognitive processes. A dissociation is thus created, which produces self-alienation with a distancing from the Self, from truth and meaning.

But since deception is unnatural, some truths manage to enter awareness. Some feelings of guilt also diffuse into consciousness, in spite of efforts to suppress them, and may be experienced as pains, aches, fears, phobias, nightmares, delusions, etc.

Narcissism and hostility certainly mix and mingle in the paraphilia known as **Exhibitionism.** When the exhibitionist exposes his genitalia, he seeks to obtain the admiration of others, narcissistically believing in the special appeal of his sexual organs. But the exhibitionist may also use the exposure of his genitals as an offensive, hostile communication, intended to startle and humiliate the unwilling onlooker.

Narcissism and hostility may, however, be absent in that minority of homosexuals who commit themselves to lifelong relationships, and to those whose makeup is truly hermaphroditic from birth. Exceptions do not make the rule, nonetheless. It is also worthy of consideration that one's "love" may cover a multitude of unloving and even hateful attitudes, such as are common in both homosexual and heterosexual relationships. All too frequently—and this applies to men as well as to women—their "loves" become contaminated by financial interest, the lure of social standing, or other worldly advantage. Many of these "loves," moreover, may be predominantly clinging, dependent, possessive, and in some cases degrading, humiliating, and destructive—making the sexual partner an object to be used and abused, an "it," so to speak.

Paraphilic sexual activities, ironically, fail to provide lasting satisfaction. And even when emotional attachment does bind paraphiliacs in their intimacy, they still find themselves empty and dissatisfied following the act. Because their bread is that of Mephistopheles (as was the bread of Goethe's Faust), which never satisfies, sexual deviants are in a state of perpetual sexual arousal and forever in search of a better partner, as well as novel and more perverse means of gratification—with a definite pull toward the forbidden, the sordid, the bizarre. Psychologist and expert on human sexuality John Money wrote as follows:

> The sex offender's paraphilia permeates every part of his interpersonal life, his specifications of the ideal partner are so eccentric and bizarre, that in some paraphilias they cannot be fulfilled . . . . (*Psychiatric News*, July 17, 1981)

The disorder designated **Polymorphous Sexual Perversion** describes a nosological entity which comprises more than one sexual "preference." It also serves to demonstrate how inordinate sexual arousal gives rise to insatiable sexual hunger and fosters appetites with cravings for ever novel and more bizarre means of satisfaction. Sexual urges dictate thus a growing variety of ways of gratification often associated with sadistic acts, and even murder—committed in the name of "love."

According to a survey of 500 sex offenders by G. G. Abel et al. (1988), these paraphiliacs required unusual imagery or acts involving nonhuman subjects, children, and other *unwilling* partners, and/or their *suffering* and *humiliation*. Most of the men surveyed were capable of normal sexual activities, yet preferred paraphilic sex. Only 10 percent engaged in just *one* form of paraphilic activity; 38 percent engaged in five or more. Fetishism, sadism, and masochism were always associated with other paraphilias.

That paraphilias have a tendency to progress beyond sexual preference may be deduced from individual case histories. Rape, for example, has been found to predispose to rape-murder. According to law enforcement agents in the Hollywood division of the Los Angeles Police Department, sexual aberrancy was a factor in 10 of the 42 cases of murder committed during one year in that precinct (*New York Times*, September 21, 1981). It is believed that the current epidemic of homosexuality has led to yet another epidemic, that of sexual abuse of children, most of whom are abused by men, not women (in a proportion of 10 to 1). **Pedophilia** most clearly defines the meaning of the word perversion. Instead of love and protection naturally extended to children, the pedophile takes advantage of their helplessness, shows callous indifference for their future, and finds pleasure in destroying their innocence. It has been estimated that among missing children (their number exceeding 500,000 in 1992, which according to the FBI is eight times as high as 10 years ago), a good number have fallen prey to the bizarre and insatiable appetites of paraphiliacs.

One thing remains certain, nonetheless, applicable to all of the paraphilias as well as to excesses in sexual activity in general: they tend to weigh heavily on the conscience and engender intense feelings of guilt. This unmistakable fact may be explained, however, on the basis of the paraphiliac's ways of being-in-the-world in general: hostile, defiant, abusive, contemptuous, harm-seeking, and destructive—attitudes that engender guilt of their own accord. Such an explanation would be too simplistic, nevertheless, and also missing an important point: even those paraphiliacs who prefer to "love" those of their own sex, who trust and care, and who are committed in their relationships, still suffer from a sense of guilt and *paranoid uneasiness*, which may intensify along a gradient and lead to a paranoid psychosis. The clinical finding to the effect that sins of a sexual nature weigh heavily on those engaged in such practices most eloquently bespeaks of the sensitivity of conscience to transgressions in the sexual realm. Almost half of the patients studied by this author (M. Niv 1980) revealed sexual excesses and deviations to have been the precipitating events to their psychotic decompensation.

Whether intended or acted out, Ego-syntonic or Ego-dystonic, **Homosexuality** is usually preceded by warning anxieties of intense magnitude, leading to phobias and often transformed into "homosexual panic." In some cases, panic evolves into psychosis, following such an encounter (p. 245). Some individuals suffer from feelings of persecution and paranoid "social phobia," which may assume psychotic proportions. In his *Interpretation of Schizophrenia*, S. Arieti (1974) finds homosexuality to constitute an important aggravating factor that might become responsible for "precipitating and maintaining psychotic episodes."

> When early in youth, the patient succumbs to the first homosexual seduction, he may go into a state of panic, leading to a schizophrenic psychosis. If a schizophrenic is homosexual, his chances of recovering decrease.

The link between paranoid fears, uneasiness, ideation, and paranoid psychoses was first perceived by one of Freud's followers, namely S. Ferenczi (1873–1933). It was later described by Freud (1911), with the famous case of magistrate Schreber serving as an example. It is of interest to note, however, that Freud—always faithful to his model of the neuroses—thought Schreber to have merely entertained homosexual fantasies. Later biographers of the magistrate, however, were able to show that he was actively engaged in homosexual practices. In this case, as elsewhere, Freud failed to perceive the cardinal difference between neuroses—illnesses predicated upon fear of transgression—and psychoses, which follow the enactment of a forbidden wish/desire. But needless to say, while engendering a variety of dysphorias, most common of which is a sense of condemnation—of paranoia—homosexuality *per se* does not necessarily evolve into a schizophrenia.

The histories of practicing homosexuals frequently reveal that one parent, or both, had indulged in some transgression in the sexual realm. The sins of the fathers usually mark their offspring, who may become homosexual. Often one hears of early seduction by a parent, relative, teacher, or someone in authority. Such seems to have been the case of magistrate Schreber. The potential homosexual may succumb thus to flattery, the need for importance, and also to his own weaknesses and cowardice. So initiated, he may continue the practice and become entrenched in a lifestyle quite unhealthy, and most unfortunate, besides. In a recent review of *Theories of Origins of Male Homosexuality*, R. J. Stoller and G. H. Herdt (1985) recognize "numerous homosexualities varying in their origins, subjective states and behaviors." For Stoller and Herdt, homosexuality represents a preference: the product of a complex and organized number of motives. Early nonerotic events and character structure (inclusive of constitutional, prenatal factors) may determine sexual preference, and "ignoring the power of personality in shaping desire, and the power of fantasy, theorists have failed to perceive that fantasy is not only an aspect of the way desire presents itself, but also that *fantasy can lead to, be the cause of desire*."

But the term "sexual *preference*" may also be a misnomer, cancelled by those whose orientation is "bisexual." What *is* the preference of "bisexuals?" French writer and Nobel laureate André Gide, whose sexual practices caused an uproar in his native country, candidly described his mixed sexual orientation in terms of "tastes," "appetites," and "gluttony" (*Ainsi Soit-Il*).

The question, however, as to why homosexuals feel as dysphoric as they do has remained largely unanswered. Is it because they feel rejected and condemned by others? Or that they sense themselves acting, in a way, contrary to the laws of nature? Whatever the case, the fact remains that even when they lead productive lives and commit themselves to long-lasting relationships, homosexuals feel defensive, because they feel guilty. They also suffer from a variety of psychological and physiological disturbances as well as from hypochondriasis, and their symptoms most commonly involve the genital organs, prostate, anus, and rectum. In a study intended to assess the emotional status of patients with AIDS and AIDS-related syndromes, as compared to homosexuals without AIDS and heterosexuals, J. H. Atkinson et al. (1988) found that 100 percent (*sic*) [100 percent is very rare in biology] of homosexual men, *negative* for HIV antibodies, had a lifetime history of at least one psychiatric disorder, as compared to 59 percent of heterosexuals. The most common diagnoses found in the homosexual group were related to anxiety and depression.

Not only homosexuals experience feelings of guilt, defensiveness, ideas of reference, condemnation, and judgment. Incest, rape, sexual excesses, as well as sex-related exploitations and abuses, all give rise to feelings of guilt and to various dysphoric states associated with paranoia.

Homosexuality and sexual excesses have been known to accompany other manifestations of a decadent society. But social disintegration *per se* would not explain the defensiveness of homosexuals, which persists even when their lifestyle is accepted by society, as it has become in recent years. The homosexuality prevailing in ancient Greece is frequently brought up in debates to justify it. Yet homosexuality was then regarded as a passing stage and acceptable before maturity and marriage. Nowhere in the writings of Plato nor in the speeches of Socrates can one find any support for carnal homosexual love, nor license for the seduction of children, which is frankly condemned. And the question as to why the "solitary sin of masturbation" gives rise to intense feelings of guilt remains unanswered still. Yet, nothing changes the fact. Even in modern overpopulated Communist China—where abstinence is fostered and abortion forced—its citizens are warned against excessive masturbation, which they are told, may cause insomnia, impotence, guilt, and even precipitate a complete "nervous breakdown."

Called sins of "lasciviousness," sexual perversions are considered "abominations" by that half of humanity adhering to the precepts of the Holy Scriptures and the Koran. "Remember the words of Lot to his people: 'Will you persist in these indecent acts which no other nation has committed before you? You lust after men, instead of women. Truly, you are a degenerate people,'" we read in the Koran (*The Heights*: 7:80). The Buddha explicitly condemns every kind of sexual perversion. For the Catholic church, sexual perversions are considered mortal sin.

Although the incidence of homosexuality is believed to keep a constant of four percent across all societies (J. Marmor, *The Harvard Medical School Medical Health Letter*, October 1985), it tends to be low in countries where it is forbidden by law, and high where it is allowed. In countries of the former Communist bloc, it was considered vice and so prosecuted by law. Among people who cleave to Islam, the incidence of homosexuality tends to be low, for it is condemned by their religion and unacceptable to their societies. The same low incidence of homosexuality is observed in those countries that follow the teachings of the Buddha. Whether bypath preferred by people, sin, or vice, this paraphilia does not satisfy the biological need for mating and procreation. Nor does it always have a cause, but, like every sin or crime, such is its nature that it flourishes wherever it can.

As is true for every paraphilia, homosexual encounters fail to provide lasting satisfaction, and, for this reason, homosexuals may engage in various other paraphilias. **Pedophilia,** for example, is more likely among men with a homosexual orientation than among heterosexuals, according to the American Psychiatric Association. Dr. A. Nicholas Groth, director of the sex offender program at Somers, believes there is an epidemic of sexual abuse of children in the United States. But the question arises whether the epidemic of pedophilia parallels the rather steep increase, currently observed, in the number of practicing homosexuals.

Delusional belief may convince the homosexual male to wear women's clothes, and the lesbian female to don men's attire. The tragicomic figure of the paraphiliac practicing **Transvestism** has now become an almost familiar sight. Carried somewhat further, the homosexual may entertain the false belief—a very common delusion—that he is actually a woman encased in a man's body (or for the lesbian, a man in a woman's body). Obsessed with such self-deceptions, some transvestites seek out castration by various means, and some even change their "sex" through surgical procedures. But, more even than the transvestite, the **Transsexual** suffers from intensely tormenting dysphorias: depression (due to a loss of Self), remorse, regret, self-reproach, shame, and guilt—all of which may contribute to the catastrophe of a psychotic breakdown. The chief complaint of these patients usually centers around their loss or lack of identity. Their act of rebellion against the Creator ends with tragedy in most cases; it may lead to suicide, uncommonly frequent in this population.

The majority of homosexuals do not reach such extremes of disturbance, however, yet are beset by various fears, social uneasiness, and a sense of rejection. These dysphorias frequently prevent them from upward mobility in career and otherwise. A vague feeling of judgment and condemnation haunts them all. But who judges them? Who is their prosecutor?

An amorphous society with an ambiguous set of values would certainly not trouble itself to invest much effort to combat homosexuality. Yet there will always be some individuals or groups of people who will seek out the black, the Jew, the homosexual, upon whom they could vent all of their hate and malevolence. But before judging homosexuals, one must remember to first take the beam out of one's own eye; and before casting the first stone, one ought to be sure of one's own sinlessness.

One must also remember that many homosexuals may be victims of circumstances—conditions that exist in prisons, boarding schools, and the armed forces, where they live exclusively in proximity to individuals of their own sex. Here, loving emotions and erotic desire may come to rest upon one near and dear. And because these feelings, admixed with erotic strivings, are based on real love and caring, they cannot be so easily dissolved. The victims of such circumstances may become entrapped. Seduction by a teacher or other figure in authority may also be responsible for sexual orientation in adult life. Whether the homosexual practices of any particular individual are sinful or not, ultimately rests with the Judge of judges to decide. The moral conscience will certainly convey His decree with abundant clarity. If those so addressed would only listen and submit.

From the vantage point of reality, the homosexual lifestyle offers little by way of stability in interpersonal relationships. This paraphilia condemns most homosexuals to suffer loneliness in later years, and deprives them of the comfort and consolation provided by family and progeny. The highest rate of suicide among the general population has been found to involve the older, alcoholic, homosexual male (A. V. Cutter, Preparatory Course for the *American Board of Psychiatry and Neurology,* 1976).

A debt of gratitude is owed to W. Stekel (1929) for his insightful interpretation of sexual perversions pervaded by **Sadism,** or the pleasure derived from the pain of another. In sadistic sexual acts, Stekel always finds cruelty toward those one "loves." Seeking to extract emotions otherwise denied him, the sadist seems to say: "If you will not love me, you must feel me and occupy yourself with me." For the sadist attempts to be supremely unique. Stekel wrote also: "Only love that has been rejected can be so ferocious." Proceeding further in his analysis, Stekel finds that the future sadist has coveted a lustful love in his breast which is nearly impossible to satisfy. Magnified by the powers of imagination and passion of desire, this lustful love may have embraced mother, sister, father, brother. The frustration engendered by the impossible fulfillment of such sexual cravings, causes these dreamers of impossible dreams to become as ferocious as those whose love has been rejected.

Masochism in sexual relationships has been frequently found associated with sadistic tendencies, and, for this reason, it has been linked together with Sadism as **Sado-Masochism,** popularly known as S&M. Such ways of sexual satisfaction are explained by Stekel on the premise that every sexual sadist loves his punishment as a guilty masochist. Similar to what occurs in obsessive-compulsive disorders, in S&M guilt is placated through punishment.

The solitary act of masturbation, considered a health hazard for body and mind even as far back as ancient Egypt, is condemned as sin by the major world religions. This "sin of self abuse," also known as the "primary addiction," is severely condemned in the Judeo-Christian tradition. Eminent psychiatrists Jean-Etienne D. Esquirol (1772–1840) in France and Benjamin Rush (1745–1813) in North America have each described the ill-effects of excessive masturbation which, they warned, endangers psychological well-being. Committed in perfect secrecy, this paraphilia—apparently injurious to no one—still needs to be considered moral transgression, if solely by reason of the guilt it tends to produce. The ill-effects of masturbation can be observed in children still tender in age, as dysphorias of guilt overtake them even before their caretakers have had an opportunity to express their disapproval. Certain moral-spiritual laws are independent of men's decrees, but exist, nonetheless, engraved in the conscience. Psychiatrists have little jurisdiction over these laws and no capacity for their cancellation.

It is of interest to note that the American Psychiatric Association's dilemma, whether to declare homosexuality a "mental disease" or not, was decided by a vote in December 1973. It was not based on clinical observation, nor derived from existing research data. C. W. Socarides et al. (1973), who polled 11 psychiatrists and added their own observations, came to the following conclusion:

> If all discrimination and punitive persecutory measures against homosexuals were stopped—as they should indeed—the inner conflicts, anxieties and frequent depressions of the homosexual would still not be eliminated.

Morbid self-love (narcissism) alone may not explain the dynamics of homosexuality, or for that matter, other paraphilias, such as **Zoophilia** (bestiality) and **Sexually-Excited Murder.**

Existentialists offer a larger view of sexual deviancy than biologically oriented psychiatrists, as they relate sexuality to the individual's ways of being-in-the-world in general. As a man loves, so will he express himself sexually. The more one loves another, different yet complementary to oneself, the less one will need to search for another, more satisfying object to love. The more one loves, the richer and deeper are one's sexual experiences liable to be. The less one loves, the more would one need to search. But the more one searches, the more is one bound to be carried by lusts on the wings of fantasy, away from loving *one*, complementary to oneself. Fantasy is a skillful liar, and in sexual matters, always leads toward the vulgar, sordid, forbidden, bizarre, and impossible. Observe the **Fetishist:** he cannot even love a whole person, only a part, and oftentimes only a garment of that part.

Sins Against Oneself:
Self-defeating Behaviors

A common denominator to all addictions is their capacity to entrap their subjects by way of short-term gratifications. Compulsive spending, as well as hoarding, gambling, overeating, drug abuse, masturbation, and many more, enter into the category of addictions. Not counting the immediate effects on physical and mental health from alcoholism and drugs, for example, the addict is liable to jeopardize his future as well. And, clearly, the easier it is to obtain gratification, the more this behavior will tend to become subject to the repetition compulsion. Empowered by their gratifying capacity, ease of availability, and reinforced by the repetition compulsion, certain transgressions—long known by the designation "vice"—are extremely difficult to eradicate. It is of interest to note that of the seven deadly sins, so declared by the Catholic church, two pertain to the self-indulging practices of gluttony and sloth.

By **Overeating,** the glutton seems to be ready to bargain away his or her physical well-being, attractiveness, as well as the social rewards derived therefrom, just for the sake of some short-lasting tickles on his or her palate and their anticipation. The compulsive overeater, moreover, frequently displaces onto culinary satisfactions some of his heart's desires, away from more precious but less tangible possibilities. Although many reasons stand behind the overeater, alcoholic, and drug abuser, it would seem these addicts are ready to trade off their future, health, family ties—and even moral principles—all for the sake of some elusive "kicks" and "highs" that other people obtain through achievement, duty fulfilled, and love requited.

Compulsive Gambling can be understood in terms of the excitement it creates and also for the illusional-delusional hope for gain it tends to kindle. Existentially, gambling betrays the transcendental strivings of the individual entrapped by this vice, namely, his affinity for "free," unearned money. For the gambler, as a rule, uses not his own, but his parents', family's, or borrowed money, so as to obtain—as his vice dictates—something for nothing. There is also a great deal of magic thinking in compulsive gambling—the gambler believing himself favored by Fortune. Even in the face of considerable losses, he stubbornly maintains the delusion that he is about to make unusual gains. This senseless pursuit of unearned monetary rewards frequently buries him—and often also his relatives family and friends—into such indebtedness that he cannot see another solution but to exit from the stage of life by way of suicide. As if making up for his losses by way of work or other gainful occupation did not exist as a possibility.

The sluggard's indolence and detachment might spare him sweat and toil, and even pain and suffering. He is bound, nevertheless, to live his days in a state of permanent "acedia," with little taste for anything that life can offer. Yet his inactivity holds but a flabby grip on his sanity, as this aimless drifter on the road of life is all too prone to become affected by a schizophrenia of the "simple" variety—**Schizophrenia Simplex,** almost untreatable (p. 271).

Common to all self-indulgent practices is their tendency to engender a sense of failure, frequently leading to chronic depression. According to J. C. Heinroth (1818), vice is so malignant because it is "opposed to reason, whereas passion and madness are merely outside of reason." Vice is nourished by desire, not need, as is characteristic of all moral transgressions. In the teachings of the Buddha, desire is equated with the Hells. But there exists a difference between vice and desire or passion, as Heinroth pointed out: "While the birth of passion is not voluntary, vice originates in the will which has made a free choice against God and which has passed to the opposite side in defiance of the call of conscience . . . ." Heinroth regards "a return to a healthy human condition to be often easy in the case of passion, but always difficult and often impossible in the case of vice."

Both William James (1892) and later Jean Piaget (1962) make a distinction between *will* and *desire*. James regards the power of will to be the *affective force* that, with effort, has the capacity to subordinate "the lower tendency of desire." Piaget also posits will against desire, and maintains that in willing there is a decentering and subordination of the actual value of desire to a higher, larger scale of values (morality). A *willful* individual follows the urges of desire and overcomes all obstacles on the way, but this does not mean that his will is strong. A truly strong-willed individual is capable of the effort that overcomes the lower tendency of desire for the sake of higher goals. Conquering one's desire is tantamount to the conquest of a world. The willfulness with which the alcoholic, gambler, overeater, overspender, etc., secures his desire is by *will*, but it is a *weak* will. James (1892) wrote thus on will:

> Our strength and our intelligence, our wealth and even our good luck, are things which warm our heart and make us feel a match for life. But deeper than all such things and able to suffice unto itself without them, is the sense of the amount of effort we can put forth. But the effort seems to belong to an altogether different realm, as if it were a *substantive* thing which we are and those were externals which we *carry*. If the "searching of our heart and reins" be the purpose of this human drama, then, what is sought seems to be the effort we can make. He who can make none is a shadow; he who can make much is a hero.

How many shadows among this, our self-indulgent Me generation, and how many heroes?

A characteristic of the **Inadequate Personality**—now deleted from the newest disease classifications—is its weakness of will. In this category we find alcoholics, overeaters, sluggards, beggars, and also individuals engaged in a great variety of vice and self-indulgent activity, or inactivity.

More accessible even than drink or drug, and more enticing, the lies of fantasy have long been recognized as dangerously psychotogenic. Such activities require neither expenditure of energy nor respect for moral constraints. But what seems so risky in the enterprise are the contents of the fantasies these dreamers conjure up, not the act of imagination *per se*. Not unlike Dostoyevsky's underground man, *(Notes from the Underground),* the young adults who are brought to experience a **Hebephrenic Schizophrenia** have entertained fantasies: delusions of omnipotence, desire for revenge, intentions to harm others, and various lusts tending toward the forbidden, some already acted out. Divesting themselves of all responsibility as well as moral constraints, these preys of illusion eventually become transformed into shadows, many swallowed up in the underworlds of a psychosis, from which but a few are fortunate to return.

Hard Data

The failure of modern psychiatry to discern the etiology of the majority of psychiatric disorders may be attributed to its vain attempts to neatly classify them, as well as to its unrealistic expectations to reach scientific validation and reliable diagnostic criteria. Unfortunately, these futile endeavors have given cause to more unnecessary squabbles and drained more precious resources than any other subject on the agenda of the psychiatric community. For an individual's psychopathology to be understood, what needs to be first recognized is his uniqueness and highly complex world. Whether in health or in disease, this world can never be reduced to the size of a code symbol, demanded by a computer for statistical analysis. What is an important life event for one individual, is not for another. And for obvious reasons, thought processes and feeling states will elude attempts at measurement and will fail to provide such data that allow for scientific validation. The "inner domain of the emotions" is not only very private and very personal, but relative to the experiencer as well. Only by empathic understanding can subjective experience be bridged and understood. The phenomenological method concerns itself, precisely, with the study of subjective experiences, which the phenomenologist attempts to understand and to interpret as well.

The study of moral transgression needs to begin with the transgressing individual, his world and ways of being-in-the-world. Exploration needs to include the individual's heredity, childhood, tradition, culture, and various other circumstances and life events, from which the exercise of his free will and choices are never to be excluded. An in-depth probe of transcendental strivings offers more insights even than the patient's historical past. Although sin is relative to the sinner, certain moral transgressions weigh heavier on the conscience than do others. Some sins—namely murder and suicide—are considered absolutely absolute by all of humankind.

In his lectures on clinical psychiatry nearly a century ago, Emil Kraepelin (1904) described the antecedents of dementia praecox as he observed them in his patients. Mostly young adults, these patients presented with the chief complaint of culpability, sin, and guilt. Not much has changed since that time, it seems, for the same laments are heard today, in spite of the fact that the notion of sin is no longer relevant to secular modern societies in general and to the psychiatric community in particular. Yet one must listen and reflect on this, the chief complaint of depressed, anxious, character-disordered, and schizophrenic patients. It may be valid. A list of opinions gathered from schizophrenic patients concerning the reasons they perceive as leading to their breakdown is here presented.

Self-assessed reasons for the outbreak of psychosis:

1. Sin. Sin caused guilt. Guilt separated me from God and other people. I became deceitful.
2. Not obeying your conscience leads you to the "other world."
3. I decided to break all the rules, commit every sin, so I could win Satan's favor and become an actor.
4. Sin. One pays for every sin. I got a girl pregnant, I was defiant, I was promiscuous. Guilt caused my suicidal attempt.
5. When you sin against God—you are persecuted!
6. Second voluntary abortion. This set it all up.
7. Beating up my son and murderous impulses.
8. It happened because I acted against my conscience, all other things are tributaries to this.
9. The reason for my illness: hate, duplicity, homosexual practices.
10. I went on an Ego trip. I thought I was as powerful as God.
11. The reason for my sickness is that I have been beating my innocent children.
12. I am guilty!
13. My problem is guilt. I knew he will be murdered.
14. Definitely related to my guilt.
15. Because I was evil, I thought only of myself. Stopped recognizing right from wrong.
16. I do not need a doctor. I need a priest.
17. My breakdown followed a bribing operation.
18. I starved in order to redeem myself from sin.
19. Nobody did anything to me. I myself did it. I am guilty and ashamed.
20. The center of the problem is guilt.
21. It all started one morning when my parents went to church and I did not.
22. Since I raped five women, I started hearing voices, which are guilt.
23. Guilt.
24. Hate. I will improve only if I could become a good person.
25. I became sick since I changed my religion.
26. First it was my guilt. Then I was told I messed up my whole life. Lost my faith. Took things into my own hands.
27. Guilt feelings are destroying me.
28. My guilt can fill this whole room.
29. I wanted money the easy way. The conscience has to be exposed.

30. My problem is spiritual. This is why I am here.
31. First guilt, then depression, then I began to feel persecuted.
32. You cannot escape your conscience. When you lie you become TWO!

A carefully recorded history of 144 schizophrenic patients, examined during their first breakdown (N = 100) and at the time of an acute exacerbation (N = 44), revealed *a crucial moral violation to have preceded their psychosis*, being its precipitating event (M. Niv 1980). Engendering inordinately intense feelings of guilt and responsible for an "explosion of conscience," the crucial moral violation/s became eventually a part of the "schizophrenic complex," thenceforth to assume sovereignty over these patients' mental processes, during and after the psychosis.

Although the sample of this study may not be sufficiently representative of the schizophrenic patient population, it allows, nonetheless, for the extrapolation of certain evident trends. The moral violations that preceded the psychotic decompensation of these 144 patients are classified in Table # 1. Given are some hard facts as real acts, not fantasies, feeling states, or mere intentions. The moral violations listed exceed the number of patients, and much remains unknown. What the list actually reflects are those moral violations that were experienced as most disturbing and which haunted these patients with nightmares, delusions and hallucinations. Adultery, for example, probably committed with equal frequency by men and women, seemed to weigh more heavily on the consciences of women. Child abandonment, much more frequently committed by men, appeared to leave them without significant emotional scars, whereas for women, the deliberate abandonment of their children was experienced as an *unforgettable* and *unforgivable* transgression. Approximately one-half of the patients studied reported transgressions in the sexual realm: excesses, with or without perversions. The inordinately high percentage of murder (4.16 percent) and assault causing injury (23.6 percent), could be understood on the basis of these patients' hostility and malevolence, characteristic of the schizophrenic premorbid personality. The violations classified as "miscellaneous" included wife-beating, abandonment of elderly parents, defraudation, and parasitism among others. For women, sexual excesses appeared to be more psychotogenic, whereas for men sexual perversions gave rise to inordinately high levels of guilty dysphorias. There is much thought-provoking material in this list of moral transgressions. Which ones are more serious? And which more likely to lead to psychosis? From the study of these patients, more of an *indication* regarding the nature of the psychotogenic stressor than a quantitative estimation of its magnitude can be derived. What can be gleaned from the life-histories and subjective experiences of the insane, nonetheless, is that sin belongs to the category of the individual, and that the courts of conscience take into account all of the circumstances involved: attenuating, aggravating, incriminating. The individual's heredity, conditions of upbringing, childhood, past experiences, true inner motivations, deliberateness, and of course, the quality and quantity of his loving, all seem to enter into the judgments of his conscience.

A brief consideration of **Suicide** may best conclude this chapter on moral transgression. According to the *National Center for Health Statistics,* August, 1993 the crude rate for suicide (all ages), was 12.4 per 100,000 population. In *Suicide Facts,* (*National Institute of Mental Health*, March 1993), we read: "Almost all people who kill themselves have a mental or substance abuse disorder; suicide is not a normal response to the stresses experienced by most people." Yet, this tragic self-induced ending is always consistent with the personality of the individual and the life he has led. Among those who murder, approximately one third (30 percent) eventually kill themselves (p. 250). As if the law of talion were here operative, decreeing "a life for a life"—executed by those who refuse to plead for mercy.

Whereas the association of depression with suicide, and the high rate of suicide among alcoholics, psychopaths, schizophrenic and borderline persons can be explained without much difficulty, the association of sexual deviations and suicide, being less clear, would need to be further explored—unless sexual deviations are regarded not as "preference," but as mental disorder.

William A. O'Connor (1948), who studied the past histories of 50 patients who committed suicide, came to the conclusion that suicide obtains its motivating force from the Superego, the conscience. He found the sexual life of the future suicide to have been (in more than 90 percent of the cases) "unsatisfactory to a marked degree, either in the direction of the heterosexual urge, or the strength of the homosexual urge, or both."

Suicide stamps the ultimate defeat of those who refuse to submit to the spiritual-moral laws as conveyed to them by their conscience. Whereas some are brought to despair with regard to their salvation, others are unwilling to accept it. Yet, repentance is an available option for everyone, and reform but a step away from such a decision. Nevertheless, pride may stand in the way and preclude them both.

A climate of brooding and isolation tends to enhance existing depression, anger, revengeful feelings, bitterness, and hate. Fortified by the powers of fantasy, sadistic, malevolent, and suicidal intentions may suddenly burst into action. Some intentions may, eventually,

Table # 1

Nature of the Moral Violation Preceding the Psychosis

n=144	Females	Males	Jailed*	Corroborated by family
Murder	1	5	4	2
Assault causing injury	2	18	7	2
Assault with intention to kill	6	8		8
Child abandonment	7			3
Adultery	7		1	3
Child abuse/neglect	11		1	2
Incest	8	1		1
Theft	3	8		3
Robbery	1	16	9	1
Repeated abortions	6			
Rape			3	3
Causing pregnancy and abortions		2		2
Sexual deviations	5	19		7
Sexual excesses	25	7		5
Fire setting	2	1		
Embezzlement of money		6	1	
Miscellaneous	7	17	1	4

* jailed for the specific violation mentioned

become irresistible compulsions. It is for this reason that all religions condemn already existing attitudes before they become acted out, for during states of isolation, clouded consciousness such as sleep, alcohol intoxication, influence of drugs, and psychotic confusion—states in which the powers of reason and control become eclipsed—the entertained forbidden intention might become translated into action.

*   *   *

The histories given by the 144 patients studied by this author and their estimation of the causes of their mental illness deserve to be further explored. Transgression of the moral code may, indeed, lead to the development of a psychiatric disorder, a "mental illness." Deductions derived from the patients' opinions as well as from observations of their manifest behaviors, signs, and symptoms of disease, may well serve to consolidate the theory this work has set to prove. It goes without saying, however, that this may be an imperfect method for the establishment of a theory. Yet this theory already has a history as old as mankind. It is validated by a host of research data, even from such divergent sources as polygraph investigations, genetics, neuroanatomy, and psychopharmacology. This "old-new" theory certainly deserves to be further explored and allowed to pass the test of validity. It might prove true after all, and even provide a key for decoding the mysteries of insanity. Some of the disorders, classified in the DSM-III-R as "diseases of unknown etiology," would then cease to be so regarded.

Chapter VII

The Psychoses:
Underworlds of Madness

En el pecado es el castigo. In sin is the punishment.
— Spanish proverb

The anxiety of the heathen is his punishment—nothing punishes as self-torment.
— Sören Kierkegaard

Subjectively experienced and objectively regarded, a schizophrenic breakdown represents a momentous catastrophe for all concerned. For the subject of a schizophrenic fall, the world will never be the same. Gone forever is some freshness of experience, lost some spontaneity in self-expression. Although a sense of "weller than well" may follow the recovery from a schizophrenic psychosis, such occurrences, unfortunately, are an exception rather than the rule. Only between 22 percent to 33 percent of those patients who recover from a single schizophrenic episode will enjoy a permanent cure. About 33 percent will suffer chronicity punctuated by exacerbations. Approximately 33 percent will remain ill, and of these 6 percent will deteriorate into a state of dementia, some prematurely—i.e., "dementia praecox" (L. C. Kolb 1973).

Coined by psychologist O. Hobart Mowrer (1974), the term "explosion of conscience" cogently describes the psychotic cataclysm, its etiology as well as its shattering consequences. Drawing from clinical observation and to some extent from personal experience, Mowrer came to the conclusion that the precipitating event leading to psychosis is a voluntarily committed crucial moral violation, unacceptable to the Self, and which engenders feelings of guilt, as well as a sense of persecution, judgment, and condemnation. The "guilty" verdict pronounced by the courts of conscience gives rise to feelings of unbearable and overwhelming dread, in addition—to permeate thenceforth the total life experience of the schizophrenic patient. A fear of something unknown, inexplicable, and recognized as irrational, produces a state of terror, or "trema"—as the soul begins to flutter before the danger of extinction. This awful possibility is revealed through the invasion of the patient's consciousness by spiritually significant symbols, which will henceforth dominate his mental processes. The psychotic thus loosens his grip on reality, but this is only a secondary phenomenon.

*   *   *

Before undertaking an analysis of the various aspects of insanity, a review of the currently prevailing theories, set against a background of past perceptions, will best serve to enhance their understanding.

According to Freud's analytical formulations (1924), psychoses result from various "frustrations," "thwarted wishes," repressions, and externally determined calamities, which lead to withdrawal from the world of reality and into an allegedly more satisfying world of fantasy. Presumably, this withdrawal from the world and its "objects" (meaning one's fellow men) represents a regression to earlier (infantile) narcissistic levels of development. A return to "archaic," more primitive, "primary process" ways of cognition, such as are characteristic of preverbal children, allegedly takes place as well. Yet evidence and logic fail to support Freud's hypotheses. While painful experiences, frustrations, and repressed desire may be endured with difficulty, and give cause to suffering and mental anguish, it is doubtful whether such experiences would lead their subjects into darker lands, inhabited by spiders, snakes, vultures, ghosts, and devils such as are characteristic of psychotic states. Would the weary of external reality conjure up fantasies more dreadful than their own predicament? Would not the refugees from painful realities attempt to reach more blissful shores instead?

With respect to physical illnesses, although they frequently allow for certain regressions in Ego-functioning to occur, these regressions by no means resemble the manifestations observed in psychosis. Moreover, physical illnesses may actually reverse the course of psychotic illnesses, as is elsewhere emphasized (p. 400), and, in some cases, even lead to recovery. Of frustrations and externally determined traumata, what painful realities can compare with the conditions of starvation, humiliation, and constant threats of a violent death, as were endured by the inmates of the Nazi extermination camps? Yet the victims of what can be considered ultimate conditions of "stress" did not flee into a world of fantasy, nor did they regress to infantile levels of functioning. Surprisingly, years later, even after 20 years, some Holocaust survivors fared better than matched "controls" in being less sensitive to stress (H. Dasberg 1987). And although others were found more vulnerable to stress and somewhat more prone to physical illnesses, they certainly did not become insane. Neither during their terrible ordeal nor afterward did they lose their reason (p. 120) on a retrospective study of Norwegian concentration camps inmates).

Regressions to earlier phases of development will fail to explain the cognitive aberrations, and especially illogical thinking, so frequently encountered in psychotic illnesses. Children think in a logical manner, stressed S. Arieti (1974). Moreover, whereas preverbal children may well be thinking by way of images, there is little evidence to suggest their visions contain the horrors that pervade the perceptions and misperceptions characteristic of the psychotic. Freud's account of the psychoses leaves out most of their manifestations, as it also fails to provide a cogent explanation of the causes and dynamic forces operative in these disorders. Frustrations and painful external realities of whatever nature would not lead their subjects to conjure up more dread-filled fantasies than the painful realities they attempt to escape.

Never advancing beyond the model of the neuroses—disorders predicated on a conflict between a forbidden wish or desire and the reality-oriented Ego-reason—Freud failed to make the all important distinction between fantasized wish, lust, or desire and its enactment in reality. This failure to distinguish between fantasy and reality has given cause to much debate and bitter controversy. To a great extent, the case of Freud's patient Anna O.—a disturbed young lady, whose father presumably was trying to seduce—is still alive today, because it now appears that the seduction actually did take place; Anna did not just imagine it. Failing also to perceive the enormous difference in degree between the anxieties that assail the neurotic and the dread that follows the enactment of a morally forbidden wish, Freud could not appreciate the enormous gap which separates neurotic illnesses from the psychoses. Focusing principally on the collapse of the Ego and its defensive armor, he failed to give heed to those forces responsible for its collapse. And for his refusal to acknowledge sin as a psychological reality and guilt as its logical consequence, Freud failed to appreciate their potency in detracting from the Ego's capacity to mediate and reason. Disposing of the florid symptoms of psychotic illnesses as nothing more than "primary process" phenomena, Freud dispensed with the need to search out their meaning. He failed to recognize the spiritual nature of psychotic experiences and to perceive their antecedents, namely transgressions of the moral-spiritual law. Had Freud dared to face and also to analyze the components of anyone's particular Id-forces, he might have solved to a large extent the etiological problems surrounding the psychoses.

Harry Stack Sullivan (1962) went further than Freud in his ability to perceive that breaches in interpersonal relationships can become precipitants to psychotic illnesses. Attributing the "disorganizing terrors," "perceptions of danger," and "need to escape" to a sudden injury to self-esteem, Sullivan failed, however, to give heed to the fact that the majority of psychotogenic events actually contain some "interpersonal crime," the perpetrator of which is none other than the patient himself. He gave no account of those events that suddenly cause injury to self-esteem, or how they bring about a plunge into the depths.

According to Silvano Arieti (1974), schizophrenia results from the "externalization of an inner reality, the purpose of which is to relieve guilt." Like Sullivan, Arieti acknowledged that a sudden loss of self-esteem and feelings of worthlessness play a role in the inner "drama" of psychosis, but failed to account for the reasons the patient finds himself suddenly in Hell. There is no mention in Arieti's writings of sin as a breach of the patient's moral code. Tracing guilt to its source would have explained why the patient suddenly feels so guilty, and why this guilt is experienced as dangerous. Arieti tended to interpret most of the symbolic representations that appear in psychosis as by-products of the disorder. Like Freud, he regarded the invasion of consciousness by spiritually meaningful symbols as regression to "paleological" ways of thinking. He thus lumped spiritual experiences into a single common category and dispensed with the need for their interpretation. Arieti did not search out the meaning of delusions and hallucinations and failed to appreciate the benefits to be derived from incorporating these experiences into the process of psychotherapy. Refusing to acknowledge the central role of the conscience in the life of the "psyche," he also failed to recognize the reasons for the emergence of feelings of guilt, and their role in psychiatric disturbances in general. Arieti did not associate feelings of guilt with low self-esteem. He perceived, nonetheless, that disturbances of thinking and defects in logic, such as become manifest in certain cases of schizophrenia, serve as defensive operations. In his therapeutic approaches he sought to bring the patient "to accept responsibility" for his actions. Arieti was fully aware of the basic and pervasive hostilities that mark all schizophrenias—representing their most universal and outstanding characteristic .

Both Sullivan and Arieti refused to recognize the validity of guilt as an authentic, spontaneous consequence of the commission of transgression. Neither could accept the fact that conscience is sensitive to laws other than those decreed by men. Arieti, for example, believed that in a predominantly homosexual society, the psychological repercussions engendered by this practice would cease to exist. Yet, even the relaxed moral attitudes and permissiveness of Western societies have not influenced the *subjective experience of guilt,* nor the sense of persecution and condemnation, that torment every homosexual. The laws of conscience do not necessarily follow those of men. Although keenly perceiving the psychotogenic effects of homosexual activities, Arieti did not entertain the possibility that such practices engender guilt because they are sinful, and could not therefore account for the cleavage of the personality and self-alienation that homosexuality induces. As for the spiritual turmoil and religious preoccupations so central to psychotic illnesses—the *Leitmotif* of these patients' laments—we hear from Sullivan and Arieti nothing but a loud silence.

For Carl Gustav Jung (1907), schizophrenia remained a psychological disease to be cured by psychological means. He accepted, nevertheless, the possibility that a specific affect, acting like a toxin, complicates the course of schizophrenia in its later stages, and introduced the concept of "affect-toxin." Jung was first to describe the "schizophrenic complex"—meaning by "complex," an affect-laden set of ideas. He perceived that a pathogenic complex(es) becomes the focal point around which most of the manifestations of schizophrenia eventually crystallize. He also wrote: "I have never met with a case of schizophrenia, that did not show a logical and consistent development" (1957). Jung insisted that uncovering the secret of the complex becomes the "rock upon which successful psychotherapy" can be built. In the face of this serious mental illness, Jung maintained an optimistic stance, nonetheless, and insisted that schizophrenia is curable by psychological means.

Following the trails of thought left by psychoanalytic doctrine, most Ego-psychologists understand the etiology of schizophrenia, as well as most of its manifestations, in terms of failures of the mature Ego to "cope" with outside "pressures" and externally determined painful realities. Thus, Ego-psychologists maintain that it is the breakdown of the Ego's defenses that allows for "the loss of control" characteristic of psychotic illnesses. For K. Menninger (1963), sin represented a symptom of disease, and not its cause: "Murder is frequently committed, according to our theory, to preserve sanity," he wrote. Menninger also believed that "murder and suicide may serve as defense against psychosis."

For Ego-psychologists and other psychoanalytically derived theories, of major import in assessment of the personality are its defensive operations, reality-orientation, judgment, and reasoning—all part and parcel of the functions of the Ego-mind. These theories fail to recognize, nevertheless, the role of the Superego in mental illness, and also the different motivations of any one's specific Id. Envy, covetousness, lust, destructive urges, or homicidal intent may thus exert undue "pressure" and become eventually enacted in reality. Neither psychoanalysis nor its derivative psychologies have ever attempted to incorporate into their treatment strategies an analysis of the patient's very personal Id—obviously avoiding the issue altogether. Modern psychologies, for that matter, have lumped into the "unconscious Id" all that is evil in human nature. Yet their theorists are well aware that making the "unconscious" conscious does not necessarily erase evil intent. Thus, hateful obsessions—solidly entrenched in awareness—might, in spite of being conscious, grow strong and dictate some "irresistible" action. When the patient is prompted by his hallucinations to murder, for example, he does not kill in order to preserve his sanity, but in order to gratify a powerful preexisting lust, or urge, or desire-become-obsession.

The position held by Ego-psychologists with regard to psychotic behavior is justified in certain conditions, nonetheless. During altered states of consciousness, wherein the Ego-mind-reason-control relaxes its grip, certain acts are often committed that normal alertness would not allow. During sodium amytal (truth serum) narcosis, for example, the patient is inclined to divulge the truth, which he would not do otherwise. In natural sleep, when dreams, internal visions, and experiences become intensified, and perceived as more real than reality itself, the sleeper will be more inclined to engage in activities that he would not dare to undertake during states of wakefulness.

Similarly, one may commit the most heinous crime while under the influence of alcohol, PCP, cocaine, or "crack," for example.

Somnambulism defines behaviors enacted during sleep, usually NREM (no rapid eye movement) cycles, or stages three and four. These acts or activities are very meaningful, nonetheless, for they betray the dreamer's inner motivations. The following cases have come to the attention of this author: one somnambulist was found on the roof, attempting to run away from a disturbed family; another was trying to open a window, intending suicide; another took a knife to slay her lesbian lover. A case of filicide during somnambulism is reported by D. J. Luchins et al. (1978). But the somnambulist can enact only that which he has long pondered, inwardly wished, and intended—and nothing more. During alcohol and drug intoxication, we say what we mean; become who we really are; and our wishes come to surface—"*in vino veritas.*" Similarly, during other "twilight" states of altered consciousness, wherein the Ego slackens its controlling operations, the truth comes forth and intention may become action.

In states of **Pathological Intoxication,** intention bursts out into action. The intoxicated individual may thus engage in wife-beating, child abuse, sexual aggression, or arson, among others. Nevertheless, even during states of altered consciousness, the subject cannot act in any way contrary to his inner wishes and intentions, but in the direction of their gratification. It would be erroneous, thus, to blame a weakened Ego for those sins and crimes committed during somnambulism, alcohol intoxication, and other such conditions—for no one can act against his wishes and intentions. This fact finds confirmation in experiments with hypnotic suggestion: when the suggested act runs against the wishes and moral code of the hypnotized subject, it may jolt him into an abrupt awakening. The mere suggestion of transgression has the power to cancel a hypnotic trance and to bring about a sudden awakening in a reluctant subject. These experiments suggest that while the Ego-mind-reason may be relaxing its powers of control during sleep, sodium amytal narcosis, and alcoholic intoxication— allowing the true wish or intention to surface in word or action—the conscience never slumbers or sleeps. The conscience might, however, become unresponsive and even deadened, as will be shown further.

With regard to the role of the Ego in psychoses, Jung maintained that the dynamism of these states has less to do with a weakening of the powers of the Ego-mind than with increases in the forces governing the unconscious Id (p. 168). But the Ego may conspire with the Id by supplying the necessary realities in the service of the commission of a sin or crime. The Ego may also provide various justifications afterward. Mobilized in the service of the Id, the Ego-mind has even the capacity to eliminate the "forbiddenness" of certain wishes or desires through the espousal of a hedonistic Weltan-schauung. Such an Ego is weak, however, and may lose its powers of control. Every complex of sin and guilt detracts from its functional capacity. But every complex of sin and guilt detracts from the integrity of the Superego also, as it tends to erode the Self. Moreover, since *every sin that remains unrepented tends to be repeated under compulsion*, it is easy to understand how the forces of the soul become unbalanced in favor of the furthering of transgression. Senseless sins and crimes may be committed by reason of this imbalance. A rapist-murderer convinced himself to murder his third victim with the argument that he had already murdered two women: "I was thinking, I have killed two, I might *as well* kill this one, too . . . [emphasis added]" (R. K. Ressler et al. 1983). His reasoning was determined not by logic, but by the repetition compulsion.

For those who with William James believe in the "living substance of the soul," it is not difficult to understand how the soul can become sick through the accumulation of moral transgressions. Just before the dawn of psychoanalysis, J. C. Heinroth (1818) wrote as follows:

> . . . No matter how sharp the distinction made by a subtle
> psychology between vice and sin in general, the true substance
> of all soul disturbances is Evil.

The etiology of madness is sin, wrote Heinroth further, reiterating a theory of insanity as old as humanity itself. It has persisted until our times—standing strong even after the zeal for scientific proof has swept it over with a flood of research data, seeking to drown its veracity.

With the currently prevailing ambiguous attitudes toward evil and immorality in general, the notion of sin may have lost its concrete-ness, yet its impact remains unchanged. Conveniently, whatever evil may be thought, intended, or committed is now considered but "reactive" to another evil, or else attributed to "sickness," in need of treatment by various "talking-out" or "down" techniques, or else managed with medicines. And the most important commandment issued by modern psychotherapists: "Love thyself first"—a prescrip-tion for selfishness, the root of all evil—only serves to potentiate every sin and crime and to corrupt the personality. When the successful "adaptation" of an individual—so highly valued by Ego-psychologists—is obtained at the expense, or even harm of another or others, it defines the essence of immorality.

Before Existentialists came to be united in a common philosophy, Heinroth wrote:

> Life not in the self, but for the self turns into sin, that is to a state where nature and destiny are opposed, and growth of the highest human being is hampered and disease results. Soul disturbances are due to selfishness.

Existentialists join Heinroth in identifying evil and sin as the substance by which every mental illness is leavened. They also insist on the need for self-detachment, since life for the self not only fails to bring forth inner peace and contentment, but very often such an existence leads to "ugly," vacuous depressions, hypochondriacal preoccupations, and an oppressive sense of failure later in life—if not to outright mental illness.

For lack of substantial scientific data to justify any one of the existing theories of mental disease and insanity in particular, psychiatry has remained entrenched in several theoretical positions—each one offering but a partial view of the larger problem. Two main streams of thought have come to prevail over others, but, unfortunately, they run in opposite directions. One stream of thought holds "chemical aberrations" of unknown origin to be responsible for the occurrence of mental illnesses; while the other—dominated by psychoanalytic theories—projects upon an unknown past (of early childhood) all sources of psychopathology, and explains the apparent mysteries of the insanities on the basis of a nebulous "unconscious." There is obviously little or no dialogue between these two prevailing currents of modern psychiatry.

Yet in spite of a wide array of theories as well as therapeutic approaches, the concerted efforts of modern psychiatry are directed toward combating the secondary manifestations of mental illnesses, namely their symptoms: anxiety, depression, dread, confusion, phobias, among many others, instead of targeting their primary causes. Nothing, however, prevents psychiatrists from attempting to eradicate the seeds of hatefulness, jealousy, envy, greed, and lusts of various kinds, among the "irrational" evil intentions of their patients' unconscious Id. In his *Disorders of the Instincts and the Emotions*, W. Stekel (1929) gave a clue as to where the seeds of evil can be found: in the pursuit of forbidden and impossible goals. One of his patients spent a lifetime wishing the death of his father; another became obsessed with sexual desire for his sister; another would have only his mother. One of this author's patients lost the woman he really loved, because he insisted on elopement rather than a conventional marriage ceremony. Greed that always seeks more; envy that has no remedy; revenge that never gives satisfaction; lust for the forbidden; thirst for power that is never quenched; these transcendental motivations—both evil and irrational—instead of yielding the fruits of satisfaction, grow into weeds of destruction. Would it not be more profitable to uproot the patient's stifling evil motivations, rather than analyze his "defensive style," as the doctrine of psychoanalysis dictates?

*   *   *

A debt of gratitude is owed to past president of the American Psychological Association, O. Hobart Mowrer, for his courage in daring to shake the dust off forgotten volumes of human wisdom and knowledge, and for implicating sin as the causative factor of the majority of mental illnesses. For Mowrer (1961, 1974), psychosis represented an "explosion of conscience" consequent to a serious moral violation(s). The conceptualization of psychosis as an "explosion of conscience" poignantly defines and describes the disorganization, terror, confusion, and spiritual experiences that erupt from the depths of the Self—wellspring of emotion and center of being. The subjects of psychosis understand the cataclysmic events that follow the verdict of "guilty," pronounced in the courts of their consciences, as being their punishment. But this punishment, they frequently lament, is far more terrible than any retributive reality could possibly inflict. The awesome verdict immediately plunges self-esteem to lower depths. It is the function of the psychosis, to "make" or to "break" those afflicted, according to Anton Boisen (1936). Unsparing of himself, Boisen, who later became the founder of the Pastoral Counseling Movement, described psychosis as he had once experienced it. A sense of danger, guilt, and fear progressively become generalized along a gradient, and produce effects similar to those of a "toxin." A terrifying fear of annihilation—"annihilation anxiety"— invades consciousness as the soul senses a threat to its very existence.

Precipitating Events

The search for specific events that could cause insanity has yielded but scanty returns up to this date. As has been mentioned before, external disasters have not been found to engender psychotic illnesses. Commenting on the effects of World War I and other catastrophes, K. Jaspers (1963) stressed that such events *per se* were hardly ever found to precipitate a psychosis. External calamities and physical illnesses were actually found beneficial and responsible for improvement of mental illnesses, even for recovery in certain cases (pp. 210, 400). It is worthy of note that the **Malignant Post-Vietnam Stress Syndrome** became converted into a psychotic nightmare only for those Vietnam combatants who had "had extensive exposure to and in the killing and dying of other people"—a *sine qua non* for the malignant development of the syndrome (R. Rosenheck 1985). Many had killed enemy civilians, women, and children—not by order but by choice—and had at times even enjoyed the experience of brutality and sadism "of a kind most people shudder to imagine." They perceived themselves, rightfully, as "animals," "vermin," and either sought incarceration, injured themselves, or courted suicide as a release from their "relentless pangs of conscience and indelible awareness of shame and guilt."

Symptoms of withdrawal, paranoia, and violent outbursts are most common among these veterans. One man described a dream that presented itself almost every night, in which he saw himself confronted with the leering, screaming heads of the children he had killed. Relentlessly, past memories invade the life-experiences of these combatants "with no respite for long periods of time," just as murder memories haunt and taunt every other killer. Upon examination of these combatants, what was missing from a complete picture of a "classic" schizophrenia was the absence of a thought disorder. But the lack of this sign is easy to understand: witnessed by others, the past misdeeds of these unfortunates needed no cover-up, and could be justified as "atrocities of war."

Not every schizophrenia can so directly be traced back to clear-cut precipitants as the Malignant Post-Vietnam Stress Syndrome, however, and not every case shows antecedents so drastic. Nevertheless, every case of insanity, when thoroughly investigated, reveals more than a single determining factor. The premorbid personality most clearly shapes the psychosis and becomes responsible for its outcome—a finding repeatedly emphasized by both L. Ciompi (1980) and M. Bleuler (1968). The structure of the premorbid personality may have been determined by certain negative traits and attitudes that became converted into morally forbidden actions. A hate-obsessed individual, for example, if not daring to enact his sadistic fantasies or homicidal intentions, will, by reason of his inner malevolence, engage in some act of this kind—which may eventually bring about a catatonic episode or a progressively disabling condition, indistinguishable from other chronic schizophrenias. Both Stekel and Freud were struck by the cowardice of schizophrenics to act out their morbid fantasies. Yet cowardice dos not sufficiently protect these individuals from committing little acts of malevolence, and does not always deter them from acting on their homicidal intentions. A passively lusting individual, cowardly evading courtship and the minor stresses of the "loving game"—which may require some humiliation at certain moments and the pain of rejection at others—may resort to obsessive masturbation, pervaded by sadistic fantasies. This may lead him to experience a psychotic decompensation, nonetheless, whose manifestations are liable to include fears of damage to the genitals, dread of punishment, and a sexual arousal more intense than at the outset of the masturbatory activity. The rebellious young adult, who during adolescence decides to disregard the demands of his conscience, who frees himself from moral constraints, and flouts the laws imposed on him by family and society, may be bound for a no-man's land filled with uncanny, threatening wonders such as inhabit the psychotic world of the hebephrenic schizophrenic. The individual engaged in antisocial activities, drug and alcohol abuse, crime, or acts of violence, may join the ranks of paranoid schizophrenics—if he does not experience a Ganser syndrome, incarceration psychosis, or similar psychiatric disturbance before. Autistic, narcissistic, and borderline persons—involved as they are in a variety of interpersonal offenses, abuses, manipulations, and exploitations—frequently find themselves close to the borders of sanity, which they may cross for various lengths of time.

While hereditary loading, parental attitudes, and emotional atmosphere during the child's critical years of development are all brought to bear upon the final mold of the personality of the future schizophrenic, factors of transcendence and intentionality retain, nonetheless, their central position. As shown by Structuralists as well as Existentialists, every individual constructs his life experiences around a vector of intentionality.

As for schizophrenia, if there were but one common characteristic that could identify the premorbid personality of the future schizophrenic early in life, it would be his lack in loving capacity. Little or no love emanates from his being. With this crucial deficiency—whether inherited or acquired—the inner attitudes of the preschizophrenic, dominated as they are by lusts instead of loves, bring to fruition but sour grapes of wrath, disappointment, bitterness, jealousy, and hate. The lovelessness of the preschizophrenic, obviously, contributes to his isolation and brooding, and creates an inner void that may become filled with alcohol, drugs, and masturbation. His loneliness, moreover, only augments his envy for the loving relationships others enjoy, and accentuates the pain of his sad predicament. The lovelessness of the preschizophrenic individual has long been recognized as a major pathogenic factor of his illness.

The spark that finally ignites the inflammable substratum of the future schizophrenic's emotional state may, however, be a trivial external event, seemingly unrelated to the life-situation of the future patient. The dynamite of schizophrenia may be conceptualized as an aggregate of preexisting attitudes which have led to sinful actions. When a critical level of accumulated sin-guilt complexes is attained, an "explosion of conscience" is liable to erupt. External events may function solely as catalysts to the psychotic conflagration—they may not be directly related to its causation.

> A 33-year-old bank clerk who had embezzled monies during the course of his employment, without his guilt lending itself to legal proof, was finally dismissed. With the monies improperly acquired, the clerk moved to another state and bought himself a condominium. Two years later, while watching a television show where he saw the gas-chamber execution of a criminal, struck with fear, he fell on the floor, and eventually developed a full-blown psychosis with delusional experiences of darkness, auditory hallucinations, somatic delusions, and a severe residual paranoid state. (From author's caseload)

The embezzlement, which produced a smoldering inner state of uneasiness, pervaded by fear and guilt, suddenly became ignited by the criminal's execution presented on a television screen. Having identified himself with the condemned, the clerk expected a similar fate in store for himself. It is worthy of note that, at the time his psychosis erupted, no externally determined real threats existed for the patient.

Benign and even "happy" occurrences may, paradoxically, become precipitants and usher a psychosis or its exacerbation:

> In this case, the happy event was the graduation from college of twin brothers, sons of a separated, middle-aged black woman. Raised by aunts from a tender age, these young men had achieved a great victory over their fate. The graduation

brought back to their mother's awareness the memory of abandoning them many years earlier. Guilt, remorse and lonely despair were suddenly reactivated in this chronic schizophrenic patient, and caused an "exacerbation" of her psychosis, set off by the apparently happy event. (From author's caseload)

As stressed elsewhere (pp. 207, 400), externally determined calamities and blows of fate, inclusive of physical illnesses, do not, as a rule, precipitate a psychosis. To quote S. Arieti (1974):

Very extenuating and taxing external or realistic events not only do not precipitate a schizophrenic psychosis, but at times seem able to prevent it . . .

Instead of burdening and enfeebling the Ego, the stresses contingent on bodily illnesses have been observed to actually produce improvement in the mental state of schizophrenic patients (C. G. Jung 1907). The following case is worthy of mention, as it brings into focus the observation that psychosis is the result of a process in which the continuity of life, inner reality, physiological state, and external events become restructured and transformed by the individual into a personal experience, in which the spiritual center asserts its preeminence.

The patient, a 63-year-old housewife, was readmitted to a psychiatric ward for an acute exacerbation of a chronic schizophrenic state. She was belligerent to the point of hitting her caretaker. While undergoing a routine medical examination, she was thought to be suffering from a heart attack, as her ECG tracing seemed to indicate. Hastily, she was transferred to an intensive care unit. When visited by the author of this report, she was completely transformed, her demeanor unrecognizable. She began "honey-ing" the therapist while conducting a normal conversation devoid of delusions, belligerence, and disordered, meaningless statements. Nevertheless, after it was established that her ECG had been misinterpreted, she rapidly returned to her previous malevolence and belligerent stance, as she became psychotic once more. The fear of death and the hereafter had returned this patient to some past, more loving attitudes and to sanity, for a brief moment—not the effects of a physical illness she did not have in reality. (From author's caseload)

*   *   *

While the arms of the law may extend long, those of the spiritual-moral law stretch even farther, in defiance of space and time.

> A sudden "act of justice" overtook a 43-year-old murderer who had already served his time in jail. Despite a spectacular recovery and comeback in career and a new marriage—in the midst of calm and happiness—he suddenly succumbed to a psychosis, which according to his interpretation was based on the murder. It remained unclear, however, whether the patient had concealed his past from his new family. (From author's caseload)

Not uncommonly, the final psychotic catastrophe explodes after a considerable build-up of its various constituents—new elements being progressively added to an existing aggregate of sin and guilt complexes. The hate-obsessed may thus, after an accumulation of small acts of malevolence, suddenly experience a catatonic episode, directly consequent to an outburst of violent behavior. Persistent homosexual activities may suddenly give rise to panic following a sexual encounter, and lead the offender directly to a hospital's emergency room for treatment of an acute paranoid disorder.

Clear precipitants do not always antecede a schizophrenic illness, however, and some insanities have been known to develop insidiously, oftentimes over a considerable length of time. Such are the **Process, Nuclear Schizophrenias** (p. 168), first described by G. Langfeldt (1939). These insanities, as Langfeldt perceived, are progressive illnesses which inexorably lead to early deterioration, and with losses of various mental capacities, eventually evolve into a true "dementia praecox." Neither neurotic conflict nor noteworthy life-events have been found to precede the development of these psychoses. They do not follow any departures from reality or conflicts of the Ego with the outside world. They do not conform to the postulations of Freud, who held psychoses to be etiologically determined by "non-fulfillment of childhood wishes." But here, as with other of Freud's insights, a kernel of truth can be found. What is basic and nuclear to this category of schizophrenia is a general, global rebellion against Providence for not fulfilling the individual's specific wishes or for not granting him some desired physical attribute, talent, or capacity, which he perceives in others, and of whom he is envious. Yet envy, covetousness, rebellion, and jealousy do not subserve biological need. They carry neither promise, nor confer any benefit of substance. For the most part, they represent but transcendental strivings.

The major dynamic forces responsible for "nuclear" or "process" schizophrenias have eluded the understanding of contemporary psychiatrists, because their criteria for diagnosing insanity have rested upon losses in reality-appreciation and other functions of the Ego-mind-reason. Yet what appears so nuclear and obvious in the etiology of these illnesses are these patients' global choices of evil as primary motivations, to which departures from sincerity and failings in reality-appreciation are but secondary manifestations.

As with every other schizophrenia, in the "nuclear" category the most powerful dynamic forces emerge as hate and malevolence. Yet, more clearly than in other schizophrenias, here malevolence transcends biological need—it is actually dissociated from it. It does not result from biologically determined aggressive urges, nor has it anything to do with the economy of the emotions. Here is a "hate without a cause" in pure form, for it is unprovoked. Characteristic of these schizophrenias is the relative absence of anger and passion, as hostilities are not directed toward any significant Other, but involve indiscriminately all members of humankind, and often other living creatures and plants as well.

Another characteristic of nuclear, process schizophrenias is their insidious appearance, usually during the tumultuous and critical years of adolescence, when a reshuffling of life-goals and values takes place and the individual creates himself anew. Outstanding in these illnesses is the lack of conflict to precede them. For these individuals choices of evil are natural and also Ego-syntonic.

Nuclear schizophrenias can serve to demonstrate that the Ego can produce rationalizations, intended to bribe the conscience into silence, through the selection of a pseudo-philosophy, pseudo-religion or cult, astrology, "voodoo" practices, numerology, or faith in plants, among others. Scientific pursuits may be chosen solely for the purpose of negating the divinely established order and existence of the spiritual Self or soul. Subversive causes and political movements may be joined for the opportunity these provide for the expression of hateful urges. But these movements offer justification as well. The Nazi movement may best serve as example: it allowed hatred for the Jews and even their extermination, while it provided as justification the need for purification of the Aryan race. In all such instances, the moral forces of the conscience suffer suppression, repression, and denial, as the Ego-mind-reason becomes accomplice to hatred and malevolence. It is common knowledge that extremist movements usually entrap individuals who choose the "means" rather than the "end" of such movements, for which "the means justify the end." In

The Possessed, Dostoyevsky insightfully cuts across the inner motivations of the revolutionaries he describes. Many among the followers of subversive causes and movements actually seek exemption from the laws established by society, if not their outright reversal (such was the case of Charles Manson and his followers, whose murders were committed for the sake of "freedom" from the restraints of society). Obviously, these individuals do not seek to satisfy any biological need, and their malevolence exceeds the scope of private vendettas or mere discharge of anger toward a significant Other. Behind their malevolence lurks not only rebellion against Providence, but more frequently than not, a lust for power and domination. Wolves at heart, clothed in sheepskins of ideological splendor, these harbingers of subversion progress more rapidly than others toward the state of premature mental deterioration known as dementia praecox. Their majority does not pass through stages of psychotic upheaval, for the simple reason that the emotional forces at the disposal of the conscience have been willfully and consciously quenched.

When does insanity begin? The answer to this haunting question becomes now more apparent: when seeds of evil begin to germinate and become *choices of evil*. Relevant to sin is its conscious acceptance. In *Crime and Punishment*, Raskolnikov's madness begins to unfold when he accepts the idea of the murder. The cancerous growth of nuclear schizophrenias is initiated by consciously undertaken choices of evil. The pursuit of evil may, however, break the continuity of time as well as of reality.

Distinct from nuclear schizophrenia, **Reactive Psychoses** develop as a reaction to certain external events, but the reaction is always fraught with sin and guilt. When guilt exceeds a certain critical level, it "explodes," so to speak, and gives rise to a "reactive psychosis," i.e., a psychosis with clear precipitant(s).

Of short duration, **Brief Reactive Psychoses** usually erupt after a serious moral violation in individuals of otherwise good premorbid disposition who may have succumbed, nevertheless, to a tempting morally forbidden wish or desire. They may have also reacted inappropriately to an external event. Reactive psychoses will be further discussed (p. 264).

*   *   *

What exactly tips the balance of sanity may forever elude our limited understanding. We do not know the weight of various transgressions, nor can we measure them one against another. We cannot estimate the quality or quantity of guilty dysphorias. Neither are the various factors that enter into the equation—hereditary predisposition, environmental conditions, degrees of heat of passion, secret motivations, obsessive premeditation, and acceptance of the transgression—given to accurate estimation. The same holds true for all the extenuating circumstances, loving actions, and beneficent deeds weighed in the balance of an individual's conscience.

Whereas the laws that govern the workings of conscience may elude our understanding—for sin belongs to the category of the individual—it would appear that the inner judicial system takes into account all that is deceptive and injurious to others, weighed against all that is honest and loving. Love, expressed in loving actions, seems to carry considerable weight against a multitude of other transgressions . . . "for love shall cover a multitude of sins" (1 Peter 4:8). The basic commandment of the Judeo-Christian religion, "Love thy neighbor as thyself," is essentially demanded by all world religions. Its observance enhances harmonious family living and ensures the functioning of the larger societies. But it is also a law that recognizes man's most cherished innermost longings and whose fulfillment brings the deepest satisfaction and happiness. Yet, nonerotic loves such as the sorrowful charity for a disadvantaged brother, the sacrificial love of parents for their children, or the respectful affection for aging parents seem more powerful in their capacity to expand the soul. And then there is Agape, the disinterested love that embraces many; it is the worthiest of all.

As is true for the seriousness of transgression, the quality and quantity of love expressed in action do not lend themselves to measurement, nor can conversion factors be extrapolated for these dynamic intangibles. Some "loves," furthermore, are fraught with sin. A speech attributed to Socrates in Plato's *Phaedrus* is worthy here of mention:

> Intimacy with one who is not in love, mingled as it is with worldly calculation and dispensing worldly advantage with a grudging hand, will breed in your soul the ignoble qualities which the multitude extols as virtue, and condemn you to wander for nine thousand years around and beneath the world, devoid of wisdom.

So much for the deceptive "loving" and exploitation of one single individual, and his fate in the hereafter.

A more pertinent question immediately begs for an answer: How do criminals avoid insanity? They do not, is the answer, but it is qualified by the factor of time. As a matter of fact, it has been estimated that between 25 percent and 75 percent of inmates in a prison population eventually become insane. In the largest New York City jail, Rikers Island, at any given time, 25 percent of inmates suffer from a mental illness (Dr. Y. Walker, health director of the prison). The madness of some criminals becomes immediately evident from their various insane self-mutilating and self-punishing behaviors as described before. These prisoners will readily attest that their self-inflicted punishments are more severe than those of the system that holds them prisoner. Other criminals court danger and succumb to various "accidents." Some criminals and sociopaths proceed directly from self-sentencing to execution, inflicting upon themselves the ultimate punishment. The most common cause of death in New York State jails in 1977, according to M. P. Paravati et al. (1982), was suicide, which accounted for 40 percent of all prison deaths. Among those associated with the criminal justice system, it is common knowledge that one of ten detainees suffers from a serious mental disorder (personal communication, Boro Park Detention Center), and this excludes those considered sociopathic. According to Mary Ann Giordano (*Daily News,* January 30, 1983), 12 percent of prison inmates would qualify for hospitalization even under the stringent admission policies of the New York State Office of Mental Health.[*] The lack of accurate data on the prevalence of schizophrenia in U.S. jails notwithstanding, Ganser's syndrome, which affects criminals on their way to court, can serve to demonstrate how guilt and fear can tip the balance of sanity. It also sheds more light on the continuum of sin, guilt, and psychosis.

Among prisoners, **Incarceration Psychoses** are far from uncommon. Some criminals, nevertheless, seem to preserve their sanity for a surprising length of time. How do they escape the "guilty" verdict of their consciences? It may well be that these individuals are protected from an "explosion of conscience" by some loving relationship they succeed in maintaining despite their involvement in antisocial activities. Such a possibility is dramatized in the story of *The Godfather.* Loving attachments to spouse, children, family, and even collaborators—the proverbial loyalty and camaraderie of criminals—might perhaps outweigh their less than "loving" criminal activities and protect them from psychosis—at least for a time. The

---

[*] The wide range of these statistics is explained by the lack of studies on the prevalence of mental illness in U.S. jails.

nature of the crime and the magnitude of its injurious effects on others may also serve to explain the temporary immunity from insanity certain criminals seem to enjoy. Many criminal acts, primarily involving damage to or loss of property, may conceivably be less guilt-provoking than crimes against a person. Tax evasion certainly makes one feel less guilty than a slanderous, untrue statement about another person. A verbal attack, humiliation of another, secret exploitation, deception, and "character assassination" all weigh heavier on the conscience than the misappropriation of material goods. It would appear, thus, that by causing injury and harm to another or others, the most basic law which demands that we love our neighbor is being violated, and this evokes a stronger response from conscience than otherwise.

The degree and magnitude of moral violations will certainly elude attempts at neat classification and quantification, and their weight against any individual's loving actions will be rather difficult to estimate. Therefore, in order to arrive at some understanding of the laws of conscience, general principles must, by necessity, be accepted. Universal laws, moreover, become subject to change when applied to the individual—the uniqueness of his world—for "sin applies to the individual and the category of sin is the category of the individual," wrote Kierkegaard (1849). This definition applies to psychiatric disturbances as well, for they affect the individual in accordance with his specific conditions. Every individual comes into the world charged with the "sins of the fathers;" grows in environments not of his making; and learns the moral law in somewhat different circumstances. Kierkegaard (1849) wrote:

> . . . in relation to sin, the ethical has its place, which employs an emphasis which is the converse of that of speculation and accomplishes the opposite development; for the ethical does not abstract from reality, but goes deeper into reality, operating essentially by the aid of the category of the individual. (*The Sickness unto Death*)

The following case may serve as an example:

> This was a case of child abandonment. The mother was herself abandoned in early childhood by her mother. She grew up in adverse circumstances, and, hungering for love and affection denied her, succumbed to seduction and begot the child of an irresponsible youth. She soon abandoned her child for realistic reasons. This injurious to her child act produced a

low-grade depression, anxiety, some paranoid uneasiness, and guilt of a bearable intensity, nevertheless. Her multiple adverse life-circumstances may have attenuated the seriousness of her transgression and guilt resulting therefrom. (From author's caseload)

*   *   *

The attempts of existential philosophers to unify and update the central tenets of the world's religions may be considered one of their most formidable contributions. In his emphasis on the possibility of a direct I-Thou relationship (between the I and divine Thou), and also with the Yous of human fellowship, Martin Buber (1970) expressed the view of the majority of Existentialists, for whom abstract moral and ethical injunctions recede into the background, as if of secondary importance. It is the nature and sincerity of relationships that are ultimately brought to bear upon the weight of sin and relevance of guilt, rather than the dogmatic laws of any given religion. And it is the divine call that represents that Reality to which one is *responsible for responding*. There is no other way of relating to the divine Thou but "in spirit and in truth." This rule applies to relationships with one's fellow men as well. Any breach in one's relationship to the Thou or Yous of one's world constitutes, therefore, transgression.

O. H. Mowrer (1961) follows the philosophical thought laid down by Aristotle, in emphasizing, as do all major religions, that it is the intentional content of a sinful act that ultimately determines its magnitude. Relevant to sin is the degree of one's acceptance of it and the conscious participation of the will (H. Fingarette 1967). "Sin lies in the will, not in the intellect," wrote Kierkegaard (1849). Thus, when a patient claims to have killed his father, he may be guilty even if he did not do so in reality, because such was his intention, not his fantasy.

The tragedy of the schizophrenic begins with his separation from the divine Thou through a deliberately committed offense against His moral injunction(s). But the schizophrenic loses also the Yous he has injured, as well as others belonging to his *Mitwelt*, the world of others, who stand to condemn him. And through the dissociation from his inner feelings—intended to ward off guilt from entering consciousness—he loses the ability to relate to himself also, and in this manner becomes estranged from his *Eigenwelt* (his inner world) as well. This is how the schizophrenic loses his world in existential terms, and how he loses himself, his soul. What is left for him to exploit is the world of inanimate objects, of *matter*—an empty world of nothingness. Schizophrenics frequently complain of being "dead" and of their soul having turned into solid matter. The schizophrenic may be compared to a star that has lost its orbit—aimlessly drifting in the vastness of the universe.

According to Aristotle, "In justice is summed up the whole virtue." It is perfect virtue, indeed, when one secures advantage for another or for others. The schizophrenic acts defiantly, in opposition to the laws of justice and virtue. O. H. Mowrer (1961) concurs with the views of Existentialists when he considers sin from both the vertical, I-Thou and the horizontal, I-You dimensions as more relevant to sin than any dogmatic abstraction. Psychiatric disturbances tend to confirm the existential position: interpersonal "crimes" weigh heavy on the conscience, more so than other offenses; and secrecy or deceptive cover-up tends to intensify the various guilty dysphorias such as paranoid uneasiness, ideas of reference, anxiety, and persecutory delusions.

The Experience of Schizophrenia

Can one wish oneself a dream and dream it? And if the dream turns out to be a nightmare, can one extricate oneself from its grip by sheer power of the will? Can one modify misperceptions by an effort of the mind? Is it possible to free oneself from irrational fears by recognizing their absurdity? Can one silence tormenting hallucinatory "voices," against which even earplugs provide but limited relief? The answers to these questions are quite obvious, and no one would deny that these experiences are *given*: they are beyond the control of volition, and cannot be eliminated by the powers of reason. Were it not so, one would be able to subdue the dread-filled symptoms of psychosis through rational analysis and control of the will. It becomes, therefore, almost insulting to shrug off the nightmarish experiences of psychotic patients as "unreal," "hysterical manifestations," or as products of their imagination. For as pain and distress resulting from a physical illness can be intensified by the indifference of others, and conversely, alleviated by compassion, the same holds true for the symptoms, suffering, and anguish of the mentally diseased. The symptoms of psychosis, moreover, cannot be compared to those of physical illness. Patients have repeatedly insisted that their experiences (or symptoms) are more dreadful and terrible than anything they had experienced or seen in a "horror movie," and which are to them more real than reality itself. And why, one may ask, would the schizophrenic want to conjure up the snakes, vultures, spiders, rats, and bats that suddenly invade his conscious mind with threats of annihilation? To what benefit would a refugee from adverse external realities or "traumata" be comforted by terrifying visions, clearly suggestive of Hell? How can insanity and its dread-filled experiences be considered but "defense" (K. Menninger et al. 1963)? Defense against what? And how can theories that blame failures of the Ego to "cope" with excessive "pressures" and various externally determined traumata—allegedly responsible for the outbreak of psychosis—explain the invasion of consciousness by spiritually charged symbols suggestive of Hell?

Obviously, the currently prevailing theories of schizophrenia suffer from a strain in logical connections that would bind existing facts. In order to stand firmly on its ground, any theory of schizophrenia would need to account for the appearance of the spiritually meaning-ful symbolic creatures that come to inhabit the world of the psychotic. And this would also apply to theories that attempt to interpret schizophrenia in terms of biochemical accidents or aberrations. How is a chemical substance (be this even a neurotransmitter) capable of creating highly meaningful experiences such as nightmares, delusions, misperceptions, and similar phenomena? Mescaline, for example—a substance used in Mexico for religious purposes—brings blissful experiences only to the faithful, whereas when taken by the so-predisposed (*vide infra*), produces experiences evocative of Hell. Neither fever, nor toxic deliria, nor organically determined confu-sional states are known to produce so vividly and creatively experi-ences perceived as Hell as are given to the subjects of psychosis.

Whereas a psychotic breakdown may "explode" without much warning, in the majority of cases the process is a gradual one. Progressively evolving and becoming more and more unbearable, the following symptoms follow one another on a continuum of severity: depression, insomnia, fears and anxieties punctuated by phobias, and panic attacks which eventually culminate in paranoid uneasiness and ideas of reference. The alarm begins to ring louder with the appear-ance of dread-provoking nightmares, which increase in frequency and intensity as the breakdown draws near. But the nightmare is not just a random occurrence: it is heavily charged with meaning. Its impact surpasses that of any given reality, and its effects long outlast its actual duration. It ought to be of great interest to biologically oriented theorists that the same nightmare may be repeated several times during one night, and the patient finally realizes that he cannot escape it. What chemical substance can produce exactly the same images and repeat them with such accuracy as the tenacious, repeated nightmare that intends to impart to its subject an important existential message? It has long been recognized that an increase in frequency and intensity of dread-provoking nightmares represents an ominous sign for an impending psychosis. And indeed, all too soon fears, visions, hallucinations, and nightmares will coalesce and produce a dread-filled delusional experience of great significance that takes precedence over everything else in the conscious mind of the psychotic patient. External perceptions become dimmed, and many patients experience a great darkness descending upon them. Misperceptions are most common, yet they do not just happen at random, but follow remarkably creative constructs—heavily charged with meaning. To one patient, people suddenly appeared deformed, resembling dogs. The meaning of this delusional state was interpreted by the patient himself, who took it as a reminder of his attitudes to others, whom he had treated "like dogs." To another patient, bulls suddenly made their appearance in nightmares and visions, as it became apparent that he had behaved like a "bully" all his life. Another patient saw a turtle in an oven, which he interpreted as meaning that he ought "to get out of his shell" and become engaged in the tasks of life at hand. The patient who complained of being tormented by a snake recovered from her "depression" only after realizing that the snake was none other than herself. As can be gleaned from these delusional experiences, their meaning is not associated with any particular misdeed, but represents rather a dramatization of the patient's deviant ways of being-in-the-world.

Whatever its antecedents, the guilty verdict pronounced by the moral conscience carries with it a sentence. It brings about a complete change in the convicted's experience of life. Feelings of guilt, a *fear of the unknown,* and overwhelming dread progressively flood the various streams of consciousness to contaminate thenceforth every thought and feeling. Complexes of sin and guilt begin to float in awareness as one or another takes precedence and thinking becomes "complex-bound." The nightmares that invade the sleep of the psychotic are carried over into the day as delusional experiences. The organs of perception bring into awareness stimuli of a threatening nature, all structured around the patient's deviant attitudes and complexes of sin and guilt. Whatever the modality of hallucinations—auditory, visual, olfactory, kinesthetic, or gustatory—their message is perceived as unmistakably punitive. To the observer it becomes apparent that the "explosion of conscience" does not necessarily follow a specific moral transgression, but represents rather an accretion of offenses, since in the symptomatology of the psychotic, several complexes of sin and guilt emerge as active.

How can the multiperceptual experience of schizophrenia best be described? It is completely new to the experiencer; it is not rooted in his past, nor is it a product of his imagination. This strange transformation of the patient's world has frequently been likened to a "big dream"—ineffable, numinous, and, to its subject, of tremendous significance. The altered perceptions (or misperceptions) cause a narrowing of consciousness in favor of newly emergent matters concerning the spiritual Me. That every soul represents a world unto itself is quite literally experienced by the schizophrenic, although he feels his world to be crumbling and in danger of annihilation. Apocalyptic visions of *the* Judgment, final destruction of the world, and a fierce struggle between Good and Evil become personal matters of utmost importance.

As a general rule, *the first psychotic episode contains elements of Heaven as well as of Hell.* Subsequent psychotic episodes become progressively less benign and more suggestive of Hell. Clinical observations tend to validate those of philosopher and novelist Aldous Huxley (1954, 1956). "Hell is confirmed in the schizophrenic's experience," wrote Huxley as he cited Carlyle's "amazing description of a psychotic state of mind":

> The men and women around me, even speaking with me, were but Figures; I had practically forgotten that they were alive, that they were not merely automata. Friendship was but an incredible tradition. In the midst of the crowded streets and assemblages, I walked solitary and except that it was my own heart, and not another's, that I kept devouring savage also, as the tiger in the jungle . . . . To me the Universe was also void of life, of Purpose, of Volition, even of Hostility; it was one huge, dead immeasurable steam-engine, rolling on its dead Indifference, to grind me limb from limb . . . . Having no Hope, neither had I any definite fear, were it of Man or of the Devil. And yet, strangely enough, I lived in continual, indefinite, pining Fear, tremulous, pusillanimous, apprehensive of I don't know what . . . as if the Heavens and the Earth beneath would hurt me; as if the Heavens and the Earth were but boundless jaws of a devouring Monster, wherein I, palpitating, waited to be devoured.

Containing all the basic elements of schizophrenia, Carlyle's account of his psychotic experience suggests the existence of a very personal and individualized Hell. From his emphasis on the "dead Indifference" which is to grind him limb from limb, one may deduce that Carlyle's ways of being-in-the-world and his relatedness to others were marked by lovelessness, automatism, and indifference. He mentions a "fear of I don't know what" (fear of the unknown), and describes a sense of "ultimate punishment by a devouring monster"— statements frequently expressed by other psychotic patients also.

As for the presence of the devil in the experience of psychosis, it may be glibly dismissed as mere symbolic representation: a vestige from medieval times, or product, perhaps, of superstitious belief or imagination. Yet in schizophrenia the devil becomes all too real, all too terrible, and disregard for this fact must by necessity represent defense by denial. The various explanations for his appearance in schizophrenia, and the blame cast on a "strict" or "Catholic" education, have failed to drive him away. His alleged surge from an atavistic past still comes short in accounting for his sudden appearance, as well as for the lack of angelic representations—also symbolic creatures from the same atavistic past—in recurrent schizophrenic exacerbations. The devil, it would seem, has no preference for any particular culture, religion, or tradition, for he appears to every schizophrenic, irrespective of origins, upbringing, religion, or education. Neither does the patient's "craziness" explain his presence in psychosis. Even in high doses, neuroleptic medications have shown themselves quite powerless in forcing him to extinction.

Attempting to relate the appearance of delusional experiences such as visions of ghosts, for example, to "sickness," Dostoyevsky wrote in *Crime and Punishment*:

> People say, you are ill, so what appears to you is only unreal, fantasy. But that is not strictly logical: I agree that ghosts appear only to the sick, but that only proves that they are unable to appear, except to the sick, not that they do not exist . . . . Ghosts are shreds or fragments of other worlds, the beginnings of them . . . and the more seriously ill one is, the closer becomes one's contact with the other worlds.

In this manner, Raskolnikov the murderer explained his visions to Svidrigailov, also a murderer and subject to similar delusional and hallucinatory experiences.

If, indeed, visions of ghosts, the devil, snakes, rats, and vultures represent but products of these patients' "craziness," of their "mental disturbance"—allowing the atavistically transmitted from past generations "unconscious," to assert itself in consciousness—how are the religious conflicts and philosophical dilemmas, universally present in the thought processes of schizophrenics, to be explained? And how is their absence from organically determined disorders to be understood? If the observation that neurologically impaired patients fail to perceive visions of Hell and do not obsess with matters of a spiritual nature is dismissed as irrelevant, how are the seemingly bizarre behaviors of schizophrenics, such as their frequent hand-washing, fasting, expiatory rituals, and head shaving, to be interpreted?

Notwithstanding the deliberate disregard, often admixed with derision, these manifestations evoke in mental health professionals, they cannot be ignored as irrelevant, just the same, because they are as constant in psychosis as are its other diagnostic signs and symptoms. The psychiatric community is thus called to accept them and seek to understand their meaning. And when during psychotic illnesses the soul, psyche, or spiritual Self emerges to assert its central position in the living processes of mind and body—crying out in pain and anguish about the reality of Hell—this cry ought to shake the healers of the soul and stir them to compassion.

But unfortunately for all concerned, the laments of the insane are mostly ignored and, feeling themselves misunderstood, many among hospitalized patients can be observed to sink deeper into themselves and withdraw into their personal prisons of alienation. Hardly by chance, a good number refuse to "cooperate" with prescribed treatment regimens. And what do these regimens consist of? Mostly medicines, coupled with instructions intended to sharpen the patients' "social skills," and added to them, doses of "reality orientation," such as the pronouncement: "There are no ghosts." For these reasons, among others, most psychotic patients prefer their solitude and the opportunity it offers them to understand this, their terrible ordeal.

In spite of the universality and centrality of the religious and spiritual preoccupations of the insane—regarded mostly as delusional—these concerns are grossly avoided, if not ridiculed by therapists, instead of becoming incorporated into the process of meaningful psychotherapy. A tendency to equate religious belief with madness has even insinuated itself into the opinions and practices of contemporary psychiatrists. In a report by a task force on religion—mandated by the American Psychiatric Association to investigate transcendental visions and other such experiences—we find the following statements:

It is of interest that many of these transient, self-limited
experiences conform to standard definitions for the first rank
symptoms of schizophrenia. The occurrence of psychotic-like
phenomena in the religious and meditative context raises
questions about possible biosocial aspects of these symptoms
in psychopathological conditions . . . . Have we come to
understand the role of cognitive and social induction in *eliciting*
and *modulating* psychosis? [emphasis added] (M. Galanter and
J. Westermeyer 1980).

The inferences are quite clear. Not only does the task force deny
personal revelatory phenomena, which the bulk of humanity acknowl-
edges as authentic, spontaneous religious-spiritual experiences, it also
implies a "social induction in eliciting and modulating psychosis,"
obliquely casting the blame on religion for the eruption of psychosis.
Yet despite the conclusions drawn by the task force of the APA,
religion has been validated by billions of men and women who
believe. According to statistics presented by H.-J. Shoeps (1968) in
his *Religions of Mankind*, only 17.5 percent of the world's population
does not belong to one of the major or tribal religions. As for the
essence of their doctrines, and even their symbols, there exist among
the various religions more similarities than differences. All religions
are grounded in a moral law, whose major precepts, albeit colored by
local culture and tradition, are universal nonetheless. All demand from
their followers a life that adheres to ethical-moral standards, and all
bind their faithful to love their fellow men, even their enemies.

As for holding religion responsible for inducing "psychotic-like"
phenomena, it betrays the stance of the APA, dominated as it is by
a biologically grounded determinism—whose approaches attempt to
heal the "psyche" without giving recognition to its existence. It
becomes evident, thus, that the APA ignores *man's most basic and
central spiritual strivings.* According to a Gallup poll taken in 1981,
96 percent of Americans stated that they were believers; yet only 5
percent among psychologists professed any religious belief; and the
highest rate of apostasy was found among psychoanalysts.

As for peoples from the former Soviet bloc—where religion was
denounced as "opium of the masses"—who had for several generations endured biosocially induced, culturally and politically reinforced
"brainwashing," their majority, namely 85 percent, persists in
believing. How would the APA explain this finding?

It is of great interest that little difference can be found between
believer and nonbeliever in their experience of psychosis. Both

believer and nonbeliever descend into an underworld of Hell during their psychotic ordeal, and both experience the presence of demonic forces over which they feel powerless. Both experience a sense of loss of the integrity of their souls, conveyed to them through spiritually charged symbols, which they all seem well to understand. And the question whether a believer can suffer from psychosis and its experiences of Hell remains ever pertinent. Yet the answer may be simple: a true believer is one who worships "in spirit and in truth;" follows the precepts of the moral law; obeys the ordinances of family and society; and proves his love for the neighbor in action. "Believing" is easy, but when faith is dissociated from truth, and love not expressed in action, it becomes hypocrisy, i.e., a lie.

That the experience of schizophrenia is similar across religions, traditions, and cultures finds confirmation in a recent report by A. Jablensky (1987) from the World Health Organization (WHO), whose findings reveal that schizophrenics across cultures around the world, even as separate as those of Nigeria and Denmark, describe their experience by "using almost identical words or phrases."

The Signs and Symptoms of Schizophrenia

a. Delusional Ideas and Experiences

Delusional *ideas*—as distinct from delusional *experiences* (or delusions *proper*)—represent distortions or falsifications of certain realities, which are held with unshakable conviction and tenacity, because they serve as *justification*. For this reason, delusional ideas are considered fixed ideas (*idées fixes*), resistant to interpretation and impervious to "reality orientation." Delusional ideas represent perfect examples of deception and self-deception. They are held with unusual conviction and tenacity, because justification is so important to the deceiver. Delusional ideas are reducible, nonetheless, i.e., they can be dissolved, provided the patient is given the opportunity to admit to others and accept the blame for some past misdeed. The following is a good example of a delusional idea:

> A 12-year-old boy breaks a window with his ball. He persists in claiming that the window was already broken before his throw, and becomes angry when contradicted.

Delusional ideas, so frequent in the communications of schizophrenic patients, may be understood even when they appear to be bizarre and devoid of meaning. The following formula is useful for their understanding:

> The delusional idea shields a complex of sin and guilt by the use of some lie or half truth, which serves as justification.

A common delusional idea is maintained by the unfaithful spouse, who persists in attempts to convince others that it is his (or her) spouse, and not himself (or herself), who is involved in an extramarital affair. The adulterer thus falsifies a known truth, for he is well aware of his infidelities, but tenaciously holds on to his accusations, which serve both as cover-up and justification. The false claims of sexual abuse in childhood, raised by some patients, serve to justify their current sexual excesses or perversions.

Delusional *ideas* need to be differentiated from delusions *proper*, so designated by K. Jaspers (1963). Delusions proper are irreducible, because they belong to the category of *subjective experiences,* which are *given*; i.e., they cannot be controlled by the will or influenced by the powers of reason. Delusional experiences comprise all perceptual modalities, and the patient is therefore justified in believing he has entered a strange, "other world." But the strange world of the psychotic is frightening and threatening, in addition. The delusional transformation of the world of the psychotic completely changes all of his life-experiences—as they become pervaded with an "atmosphere of unbearable dread, charged with meaning." It is of great interest that the delusional experiences of psychotic patients strikingly resemble the descriptions of Hell given by Swedenborg. After death, according to Swedenborg, those destined to eternal Hell enter their own specific, individualized hellish society—all in accordance with the intentions and evils of the life they had led (*Heaven and Hell*). In their new "strange other world," patients experience something of a very private, very personal Hell, where sin and punishment go hand in hand. In delusional experiences the patient's aberrant ways of being-in-the-world are clearly and concretely exposed, as they are also punished according to the laws of talion:

1. A patient who was, by his own admission, a "pretender"— ingratiating himself in order to obtain favors—suddenly perceived himself in a world where everybody was an "actor."

2. A patient who refused to work saw himself wandering in eternity as a lonely vagrant.

3. A racially biased young man, suffering from obsessive hateful thoughts, saw himself, during his psychosis, as a defendant in the Nuremberg trials.

4. A homosexual man, engaged in promiscuous sexual relationships, suddenly experienced labor pains, as he was travailing to give birth through the rectum.

Delusions proper carry a warning that is quite clear and often well understood by the patient. When the meaning of a delusion is correctly interpreted by patient or therapist, it may bring about its dissolution. Not unlike the dream, the delusional experience creatively combines external as well as internal realities, which conspire, so to speak, in their efforts to create an atmosphere of dread, intended to jolt their subjects into repentance and convince them to reform.

b. Hallucinations

Unlike the delusional transformation of the world that occurs in psychosis—where all modalities of perception become involved in the service of the spiritual center of the personality—hallucinations employ one, two, or several channels of perception to convey their message, leaving consciousness relatively clear and open to stimuli from the outside world. The hallucinations of schizophrenia, moreover, occur, according to P. Hoch (1972), "in a clear setting," i.e., they cannot be compared to those produced by hallucinogenic substances, or to those occurring during states of clouded consciousness based on organic cerebral damage or metabolic aberrations. Despite their intrusive character and tendency to dominate the conscious mind, the *hallucinations of schizophrenia cannot be repressed or suppressed at will*. The patient feels as if "possessed" by his hallucinations, for they detract from his ability to concentrate. The distracting pull of hallucinations may be of such intensity as to prevent the patient's functioning on the most basic level, such as dressing, washing, cooking, cleaning, and generally caring for himself. When not organically determined, hallucinations occur spontaneously and are meaningful and organized in the majority of cases. They cannot be shut off at will, as can fantasy. The currently prevailing interpretations of hallucinations, which hold the patient responsible for "hallucinating," hardly do justice to these essentially involuntary phenomena, nor do they offer comfort and needed compassion to these dread-stricken individuals. Recognized as incongruous to the thought configuration of the conscious mind at the given moment, it becomes logically untenable to regard hallucinations as products of wishful fantasy or imagination. All modalities of perception may become channels of hallucinations, but in some disorders specific channels are involved more commonly than others. Cocaine intoxication, for example, characteristically produces tactile hallucinations; in alcoholic hallucinosis, auditory hallucinations tend to predominate. In schizophrenia all modalities of perception may be involved, but auditory hallucinations are most common, with visual, tactile, and olfactory following suit.

It has long been recognized that, as a general rule, the frequency and intensity of hallucinations tend to parallel existing psychopathology. When hallucinations are experienced by otherwise psychologically intact or mildly impaired individuals, they are considered "hysterical" in nature. Yet they are hallucinations, just the same, even if their subjects are different. The sudden appearance of the devil to the student-housewife mentioned above (p. 133) would be categorized as "hysterical"; whereas the same vision, when appearing to a schizophrenic, would be classified as a "florid" psychotic symptom. The function of the vision is similar to that of the delusional experience, serving as a warning, and prompting the visionary to correction and reform. When the warning is heeded—as it was by the student-housewife—it frees the subject from his symptoms. Visual hallucinations tend to appear primarily in the dark, and for this reason many patients keep their lights on during the night; they may also engage in various activities, so as to crowd out the appearance of these frightening visions. Visual hallucinations may appear in all categories of mental illness, but are believed to be more characteristic of the "hysterical" and the alcoholic. Auditory as well as other perception-modality hallucinations may occur in various situations of danger, sensory deprivation, influence of drugs, and nearness to death. Notwithstanding, most patients are reluctant to divulge their hallucinatory experiences.

In schizophrenia, auditory hallucinations are liable to appear in all stages of the disease-process: acute, subchronic, and chronic. They also occur in later stages of alcoholism and intensify during situations of crisis and isolation. Their first appearance usually arouses an inordinately intense sense of dread. One patient gave up ten years of antisocial adventures and reversed the course of his life after hearing a threatening voice for the first time. According to P. Hoch (1972), auditory hallucinations cannot be reproduced experimentally by any drug or substance. They occur not only in the confusional stages of psychosis, but also in a clear setting, when there is no narrowing of consciousness, as in chronic states of schizophrenia, alcoholism, and severe depression.

While some drugs may induce visual hallucinations, such as are perceived during early use of LSD, for example—appearing as colors, shapes, and geometric figures—auditory hallucinations have a definite content and meaning. For this reason, drug-induced hallucinations are considered "perceptual," while auditory hallucinations are regarded as "conceptual." Congenitally deaf individuals do not experience auditory hallucinations. Some patients find relief from their tormenting and accusatory "voices" by the use of earplugs. The presence of other people and extraneous noises have also been found useful in reducing the intensity of auditory hallucinations, yet they cannot completely eliminate them. It is worth mentioning that several patients have come to attention for having undergone *repeated operations* on their eardrums, in an attempt to tone down their auditory hallucinations. Among the homeless, many prefer to sleep on the street whose noises dampen somewhat the intensity of their hallucinatory "voices."

Hallucinations are still poorly understood subjective phenomena. A wide array of interpretations and speculations have been offered to explain their origin. Unfortunately, their significance and potential usefulness for psychotherapy have impressed but a few. Freud (1937) held delusions and hallucinations to be related to "something in the past, which has been forgotten"—representing "unconscious" wishes which suffer distortions imposed by external realities. Most widely accepted is the theory that regards auditory hallucinations as experiences, whereby one hears "one's thoughts spoken aloud"—an interpretation frequently given also by patients so affected. Other patients become enraged at the mere mention of this suggestion. For Arieti (1974), auditory hallucinations represent the "perceptualization of a concept," a view shared also by Hoch. According to this notion, an idea is perceived as if derived from the external world. Certain thoughts are thus first "projected" outside, and then perceived as auditory stimuli. Yet the conceptual makeup of hallucinations is a persistent, sustained, and organized set of ideas, which more frequently than not is experienced as Ego-alien. Many patients become indignant by this "projection" interpretation of their hallucinatory experience and claim, furthermore, that their "voices" frequently speak in a foreign language; belong to the opposite sex; and may even comment or argue with other voices concerning them. A great number of patients have understood their hallucinations as being the voice of their conscience, accusing and condemning them for past misdeeds.

It is generally agreed that hallucinations possess negative, disagreeable, and, at times, disturbing qualities. Except in cases of hebephrenic schizophrenia and later stages of deteriorative illnesses, auditory hallucinations are either accusatory, derogatory, mocking, denigrating, or commanding in nature. More often than not, the accusations are exaggerated and the commands given by the halluci- natory "voices" run contrary to the patient's best interests. This observation alone raises serious questions concerning the derivation of auditory hallucinations. Would the moral conscience advise the patient to commit rape, murder, or suicide? And why do command hallucinations never order the patient to visit a sick relative, help a friend, or otherwise engage in some charitable activity? It is also worthy of note that accusatory hallucinations always magnify the moral transgressions for which the patient feels already guilty. And when the "voices" command yet another crime, or rape, or prompt the patient to punish himself, or commit suicide, they are merely exploiting the patient's weaknesses, his tendency to act out the dictates of his "repetition compulsion," and his urges for self- punishment.

> A mother of four complained that her "voices" were com- manding her to drink the bleach Clorox. When further ques- tioned, she admitted to having given Clorox to her small children, many years before, intending their destruction. (From author's caseload)

Whereas command hallucinations have been used in insanity pleas and even held responsible for a number of crimes, the patient's "voices" cannot by themselves compel him to commit an act not previously intended or committed. The crime, moreover, ordered by the hallucinations must hold a certain appeal for the subject, for otherwise he would not be tempted to commit it. For these reasons, auditory "command hallucinations" ought to be barred as legal defense, because the patient who is guilty has acted out but his own intentions. He would refuse otherwise to yield to the commands of his hallucinations.

As a general rule, the content and meaning of hallucinations follow a pattern quite distinct and more complex than that of the nightmare and delusional experience, whose messages tend to be rather direct and concrete. But one can always find "a kernel of truth" in halluci- nations, as Freud observed. This truth can be extremely useful in psychotherapy, as the following case illustrates:

A patient who appeared to be suffering from an organic brain syndrome with an admixture of schizophrenic symptomatology heard a voice calling her "Vodka Collins," instead of her true name "Anna Collins"—betraying thus her secret drinking habit. Her hallucinations revealed the correct diagnosis—Alcoholic Hallucinosis—which paved the way for meaningful psychotherapy. (From author's caseload)

In his interpretations of hallucinatory phenomena, Hoch emphasized that hallucinations are both persistent and consistent in their representation of something, but this "something" is always incongruous with the conscious content of thought. The most striking common denominator of auditory hallucinations, however, is their capacity to evoke all that is failing, ugly, and evil in the personality of their subject, which the "voices" tend to exploit and magnify. It is also of interest to note that auditory hallucinations always pronounce themselves against religion and its precepts. Hallucinatory "voices," moreover, consistently try to sound the trumpet of doom—as if the patient were already lost and no possibilities existed for his redemption.

Hoch believed auditory hallucinations to be derived from the patient's "unconscious." But this "unconscious" means different things to different thinkers. For Freud the "unconscious" contains elements of an atavistic past, instinctual urges, and stored memories. For Jung (1957), the soul is continuous with an "unconscious" that corresponds to the "mythical land of the dead" and to a vast world of the Unredeemed. The patients' experiences of some "other worlds" are described by contemporary research psychologist W. Van Dusen in his book *The Presence of Other Worlds* (1974). Swedenborg, for whom Heaven and Hell were unquestionable realities, thought the spiritual world to be inhabited by those whose final eternal destination was uncertain still. An elaborate description of the "other worlds" can be found in Swedenborg's work *Heaven and Hell*, and in many of his other writings. The "unconscious" has also been regarded as center of creativity, love, and transcendence. The views of Freud and Hoch on the "unconscious," and those of Jung, Swedenborg, and Dostoyevsky—claiming the existence of some "other worlds"—may perhaps be reconciled by regarding the "unconscious" as being a window that opens onto a spiritual world, allowing glimpses to some subjects in certain circumstances.

It is of great interest that a set of delusional and hallucinatory experiences has come to be recognized as characteristic for schizophrenia and even established as a criterion for its diagnosis. These so-called "first-rank symptoms," described by Kurt Schneider (1959), comprise, among others:

- the conviction of being controlled by outside forces
- the belief that one's thoughts are being inserted, or else withdrawn
- the sense that one's thoughts are being read and broadcasted
- a set of hallucinations that comment on the patient and his thoughts

To the schizophrenic in the clutches of these symptoms, the "other worlds" of evil, darkness, and threats appear all too real, all too terrible. He hears the call of the Unredeemed, and, through his visions, nightmares, delusions, and hallucinations, becomes aware of an unavoidable, impending punishment. He senses his evil intentions loudly proclaimed. He also interprets the glimpses granted him from those "other worlds" of darkness and evil as representing a warning.

c. Meaning

In all the stages of his illness, the schizophrenic patient perceives a particular meaning in even the most ordinary, insignificant objects and events. One patient—who came to believe she had lost her soul and had become solid "matter"—felt metallic objects to be attracted to her. In this case it seemed as if matter had won over spirit. Another patient would not eat Hellman's mayonnaise, because the inscription on the jar was read by her as "Hell-man," which she took as a warning.

> A patient who had simulated physical illness in order to receive disability benefits heard the television set broadcasting his laziness and deception. (From author's caseload)

d. Paranoid Fears and Ideas of Persecution

Traditionally, paranoid fears and ideas of persecution have been understood as representing hostilities projected onto others, the outside world. But projections have also been thought to serve as defense: "They hate me" being felt as less dysphoric than "I hate them." Paranoid fears of persecution have been explained also on the basis of some patients' grandiose self-perceptions. Believing themselves superior to others, paranoid individuals, allegedly, expect this superiority to provoke jealousy, envy, resentment, and thus give reason for their persecution. Yet, more often than not, projections of blame represent delusional ideas which serve as justification.

In a survey of mental patients treated in a municipal hospital center, 97 percent, mostly schizophrenics, felt themselves judged, condemned, and persecuted by others. Only 3 percent, the majority of whom were depressives, did not entertain such feelings. (Study presented at the 1994 3rd Schizophrenia International Convention, to be published.)

In authentic **Paranoia**, the sense of being judged is most central. Intensifying along a gradient, it leads to feelings of condemnation, persecution, and impending punishment. The intensity of paranoid fears always parallels the magnitude of the transgression as well as the secrecy with which it has been maintained. Paranoid fears and ideas are present in all mental diseases belonging to the schizophrenic spectrum (Diagram # 2, p. 140). With respect to the punishment expected, the fear of castration contained in the Oedipus complex, for example, is not only entertained by the child who is sexually attracted to his mother, but by all who transgress in the sexual realm. The fear of cancer, **Cancerophobia,** perturbs those who abuse their physical bodies, and, paradoxically, narcissistic individuals also, who idolize their physique and indulge in sensual pleasures. Paranoid fears of persecution have been interpreted by Arieti (1974) as defensive operations by which "internal dangers" become externalized. Arieti did not clarify, however, whether the "internal dangers" represented fears of acting out a forbidden wish/desire—as the neurotic model of mental disease demands—or were associated with derivatives of guilt, fear of the unknown, and expectations of punishment. Projections and "externalizations" become advantageous only when culpability or blame can be cast on others or external circumstances.

Psychoanalytical theories have correctly linked paranoid ideas of persecution to homosexual tendencies and such practices. The association between homosexual activities and paranoid fears of condemnation, persecution, and punishment has never been questioned. Yet the association between paranoia and moral transgressions other than homosexuality—no less evident—has failed to impress modern psychologists and psychiatrists. But then, the psychiatric community has refused to acknowledge the stressfulness of moral transgression in general, as it has also failed to recognize guilt as a valid emotion.

Notwithstanding the experts' interpretations, popular opinion has always considered feelings of persecution to be associated with secret legally, socially, or morally forbidden acts or activities. Patients, in fact, frequently refer to their paranoid feelings as nothing more than "guilt trips." Fifty years of clinical experience with schizophrenic and paranoid patients have led French psychiatrist Henri Baruk (1976) to conclude that "it is the disturbed conscience, which is found hidden behind paranoid delusions." But since contemporary psychiatry has remained entrenched in Id and Ego-psychologies, disregarding the central role of the Superego in mental illnesses, the majority of psychiatric patients are doomed to misunderstanding. Inflated self-esteem and grandiose self-perceptions do not necessarily create feelings of persecution. Many lowly, self-effacing, and "creepy" sexual perverts, furthermore, are known to entertain paranoid fears of immense intensity. Grandiosity and projections of rage, hate, jealousy, and anger onto others do not explain it all. "The wicked flee when none pursueth," observed wise King Solomon a long time ago. Homo sapiens seems to respond to danger—whether internal or external—by the same reactions of fight, fright, or flight, as do all creatures belonging to the animal kingdom. The frightened schizophrenic, who attempts to flee or fight in self-defense, responds to a threat, but it originates deep within himself.

Not only breaches of the law, which are subject to legal prosecution, engender paranoid fears and ideas of persecution, but also crimes committed in the interpersonal context. As a matter of fact, the most intense feelings of judgment, persecution, and condemnation are experienced when a moral violation has no witnesses other than the perpetrator's conscience, and when the victim is unaware of the abuse, crime, or exploitation. As a rule, *the more secret the act, the louder the voice of conscience*. Misrepresentations, deceptions, sexual and other abuses or exploitations—all belong to the category of moral violations for which the Ego forewarns of social or interpersonal repercussions, and for which the Superego issues guilty dysphorias that may lead to panic states, paranoid delusions, disorganization, and frank psychosis. Persecution is logically expected by those who have broken the law—whether in the legal, interpersonal, moral, or spiritual realm; and legal prosecution, condemnation, ostracism, as well as providential retribution are reasonably feared. Paranoid fears are frequently associated with undue suspiciousness. Contemporary psychiatry regards suspiciousness as due to a failure in the development of "basic trust" during infancy. But popular opinion has it otherwise. It is condensed in an old Milanese proverb which claims: "There is none so suspicious as the guilty."

A chronic schizophrenic patient, Mrs. Polly T. summed it all up when she defined paranoia by the following statement: "*When you sin against God, you feel persecuted . . . !*"

e. Fears and Phobias

The fears and phobias that pervade the life-experience of schizophrenics are too numerous to be described. Being also specific for the individual, they defy accurate systematic classification. Nonetheless, fears may be divided into two main categories: fears contingent upon what one might do in the future, as are the fears of the *neurotic,* and *dread* of impending disaster for what one has already done in the past, characteristic of the *psychotic.*

One patient feared open windows, for they tempted him to suicide; another felt fearful of the street, for she was tempted to fall in front of speeding cars; another dreaded knives and sharp objects, appealing to her because of her homicidal intentions. Fear of certain animals may symbolize a specific undesirable trait in one's personality. To an adulterous woman who had betrayed her husband in the past, **Gatophobia,** or fear of cats, represented a fear of treason. Yet the dread that follows the commission of a crucial moral violation is much more intense than the anxiety of the neurotic; it pervades every object, situation, and prospect in the patient's life. In a state of permanent danger, all the senses of the schizophrenic become sharpened, just as they do in animals exposed to danger. Most widely recognized is the schizophrenic's intolerance to noise, which he experiences as louder than in actuality—a symptom known as "hyperacusia." An attitude of "hypervigilance" has been described by Arieti (1974). It may well be that hypervigilance is actually responsible for the perception of subliminal stimuli, arising from those "other worlds" beyond the reaches of "normal" individuals under ordinary circumstances.

The dread of the schizophrenic pervades all aspects of his life, from the realm of imagination and "what might be," to the realistic "here and now." Fear prevents him from experiencing pleasure, a symptom known as anhedonia. Fear exaggerates every ache and pain arising from his body and contributes to his hypochondriasis. Fear of condemnation and persecution sends the schizophrenic into a private prison of isolation and alienation. Fear prevents him from venturing into new experiences—a symptom known as **Neophobia.** Fear of the new may prevent patients from traveling, from moving to a new location, or into a new home. Job interviews are highly dreaded events, for they are equated with interrogation. Every attempt, every movement toward advancement and success is blocked by fear. Their fear of self-exposure creates the impression that schizophrenics are inaccessible, while they are actually hiding. But of all the myriad fears with which he is beleaguered, most powerful and overwhelming for the schizophrenic is his fear of death, of impending judgment, and punishment to come.

f. Alienation

A poignant description of sudden alienation is given by Dostoyevsky when he relates Raskolnikov's experiences following his commission of a double murder. As Raskolnikov's reasoning powers begin to falter while surrounded by officers in the police precinct after his arrest, he feels:

> . . . a gloomy sensation of agonizing, everlasting solitude and remoteness too conscious—forming in his soul . . . . If he had been sentenced to be burnt, at that moment, he would not have stirred, would hardly have heard the sentence till the end. Something was happening to him entirely new, sudden and unknown. It was not that he understood, but felt clearly with all the intensity of sensation, that he could never more appeal to these people in the precinct with sentimental effusions, or with anything whatever, and if they had been his own brothers and sisters, and not police officers, it would have been utterly out of the question to appeal to them . . . . He had never felt such a strange and awful sensation . . . a direct sensation, the most agonizing of all sensations he had ever known in his life . . . .

Alienation painfully tears through the substance of human aspirations—canceling prospects for love, affection, and understanding. Alienation breeds despair. Wandering alone on various descending paths, devoid of purpose, bereft of hope and guiding reason, the schizophrenic begins to relate to and converses with his "voices"—his hallucinations. He enters thus into communication with the Unresolved and Unredeemed, but exposes himself, in this manner, to the danger of being swallowed up in the uncharted realms of darkness.

The Schizophrenic Complex

A psychiatric glossary defines the complex (any complex) as:

> A set of associated ideas, bound by a strong affect (emotional tone), mostly unconscious and which has an influence on ideas, attitudes and behavior. (*Comprehensive Textbook of Psychiatry*, II, A. Freedman et al. 1975)

Several complexes have become popular in recent years, and their significance well understood: the "mother complex," for example, applies to the weakling, attached to his mother's apron strings; the "Napoleonic complex" has become almost synonymous with the power hunger that drives the short of stature to seek preeminence; and the "inferiority complex" is held responsible for the realization of as many achievements as it is blamed for undermining.

For Freud (1940) and his followers, the Oedipus complex represented a milestone in the development of every child. This complex was also considered by him to be the foundation of the moral law—the origins of conscience being "but heirs to the Oedipus complex." Analysis of this complex *par excellence* reveals that it contains two principal elements: a forbidden wish and a warning anxiety. In the Oedipus complex the forbidden wish represents an incestual striving, desire, fantasy, or intention with which affection for the parent of the opposite sex becomes tinged, whereas "castration anxiety" summarizes all the warning dysphorias and fears that are reflexively produced by the sinful striving. Thus, by reason of entertaining such wishes, the child who secretly lusts after his mother experiences warning anxieties in addition to feelings of guilt.

Fears generated by forbidden wishes and desires may become displaced, however, onto external objects that symbolize the tempting object or situation. Such was the case of "little Hans," described by Freud (1909). This 5-year-old boy was terrified of horses, which somehow reminded him of the fear and hatred he felt toward his father.

Every neurotic complex is constructed along a configuration similar to that of the Oedipus complex, and contains: 1. a morally forbidden wish/desire, and 2. an array of warning anxieties, phobias, and fears of punishment, liable to escalate into panic. But the neurotic complex contains also feelings of guilt, generated by thoughts, feelings, or intentions, which run contrary to the moral code of the conscience. The neurotic complex can be represented schematically as a molecule containing two basic elements, as shown in Diagram # 5.

Diagram # 5

The Neurotic Conflict as a Complex

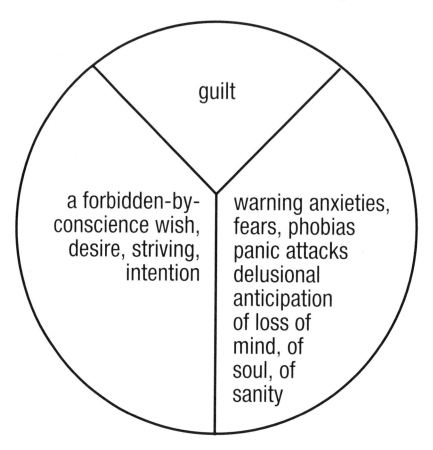

guilt

a forbidden-by-conscience wish, desire, striving, intention

warning anxieties, fears, phobias panic attacks delusional anticipation of loss of mind, of soul, of sanity

The neurotic complex contains two basic elements: the morally forbidden wish/temptation and the warning anxieties issued by the conscience and the Ego-mind-reason. A low-grade sense of guilt for entertaining the forbidden possibility is also present. The Oedipus complex, for example, contains incestual strivings and a delusional fear of castration.

What differentiates the neurotic complex(es) from that of schizophrenia? C. G. Jung (1907) attempted to compare them. Both the neurotic and the schizophrenic complex(es) remain, according to Jung, in a constant state of repression, meaning that they are hidden from the view of consciousness. In neurotic states, and especially in hysteria, the complex becomes dissociated from yet does not lose contact with the Ego, which remains the directing force in conscious thought. The complex does not shatter the Ego's integrity in neurotic disturbances; whereas the reverse holds true for schizophrenia. In neuroses, the complex remains subjugated to the Ego, whereas in schizophrenia the complex becomes autonomous and reigns sovereign over the Ego, weakening its powers. Jung thus regarded the weakening of the Ego as secondary to the complex. Whereas in the neuroses, inclusive of hysteria, wish-dream and delirium may be overcome and mental equilibrium reestablished, the schizophrenic complex becomes fixed and cannot be overcome. The psyche in schizophrenia can never rid itself of the complex, and escapes at best with psychic mutilation and scarring.

Jung's comparisons may be analyzed in existential terms: whereas in neurosis the subject is involved in a struggle against an unacceptable wish/temptation, in schizophrenia the forbidden wish/desire has already been fulfilled—against the warnings of the Ego and the Superego. The subject has yielded to the tempting possibility and can never rid himself of his action(s). The act is done and cannot be retrieved from the past.

The schizophrenic complex is incomparably more powerful than that of the neuroses, and its autonomy becomes so absolute as to "take possession of the conscious mind." The complex, moreover, encroaches upon every area of association and causes a lowering of the level of mentation (P. Janet, 1859–1947) with characteristic one-sidedness, clouding of judgment, weakness of the will, and disturbances in verbal communication. Vague statements, broken sentences, loose associations, blockings, perseverations, stereotypy, verbal-motor superficiality, alliteration, and assonance may all enter into the verbal communications of the schizophrenic. These peculiarities in the schizophrenic's verbal expressions are best understood as manifestations of "formal thought disorder" *(vide infra)*. The complex shows a tendency toward assimilating everything that comes near its orbit, and can be activated by even the most far-fetched stimuli. Perseverations and "clang associations" occur whenever the complex is being "hit," which occurs quite frequently, because associations revolve entirely around it. Needless to say, such interference with thought-processing renders the task of adaptation to the exigencies of external reality exceedingly difficult.

Jung firmly held psychological factors responsible for the causation of schizophrenia, acknowledging, nonetheless, the effects of psychological disturbances on the metabolism and physiological processes in general. Furthermore, Jung (1957) saw that schizophrenia shows a logical course: "I have never met with a case that did not show a logical and consistent development of the disease," he wrote. Most formidable of Jung's insights, however, might well prove to be his intuition regarding the existence in schizophrenia of an affect, which eventually becomes "toxic," and responsible for causing damage to the central nervous system in protracted illnesses.[*] Intuitively, Jung perceived the major role of subcortical centers in emotional transactions. All this he discovered several decades before the consolidation of the dopamine theory of schizophrenia, and before the availability of techniques for investigation of brain anatomy and physiology (i.e., CAT scans, MIR and PETT techniques).

Essentially, the dopamine theory of schizophrenia implicates the endogenously manufactured catecholamines dopamine, epinephrine, and norepinephrine as major participants in this diseased state, especially in its more acute stages (Chapter III). When dopamine-agonistic substances such as Disulfiram or L-dopa are introduced into the body, a schizophrenia-like emotional state can be produced, manifested by agitation anxiety, fear, paranoid suspiciousness, and intense aggressive urges, which may lead to combative behaviors. The same effects are produced by the use of substances that in lower doses produce "excitement," but in larger amounts produce effects much similar to those contingent on increases in dopamine turnover, as observed in schizophrenia.

Whereas chemical compounds may produce symptoms suggestive of schizophrenia, this does not, by necessity, identify them as etiological to psychotic states. And just as during other states of danger the organism releases the hormone of stress adrenaline (epinephrine) in order to prepare the body for fright, flight, or fight, the threat of spiritual annihilation perceived by the schizophrenic may well be the stimulus for the release of such substances in the brain. A twofold increase in the release of epinephrine was found associated with the stress of public speaking (J. E. Dimsdale et al. 1980). An increased release of norepinephrine, on the other hand, was found

---

[*] The "affect-toxin" of C. G. Jung may well be the biological equivalent of hate, guilt, fear, and other negative emotions transmitted through Dopamine-coded messages.

associated with physical exercise (as pleasurable activity). An increased release of dopamine at specific cerebral sites (and an accelerated turnover) was repeatedly demonstrated in acute stages of schizophrenic illnesses, yet the increase in turnover of dopamine does not necessarily implicate this neurotransmitter as responsible for schizophrenic states. One is justified, nonetheless, in assuming that certain conditions (i.e., public speaking, physical exercise), as well as internal pressures and threats, are capable of releasing substances in the body that can influence physiological processes as well as functioning of the central nervous system.

In their study on patients suffering from coronary heart disease mentioned above (p. 2), A. Rozanski et al. (1988) found that not the act of public speaking *per se*, but the mental stress involved in specifically admitting one's personal faults and undesirable habits in public, "produced the most frequent and greatest abnormality according to all markers of cardiac ischemia." Wall motion (of the heart) abnormalities and other parameters of cardiac ischemia were found in 72 percent of the patients studied. The pain of recognizing one's faults and admitting them in public was hurting these patients literally "deep down in their hearts."

It may appear quite paradoxical, in this context, that researchers in the field of medicine seek to compare the various mental stresses and to assess their impact upon body function, whereas psychiatrists, whose main interest ought to be focused on the "psyche," attempt to explain emotional disturbances on the basis of chemical compounds and somatic-physiological changes. In the case of schizophrenia, the inner danger experienced by these patients, which to them is all too real, creates changes in the body much like those of a threatened animal preparing for fright, flight, or fight. And if, indeed, the schizophrenic complex of sin and guilt has the capacity of generating threatening dysphorias pertaining to guilt—biochemically translated into increased dopamine transactions across specific synaptic clefts at specific cerebral sites—this would reconcile psychological with biochemical theories of schizophrenia and strengthen the hypotheses advanced by Jung. Certain stimulants such as amphetamines, cocaine, and PCP—known for their capacity to create subjective states of fear, anxiety, suspicion, and combativeness—can simulate the symptoms of acute schizophrenia. Inducing dread and fright-filled anticipations, the psychological and behavioral effects of these substances are quite similar to those resulting from an increase in dopamine availability. But they also induce alterations in the physiology of the organism, as occur in other states of danger.

The neurotic complex is further distinguished from the schizophrenic complex by the presence in the latter of what Jung described as "archaic material." Jung attributed the invasion of consciousness in psychosis by this archaic material to influxes from a "collective unconscious" whose symbolic representations are universally shared and understood by all members of the human family. Designated "archetypes" by Jung, the symbols pertaining to the "archaic unconscious" are experienced as endowed with a highly impressive, numinous quality. Unfortunately, a good deal of confusion came to be associated with Jung's "archetypes," the "collective unconscious," and the invasion of consciousness by spiritually meaningful symbols.

Whereas Freud relegated the "unconscious"—which he believed to contain stored past memories and various instinctual urges—to the basement of the mental edifice, for Jung the unconscious contained much more. The unconscious of Jung and later of Victor Frankl also (*The Unconscious God*, 1975), is not located at the bottom of the mental edifice, but at its center—the spiritual center of the personality. It contains, first and foremost, the moral conscience—sensitive to counsel emanating from the Divine. But the spiritual center is also the source of creativity, love, and transcendental strivings. During times of inordinate stress, cataclysm of psychosis, or nearness to death, the symbols of this unconscious come to assert their primacy, centrality, and supremacy in the life of the soul.

The schizophrenic complex contains the following three basic elements:

1. a secret, that needs to be repressed
2. a strong affect that becomes "toxic"
3. archaic symbols belonging to a collective as well as a personal unconscious, which gain dominance in the conscious mind

Jung conceptualized this complex as a macromolecule of multiple valencies which attracts to itself various thoughts, some unrelated. Eventually, the schizophrenic complex assumes preeminence and will "reign supreme" (C. J. Jung 1907) in the mental processes of the schizophrenic patient.

*   *   *

In *The Psychogenesis of Mental Disease* (1957), Jung wrote that only an insoluble conflict can lead to insanity. The psychotic patient, who has acted in favor of the forbidden wish/desire, renders his conflict insoluble, for the deed has been already done, and cannot be undone. His conflict becomes insoluble also by reason of the inviolability of certain moral-spiritual laws and the irrevocability of the verdicts of conscience. The commission of a serious moral violation may very well be that event, alluded to by Sullivan and Arieti, that suddenly plunges self-esteem to a new low. *But with the sudden loss in self-esteem, the schizophrenic senses a loss of Self in addition—a spiritual degradation, a fall.* The art productions of schizophrenic patients are replete with their sense of losses of Self— visible in their depiction of faces devoid of certain features and bodies lacking in some parts.

The drawing reproduced below depicts the constricted world of a schizophrenic patient. Nothing much is left here but the sexual act. There is near fusion with the sexual partner. The neck and the limbs are missing, as are the ears. The mouth and sexual organs are condensed into one; the fused bodies are shrunken into a rim of substance. The brain of the female (the patient)—the mind—is minimally represented, as compared to that of her male partner.

The awesome experience of spiritual degradation and their sense of a fall motivate some schizophrenic patients to embrace their original religion with renewed fervor. Others seek for themselves some new religion or philosophical solution. Redemptive acts and expiatory rituals are frequently undertaken, as are self-inflicted penalties. Paradoxically, instead of motivating them to reform, spiritual degradation leads many schizophrenics away from prior beliefs altogether, and a good number among them become negativistic, subversive, or cynical. They frequently attempt to convince themselves (and others) of the absurdity in believing in a Higher Power—a power other than their own. Delusional beliefs may lead schizophrenics to convert to another religion, which is often far removed from their original creed. Some religions, such as Buddhism, for example, may be sought simply because they *seemingly* lack in moral injunctions. Quite commonly, schizophrenic patients embrace religions that are no religions at all, but cults devoid of moral constraints. Some schizophrenics become worshippers of the devil.

In an effort to elucidate the religious conflicts and philosophical quandaries of schizophrenics, this writer (M. Niv 1980) investigated a total of 144 patients with respect to their religious beliefs, Weltanschauung, and life-philosophy. The findings of this inquiry are summarized in Table # 2.

Table # 2
**Religious Beliefs and Reported Changes
of 144 Schizophrenic Patients
During an Acute Psychotic Breakdown or Exacerbation**

	N	%
Kept their original beliefs	14	10
Refused to give information	19	13
Wished to return to their original creed but could not	17	12
Rejected their original beliefs	25	17
Changed their religion to a less or not morally binding creed: brotherhood, yoga, witchcraft, plants, the occult	27	19
Nihilistic	20	14
Made themselves the Lawgiver, the Most High	16	11
Believed Hell to be here and now	6	4

As shown in the table, many patients wished to return to their primary religion but could not, due to a sense of separation from the divine Thou, whose laws they knew they had trespassed. Their sense of spiritual degradation led one-half of the group to abandon their prior beliefs altogether. Of these, a majority chose a system of beliefs less morally binding or one devoid of moral injunctions. Some of their chosen creeds betrayed these patients' basic nihilism, as many became devoted to astrology, Scientology, numerology, signs and amulets, brotherhood, botania, etc.—allowing themselves to act thenceforth "as if all were permitted" (*vide infra*). The delusional beliefs of some patients clearly served to exalt their pride as well as to place them above the laws of morality. Others experienced the world as threatening, as though Hell were in the here and now. The results of this study may serve to demonstrate the profundity of the schizophrenic fall and its shattering effects. Only 14 patients in this series were able to return to their original religion. For a minority this was felt to be impossible, and for a majority their choices betrayed their defiant stance.

*   *   *

The following two case histories may serve to clarify as well as summarize the nature and effects of the schizophrenic complex:

> A 24-year-old college student was found by the police one early morning swimming in the icy waters of a lake in a public park, with his clothes on. He was singing to himself, so as to "feel innocent as a child again." He complained of seeing double (diplopia) and of having a reading disability (dyslexia), which were not organically determined. He had changed his original religion to one of Brotherhood. Later he admitted to having a homosexual encounter in the park, which generated in him a state of panic with "voices," visions, and other subjective experiences. He hoped he could be purified by the waters of the lake. He embraced the new "Brotherhood" religion in order to justify himself, and as license for continuing homosexual activities. (From author's caseload)

*   *   *

> A 25-year-old man requested to be circumcised and have also a tonsillectomy, while on the acute ward of a mental hospital. He believed himself afflicted with various venereal diseases and experienced other fears as well. Both the patient and his sister confirmed that he had engaged in various perverse sexual activities and excesses. His delusions contained the punishment expected for past sexual transgressions: venereal disease. He believed that the tonsillectomy and the circumcision would serve as a surgical cure, an act of penitence, as well as a religious conversion. (From author's caseload)

Diagram # 6

The Schizophrenic Complex
as a Macromolecule of Multiple Valencies

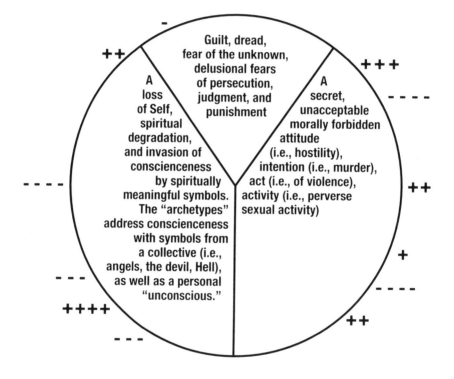

The schizophrenic complex contains three basic elements:

1. the secret morally forbidden act or attitude;
2. feelings of guilt, dread, and persecution, and
3. a sense of loss of Self, a spiritual degradation conveyed to consciousness through spiritually meaningful symbols (i.e., angels, the devil, Hell).

The multivalency of the complex accounts for its attachment to various thought-stimuli; for its encroaching upon every area of association; and for sucking to itself far-fetched stimuli, as thinking becomes "complex-bound." Attention becomes focused on the spiritually charged symbols that invade now consciousness. The schizophrenic complex floods all mental processes with fears, guilt, and dread, as it assumes sovereignty and autonomy. Unlike the neurotic complex, the schizophrenic complex is neither subject to the Ego-mind-reason nor to volition.

All the elements of the schizophrenic complex find here representation:

1. A serious moral violation or sin, unacceptable to the Self and which needs to be repressed, becoming a "secret."

2. A conviction by the court of conscience, which generates various dysphorias pertaining to guilt as fear (the major affect of schizophrenia—its "toxin").

3. Intrusion of "archaic symbols" into consciousness (through voices, visions, nightmares, misperceptions, etc.), charged with a spiritual message and imparting a sense of spiritual degradation and doom.

The sense of a spiritual fall, grasped by these patients, led some to engage in various expiatory activities and motivated a good number of them to change their original religious beliefs.

It may not be possible to analyze further the various elements of the schizophrenic complex, as sin, guilt, and dread—connected by reflexes—become interwoven with archaic symbolism. Dread and fears of every kind seep into the conscious mind of the patient, and flood it eventually with anticipations of a retributive justice, from which there appears no way of escape. It is worth repeating that, as a general rule, during the first psychotic episode, the spiritually meaningful symbols allow for glimpses of Heaven as well as of Hell; they become, however, more clearly infernal with each new exacerbation. The anonymous psychologist, cited above, wrote as follows:

> The schizophrenic is motivated in the first place by Fear. What is a schizophrenic? A terrified conscience-stricken crook, whose favorite commandment is the Eleventh: Thou shall not be caught! (Anonymous, 1958)

The presence of extreme anxiety and fear in schizophrenia finds confirmation in studies with the polygraph. Investigated by expert polygrapher S. Abrams (1974), the records of schizophrenic patients "could not be clearly differentiated from those of individuals whose psychological condition demonstrates a state of extreme anxiety, of *fright*" [emphasis added].

The schizophrenic reacts to his guilty state by way of muscular tension, increase in cardiac output, breath-holding, and hypervigilant anticipation, just as the guilty during polygraph examination. Defensive rage is frequently activated by guilt-provoking stimuli, and may compel the schizophrenic to fight without apparent reason. Vague and misleading, the schizophrenic flees from others in speech as well as in behavior. He may take flight in aimless walking ventures, or abandon his lodgings altogether—roaming the streets as a homeless person. He fears encountering himself also, and hides his complexes from his inner Self with layers of deception. But what the schizophrenic fears above all else is his own demise and the decree of divine Justice, from which he knows he cannot flee.

*   *   *

In attempting to overcome the insolubility and irrevocability of the schizophrenic complex(es), patients may engage in self-imposed punishments, by which they seek to attenuate their feelings of guilt. W. Stekel (1929) wrote on self-punishment:

> We shall find everywhere as the motif of self-accusation and self-mutilation the consciousness of guilt, which forces the original sadist to masochistic acts of atonement, that he may escape the punishment of the Supreme Judge.

The following cases, from this author's caseload, serve to demonstrate the insanity of such a solution:

> A wealthy heiress, in the habit of stealing by reason of insatiable greed and materialistic strivings, became increasingly disturbed after having stolen an object from her best friend's home. This theft, causing an acute exacerbation of her psychosis, prompted the patient to set on fire all of her belongings, in an attempt to punish herself as well as to "destroy the evidence."

> An educated, able-bodied young man refused to work and assume family responsibilities. With the progressive worsening of his "schizophrenia simplex," he began, several years later, to search the contents of garbage cans, with which he fed himself as deserved punishment for refusing to earn his keep.

In some cases, self-imposed penalties seem determined by a psychological reflex, so powerful seems the compulsion. A deeper analysis of the manifest symptoms and behaviors of psychotic patients reveals that their acts of self-punishment conspicuously betray the sin that gave them cause, following as they do, the laws of talion. This fact was keenly observed by Stekel, who wrote:

> We shall find again and again, a torturing consciousness of guilt as the source of self-mutilation, dictating severe punishment according to the laws of talion. The patient thus combines in one person judge, accused and executioner.

Most remarkable, indeed, is the consistency with which self-inflicted punishments betray the sin or sins that gave them cause. The inordinate power of the compulsion explains certain absurd self-mutilative acts, as for example, the enucleation of one's eye. Such was the case of a patient who attempted to enucleate his eye as punishment for lusting and consummating an adulterous relationship, in which a violent act was also involved. Self-punishing behaviors raise the question as to whether one can judge oneself unjustly. According to Aristotle, no one can (*The Ethics of Aristotle*). In an overview of the statistics of violence (*American Academy of Psychiatry and the Law*, 1976), S. Halleck reported that of all men charged with homicide, between 18 percent and 33 percent eventually committed suicide.

Considered from the vantage point of the laws of talion, certain self-inflicted penalties cease to appear cruel, unjust, and sadistic. The moral conscience may have good reasons for its decrees and penalties, nonetheless, even if reason fails to grasp them.

In order to explain self-punishing behaviors, which frequently appear to be unduly severe, Freud invoked "unconscious" guilt as their motivation. Nevertheless, he never sought to relate the severity of punishment to the seriousness of the transgression; but then Freud denied sin as a psychological reality altogether. He was ready to concede, however, that the strictness of the conscience could not be traced back to harsh and punitive parental attitudes during childhood (S. Freud 1933). Unable to explain adequately the psychology of self-punishment, he suggested that the sadism of the Superego derives from the dark forces of the unconscious Id (p. 113 for another interpretation).

With respect to the existence of "unconscious" guilt and the burial of the schizophrenic complex into deeper layers of consciousness, it would appear that irrespective of depth, every complex of sin and guilt eventually comes to surface. No matter how skillfully the deceiver covers his transgression through projections, denials, suppressions, and repressions, the truth about it is ever before him.

When defiantly entrenched in an unrepented position, the sinner might be compelled to execute on himself such punishments as fit his "crimes."

*   *   *

When does insanity begin? This heavy question, asked by Dostoyevsky's Raskolnikov, returns to haunt our understanding. Does insanity begin with malicious thoughts and obsessions? With perverse and morbid sexual fantasies? With their enactment in reality? Or with their aftermath? With insane acts of self-punishment?

According to current trends in psychology and psychiatry, all negative emotions such as envy, hostility, anger, and vindictiveness, among others, represent but *reactions* to faulty parental attitudes, adverse environments, various accidental calamities, or blows of Providence. Reflecting the *Zeitgeist*, what is now considered "sick" is not the maliciousness or perversion of the patient, but rather his compulsions and rituals, which serve as means for attenuating the torments of his guilt. Yet, what is to be regarded as more irrational: to hate obsessively, or to act compulsively with rituals and self-inflicted penalties, intended to erase guilt? What is to be considered more insane: to act sadistically in a "loving" sexual relationship, or to impose upon oneself some cruel punishment afterward? Where does madness begin? Should the wealthy heiress be considered insane, when she sought through theft to add to her possessions, or when she set her belongings on fire?

Whether generated by "unconscious" guilt or executed through the operation of a psychological reflex, self-inflicted penalties in no way alter the offender's basic guilty condition. And needless to say, such palliative solutions only serve to obstruct the way to authentic healing. They certainly prevent contrition, i.e., the sorrowing over one's failures and desire to reform. They allow, moreover, for moral transgressions to become entrenched as positions, rendering them ever more resistant in this manner. Self-imposed penalties seem to follow the same psychological laws as the "repetition compulsion" described by Freud (1920), but they frequently become habitual and enter then as components of the character structure.

The inordinately high rate of recidivism among criminals, estimated at 85 percent for at least one rearrest (S. Guze, 1976), and higher for sex offenders, is difficult to explain otherwise than as due to the operation of a certain psychological pattern or reflex. According to Guze's findings, neither length nor manner of punishment, family history, or background have any bearing on the rate of recidivism. The single most important factor in the prediction of recidivism among convicted criminals was found to be related to the extent of their previous criminal career. What is true for criminals seems to apply to schizophrenic patients as well. Their life-histories and psychiatric records reveal with remarkable consistency that whatever moral violation had caused the outbreak of the first psychotic illness was repeated, as if under compulsion. It would appear as if the schizophrenic complex insists on being repeated, and, needless to say, this further compounds existing psychopathology. But the repetition compulsion may not be dictated by a psychological rule or reflex altogether, but by *a spiritual law, whereby every unrepented sin compounds itself—because of its remaining unrepented—by a compulsion demanding its repetition.*

*   *   *

The most misunderstood and, perhaps for this reason, most neglected aspect of insanity has been the third element of the schizophrenic complex, namely the invasion of consciousness by "archaic material" and the sense of spiritual degradation its symbols tend to impart. Regrettably, it has become almost tradition to regard the "florid" symptoms of schizophrenia—misperceptions, delusions, and hallucinations—as regressive, "primary process phenomena"; bursts from the unconscious Id which the Ego had failed to contain. And, in spite of their relevance to etiological determinants and their possible usefulness for psychotherapy, the florid symptoms of psychosis have come to be regarded as nothing more than obsolete by-products of the patient's "craziness," and so dismissed. Primary in importance, the "archaic material" that makes its appearance by means of spiritually charged symbols during a psychotic illness, carries a message of utmost importance to the patient, nonetheless. Its meaning needs to be decoded and incorporated in the process of psychotherapy.

Jung (1907) dared to seek and penetrate the meaning not only of dreams, but of other subjective experiences as well:

> There is nothing astonishing in finding archaic, dreamlike material products with their characteristic numinosity in situations which threaten the very foundations of the individual.

Representing a most serious existential catastrophe, it is hardly surprising that during the eruption of an acute psychosis—when the soul is threatened with extinction—spiritual symbols come to assert their preeminence in the conscious mind. But the "archaic material," which gains access into consciousness and eventually takes precedence over other mental processes, contains not only elements belonging to a "collective unconscious," such as darkness, light, angels, and the devil, but symbols of deep personal significance as well. And while the overall atmosphere of psychosis is permeated by dread, and its symbolic representations are perceived as infernal (except for the first one or two psychotic episodes), the patient's delusional experiences transform his world, as he finds himself in a very personal, very individual Hell.

With striking creativity and clarity, the archaic symbols address consciousness in a language that is well comprehended. The impact of the message gives cause for reflection as well as for self-examination. The symbols may bring forth a passage from the Holy Scriptures, evoke heroes from Greek mythology, bring memories from events long past, and even make use of fairy tales, when these are of particular significance to the individual. Appearing in critical moments of existence, these subjective experiences may be understood as phenomena on the order of personal revelation. "The images of the unconscious place a great responsibility upon man," wrote Jung (1957), and further: "Insight into them must be converted into an ethical obligation."

It is not that during the critical state of psychosis the afflicted individual is invaded by atavistically transmitted "archaic" rubble from his disintegrated psyche, but rather that during this cataclysmic-to-existence event, the symbols belonging to the personal history of his soul are brought back in order to speak to his awareness in this persuasive manner. Yet the symbols must have a particular meaning for the individual so addressed, for they would not otherwise make their appearance at the moment his soul is perceived to be in danger of extinction. The windows of perception seem to open wider then— allowing for glimpses of some other worlds: blissful pastures of Heaven or dark pits of Hell.

Religious symbols do not appear by chance in psychotic illnesses. Their constant appearance in the experience of schizophrenia strongly suggests a causal link. It is indeed surprising that in spite of their universality, the philosophical dilemmas and religious preoccupations of the insane have been met with such disdain by the healers of the soul. Not only patients who had received a religious education suffer from religious difficulties, and not only those intellectually inclined become involved in problems of philosophy. Mental health professionals, it would appear, have failed to realize that behind the insane's religiosity and interest in philosophy stands a search for redemption and an attempt to overturn the guilty verdict of the conscience.

For true believers, religion is most central to their being. They live by faith and for its sake are ready to renounce much of the rewards offered them by the world. Religion directs their paths, and the subjective experience of the divine Being fills them with a basic trust and confidence. To the religious, the experience of Being is more real than any of the realities perceived by their senses. And when the spiritual Self, or master of the chariot, assumes command, it charts its course and final destination. The chariot will not be driven merely by emotions (wheels of the chariot), and may even go against their pull when its master is answering a call of duty or a demand for sacrifice. When the spiritual Self or soul truly assumes command, it rules over the Ego-mind-reason (the charioteer) and directs it to strive for higher reaches.

The language of the soul is quite distinct from that employed in thought and in communication. In states of danger, sorrow, or during the sharp turns of life, such as crises of existence and nearness to death, one ought to stand still and listen to the deeply personal messages conveyed by way of symbols: in a verse of poetry, a melody, a passage from the Scriptures, a hymn forgotten, a face beloved. One ought then to listen and reflect.

The Thought Disorder of Schizophrenia: A Major Defensive Operation

The thought disorder characteristic of schizophrenia has always enjoyed a status paramount in importance from a diagnostic viewpoint, as well as for its predictive value in prognosis. Disturbances in associative thought (thought connectedness) were regarded by E. Bleuler (1911) as a cardinal symptom of this diseased state, and, for some researchers, one responsible for its other manifestations as well. The subject of thought disorder in schizophrenia has given cause to much debate, numerous speculations, and countless studies, often leading investigators to succumb to the temptation of achieving technical precision at the expense of genuine understanding. Here as elsewhere, scientific truth became buried in an avalanche of detail. Yet a global view of the thought disturbances observed in schizophrenia would immediately force the following conclusion: these apparent aberrations serve a defensive purpose.

Before undertaking a deeper analysis of the various disturbances in the thought processes and communications of schizophrenic patients, it is useful to remember that thought disturbances can occur in moments of undue stress, and may be present in highly creative individuals, such as writers, comedians, political speakers, etc. According to N. Andreasen (1979), thought disorder may also be present in other mental disturbances, albeit to a lesser extent.

Thought disturbances, moreover, wax and wane with the various phases of the illness, and at times disappear altogether. Considering "paraphasias" choice and not mishap, H. W. Gruhle (1926) poignantly asked the question: "How can a basic thought disorder exist when it completely disappears during an intercurrent physical illness?"

A distinction between disordered thinking and disturbed communications needs to be made first, nevertheless. The guilty schizophrenic does not necessarily communicate what he thinks; and what he actually thinks is determined to a large extent by the schizophrenic complex(es). Described first by Jung and later by Hoch, the thinking of schizophrenics becomes, essentially, "complex-bound." Comparing patients suffering from organic impairments with those affected by functional mental illnesses, expert and pioneer worker on thought disorders, J. S. Kasanin (1964), strongly emphasized that "the organic patient desperately tries to make himself understood, while the schizophrenic has no intention of changing his highly individual method of communication and seems to enjoy the fact that you do not understand him . . . ." More on the subject is said by the Anonymous psychologist who defined the schizophrenic as "a guilty, conscience-stricken crook" and the state of schizophrenia as "the cultivation of a lie."

> Whatever words he actually uses are employed as self-defensive weapons. A semi-instinctive stratagem leads schizophrenics, like pursued rabbits, to "zigzag," thus baffling the pursuer's expectations. The proximal goal is to avoid being understood, the ultimate goal is to avoid punishment. (Anonymous 1958)

Are all the communications of the schizophrenic that we fail to understand intended to baffle us in order to conceal some hidden truth? If and when denial of a known truth is consciously and creatively undertaken, and cognition becomes mobilized in the service of dissimulation or justification, communication ceases to represent what is actually thought, and duplicity is created instead. A schizophrenic patient put it this way: "When you lie, you become TWO."

We cannot exactly know what is being thought, but we do know that in schizophrenia, thinking becomes largely complex-bound. As was previously emphasized, the schizophrenic complex behaves like a macromolecule in the thought processes of the schizophrenic patient. It encroaches upon every area of association and assimilates into its orbit every thought that "hits" the complex. Even the most far-fetched words or ideas are liable to be caught in the vortex of the complex, causing difficulties in concentration as well as impairment in judgment. Whenever the complex is hit by a question or thought near its orbit, a pause is liable to delay the response (just as the deceiver's responses slow down during polygraph investigation), while the answer given may be idiosyncratic, meaningless, silly, and vague. The question may also evoke perseverations, stereotypy, neologisms, etc. The complex thus may magnetically attract to itself and "overinclude" various stimuli; it may also repel certain associations closely related to the complex(es). During an interview, when the patient appears to have "loose associations," he may be skirting the issues pertaining to his sin and guilt complexes, or avoid them by various distracting tactics. In psychiatric terms, the patient's thinking is circumstantial, tangential, his thoughts "derail," and his associations are "loose." In colloquial language the patient will be described as "beating around the bush."

In schizophrenia, what is thought "in the heart" is determined largely by the complex. What is communicated is also conditioned by the complex, but verbal behavior does not necessarily reveal it. Concluding a study on the thought disorder manifested by schizophrenic patients, M. Harrow et al. (1978) dismissed disturbed logic as responsible for producing thought disturbances—as originally postulated by E. Bleuler; nor could they confirm older formulations that consider the intrusion of "drive material" into the stream of thought as causative of what appears disturbed thinking. Harrow et al. reported, however, that certain "intermingling of idiosyncratic material" related to the patient's personal life—past and present—intrudes in the thought processes of schizophrenics and disturbs the flow of thought. But what intermingles in the stream of thought shows itself to be none other than the schizophrenic complex, whose polyvalency draws to itself various thought-stimuli (quite far-fetched at times), as the patient's thinking becomes complex-bound.

Delusional ideas or delusions proper are common in the communications of schizophrenic patients. Although delusional ideas often appear far-fetched, bizarre, and devoid of logic, these false beliefs represent nothing more than deceptions and self-deceptions entertained for the sake of justification. Delusional ideas may be constructed around a falsified reality. Indeed, they frequently contain half-truths and various distortions, some of which may strain logic to its breaking point. The illogical thinking so characteristic of insanity is explained by S. Arieti (1974) in the following manner:

> As long as the patient interprets reality with Aristotelian logic, he is aware of the unbearable truth, and the panic persists. Once he sees things in a different way, with a new logic, his anxiety decreases or changes in character.

Arieti understood illogicality to be the consequence of anxiety-laden themes, and perceived that:

> Another characteristic of the schizophrenic is to find logical justifications—rationalizations to project the blame. The far-fetchedness of their rationalizations seems to be proportionate to the severity of the disorder.

A. Angyal (1964) advanced the suggestion that:

> Perhaps the patient is using an otherwise intact tool (that of thinking) in an incorrect way because of certain difficulties . . .

Not infrequently, "oneroid" or dreamlike material intrudes into the patient's consciousness. He may become distracted by his hallucinations, visions, or misperceptions, which interrupt the train of his thoughts and interfere with verbal communications. Freud considered these intrusions to represent "regressive," "primary process modes of cognition," presumably employed by preverbal children. Yet, whereas children may well think by way of images before their thoughts become formulated into words, there is nothing to indicate that their inner visions are charged with the horrors pervading the experiences of the schizophrenic. The oneroid images, appearing to the schizophrenic by way of dreams, illusions, visions, nightmares, delusions, and hallucinations, moreover, are endowed with unusual vividness, almost indistinguishable from perceptions processed by the senses. Very often, "eidetic" imagery is perceived as "more real even than reality itself." The ever changing terms and sets of labels given to the oneroid material that intrudes into the consciousness of the insane have contributed little, if at all, to their understanding. Why do these "endocepts" (Arieti), "primary process imagery" (Freud) and "archetypes" (Jung) suddenly make their appearance in the consciousness of the insane? What is their meaning?

A closer look into the *contents* of these phenomena immediately clarifies their essentially spiritual nature. Representing personal revelatory phenomena, *the oneroid material intrudes into consciousness in order to convey a message.* Yet in insanity, the oneroid images are mostly of a threatening nature, due to the perilous condition of the soul in this particular state of being, and urgency of the message. The meaning of the message is usually understood as representing a warning. In view of correction, and not as a punitive measure, the threatening images seek to impress upon the subject his closeness to the abyss, so as to "keep back his soul from the pit . . ." (Job 33:18).

*   *   *

The following is a brief review of the most common aberrations manifested in the thought processes and communications of schizophrenic patients, explained in accordance with the contents of this text:

1. *Concreteness of thinking*—reflects the inability of the schizophrenic to detach from his autistic, egotistic, egocentric Self, as well as from his schizophrenic complex(es). The proverb "One swallow does not make for spring" was interpreted by a lazy, dependent schizophrenic young man to mean that "in spring you do not have to leave the nest (his parents' home) and go out to work."

2. *Poverty of speech*—may reflect the impoverished world of the chronic schizophrenic; it may also be a consequence to conscious withholding of incriminating information. Large quantities of medication over a long period of time have also been known to produce cognitive deficits and losses in the capacity of verbal expression.

3. *Mutism*—may be used as a hostile exclusion of others; it may also serve as an all-out defensive operation.

4. *Overinclusion*—represents the assimilation by the complex of far-fetched stimuli and the endowment with meaning of remote, neutral objects.

5. *Loss of goal, or "derailing"*—occurs when speech wanders from topic to topic and sentences break in the middle, without ever reaching a goal or conclusion. In speech, this loss of goal is due to interference by the complex(es) and reflects also the loss of meaning experienced by the schizophrenic patient.

6. *Blockings*—represent silences that precede an answer, allowing time for the elaboration of a lie or another defense whenever the complex is being hit.

7. *Perseverations*—are vain repetitions of a word or sentence. They may fill in the vacuum in the thought processes of the schizophrenic. They may be present as symptoms in the organically impaired as well. Perseverations allow time for the schizophrenic to formulate a defensive, justificatory, or dissimulatory appropriate answer, whereas the organically impaired uses them as an opportunity for finding alternatives to forgotten words or sentences.

8. *Circumstantial and tangential statements*—are given with the purpose of "skirting the issue," avoiding the complex, the truth. They are literally a centrifugal way of thinking, away from the complex of sin and guilt, and away also from the Self, center of being and meaning. In verbal communications "beating around the bush" is recognized as a deceptive tactic.

9. *Loose associations*—are disjointed thoughts or ideas. They are usually due to the presence of the schizophrenic *complex. The complex both attracts far-fetched thoughts and repels certain thoughts that hit it.* Associations thus appear loosely connected to each other as well as to the topic.

10. *Clanging*—refers to the tendency of schizophrenic patients to use rhyming instead of meaningful words. Puns and jokes may be similarly derived, their connection being based on sound and not on meaning (in German, *klang* = sound).

11. *Neologisms, metonyms, etc.*—are used by creative schizophrenic individuals with the purpose of baffling, distracting, and impressing others with their wit.

As every communication reveals some of the thoughts and ways of being of the communicant, the verbal expressions of the schizophrenic expose some of the characteristics of his condition:

1. An impoverished world and threatened existence.

2. Autistic concerns and egocentricity.

3. Complexes of sin and guilt that assimilate all thoughts in their orbit and produce "complex-bound" thinking.

4. Deceptive operations intended to shield sin and guilt from the Self as well as from others—executed by various defensive operations, such as projections, denials, half-truths, distractive stratagems, silences, puns, stereotypy, perseverations, mutism, and more.

5. Intrusion into the stream of thought of symbolic representations whose content is spiritual in nature, and which persist in reminding the schizophrenic of the need to mend his ways.

Intellectually endowed individuals avail themselves of distracting stratagems, manifested as loose associations and centrifugal ways of communicating. But later, when deterioration sets in, the meaningless existence, impoverished world, and damaged intellect of the schizophrenic become manifest by what has been termed "negative thought disorder" (N. Andreasen 1979), i.e., communications pervaded by mutism, stereotypy, and perseverations, which convey little information.

As has been long recognized by researchers in the field of schizophrenia, this *diseased state may exist without the presence of a thought disorder*. K. Schneider's (1959) first-rank criteria do not include thought disorder; thought disturbances are also absent from the diagnostic criteria enunciated by J. P. Feighner et al. (1972). What differentiates schizophrenias in which a thought disorder is present from those illnesses in which it is absent?

Both thought-disordered and non-thought-disordered schizophrenics suffer from the same visions, nightmares, delusions, and hallucinations, and the life-experience of both is pervaded by fear. Yet they differ by a basic and crucial attitude: whereas the thought-disordered schizophrenic engages in self-justification, cover-up, projections, denials, deceptions, and self-deceptions, the non-thought-disordered schizophrenic admits to wrongdoing and accepts its consequences. Needless to say, the deceptive and self-deceptive stratagems of the thought-disordered schizophrenic remove him further from his fellow men as well as from his true Self, and this alienation greatly contributes to his eventual deterioration. According to J. S. Kasanin (1964), "When a formal thought disorder becomes apparent, the prognosis becomes ominous." A. T. Boisen (1936) expressed a similar opinion. A study by M. Harrow et al. (1981) of 125 patients with a two-year follow-up led these researchers to conclude that: "Persistently thought-disordered schizophrenic patients represent a group with a very poor outcome."

The Premorbid Personality
and Its Brand of Schizophrenia

Were schizophrenic illnesses but the results of some biochemical mishap or aberration—conditions predicated on faulty neurotransmission due to excesses or defaults of this or that neurotransmitter—the structure of the premorbid personality would be of little import to the outbreak of a psychotic illness. Accumulated research data and clinical observations tend, however, to point in the opposite direction. Whether reversible functional disorders or not, schizophrenic psychoses never emerge *de novo*, but are continuous with the premorbid personality, engrafting themselves upon its defects and weaknesses. The premorbid personality, moreover, not only molds the particular brand of schizophrenic illness, but determines its structure and eventual outcome, as well. To the wise of ages past, the findings produced by modern research, indicating that the personality and its functioning have a decisive influence on psychic well-being (or else, on dis-ease), would appear but superfluous assertion of obvious facts.

From a long-term longitudinal study of 502 schizophrenic patients, with an average of 22.4 years' duration of their illness, spanning over 14 years, G. Huber et al. (1980) found that among their patient population, 22.1 percent achieved a complete recovery; a noncharacteristic type of remission was observed in 43.2 percent; and a characteristic residual defect state (with cognitive deficits, loss of volition, abulia, loss of energy, reduced tolerance to nonspecific stress, and changes in the personality, among others) affected the remaining 34.7 percent. Neither family background nor the nature of the initial symptoms were found predictive of outcome, but in "markedly abnormal personalities, remissions were absent and more characteristic residues were frequent (48 percent) in this group." A "nonschizoid premorbid adjustment," on the other hand, was found predictive of a better outcome than otherwise (G. Vaillant 1964).

The longest catamnestic study to be reported in the psychiatric literature, spanning a period of 37 years, by L. Ciompi (1980), confirms personality factors to be the carriers of distinct prognostic weights. Personality factors associated with good premorbid functioning, as well as familial and professional adaptation, were found of primary importance in predicting a favorable outcome. These factors were found to "exercise such force that they influenced decisively the psychic well-being throughout the entire life." In earlier publications, G. Vaillant (1962) reported research data very similar to those of G. Huber and L. Ciompi.

It is noteworthy that the premorbid personality was assessed by its functioning—an evaluation dependent upon the summation of actions as behaviors, not feeling states. Harmonious existence within the family and society-at-large entails, precisely, the overcoming of certain feelings and individual idiosyncrasies. There is no satisfactory relationship or goal that can be achieved without the overcoming of certain feelings—a painful process more often than not. But since the will is also an emotion, it can be mobilized in order to subdue other feelings, for the sake of higher goals or benefit to others, the larger community.

According to Huber et al. (1980), acute psychoses carry a prognosis "significantly more favorable, with only 24 percent characteristic residues, whereas the reverse is true for insidiously progressing psychoses."

Most researchers concur that acute psychotic illnesses, indeed, augur a better prognosis than otherwise (P. Hoch 1972, G. Vaillant 1962, 1964, S. Arieti 1974). Acuteness of onset was also found to be "correlated with the primary personality" (G. Huber 1980). Insidious onset, on the other hand, was found "more frequent in deviant personalities than in nonaberrant or slightly aberrant personalities." Ciompi considered the "structural disease factors" as entirely reflected in the time-honored principle that has been repeatedly verified: the disease tends to run a more favorable course the more lively, the more acute, the more mobile its onset. But here again, "the structural disease factor is related to the premorbid personality." Obsessive-compulsive disorders, for example, evolve into a schizophrenia of the catatonic variety in 1 percent to 12 percent of cases. (E. Bleuler 1911, S. Arieti 1974, *The Harvard Mental Health Letter*, October, 1985). If these data are accurate, they would tend to implicate psychological factors—always intricately interwoven within the personality—in the development of a schizophrenic illness. The old adage that man's character to a large extent forges his destiny finds corroboration through a wealth of research data on the etiology and evolution of insanity. Much can be conjectured, however, about the constituents of character and the determinants of its final mold. One may be justified, nonetheless, in assessing the character of any one individual by his repetitive manifest behaviors (inclusive of verbal communications)—given that behavior represents the final outcome of consciously undertaken decisions. Decisions, in turn, result from a complex interplay of forces with inputs from the Ego-mind-reason, its reality assessment, its judgment, feeling states, past experiences, transcendental strivings, and much more. Whatever their determinants, behaviors represent the summation of mostly voluntary coordinated actions, which when repetitive, enter as building blocks in the structure of the personality.

Expressing the views of most Existentialists, Sartre (1946) writes in *Existentialism is a Humanism*:

> Man is nothing else but what he purposes, he exists only insofar as he realizes himself, he is therefore nothing else but the sum of his actions . . . .

It is thus hardly surprising that when psychotic illnesses make their appearance, their occurrence, structure, and outcome are largely determined by the premorbid personality, i.e., by the individual's character as summation of his actions. This does not mean that the schizophrenic *chooses* to descend into the underworlds of psychosis, but that he is suddenly brought to experience some of the consequences of his actions as the continuity of his life is interrupted by a spiritual-psychological breakdown. The profile of the future schizophrenic would show thus: that in the past he had acted almost exclusively in his own interest; that autistically and egotistically he had submitted to the dictates of mostly his own will and desires; that he had defiantly disregarded the needs and benefit of others; and that in full consciousness he had undertaken the suppression of the dictates of his conscience. Regardless of motivation, whether unconscious or not, coordinated activities cannot be executed without participation of the Ego-mind—although its reason and control might become temporarily eclipsed in the heat of passion, anesthetized by drugs or alcohol, or suspended in the state of sleep.

Existential psychiatrists are thus justified in their insistence that the soul may suffer loss of its substance, but only for actions that run against the laws of its existence, not for feeling states or fantasies. And whatever the given circumstances—heredity, birth, upbringing, adversity, or blows of fate—the Self or soul cannot suffer from disease, spiritual degradation, or loss of its integrity unless its owner—free to make choices—has taken the decision to cause harm, damage, hurt or destruction, in violation of the moral-spiritual laws engraved in his conscience.

With respect to moral transgression, a major qualitative difference exists between sin that has become ingrained within the personality—deception or hatred, for example—and sin committed suddenly, in isolation, as capitulation to a pressing temptation. In the first case, where sin is structured within the personality—which may contain other negative traits as well—an insidious type of illness with a progressively deteriorative outcome is more likely to ensue. In the second instance, where sin is committed by reason of an overwhelming power arising from desire, temporarily victorious over the forces of morality, a "reactive" type of psychosis—singular event, lively and dramatic—is liable to occur, carrying a good prognosis as a general rule.

G. Langfeldt's (1939) dichotomy, which separates core, Process or Nuclear Schizophrenias (p. 168) from Reactive or Schizophreniform Psychoses carries distinct prognostic markers that have been repeatedly validated by research findings. Whereas the process, nuclear variety leads to early deterioration and dementia, reactive and schizophreniform psychoses have a course and outcome quite benign. From the existential perspective, the dichotomy is justified as well, because the insidious, process variety involves consciously undertaken choices of evil, whereas the reactive variety represents merely a response to temptation.

a. Brief Reactive Psychoses, Transitional Psychotic Episodes,
and Hysterical Psychoses

These acute psychoses have traditionally been differentiated from true schizophrenias by their short duration and generally benign course and outcome. **Reactive, Schizophreniform Psychoses** and **Transitional Psychotic Episodes** are known to affect otherwise "good" premorbid personalities. As a general rule, these illnesses subside within a short period of time and do not leave much of a residual state. Despite their drama, liveliness, confusion, delusions, and hallucinations, they subside within one to six weeks, with or *without* treatment. Known the world over by various designations, their symptomatology is heavily colored by local customs, traditions, and religious beliefs. Nonetheless, these psychoses, offer a good opportunity for the investigation of the precipitants to psychoses in general. In Laos, brief psychoses are known as Baa; in Siberia as Nagi-Nagi; in Malaya as Koro. **Koro** is a state of intense fear—a panic-merging-with-psychosis state whose subject entertains the possibility of losing his genitals. The dread and delusional fear in the psychotic state of Koro follow the actual practice (not fantasy) of either sexual excesses, incest, perverse sexual activities, or the infringement of another sexual taboo. Koro brings to mind the famous "fear of castration," pivotal to psychoanalytical theories. This panic state may serve to explain delusions in general as representing threats of punishment justly deserved—in the case of Koro, for incest, deviancy, or excessive sexual activity.

As for **Hysterical Psychoses,** there is nothing primitive or imaginary about them. Colored by culture, tradition, and religious practices, the symbolic representations that invade consciousness during their more acute stages have come, unfortunately, to be regarded as *causative*, i.e., as etiologic to these psychotic distur-bances. Nothing can be further from the truth than such an interpreta-tion. Affecting otherwise well-functioning premorbid persons, brief reactive "hysterical" psychoses result from capitulation to a tempting but morally forbidden wish/desire. Whatever the reasons behind the breach of the moral law or infringement of a social taboo, they do not prevent the conscience's system of justice from taking its course. As with other psychotic illnesses, the verdict of the conscience brings to awareness both the moral offense as well as its penalty. And similar to other "explosions of conscience," elements from a collective as well as a personal "unconscious" make their appearance in awareness—addressing consciousness with symbolic representations of significance to the spiritual Me, to the soul.

If we were to compare the healing practices of "primitive" peoples with those of the civilized Western world, we might be surprised to find a sounder judgment and rationale in the treatment approaches of the primitives. In their cultures and traditions, sin is acknowledged as a reality, representing a personal failure, not any "sickness" or product of "craziness." Guilt is recognized as the unavoidable consequence of moral transgression. The healing strategies of the "primitives" thus require the psychotic to make a public confession, to repent in sincerity, and to renounce the particular sin in question. The penitent may then be asked to plead for forgiveness and to undergo certain ritual(s) of penitence and purification. After the social group extends forgiveness and acceptance to the failing individual, he is eventually reintegrated within the family and his society. Denying the reality of sin—and guilt as its unavoidable consequence—Western therapeutic approaches have sought to effect a healing of the psyche by the use of medicines and enforced resocialization. Yet, for bypassing the process of confession, contrition, repentance, and desire to change; and for failing to require from the patient to humbly seek forgiveness from the injured other or the group, secular therapists can count themselves guilty of abandoning their patients while they are bleeding from their spiritual wounds.

b. Catatonic Schizophrenias

Catatonic schizophrenias represent mobile, acute, and dramatic psychoses which often engraft themselves on obsessive-compulsive disorders (p. 165), as reported by Arieti, E. Bleuler (1911), and Jung. The premorbid characteristics of those eventually affected by catatonic schizophrenia include: excessive stubbornness, negativism, willfulness, withholding, a pervasive hostility which may be expressed by sadistic behaviors, passive-aggressive obstructionism, and defiant attitudes in general. In excited catatonia, aggression, hostility, and destructive rage come to the fore, as the basic negativism and malevolence of these patients become grotesquely exaggerated and often acted out. W. Stekel (1929) commented on the hatefulness of the obsessional neurotic:

> We must consider that every hatred in its final issue is deadly. The "death" clause is absent from no obsession. The parapathic (obsessional) neurotic is a criminal without the courage to commit the crime. He is ill of this division of his nature—*he oscillates between good and evil* [emphasis added].

In his characterization of the obsessional neurotic, Stekel brings into focus a cardinal sign of schizophrenia, namely ambivalence—one of Bleuler's four "A's." Ambivalence seeps into the mental processes of both the obsessional neurotic and the schizophrenic and renders their decision-making difficult. Ambivalence characteristically mars all of their relationships. Hatefulness may thus be entertained together with love, but this love is mostly of a clinging, dependent, possessive, and exploitative kind. In most of the relationships of both the obsessive and the schizophrenic, hatefulness tends to predominate. In catatonic schizophrenia, ambivalence may become manifest by alternations of willful defiance with periods of automatic obedience. In excited catatonia, pent-up aggression and malevolent intentions break loose in a frenzy of destructive and injurious activities. In stuporous catatonia, on the other hand, the subject is held in dramatic suspense by visions of Hell, the devil, and destruction of the world— fear and terror holding him hostage to the point of paralysis. Powerful aggressive urges might thus be held in check by an effort of the will. These patients often give the appearance of waxy, cataleptic statues— motionless from fright, as if under the spell of a terrible nightmare.

The visions, delusions, and hallucinations of catatonic schizophrenia, permeated as they are by infernal symbolic representations, cause a state that P. Hoch (1972) termed "narrowing of consciousness," meaning that the subject's attention becomes focused on the inner drama of his psychosis. In catatonic schizophrenia, where spiritual matters assume precedence over matters of biological import, this narrowing of consciousness becomes so extreme that it obliterates even signals of pain emitted by the body. Painful stimuli may actually be completely suppressed (denied entry in consciousness). Surgical procedures can be performed on some catatonic patients without the need for anesthesia. Two such cases are described by Benjamin Rush. This author has witnessed the realignment of a fracture in a catatonic patient, which required no anesthesia at all.

c. Paranoid Schizophrenia and Paranoid States

According to French psychiatrist Henry Ey, a nucleus of paranoia is present in every case of schizophrenic illness. Therefore, to Bleuler's four "A's" one is justified in adding the letter "P," standing for paranoia. And whereas any one of Bleuler's four "A's" may be missing from the manifestations of a particular patient (as disturbances in associative thought, for example), *paranoia is the most outstanding symptom of schizophrenia, invariably present in each and every case.* Predicated as they are on complexes of sin and guilt, paranoid fears, ideas, and delusions do not appear by chance, but represent reminders of the patient's guilty state, as the moral conscience comes to assert its central position in the life of the psyche. The never absent symptoms of paranoia reveal not only the source of the disturbance in a particular case, they also clarify much that is unknown in the etiology of the disease in general.

Paranoid Schizophrenia came to be regarded as a separate disease entity, characterized in the DSM-III-R by the following dominant features: persecutory delusions, grandiose delusions, jealousy delusions, and hallucinations with grandiose or accusatory content. In actuality, all of the above are present to some degree in the majority of schizophrenic illnesses, and as they progress over time, every brand of schizophrenia comes eventually to resemble the others, as well as the single syndrome known as **Chronic Undifferentiated Schizophrenia.** Yet, the main reason for their similarity seems to be the common pathogenesis of these illnesses, and not their chronic course. What differentiates paranoid from other schizophrenias?

It would be erroneous to assume that every paranoid schizophrenia is contingent upon a premorbid **Paranoid Personality,** although some schizophrenias are so determined. Two major characteristic traits distinguish the paranoid personality: hypersensitivity and self-reverence. When subjected to existential analysis, however, these personality traits reveal themselves to be but the opposite sides of one and the same coin: that of *hubris*—the sin of arrogant pride. Being aware of their inflated self-perceptions, paranoid individuals feel continually threatened by the prospect of their true value being revealed. The achievements and positive attributes of others are also perceived as threats to the illusion of superiority they tenaciously maintain. The paranoid is thus motivated to engage in endless struggles, verbal and otherwise. He must assert his superiority, no matter what, and in debate he will prove himself "right" even at the cost of logic and in the face of an altogether different reality. His delusion of superiority often compels the paranoiac to humiliate and dominate others, which may entail the "putting down" (figuratively and literally) of the objects of his amorous entanglements. The hypersensitivity of the paranoid personality may be disguised as excessive "shyness," but its central dynamism remains as nothing more than the dread of rejection. The slightest "slight" is stored by the paranoid individual for future reference and revengeful action. Rejection may send the paranoiac into a state of depression. In the social sphere, the paranoiac's attitudes evoke rejection instead of the much craved love and admiration. But the paranoiac perceives rejection as a deadly blow to be avenged. The most common event to trigger homicide among schizophrenics, according to H. L. Lehman (1975), is the trauma of rejection. The sin of pride, which emerges as the crowning defect of this personality, reaches its full expression during a psychotic illness, when the paranoiac declares himself King of Egypt, Napoleon, Hitler, or some other odd celebrity. In reality, the sin of pride, instead of magnifying, reduces these unfortunate self-idolaters and brings them to a most pitiful paradox, as they parade in their pajamas on the wards of mental institutions.

Thus, by reason of his personality, the paranoiac emerges as a lonely, proud, and absurd hero on the stage of life, whose fall appears all the more tragic, considering the lofty heights of his self-estimation. When the paranoiac strikes out, propelled by aggressive urges, his attack is not the outcome of an unresolved conflict, but an act committed "out of fear, behind which hatefulness can always be perceived" (H. Baruk 1976). Injured pride combined with hatefulness, combative urges, and revengeful feelings may combine and dictate ferocious acts of retaliation. For daring to reject him, the paranoiac is liable to destroy even the object of his "love." In his amorous pursuits, he usually persists, in defiance of reality and reason and in spite of clearly communicated rebuke. He may resort to random homicide or a similarly insane act. The attempted assassination of President Reagan, for example, was designed to win the favor of a "love" object. But it is the object of his "love," who dares to reject him, that the paranoiac most commonly destroys. Not infrequently, he commits suicide following the act.

According to A. T. Boisen (1936), paranoid schizophrenia can be differentiated from other such disturbances by the defensive style of the patient. In paranoid schizophrenia, the patient resorts mostly to projections, denials, and justifications. P. Hoch (1972) writes on the subject:

> While in depressive disorders such as manic depressive or involutional psychoses, paranoid delusions are usually secondary to strong guilt feelings and are self-accusatory in nature, in paranoid schizophrenia, there is *more massive projection and no self-recrimination.* [emphasis added]

On massive projection and absence of self-recrimination hinges not only the difference between paranoid and other schizophrenias, but prognostic outlook as well. As a general rule, paranoid schizophrenias carry a poor prognosis compared to other schizophrenias, whose outcome is mostly favorable. Self-recrimination implies the recognition of one's error, which may lead to repentance and reform. And just as the presence of thought disorder with its deceptions and justificatory operations augurs an ominous prognosis, so do projections and denials. According to E. Kraepelin (1904), the projections and denials so frequently employed by paranoid individuals serve to "reject from consciousness some intolerable accusation against themselves," which is then projected onto others. The validity of self-accusations has never been investigated, however, much less the reason for their intolerability. But the same self-accusations, which dictate projections and denials, create also the need for justifications—the substance of delusional *ideas*. The massive deployment of defenses such as projections, deceptions, denials, and justifications usually signifies that the schizophrenic has resolved to take the crucial decision—dictated mostly by his pride—to defend himself and cover up his past misdeeds. Unfortunately, this decision sets him on a futile journey further removed from the possibility of recovery.

Paranoid States represent rather "circumscribed" disturbances in which a delusional complex has become "encapsulated," yet dominates the conscious life of otherwise apparently well-functioning individuals. Paranoid states are most commonly observed in the middle years of life. These conditions are curable, however, provided their subjects allow the delusional capsule-complex to be opened and its contents spilled out. Engaged in some secret sinful activities such as cheating in business, involvement in extramarital affairs, gambling, drug dealing, etc., these individuals experience their secret activities as such a threat to their self-esteem and honor, that their apparent good adjustment eventually crumbles under the strain of their deceptions, projections, and justifications. Preoccupations with the "encapsulated" complex of sin and guilt eventually drain most of their physical and mental energies, and lead them to collapse. Such was the case of:

> a 66-year-old man who went to painstaking lengths and legal battles to prove his landlords were in league with his neighbors in a conspiracy to evict him. Eventually, he admitted that he was actually shielding secret adulterous relationships. He feared that his neighbors knew, and attempted to evict him for this reason. (From author's caseload)

d. Paraphrenias

So designated by E. Kraepelin in 1912, **Paraphrenias** comprise a set of paranoid disorders whose onset is insidious and which make their appearance at a relatively late age. In paraphrenias, odd delusional ideas are frequently expressed, but what is outstanding in these disorders is the premorbid personality of the paraphreniac, dominated as it is by egotism, emotional "coldness," jealousy, and hostility, coupled with suspiciousness. The grouchy old lady from the lower floor, who persistently complains of noises and who accuses her neighbors of spying, stealing, and deliberately attempting to disturb her peace is, in all likelihood, a paraphreniac. An existential analysis of her past and present ways of being-in-the-world is liable to reveal the presence of low-grade, smoldering resentments, bitterness, righteous indignations, and petty jealousies, expressed by way of malicious gossip and/or trivial acts of animosity. During long nights of sleeplessness and agitation, the paraphreniac is liable to become, nonetheless, subject of various visions, illusions, delusions, and hallucinations, not much different from those experienced by the frankly schizophrenic. Yet, since lifelong malevolent ways of being can be brought into the field of vision of the paraphreniac only with considerable difficulty, little by way of recovery from this serious condition can be expected. And as is true for other paranoid individuals, the hostile old lady who persists in maintaining projections, denials, and justifications as defenses in order to retain her most prized possession, namely her pride, might find herself reaching a state of dementia (often written off as Alzheimer's disease) with no possibility of return.

e. Hebephrenic Schizophrenia

First described by E. Hecker in 1843, **Hebephrenic Schizophrenia** is so named for the silly dementia that characteristically affects young adults. Divesting themselves of moral constraints and pursuing mostly hedonistic goals, these rebellious youngsters frequently become prey to their own fantasies. Giving themselves up for the sake of gratification of youthful lusts and passions—in flagrant disregard for parental authority and the dictates of their consciences—they descend eventually into an underworld of madness from which they seldom return. The chaotic clothing style, senseless and disjointed utterances, the wit and contagious silly laughter of the hebephrenic make the observer wonder whether to laugh or to cry.

f. Simple Schizophrenia (Schizophrenia Simplex)

Representing a non-choice rather than a reaction to adversity or special external circumstances, **Schizophrenia Simplex** (E. Bleuler 1911) gives some indication regarding the structure of the psychosis as well as the premorbid personality which succumbs to it. The simple schizophrenic is one who shuns commitment in any kind of relationship; who cares for no one in particular; and who refuses to earn his keep. In spite of being profoundly "bored," he will not engage in any meaningful activity, except perhaps to strum on his guitar or "express" himself in some visual art. He is the hobo of the road, the alcoholic in the gutter; she is the "bag lady" on the corner. Many are homeless, a substantial number engage in panhandling, and some prefer to eat from garbage cans, i.e., from refuse. Good intentions and charitable zeal on the part of family and society stand powerless in their attempts to soften the decrees and punishments issued by the guilty consciences of these individuals. Truly acedic, "simple" schizophrenics suffer deeply from a lack of the joy that rewards those who sweat and toil. Drink or drug can provide them with not much more than a fleeting, artificial "high."

*   *   *

Whether detached "schizoid" or stormy "schizotypal," the personality of the future schizophrenic shows several common weaknesses, defects, and deviations. A central autism may show itself as an egotistic variation of narcissism. Translated into existential terms, autism is a way of being-in-the-world that seeks to extract all that can be of benefit exclusively to the individual himself. Bound neither by attachments of love nor by the laws of morality, the future schizophrenic experiences his identity and existence as precarious. "Who am I?" he asks, as if he had no identity. Having made little or no impact on the world, except perhaps in a negative sense, his existence brings confirmation to the comment made by Rabbinical Patriarch Rabbi Hillel: "If I am only for myself, I am nothing." The question then arises as to whether the "nothingness" of those pursuing strictly self-serving goals can in any way be changed; and whether the deviant premorbid personality of the future schizophrenic needs to first be rent by an "explosion of conscience" before it can be rebuilt upon a sounder foundation.

Existential philosophy might provide some answers to these questions, more satisfactory perhaps than those of psychoanalytically derived developmental theories. According to this philosophy, behaviors are the resultants of decisions, determined primarily at the center of the personality as *vectors of intention*. "Intention is the actual person, not thought, except as it is derived from intention— intention is a person's nature or bent," wrote Swedenborg (*Heaven and Hell*), who defined the personality by its affections, its "loves," and its intentions (*Divine Providence*). If indeed, an individual's nature is determined by his loves and intentions, it becomes understandable how small changes in the center of the personality might create big differentials in outward behavior, and consequently in the structure of the character.

If the hate-obsessed individual can be persuaded to transform his hatefulness into, at least, a "love" for some benevolent cause, such a change would immediately produce effects that become manifest in outward behavior, as it would also transform the individual's character and disposition. If the excitement sought in gambling, for example, could be exchanged for the thrills provided by adventurous traveling expeditions, this would not only enlarge the world (and soul) of the adventurer, but transform his behavior and disposition as well. (See Diagram # 7.)

The spotlight of both psychoanalysis and existential analysis focuses upon the analysand's "unconscious" inner motivations, for these are recognized as moving the will to action and determining behavior. From this point on, however, existential analysis parts ways with psychoanalysis, as their objectives tend to diverge.

Whereas psychoanalysis may content itself with the relief of the analysand's symptoms of distress and the improvement of his overall functioning, treatment frequently tends to foster such goals as benefit primarily the patient himself: sexual gratification, self-assertive actions, advancement in business or career—often with disregard for the interests of others, the family, society.

Existential analysis also begins with uncovering of the patient's true motivations, but proceeds further in attempting to explore the totality of his ways of being-in-the-world, and to correct them, if need be. Not only his childhood, but all of the patient's past is laid out. All his relationships are explored: to the Yous of his world, to the divine Thou, to himself, and to the "its," or world of inanimate objects. Attempts are also made to expose the analysand's transcendental strivings. Existential psychotherapy (Chapter X) does not content itself with the accumulation of data, and improvement in the patient's mental condition, but proceeds further in promoting self-detachment in view of *expanding the soul's boundaries*. This may be achieved through love, an act of courage, fulfillment of duty, or response to a call from one's destiny. But unless the Self can detach from the Me-myself, it can be neither rebuilt nor expanded. The healing strategies currently in vogue—which stress love for one's self as "number one," foster self-assertion no-matter-what, and promote self-interest above all else—may not be therapeutic after all.

The precarious existence of the schizophrenic and his tenuous sense of identity need always to be taken seriously. In order to promote a sense of anchorage, the patient must be urged to relate to others in a more loving, disinterested manner; he must be taught to give, even sacrificially. Respect for the will of an Other or others and submission to their wishes is a way of self-detachment which enhances self-esteem and promotes a sense of belonging. There is no other way for a meaningful relatedness to the divine Thou but through

Diagram # 7

Motivation, Behavior, and Character Structure

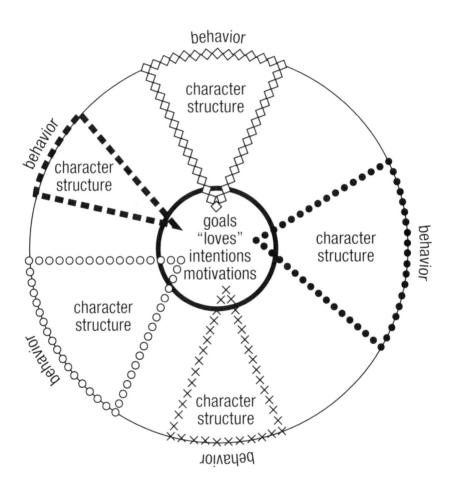

Small changes in the center of the personality as goals or "loves" create big differentials in behavior and influence the structure of the personality.

submission and obedience to His moral laws. And there seems no other means for acquiring a sense of identity than through love for an other or others. Even the sense of identity depends on fulfillment of the basic spiritual-moral law which requires that one love one's neighbor as oneself.

The Lonely Journey of the Schizophrenic

Preference or destiny? It would be difficult, if not impossible, to determine with exactitude the reasons that motivate the alienated to shun the company of others and choose conditions of isolation instead. Alienation may not always be conditioned by premorbid inclinations (as those of the schizoid, for example), for many previously gregarious, extroverted, and "stormy" personalities suddenly withdraw into seclusion after the shattering experience of a psychotic ordeal. All schizophrenics feel judged, persecuted, and condemned by their fellow men; they all share the experience of Raskolnikov in the police precinct: "an indescribable anguish and separation from others, more painful than anything experienced ever before . . . . " They all seem also to concur with the opinion of Mrs. Polly T. (mentioned above): "When you sin against God you feel persecuted; and while God is forgiving, men are not."

The separation of schizophrenics from their fellow men is reinforced further by a certain "eerie," "praecox" feeling that schizophrenics, characteristically, tend to evoke in others. Neither their eccentricities and bizarre utterances, nor their peculiar aloofness can account for the revulsion and "eeriness" these patients engender. And needless to say, their lack of honesty, deceptive manipulations, and generally devious ways of relatedness are strongly resented. But above all else, the insane are experienced as menacing—a true perception of their homicidal and destructive potential. The question whether the fears others experience of the insane are justified or not is answered in the affirmative by the "man on the street," who instinctively avoids them; and who is frequently exposed to reports of horrifying crimes perpetrated by ex-mental patients. Living in a state of perpetual fear, the families of ex-mental patients have even more to tell about their personal experiences and reasons for alarm. Yet in spite of all the evidence, which overwhelmingly incriminates mental patients in acts of senseless violence, sexual assault, arson, and destruction, the majority of mental health professionals remain incredulous with regard to the dangerous potential of the mentally ill, until they become victims themselves. Given that every schizophrenic harbors in his heart hostilities of homicidal proportions, who can guarantee that, even if submerged to subconscious or preconscious levels, these hateful urges will remain there and forever in check? Investigating the justification for fearing the insane, J. M. Lagos et al. (1977) examined the records of 321 hospitalized patients and found that 36 percent of them (excluding drug addicts and alcoholics) had manifested violent behaviors which led to their hospital admission. In an analysis of the *Psychodynamic Aspects of Violence,* S. A. Halleck (1976) found the association between psychotic illness and violence "intriguing." Ex-mental patients have much higher arrest rates for aggravated assault, burglary, and rape than the remainder of the population (A. Zitrin et al. 1976). They have five times the arrest rates of other individuals from the same catchment area and commit five times as many violent crimes (J. Mullen's, study, quoted by S. Halleck 1976). These data may still be underrepresentative of all the violent crimes committed by insane individuals, however, for some family members remain reluctant to report their relative's behavior to the legal authorities. Statistics of arrests may not be relied upon as indices of crime, either, since the number of arrests may reflect more accurately the capacity of the police to apprehend offenders than the actual number of committed crimes. Motivated by shame, embarrassment, and pity, most families remain tight-lipped even vis-à-vis the hospital authorities. As for the effects of the schizophrenic on his family, they have not been deemed sufficiently important to deserve the attention of psychiatrists and mental health administrators. In a monograph entitled *Trapped Families and Schizophrenia,* L. L. Rogler and A. B. Hollingshead (1965), who studied 40 Puerto Rican families, describe some of the consequences of sharing life with a schizophrenic individual:

> When a husband is affected with a schizophrenic illness, the rate of physical illness for his wife is four times higher than that of the control group. A schizophrenic wife causes corrosion in the marital union, while her children feel trapped in a chaotic and disorganized family.

In Puerto Rican culture, moreover, to be insane, or *loco,* means to be truly outcast from others, from society.

How can the schizophrenic patient and his family be helped? Family therapies (Chapter X), based as they are on negotiated rules and regulations, prove ineffective for such families, because their proud, defiant, and hostile schizophrenic member will refuse to abide by any set agreement. Self-willed and seeking to dominate others, the schizophrenic will skillfully undermine any negotiated contract, while the family's sense of frustration is bound to intensify. Only treatment approaches that support the family in its efforts to contain the insane member; that offer alternatives in eventual emergencies; and that relieve the family's shame and guilt, are of any value and meet the needs of these unfortunates. "Systems theory" approaches, which subtly blame the family, are extremely inappropriate and even onerous for families burdened with the care of a schizophrenic member. Precisely because of the schizophrenic's rebellious tendencies, need to dominate, and his deliberate attempts to disrupt the harmonious functioning of the family unit, no limit-setting is of value. If and when no other recourse is available, and the schizophrenic needs to be extruded from his family, full support and understanding need to be extended—for no one ought to judge or burden the tolerance of others.

Regarding the peculiar characteristics of patients considered "burnt-out" schizophrenics—their lack of spunk, limitless dependencies, subdepressive and depressive moods, demandingness, suspiciousness, and manipulativeness—these traits, instinctively perceived by others, render them socially unattractive, and needless to say, their company is shunned.

It becomes quite evident from the foregoing that a multiplicity of factors contribute to the alienation that becomes the lot of the schizophrenic individual, and the problem does not lend itself to any one easy solution. At the termination of the previously mentioned catamnestic study by L. Ciompi (1980), which followed patients 37 years after their first hospitalization, the majority were found to be "definitely poor in their social relations." Only 17 percent were married, while the remaining 83 percent were either single, separated, divorced, or widowed, and only 12 percent of the whole group were completely free from any disturbance.

In addition to their isolated, secluded existence, it has been noted that schizophrenic individuals tend to drift to lower occupational, social, and economic strata, as if they were being demoted. This "downward drift" occurs with such constancy that it has become a diagnostic marker in the DSM-III-R. It represents an actual descent on all levels of communal life, yet it is contingent on the consequences of the illness, and is not its cause. The question then emerges: do the alienation and demotion of the schizophrenic represent a fate forever sealed? But before this question can be answered, another more compelling problem comes to surface and disturb our understanding: What makes "normal" sinners so different from "guilty, conscience-stricken" schizophrenic individuals? For sinners we all are, and our "imaginations are evil" from our youth; we also "enlarge desire as sheol," to quote from Scripture. A good number of those considered normal have certainly committed offenses very similar to those for which the schizophrenic is finally brought to condemnation. What makes the difference? A logical way for solving this problem would be through the extrapolation of common characteristics as denominators for the premorbid personality as well as the frankly schizophrenic, which could then be compared with those of normal persons. Investigations derived from studies on childhood and heredity (Chapter IV) have ferreted out certain characteristics that distinguish future schizophrenics early in life and through adolescence: hostility, defiance, negativism, willfulness, and incorrigibility. It is quite possible that in schizophrenic individuals, these negative traits attain an unusual measure of intensity and potency through mutual reinforcement, as are seldom present in healthy, normal people. What seems certain is that, quantitatively and qualitatively, the schizophrenic has harbored more hatred and anger in his heart than warranted by the provoking act, situation, or event. But often his malevolence draws from no other source than envy, jealousy, covetousness, or revenge. Hostility endows the schizophrenic with a sense of power also, and power is his *primum mobile*. The passionate spite and viciousness of the borderline schizophrenic, so well described by Dostoyevsky in *Notes from the Underground*, are tenaciously maintained for the simple reason that they are enjoyed "with voluptuous pleasure." In cowardice, the preschizophrenic burrows underground and directs to the outside world all the poison of his malevolence, precisely because in rebellion, he refuses to acquire by effort all those worldly goods, attributes, and satisfactions that reward the sowers of good will. In defiance of the laws of men and the warnings of his conscience, the preschizophrenic acts in a manner injurious to others and suffers thenceforth from the consequences of his actions. The past cannot be retrieved, nor the laws of conscience altered. But the future schizophrenic has in all probability been forewarned by fears, phobias, panic states, and nightmares, yet has failed to heed their message. He may have been granted some visions of Heaven and Hell in addition, but in all likelihood, he has chosen to ignore them, or else has sought to drown them in excitement, drugs, or alcohol.

With regard to sin, most religions insist that throughout our journey to Eternity, what seems to be of importance has more to do with our willingness to admit error, bear the shame, and cry for mercy in contrition—all the while attempting to redress wrongdoing and avoid its repetition—than with any particular sin or sins.

Quality and magnitude of transgression notwithstanding, the doors of repentance stand forever open for those who wish to enter in humility and reverence. For the proud, defiant sinner who has respect for laws mostly of his own making, who follows pseudo-philosophies that extol the meaninglessness of life and stress the advantages to be gained from hedonistic pursuits in the here and now, for such an individual—deeming himself above Good and Evil—repentance becomes nearly impossible. In pride, the schizophrenic may refuse to take the road that leads to recovery, for it requires that he admit wrongdoing and seek with humility the forgiveness of those he has injured. *In pride, he may seek justice, and justice he will obtain.* Unconsciously, subconsciously, and consciously, he will pluck out his eye, cut his wrists, serve unending terms of alienation and various penalties, inclusive of solitary confinement, yet will refuse to repent.

Paradoxically, the proud, defiant, all-powerful paranoid schizophrenic is found in mental institutions, in single-occupancy hotel rooms, on the streets, and in the gutter. Greater humiliation and degradation he need no longer fear. His body frequently molds itself around his crooked inner being, assuming eventually its deformed shape. Rejected and rejecting, he relates now mostly to his "voices" and talks to them with grimaces and gesticulations.

Many schizophrenics believe they have reached a state they qualify as "sub-human," and so they are also perceived by others. They often eat with their bare hands and quarrel for no obvious reason. They may discharge their excretory and sexual urges openly, in public places. They wallow in shabbiness and utter self-neglect. They laugh at things spiritual. They also laugh when told the truth about their past misdeeds. They can no longer cry, but show their fist in anger. When asked to give up their malevolence they flatly refuse, for it endows them with a sense of power. They delight in obtaining by begging, and engage in stealing as an occupation. They proudly carry their shopping bags, stuffed with the most absurd possessions. They hoard what they do not need. Eventually, they divest themselves of all pretense—naked in their lusts and sadistic satisfactions—spiritless creatures, symbols of the lost. With their shadowy state of being, these unfortunates vividly serve to model the reality of *death in life—*

the lot of those who invest all their treasures in this world, and none in Heaven.

The following verses, quoted from Carl Orff's *Carmina Burrana*, well apply to the end-state of spiritlessness deteriorated schizophrenics may attain:

> I am entangled in vice
> and unmindful of virtue.
> Greedy more for lust
> than for welfare,
> dead in soul,
> I care only for my body . . .

The fateful decision taken by some schizophrenics to seek justice instead of mercy eventually brings them to justice. And here, perhaps, they attain the height of their madness—believing they can justify and defend themselves, or escape somehow the guilty verdict pronounced by their consciences.

Course and Outcome

Just as the configuration of a psychosis, if and when it occurs, depends on the characteristics of the premorbid personality, so is its outcome ultimately determined. A return to sanity is contingent upon the reaction of the psychotic to his illness as well as to its precipitants, of which the patient is usually aware.

In spite of all their drama, liveliness, visions, horrors, delusions, and hallucinations, acute psychotic illnesses tend to subside gradually. Their duration is variable, lasting from several days (three-day psychoses) to several months, with an average of six weeks. Sleep disturbances, nightmares, fears, phobias, paranoid uneasiness, and a loss of capacity for concentration may last, however, for up to one year.

It is worthy of note that the final outcome of a schizophrenic illness markedly changes with a second episode, after which the risk of personality deterioration rapidly increases (H. E. Lehman 1975). The spiritual message conveyed during the first psychotic decompensation, with visions of Hell along with glimpses of Heaven, becomes increasingly urgent and its contents more threatening. In other words, the visions turn more infernal with every new psychotic fall. Every new psychotic episode, moreover, erodes the integrity of the personality and leaves residual defects. According to G. Huber et al. (1980), pure "residual defects" become evident in the first three years of illness in 43.2 percent of patients. These defects represent a "dynamic insufficiency," or a lack of spark, which Huber perceives as due to an "irreversible loss of psychic energy." Residual symptoms may be divided into those derived from the "affect-toxin" of schizophrenia and related to fear, such as intolerance to noise, sensitivity to weather conditions, various attention deficits, somatic and cognitive disturbances, and symptoms that result from a *spiritual loss*, such as loss of spontaneity, innocence, energy, and drive (replaced by suspiciousness and subdepressive moods). Something of the spark of life, ignited by the Spirit, is felt as being lost. Affected in this manner, they suffer from a loss of power for ascendance, and this loss affects much if not all of their life-endeavors.

From the 37-year-long-term study of L. Ciompi (1980) mentioned above, the following findings were reported: at the end of the study, 20.1 percent of the patients had recovered from their initial psychosis; 42.6 percent had improved; 17.3 percent had reached an uncertain psycho-organic end-state; and 8 percent presented a complete dementia syndrome. Late exacerbations 20 and even 40 years later and 5 cases of surprising improvement were also observed. A follow-up study conducted by M. Bleuler (1968), spanning 23 years and involving 208 patients, yielded almost identical results.

When does madness finally end? Existentially, the guilty, *un-repented,* conscience-stricken schizophrenic stands, in all appearances, as if on trial. He resorts therefore, to such maneuvers as a defendant would:

- justifies himself through perjury or makes use of half-truths
- accuses others, the judges, for their misdeeds—so as to prove himself less guilty—as he bemoans the lack of justice in this world (H. Baruk 1976)
- denies his deeds, circumstances, reality
- projects the blame on those he has actually victimized: spouse, siblings, parents, partners, etc.
- diverts the attention of his "judges" by circumstantial and tangential statements, puns, jokes, etc.
- makes himself the Lawgiver, Judge, Christ, or else claims to be Napoleon, Stalin, Hitler—giving sanction to his crimes in this manner
- changes his moral code by escaping into another or less demanding religion

- abandons religion altogether and chooses such "creeds" as serve his purposes: astrology, numerology, botania, the occult
- sentences himself to serve various terms of isolation-penalties or self-inflicted injuries
- condemns himself to death and commits suicide

The majority of schizophrenic patients sentence themselves to a prison of isolation. Reminded by mocking and accusing "voices" of their past misdeeds, their hallucinations may compel them to repeat some past offenses; they may also "advise" some punishment. These unfortunates feel now excluded and rejected—as if they no longer belonged to the human family.

Who recovers from schizophrenia and what factors influence the course of the illness? A retrospective study of 60 recovered patients by G. Vaillant (1962) identified the following factors as predictive of a favorable outcome: 1) acute onset, 2) confusion and disorientation during the psychosis, 3) absence of a schizoid premorbid personality, 4) a clear precipitating event, 5) the presence of depression, and 6) onset of illness less than six months before the psychosis. It is worthy of note that approximately one-half of those who recovered did so *without receiving any treatment* at all. When the factors that tended to favor recovery were applied on a "yes-no" basis, it was possible to separate 83 percent of patients who did eventually recover.

In addition to the premorbid personality factors already discussed, and their association with the structure of the psychosis (whether acute or chronic), the prognosis of schizophrenia was also consistently found correlated with the presence of affect, clear precipitants, "formal" thought disorder, and defensive projections and denials.

With respect to the "undulating" course of some schizophrenias, little by way of explanation can be found in the current psychiatric literature, except for mention of relapses following withdrawal of neuroleptic drugs or noncompliance with prescribed medication. Exacerbations of psychoses following the withdrawal of medication can be understood, however, as representing *reactions of withdrawal*, such as occur with any drug that has been used for a long period of time.

Yet it is psychological and spiritual factors that are more commonly responsible for the recurrence of psychosis. Certain external events, when they cause a new surge of hatred, anger, revenge, or jealousy, and lead to behaviors spurred by these dynamic forces, are known to predispose to acute exacerbations. The death of a close relative, for example, is often implicated in the upsurge of an otherwise smoldering psychosis, but such an exacerbation has less to do with the sadness of mourning than with the inevitability of death this event brings to awareness. Furthermore, when the schizophrenic had hated the departed, abused him when still alive, or simply wished him dead, his mourning might become pathological—**Pathological Mourning**—and responsible for precipitating a new psychotic illness.

It is striking to observe, however, that in the majority of cases, the same antecedent that had led to the initial hospitalization is found operative in subsequent ones as well. The hospital records of schizophrenic patients reveal with remarkable monotony the same or similar circumstances to have anteceded the new exacerbation. It often appears as if admission notes had been copied one from another. The same transgression that had caused the initial psychosis is found repeated with little or no variation.

> A first psychotic episode of a 27-year-old-homosexual man occurred after he had "made a contract" on the life of his seducer. Two years later, he made another such "contract," and suffered a new psychotic exacerbation shortly thereafter. (From author's caseload)

For most contemporary psychiatrists the exacerbation of psychosis is understood as a "new outbreak of craziness"—the consequence of a mysterious interplay between brain neurotransmitters. Strangely enough, such an interpretation is not only accepted, it has also served to tranquilize a good number of mental health professionals to the point of indolence. "Craziness" *per se*, however, could not explain certain behaviors antecedent to psychosis, some of which require the mobilization of considerable effort and also well-functioning mental faculties, such as reality assessment, judgment, planning, and execution. The man who decided on making a "contract" to kill his seducer did not plan the murder because he suddenly became crazy, but became so while preparing the act.

Unrepented sin, moreover, not only tends to be compulsively repeated, but shows also a growth in potency and versatility, in spite of all the warning anxieties, phobias, and panic states issued by the conscience and reasoning powers of the Ego. A certain "contamination," or spreading of morally forbidden activities to other areas of the patient's life, is frequently observed. Such was the case of a 16-year-old student (later affected by a relentless-course schizophrenia) who could not understand her motivation for suddenly beginning to steal books from the public library. She was secretly engaged in various sexual activities at the time, which necessitated a great deal of deception in order to ward off her parents' disapproval.

a. Premorbid Personality Factors

Among the hierarchy of factors most reliably predictive of the course and outcome of a schizophrenic illness, those related to the premorbid personality were found to rank highest in importance (L Ciompi 1980). "Good premorbid, familial, social and occupational adaptation were significantly associated with favorable disease course into old age." Intelligence, education, family relationships during childhood (investigated retrospectively), and, surprisingly, familial history of a schizophrenic illness or other type of mental disorder, as well as constitutional factors, *did not* significantly influence long-term course, according to this study. M. Bleuler (1972) found the course of illness to be simple-progressive in 43 percent of the cases he studied, with 18 percent reaching "a most severe end-state" and 23.9 percent a moderately severe end-state. About one-half of Bleuler's cases developed favorably; that is, these patients were able to achieve recovery or a mild end-state. Complete recovery was achieved by 26.6 percent of the patients. "Even in advanced age, schizophrenia in no way assumes the character of a typical organic disease," observed Bleuler. The major influences on long-term course (based on this and other research findings), were certain premorbid personality factors and, possibly related to them, structural disease factors.

Studies that follow the long-term course of schizophrenic illnesses make a good case for those who argue that man is capable of freeing himself from the chains of heredity, early childhood experiences, family relationships, and even constitutional factors. And in spite of all the limitations imposed on him by a schizophrenic illness, the individual so afflicted might still be capable of producing changes in himself, thereby influence the outcome of his illness as well as the course of his destiny.

The long-term prognosis of acute-onset psychoses was found to be significantly more favorable than otherwise—leaving only 24 percent of cases with characteristic residua, whereas insidious-onset psychoses left 58 percent with characteristic residua (G. Huber et al. 1980). It may seem paradoxical that psychoses with a more severe symptomatology—acute illnesses with stupor, confusion, disorientation, hallucinations, and delusions—carry the best prognosis among the whole array of schizophrenic illnesses. The favorable outcome of reactive, catatonic, hysterical psychoses and "acute schizophrenic deliria," or "acute turmoil schizophrenias" may be explained, however, on the basis of the premorbid personality and its moral forces, capable of waging even a minimal struggle against the onslaughts of some forbidden wish or temptation. Moreover, since the purpose of the psychotic catastrophe is to provoke a crisis (A. T. Boisen 1936), those in the throes of an "explosion of conscience" may well be more predisposed to heed the message of their awesome experience than those who consistently refuse to obey the dictates of their conscience and disregard its warnings. A psychotic catastrophe may well act similarly to "hitting bottom"—an event, described by recovered alcoholics, and believed by them to have been the most powerful factor in bringing them back to sobriety.

In contrast to acute confusional psychoses, the insidious-onset schizophrenias do not result from any particular struggle with the moral forces of conscience, nor from any conflict, for that matter, but engraft themselves, as previously noted, upon markedly abnormal personalities (G. Huber et al. 1980). The "nucleus" of these insidious, "process" schizophrenias resides, indeed, in the core of the personality, wherein life-goals, "loves," and crucial choices are being determined. In these illnesses, however, the vector of intention swerves toward the negative—indicating *choices unmistakably evil.* The malignant course and outcome of insidious schizophrenias are thus contingent upon the acceptance of sin by the will and participation of the reasoning Ego in this choice. Here, the reasoning powers of the Ego provide bribes and justifications and may even supply some pseudo-philosophy, pseudo-religion, or pseudo-humanitarian ideal, purposing to still the moral forces of the conscience in this manner. Sin may also become so thoroughly ingrained within the structure of the personality as to become responsible for its permanent deformity. The "markedly abnormal personality," described by Huber, produces a schizophrenia that takes a relentless course and leads to progressive deterioration. A compulsive need to exploit others, for example, backed by a philosophy of "everybody does it" and involving the faculties of the Ego-mind-reason, might suppress the guiding forces of the moral conscience and become so pervasive as to lead to alienation, self-alienation, and an inauthentic existence. Such are the ingredients that make for schizophrenias from which there is no return.

Similar to nuclear schizophrenia, the hebephrenic, silly variety grows out of the conscious pursuit of hedonistic goals, coupled with a defiant mockery for the laws of morality. Hebephrenic schizophrenia marches relentlessly toward early deterioration. In the schizophrenias labelled "simple," there is a conscious acceptance of sins of omission in the most global sense. A state of "spiritlessness" and dementia eventually overtakes unrepentant schizophrenics from all categories, especially those belonging to the nuclear, hebephrenic, and simple varieties.

b. Affect and Depression

Although a consensus has now been established to confirm the observation that the presence of affect in schizophrenia, especially depression, augurs a better prognosis than otherwise, much diagnostic confusion and uncertainty about the role of depression still exist. Many depressive illnesses, as a matter of fact—with or without delusions—have become classified outside of the schizophrenic spectrum by the DSM-III. Such a classification fails, however, to give recognition to the long-confirmed observation that in its initial stages schizophrenia may present as depression. The reasons for the confusion may be found in deficient history-taking, but it may also reflect the tendency of the psychiatric authorities to focus on a particular symptom of the illness—in this case, depression—instead of its underlying causes.

The nosological entity **Schizo-Affective Psychosis,** so termed by J. S. Kasanin in 1933, describes illnesses schizophrenic in essence, but whose symptomatology is pervaded by emotions, mostly depressive in nature. The prognosis of these illnesses has always been considered more favorable than that of other schizophrenias, but less favorable than that of manic-depressive illnesses, where reconstitution between episodes is the rule rather than the exception. In a review that emphasizes the difficulties inherent in the separation of "schizo-affective" illnesses from schizophrenia and manic-depressive psychoses, W. Procci (1976) warned against the diagnostic reliance on clusters of symptoms in acute stages only. In a study of recovered patients by G. Langfeldt, cited by Procci, the following features were associated with recovery: acute onset, psychogenic precipitants, and affective symptoms, especially depression. In studies conducted by C. Astrup et al. (1966), the presence of affective symptoms, especially depression, was found "most important for reducing the risk of deterioration." With the aid of a computer, an accurate prediction of the outcome of schizophrenic patients was possible for 80 percent of the cases—a figure similar to that produced by G. Vaillant (1962) from his retrospective studies. Changes in character, emotional blunting, and insidious onset were of the strongest predictive strength for deterioration, while depression, excitation, and confusion were negatively correlated with poor outcome (C. Astrup et al. 1966). G. Vaillant (1964) found that a concern with death was also associated with a more favorable outcome than otherwise.

The factor of depression emerges again in conjunction with post-psychotic states pervaded by depressive feelings, which may last from a few weeks to a year and even longer (T. McGlashan 1976). Although these depressions had greatly incapacitated their subjects and had even led some to suicide, a depressive state was found to carry a more favorable outlook for the long-term outcome of schizophrenia in general.

It is of great interest that **Post Psychotic Depression** usually follows the first schizophrenic episode and appear less frequently with acute exacerbations. This phenomenon has received little attention in the psychiatric literature, except for engendering interpretations according to which the psychosis represents a loss and the depression a reaction to this loss. From a purely medical standpoint, it would appear rather strange that the complication of one disease (schizophrenia) by another (depression) can favorably affect the prognosis of both. This paradoxical effect of depression on the ultimate outcome of schizophrenia can, however, be logically explained in quite a different manner than hitherto theorized. As was previously emphasized, the crucial decision that confronts the "guilty, conscience-stricken" schizophrenic is whether to engage in self-defense through various strategies of cover-up, deceptive operations and justifications, or else to admit wrongdoing, sorrow over it, and attempt all the while to reform. There is no question that the admission of guilt is always fraught with considerable shame, anguish, remorse, and self-recrimination. Yet the sorrow and contrition that follow confession and true self-understanding, known in psychiatric circles as "emotional insight," have long been recognized for the enormous sense of relief they provide, as well as for their long-term beneficial effects.

Theories notwithstanding, depression in schizophrenia may be seized upon as an opportunity for growth and healing; it need not be regretted as an undesirable mishap. Not every schizophrenic suffers from a post-psychotic depression, but those who do "have a good chance to attain the best Ego functioning and recovery," concluded S. Roth (1970). Conversely, the loss of emotional capacity or "flattening of affect," known otherwise as "apathetic withdrawal" or "abulia," forebodes, as a rule, an ominous prognosis and a deteriorative end-state. This apparent loss of emotional capacity may be interpreted in several ways, nonetheless. A voluntary suppression of emotion, undertaken in view of warding off guilty dysphoria from flooding the various strata of consciousness, can certainly not be ruled out. Such a possibility finds actually confirmation in the sudden outburst of crying that frequently takes place at some critical moments in psychotherapy. The patient who complains of having lost the capacity for crying and feeling may suddenly find his emotions "released" by a *confession of guilt*. This is always a dramatic event. The loss of emotional capacity in some schizophrenias may also be explained on the basis of their spiritual degradation, part and parcel of the schizophrenic complex(es). Spiritual degradation may be responsible for depriving even repentant schizophrenics of some enthusiasm, spontaneity, liveliness, capacity for emotion, and zest for life.

The better prognosis associated with confusion during a psychotic illness may be explained on the basis of these patients' ambivalence and general indecisiveness. It is conceivable that during the psychotic ordeal, conflicting choices with regard to life-goals and philosophy are caught in the general turmoil before becoming finalized. A concern with death may signify that the schizophrenic still fears the loss of his soul and opportunity for salvation.

*   *   *

When does madness end? And how? One of its highest points is certainly reached when the "conscience-stricken" schizophrenic decides to deny his guilt and proceeds in defending his cause. Existentially, this is madness in its truest sense, for it represents Self-denial, denial of the Spirit, denial of reality, truth, as well as a defiant disregard towards the One, giver of the Spirit.

At the juncture where the prognostic roads for schizophrenia sharply divide to run thenceforth in opposite directions, the road signs read as follows in the "Destination" chart on the following page.

With respect to those patients who choose to justify themselves, S. Arieti (1974) came to the following conclusion:

> The more the patient projects toward others and exonerates himself, the more severe the psychosis. If, on the other hand, he believes that he is persecuted because he is guilty and responsible, the prognosis is better.

Commenting on the psychotherapeutic approaches to post-psychotic depression, E. Semrad et al. (1964) wrote as follows:

Too often the therapist allows the patient to believe that his actions are excusable and inconsistent, but every time he allows the patient to excuse himself, he lowers the patient's self-esteem. To go along with the idea that the patient is not responsible for his illness is to rob him of the continuity of his life.

With these statements, Arieti, Semrad, and co-researchers come closest to the recognition that the patient needs to work out his guilt in sorrow and contrition.

Destination

RECOVERY	NO-MAN'S LAND—OF MADNESS
admission of guilt: confession	defense of self, rationalizations, justifications, denials
repentance renunciation of sin	projections, cover-up, delusional ideas serving as justifications; changes in life-philosophy and/or religion
humility, sorrow, contrition, depression	denial of guilt, loss of emotional capacity
experiences of guilt and pain	fears of various kinds
plea for forgiveness	a sense of persecution, prosecution, and condemnation
Reform: a "change of heart," of goals, intentions, motivations	a sense of abandonment, alienation
LIFE OF THE SOUL	DEATH OF THE SOUL SPIRITLESSNESS

In *The Sickness unto Death*, Kierkegaard (1849) went even further by condemning the despair which may follow sin as yet additional offense, for it bespeaks a lack of authentic faith. He did not believe the despairing individual is in need of consolation, either. "There is but one antidote to despair," wrote Kierkegaard, "and it is faith." Every unrepented sin, according to Kierkegaard, represents new sin, and every moment it remains unrepented adds to it. Kierkegaard was able to triumph thus over his own sickness and despair.

The possibility of repentance remains ever present for a good number of schizophrenic patients. Statistics are changed by individual decisions. At all times, the schizophrenic needs to be reminded that *he can be forgiven*. Even if "our hearts condemn us, God is greater than our hearts and knoweth all things . . . " (1 John 3:20). The promise of forgiveness runs throughout the Holy Scriptures:

> Again, when the wicked man turns away from all his transgressions that he hath committed, and doeth that which is lawful, he shall save his soul alive (Ezekiel 18:27).

> If we confess our sins He is faithful and just to forgive our sins and cleanse us from all unrighteousness (1 John 1:9).

Chapter VIII

Heaven and Hell

Behold, the Kingdom of God is within you.

—Luke 17:21

There are also windows in the soul through which we can see images created not by human, but by divine imagination.

—George Russell, *Candle of Vision*

Since the advent of psychoanalysis less than a century ago and the subsequent flood of "discoveries" in the psychological sciences, much has been said and written about some dark regions of the mind, which came to be designated the "unconscious." Relegated for some reason to the basement of the mental edifice, the "unconscious" allegedly serves as a repository of stored memories—archives, so to speak, of the individual's past. Presumably, it also contains the dark forces of desire—instinctual urges dictated by Eros and Thanatos—from which emotions are derived. Neatly devised and structured, psychoanalytic theories have, nevertheless, been frequently assailed for blanketing as unconscious all that is unknown about the operations of the mind and most of what is evil.

In addition to a personal unconscious, the mind has also been thought to contain symbolic representations, atavistically transmitted from generation to generation, whose significance is understood by all members of the human family irrespective of race, cultural background, tradition, or geographical location. These universally shared symbolic representations were extensively studied by Carl Gustav Jung, who termed them "archetypes." Making their appearance in art work, dreams, nightmares, and other subjective phenomena, archetypes are considered to belong to a "collective," as distinct from a personal unconscious. The symbols of the dragon, mandala, angels, and the devil, for example, belong to the collective unconscious. The origins of these symbols have given cause for much debate and controversy. Were the archetypes but flashbacks from a distant past, they would have tended to occur more or less at random. They would not have the capacity to become so intimately interwoven with the life-experiences of their subjects, nor would they have the ability of addressing consciousness with such directness and logic as they do. "It is insufficient to claim that archetypes represent symbols," wrote G. Bachelard (1948), "one must add that these symbols are dynamic, moving symbols."

Harmoniously, the symbols move with the spiritual and psychological needs of the experiencer, conveying an important message to his awareness. Visions of the Judgment, for example, do not suddenly appear from nowhere, but at that critical moment when the conscience pronounces a verdict of guilt and the soul flutters in dread of annihilation. The subjective experience of being judged and condemned, with threats of penalties and retributions—grasped by way of feelings, visions, and hallucinations—does not appear at random during a psychotic "explosion of conscience," but follows closely the needs of the subject as a distinctly personal message is conveyed to him in this manner. In addition to symbolic representations suggestive of Hell, the message, conveyed by delusional experiences, reminds their subject of the sinful act or actions for which he stands judged and condemned. The Hell of the schizophrenic thus contains elements from a collective as well as a personal unconscious. It is lived in the here and now, and reminds the schizophrenic of possible penalties for past and present transgressions. The descriptions of Hell given by Swedenborg in *Heaven and Hell* and *Divine Providence* strikingly resemble the experiences reported by schizophrenics, and contain much to suggest the existence of a general as well as a personalized Hell. After death, according to Swedenborg, those bound for Hell enter the infernal society most suitable to the life they had led.

Subjective Spiritual Experiences

Does Hell exist? Is there a Heaven? No more tangible proof of their existence may be available than that provided by subjective experience. Whereas the borders of consciousness lend themselves to much expansion—and carried on the wings of imagination, the mind can visit distant lands, and even logically and intuitively predict the future—subjective experiences are *given*. They are beyond the reaches of the will and need to be distinguished from consciously undertaken fantasy, with its creations of imagination. Subjective experiences—or the mind's capacity to perceive realms of reality never perceived before—belong to what writer and philosopher Aldous Huxley has aptly termed the Superconscious of the mind. This Superconscious can reach, according to Huxley, some *Terrae Incognitae*—worlds heretofore unknown to it:

> Like the earth of a hundred years ago, our mind still has its darkest Africas, its unmapped Borneos and Amazonian Basins. A man consists of what I may call an Old World of personal consciousness, and beyond a dividing sea, a series of New Worlds—the not too distant Virginias and Carolinas of the personal subconscious and vegetative soul; the Far West of the collective unconscious, with its flora of symbols, its tribes of aboriginal archetypes; and across another, vaster ocean, at the antipodes of everyday consciousness, the world of the Vision-ary Experience. You do not invent these creatures any more than you invent marsupials . . . . A man cannot control them. (A. Huxley, 1956)

The healthy mind, indeed, has the capacity for grasping and intuitively sensing much more of truth and reality than gathered by the senses; and this knowledge surpasses merely integrated percep-tions, cognitively evaluated (function of the right cerebral hemisphere, see Chapter III).

Intuitive knowledge needs to be distinguished, however, from subjective experiences such as dreams, visions, and hallucinations. Whereas intuitive knowledge may become somehow facilitated by meditation, and acquired to some measure through a conscious effort of concentration, we cannot will ourselves a dream, a vision, or for that matter, any kind of subjective experience, any more than we can fight off the onslaughts of a phobia, delusion, or obsessional preoccu-pation by sheer power of the will. Subjective experiences have been likened to a "wider opening of the windows of the soul," yet the "inscapes" thus revealed entirely depend upon the visionary's inner world. Subjective experiences have also been likened to voyages directed inwardly, but here again, the landscapes discovered cannot reflect but existing inner realities. According to Huxley, a journey inward can best be achieved by way of "shutting the doors to outer perception" (*The Doors of Perception*, 1954).

An increased state of subjectivity, or the expansion of the mind's capacity, may be achieved through various chemical substances which have the ability to produce synaptic inhibition in the central nervous system. LSD-25 and psilocybin are such substances, for they not only have the capacity to shut afferent channels (through synaptic inhibition of certain neuronal pathways), but cause an enhancement of subjectivity through increase in general arousal as well. Substances so endowed have been termed "psychedelics"—i.e., mind expanders. No substance exists, however, that could secure one heavenly visions, and by shutting the doors to external perception, the visions experienced may become rather appalling. Antecedent prayer, fasting, retreat, and contemplation may bring forth bliss-filled heavenly visions, but this again depends on the state of the subject, on his "inwardness" at the given moment.

Hypnotic or "twilight" states can bring forth only that which exists underneath. In conditions of sensory deprivation, due to a paucity of external stimuli, subjective phenomena tend to increase in frequency as well as in intensity. Their contents, however, remain entirely dependent upon existing inner reality.

"The Inferno is psychologically true," wrote Huxley, "and it is lived in the schizophrenic's experience." The visions of the schizophrenic are always appalling (except perhaps during the first and second psychotic episodes). Fear, hatred, anger, and malice are guarantees that the visionary experience, when it comes, will be infernal rather than blissful. Infernal experiences abound in the writings of men and women from all times. The visions of horror described by Guy de Maupassant in *Horlá* , by Franz Kafka in *The Trial, Metamorphosis*, and depicted by Goya during his "mad" period, are very similar in content. They resemble those of innumerable men and women stricken with insanity, interpreted by almost all of them as representing glimpses of Hell. The visions of the schizophrenic Renée, subjected to psychoanalytic investigation, have been described by M. A. Séchéhaye (1952) and quoted by Huxley:

> . . . an intense electric glare without a shadow, ubiquitous, and implacable. Everything that for healthy visionaries is a

source of bliss brings to Renée only Fear and a sense of unreality. The summer sunshine is malignant . . . every object when seen at close range and out of its utilitarian context is felt as a menace. And then, there is the horror of infinity . . . "the System," the vast cosmic mechanism which exists only to grind Guilt and punishment, solitude and unreality.

Had Huxley related Renée's visions to her hate, anger, and malice, as well as her actual intention to murder her father by placing boulders on the railway tracks of the train he was traveling in, the reasons for her fear, solitude, and infernal visions would emerge logical and clear. Renée did not put blocks on the railroad tracks because she was "crazy," nor did she experience infernal visions because she was mentally "ill." Renée was a hater, a murderer at heart, as are all schizophrenics; but she was also guilty of the action of placing boulders on the railroad tracks, which endangered the life not only of her father, but of other passengers as well. Her visions became infernal for this reason. All of her fears centered now around doom and Hell. In her delusions, and visible in her drawings, is the experience of being crushed by boulders, which paralyze and finally destroy her.

Subjective experiences (whether spiritually meaningful or not) represent creative constructs, which integrate elements from internal as well as external realities, both contingent upon accumulated life experiences. In psychoses, however, it is inner reality that determines to a large extent the contents of consciousness at any given moment; external occurrences merely serve to turn the attention of the experiencer to his central, spiritual Me as well as to his complex(es) of sin and guilt:

A drug abuser's attention was magnetically drawn to the colors red and black in the office where he was treated for a paranoid schizophrenia. He was unable to perceive anything but the red and black objects in his environment in general. By his own admission, he was guilty of shedding the blood of a black man in the not-so-distant past. (From author's caseload)

Dominated by his schizophrenic complex, the consciousness of this drug abuser directed his attention to the colors red and black in order to make him aware of his past offense and induce in him the desire to confess and to repent.

In acute and subacute schizophrenic illnesses, sin and guilt complexes and inner reality supersede in importance external events.

In the consciousness of the schizophrenic, the doors to outer perception become shut, so to speak, due to the intensity and pressure exerted by internal stimuli. In more chronic cases, the doors to outer perception remain partially open, but stimuli arising from the outside world suffer transformation and become threatening visions of Hell. This transformation in schizophrenia is recognized by psychiatrists and termed "misperception." Huxley (1956) wrote on the experiences of the insane:

> For them the universe is transfigured, but for the worse. Everything in it, from the stars in the sky, to the dust under their feet, is unspeakably sinister or disgusting; every event is charged with hateful significance; every object manifests the presence of an Indwelling Horror, infinite, all-powerful, eternal. The negative visionary finds himself associated with a body that seems to become more dense, more tightly packed, until he finds himself at last reduced to being the agonizing consciousness of an inspissated lump of *matter*—no bigger than a stone . . . .

The light that embellishes all objects with fluorescence in the blissful visionary experience of the saintly, is perceived by Renée the schizophrenic as an "electric glare without a shadow, ubiquitous and implacable."

For the visionary of blissful experiences, the everyday universe is transformed also. Some of the light's brightness is reflected back from the commonplace, which is rendered brilliant and sublime. The landscape of the blissful visionary is multidimensional and shines with fluorescent colors:

> Clusters of gems, most intricately arranged, emit preternatural light, brilliance, preternatural color and preternatural significance—such is the stuff of the heavenly vision. (A. Huxley 1956)

Blissful experiences are generally associated with flying and a sense of separation from the body. The assertion made by Jesus that, "The Kingdom of God is within you," is confirmed by data derived from the science of human experience. It is psychologically true and means that in certain instances, internal reality not only allows for glimpses of the heavenly abodes, but transforms external reality also, so as to make even the commonplace shine with preternatural splendor. The blissful experience is primarily an experience of light.

Psychologist William James (1902) described the blissful visionary experience as joyful, noetic, and ineffable. "Joy, Joy, Joy," gushes out from Blaise Pascal even during lonely nightwatches. "Freude, Freude" sings Beethoven's Ninth Symphony. The light and melody of these works seem to derive from the Kingdom within.

Just as dreadful inner realities spill over to color the external world and transform it into a threatening, horrible inferno, blissful experiences may cause "the everyday universe to be transfigured," in the words of Huxley, as he wrote:

> I was sitting on the seashore, half listening to a friend arguing violently about something which merely bored me. Unconsciously to myself, I looked at a film of sand I had picked up on my hand, when I suddenly saw the exquisite beauty of every little grain of it; instead of being dull, I saw that each particle was made up of a perfect geometric pattern, with sharp angles, from each of which a brilliant shaft of light was reflected, while each tiny crystal shone like a rainbow. The rays crossed and re-crossed, making exquisite patterns of such beauty, that they left me breathless . . . . (A. Huxley, *Heaven and Hell*)

The blissful visionary experience—as strongly emphasized by Huxley—almost never contains images that remind their subjects of anything from their own past (compared to the experiences of schizophrenics, which always do). The blissful visionary is not remembering scenes, persons, or objects, nor is he inventing them. "The view of the world," wrote Plato, "is a vision of blessed beholders; for to see things as they are in themselves is bliss unalloyed and inexpressible."

Through a gentle melody, the beauty of a landscape, or harmony achieved through a work of art, the mind's vision acquires somehow an impression—just a subtle suggestion—of what Heaven might actually be. Heaven acquires then a certain reality. The aesthetic, nevertheless, remains on a lower plane than the spiritual, although it leads to it.

Of the ways one is liable to attain blissful visionary experiences, Huxley (1956) wrote: The brute facts of psychological experience indicate that virtue is not the sole or sufficient condition of blissful visionary experience. Eschatologists know that works alone are powerless to do so, and that it is faith, or loving confidence, which guarantees that the visionary experience will be blissful. The nature of the mind is such that the sinner who repents and makes an act of faith in a Higher Power is more likely to have a blissful visionary experience than is the self-satisfied pillar of society with his righteous indignations, his anxiety about possessions and pretensions, his ingrained habits of blaming, despising, and condemning. (*Heaven and Hell*)

The amazingness of grace consists precisely in its power to pervade consciousness with a sense of heavenly bliss, all *in spite* of the presence of adverse external realities.

Where are the hells located and how far removed are the heavenly abodes? Their maps could only be traced by subjective visionary experiences. Yet these seem to carry a heavy weight of reality, for their truth is unduly impactful as it becomes engraved in the memory, where it leaves permanent traces. These phenomena are neither subject to the will nor products of imagination; they may actually invade consciousness against the will and defy attempts to shake them off.

"Are we a nation of mystics?" asked A. M. Greeley and W. C. McCready (1975) from the University of Chicago's Center for the Study of American Pluralism. In a survey conducted by these investigators, "four out of ten Americans reported the experience of a powerful spiritual force, which seemed to lift them out of themselves." Some of these "altered states of consciousness" could be induced, but most of them occurred spontaneously. Out of the 1,500 persons questioned, 600 reported having had at least one "religio-mystical experience" of a very intense nature. Those who reported such "peak experiences" were rather more advantaged than disadvantaged with respect to education and financial position. When examined for psychological impairment, the subjects of these experiences were found to score high on the "Well-Being Scale" of N. Bradburn, who stated that the relationship between frequent ecstatic experiences and psychological well-being, which was found to be 0.40, was "the highest correlation ever observed with this scale." Only one of those examined reported having had a negative mystical-religious experience: the world was perceived by him as dark, hostile, and vindictive—a "dark night of the soul." Fifty-eight percent of the subjects studied reported their experience as giving them a feeling of deep peace; 48 percent a certainty that all things work for good; and to 43 percent a conviction was imparted that *love is at the center of everything.*

Although our faith in a Supreme Being, merciful and just, may well be an illusion, dictated by our helplessness and inability to accept the finality of death, for what purpose would we want to invent or imagine the tortures of Hell? Hopes of heavenly rewards might well support us during our earthly journey, but who could find delight in conjuring up visions of Hell?

For contemporary psychologists and psychiatrists, spiritual experiences represent nothing but "schizophrenia-like, socially induced" departures from reality, illusions, delusions, or mass hysteria, "auto-hypnotic" phenomena (S. Arieti 1974), and for S. Freud (1927) "regressions to primary process" modes of cognition. And regardless of content, it has become customary for our materialistic psychological scientists to automatically label such experiences as "psychotic." It is most unfortunate that such interpretations have gained acceptance, however, because more than the various psychological and "projective" tests such as the Thematic Apperception Test (TAT) and the Rorschach ink-blot, subjective experiences give an indication of the individual's mental health, or else his psychopathology. But they also mirror his existential position at the given moment. It is this failure of behavioral scientists to correlate blissful spiritual experiences with superior mental health that is so surprising. But then, it could be said of behavioral scientists that they often avail themselves of the mechanism of denial.

Before further fanning the dust of confusion and flames of controversy in professional circles about the subjective experiences of schizophrenics, all sides agree that the majority of, but not all, such phenomena are absolutely Ego-alien. This means that they force themselves upon consciousness with such unspeakable dread that it is inconceivable to regard them any way close to being the products of imagination. To the schizophrenic, these experiences are perceived as more real than reality itself. There is no question that he cannot wish himself a vision, a dream; and no doubt that he is powerless to fight off the onslaughts of a nightmare, delusion, or hallucination. There is no participation of the will in these experiences and no reason for conjuring up such threatening fantasies.

But the nature of the soul and its inner experiences will forever elude the understanding of those who refuse to give them recognition. Closely adhering to the tenets of classical psychoanalysis, one of its chief proponents, C. Brenner (1974), wrote on the "secret language" people use unconsciously, without consciously understanding its symbolism:

> The list of what may be represented by symbols is not very long. It comprises the body, its parts, particularly the sex

organs, buttocks, anus, urinary tracts and the breasts; members of the immediate family; certain bodily functions and experiences such as sexual intercourse, urination, defecation, eating, weeping, rage and sexual excitement; birth, death and a *few* others. [emphasis added]

Needless to say, such a reductionistic, purely biological interpretation of symbolic representations fails to do justice to the richness of human experience and eloquence of the spiritually meaningful symbols one encounters in dreams, visions, and other subjective phenomena. Not always is the psychology of man associated with biological function, and when the "psyche" becomes solely identified with the functions of the body, one is justified in suspecting schizophrenic deterioration.

The reductionistic interpretation of psychoanalysis as well as its tendencies toward overvaluation of sexual functions have often stirred up revulsion. Persisting in its attempts to explain the dynamics of the "psyche" and operations of the "mind" in terms of sexual and other physiological functions, it can be said about psychoanalysis that it has frequently come close to the borders of the absurd. In his efforts to explain maternal love on a basis more fitting to his theories, for instance, Freud (1917) proposed the idea that this love actually represents a "wish for the phallus"—the male sexual organ being similarly small as is the infant—*das Kleine*. The comparison obviously violates the laws of logic and may best serve to illustrate the general trend of psychoanalysis to ignore the "psyche" and the laws that govern its functioning—laws biological, psychological, and spiritual. While maternal love may well be biologically determined, it provides psychological satisfaction as well as opportunity for self-detachment, self-sacrifice, self-transcendence, and spiritual ascent. It becomes thus obvious that those who persist in denying the primacy of the spiritual forces that govern the life of the soul will by necessity fail to understand its symbolic language, and decode the meaning of the messages conveyed. Thus, when infernal symbols make their appearance by way of nightmares, delusions or hallucinations and become "projected" in various self-expressive tests and productions, these symbols are read by psychoanalysts as meaning that a collapse of the defensive mechanisms of the subject is imminent. As if all mental disturbances were predicated upon neurotic conflicts and defensive operations; as if psychoses were solely determined by the loss of defensive armor and failure of the reasoning Ego to control the urges arising from the subterranean Id.

*   *   *

We do not know how to answer the why of our existence, nor can we hope to derive an adequate response from the findings produced by scientific research. We have no means to prove the substantial essence of the soul, nor can we produce convincing evidence of its immortality.

The first question to be asked regards consciousness: What is it that determines its content at any given moment? Are we solely governed by the Ego-mind, its reasoning, reality-testing, mediating, and controlling powers? Is the Ego-mind our master? We seem to know much more than the realities the Ego can perceive; we also frequently ignore the counsel of the Ego-reason, when for example, we trade the worldly in favor of eternal bliss. Upon one point, philosophers have tended to agree, nonetheless: intuitive knowledge is superior to knowledge acquired through the senses. Socrates taught, as did Plato, that the soul comes into the world carrying true ideas.

G. W. Leibnitz (1646–1716) wrote:

> Ideas and truths are innate in the mind as tendencies. All ideas must be contained in the monad—man. Experience merely brings these ideas to the forefront. The senses can arouse, justify and verify such truths, but not demonstrate their eternal and inevitable certitude.

We all seem able to distinguish right from wrong; we sense intuitively that sin is followed by guilt, and we fear forthcoming punishment. We also sense that all our suffering is not in vain, and all the goodness we have bestowed on others will be somehow, sometime rewarded. We feel as if our loves are bound to grow and flower, and our efforts eventually bear fruit. But we also have a certitude that we will need to pay due penalties for each and every transgression of the moral-spiritual law; and that the punishments decreed by conscience are independent of the laws of men. Subjective experiences such as paranoid feelings of condemnation and persecution, for example, or the compulsion to self-punishment, well serve to prove this point. Even as homosexual practices are now more or less tolerated by enlightened societies, and do not prevent homosexuals from holding office in some modern churches, these sexual activities produce shame, guilt, and paranoid feelings of persecution, notwithstanding.

That the counsel of the reality-oriented Ego may be ignored, as, for example, when we trade the present for an uncertain future, or when we lose by giving sacrificially, or when we dare to take a "leap into faith" (S. Kierkegaard 1843) in our attempts to reach the Supreme, only proves that the Ego-mind is not our master. It is but servant to intention and, certainly, not its initiator.

The language we use unconsciously reflects much of the spiritual strivings that move our being. Even in our commonplace, routine conversations, when we speak of *lofty* goals and *higher* aspirations, when we say that "things *look up,*" and when we feel *elated,* we subconsciously acknowledge the supremacy of the Spirit. We strive for *higher* values, and frequently we try to *sublimate* certain desires. We fear, however, *darkness* and *lift* our gaze toward the *light.* All we experience as evil is associated with a *fall,* with *gravity,* with *matter.* We condemn the *base* in character and their *lowly* motivations. We seem to fear an *underworldy* power, which Freud called Id and G. Groddeck (1866–1934) "it," both men agreeing, nonetheless, in their perceptions of its dwelling place in the lower regions of the earth, as well as in the basement of the mental edifice. Like growing trees, we strive upward, our flame burning vertically in righteousness, as matter becomes transformed into Spirit (G. Bachelard 1943). We live, in the words of N. Kazantzakis (1961), in order to transubstantiate from weighty matter into spiritual ether. Even the "dumb" computer mentioned before spilled out conclusions very similar. When the computer was "fed" the random conversations of "normal people," the contents of their verbal productions revealed concerns with family, friends, and themes of *ascendance* (S. T. Rosenberg et al. 1979).

We come to know our soul, our inner spiritual Self, in times of illness, distress, loneliness, sensory deprivation, and nearness to death. In panic states and phobias, what we fear most is not damage or loss of the genitals—as psychoanalytic doctrine would have it—but the awful possibility of losing our sanity, our mind, our soul. During an acute schizophrenic psychosis, it is "annihilation" of the soul (often presented with images of cannibalism) that is so intensely dreaded. The substantial reality of the soul is also experienced when the conscience condemns by way of guilty dysphorias; when self-esteem suffers a loss; when depression stifles the spirit; and when anxiety presaging spiritual death floods the conscious mind.

But for those healers of the "psyche," who refuse to recognize the laws of conscience as valid, who deny the ascending aspirations of the soul, who themselves repress the moral forces of their own consciences, and who are all too ready to provide others with "therapeutic absolutions," danger lurks for them, for they may come to suffer a fate similar to that of their patients. Amid the circle of pioneers and devotees to the cause of psychoanalysis, nearly 10 percent succumbed to madness and/or committed suicide. It is also worthy of note that the rate of suicide among physicians is highest for psychiatrists, which at the rate of 67 per 100,000 is six times higher than that of the general population (11 per 100,000, according to Dr. Nathan Kline, Biennial Meeting of the New York State Psychiatric Association, November, 1976). Psychiatrists, moreover, tend to have a higher rate of mental disorder than the general population, and this might have less to do with their "genius" than with their refusal to acknowledge the existence of a spiritual Self, or soul. Could it also be related to their failure to guide morally those who come to them for help? Who could prove the soul's existence? Contenting themselves with theoretical constructs that explain the workings of the human "mind" to *their* satisfaction, many behavioral scientists ignore the laws that govern the life of the "psyche," yet give every consideration to the laws of physiology, respecting its laws to the minutest detail. Every deviation from, and every trivial violation of the principles of homeostasis, for example, are scrupulously evaluated and rapidly remedied, whereas the laws that govern life of the soul—biological, psychological, and spiritual—are paradoxically ignored.

*   *   *

The stirrings of the soul are frequently brought to awareness by feelings of sorrow and empathy for another, by the beauty of a landscape, wonders of nature, a moving melody, a work of art, or by some insight about ourselves. In lonely isolation, during prayer, meditation, and contemplation, we come closer to our spiritual selves and the whisper of our souls may then become audible. The encounter with our Selves, our souls, may also come about by means of drugs, during transcendental meditation, and, to a certain degree, during sleep. The outcome of the encounter, however, is quite unpredictable and beyond the control of the will. A journey inward and confrontation with our Selves may not be all that beatific, and might even prove disastrous. But if and when we are able to detach from the world and loosen ourselves from compulsions and routines—to which we may have become enslaved—and let ourselves just be, we might also be able to reach a delightful state, frequently imparting an "oceanic feeling" of Unity with the Universe, and a sense of inexplicable inner peace. We feel then as if the Kingdom of God is within us, and all its gifts are our possessions. Our inner vision becomes then crystal clear.

It is precisely this inner peace that Transcendental Meditation (TM) seeks to achieve for the meditator. TM calls for a withdrawal of attention from the world outside and a suspension of all attachments. While silence, body immobility, and monotonous repetitive chanting (at times incomprehensible to the meditator) may aid in subduing external stimuli to a minimum, and shut in this manner (at least to some degree) the doors of perception, the technique itself by no means ensures that a state of peace will necessarily ensue. What actually occurs in such conditions depends entirely upon the subject's inner reality at the given moment. Anger, hatred, bitterness, and revengeful intentions may actually become enhanced and, instead of the peak state of Nirvana, may bring the meditator to a state of panic.

Adverse effects with psychotic-like experiences and frank psychoses have been known to occur during sessions of Transcendental Meditation (R. Walsh 1979). Whereas meditation may bring about peaceful, so-called "zero-states" (during which synchronized alpha waves appear on the electroencephalogram), it might also cause the whispers of the soul to become loud and threatening. A similar process occurs when the patient with a borderline character disorder focuses his attention inwardly—and deprived of external stimuli other than the ceiling of his therapist's office—suddenly "breaks down on the couch."

In addition to sensory input derived from the outside world, consciousness receives stimuli from various parts of the body. When the body cries in pain and signals threats to its integrity, attention is immediately diverted to that locus. The flow of somatic stimuli arising from the body frequently silences for a time perceptual streams arising from the subject's psychological inner state. The capacity of somatic distress to subdue or even obliterate internal realities may account for the fact that schizophrenic patients "feel better" during a physical illness. Somatic distress and disease threatening the integrity of the body cause the schizophrenic to "forget" temporarily the threats to the integrity of his soul. In a similar manner, emotional anguish, suffering, and pain caused by blows of fate, adverse external circumstances, or general disasters may paradoxically bring about improvement in certain cases of schizophrenia through a temporary release from dread and anguish arising from within (pp. 207, 210, 400).

It thus appears that those stimuli that reach the central computer—the "mind"—continuously compete against each other for a "fair hearing" in consciousness. The question asked by M. E. Scheibel and A. B. Scheibel (1962) is very much to the point:

What are the basic mechanisms that disengage the sensory-reporting apparatus from the real inputs or give more weight to inputs of internal origin? This very question implies the existence of a system that "reads the tape as it leaves the computer."

As mentioned before an answer to this question is provided by William James (1892), who assigns hierarchical superiority to the spiritual Me. For the wise of the past as well as for modern Existentialists, the question regarding who "reads the tape" and decides whether to grant priority to external stimuli or to those arising from within, is answered by their recognition of man's soul or Self as central regulator. It is this central regulator that masters the chariot, instructs the Ego-mind, and decides ultimately upon the chariot's direction.

With the body in reduced motion, in the darkness and stillness of night—conditions under which sensory deprivation naturally occur—the central regulator, after having read the tape, brings forth into the sleeper's awareness that which it considers top priority. It may be some painful sensation derived from the soma-body; it may have to do with some realistic concern. Top priority may also be given to matters of conscience, as occurs in schizophrenia. In every phase of this diseased state, the complexes of sin and guilt assume preeminence in consciousness, even during sleep, and when threats of impending punishment produce dread of sufficient intensity, they often reverse the state of consciousness from sleep to wakefulness.

In a study of the "most recent recalled dream," 40 paranoid schizophrenics, 40 psychotically-depressed, and 40 medically-ill patients were investigated by M. Kramer et al. (1968). The paranoid schizophrenic, typically, finds himself with a stranger in an implausible situation, in which he is *the victim of hostility* (punishment dream); the depressed patient finds himself with a family member in a plausible situation, which is hostile half of the time, and in which he may be either the aggressor or the recipient of aggression; the medical patient usually finds himself with a friend in a plausible situation, which is only rarely hostile.

According to L. J. West (1962), the dream is an experience during which, for a "split second," the sleeper has at least some awareness of the stream of data processed. This is borne out by the observation that during sleep, the ever wakeful regulator imparts an awareness of the dream's meaning, and not infrequently allows even for the solution of a difficult problem, to be grasped by the conscious mind.

In states other than sleep, quantitative changes in sensory input can cause alterations in perception and become responsible for the occurrence of hallucinatory or delusional phenomena, such as are commonly experienced in conditions of sensory deprivation.

Sensory Deprivation

During experimentally created conditions of sensory deprivation, affectively colored perceptions—internally generated and unconsciously determined—may "seduce," so to speak, the patient partially or completely away from the world outside. Certain occupations more than others expose individuals to naturally occurring conditions of sensory deprivation. Such is the lot of some pilots, for example, who spend long flying hours in monotonous solitude. Confusion, disorientation, and even delusions and hallucinations have been reported by individuals subjected to conditions of sensory deprivation. In his book *Night Flight*, Antoine de Saint-Exupéry describes what it means to be sensorily deprived. In *The Little Prince* he gives an account, perhaps, of his own experiences in the desert. In *Terre des Hommes,* he describes being lost in the Sahara desert, suffering hunger, thirst, complete isolation, and a near certainty of imminent death. But since the contents of delusions, hallucinations, and visions are entirely dependent on, and vary with the subject's internal reality, it would appear as if Saint-Exupéry's experiences of sensory deprivation enhanced, actually, his creativity and provided him with important spiritual truths. From what he tells his readers, his visions and experiences served to strengthen his religious faith, and authenticated for him the prospect of eternal heavenly bliss.

In an experiment on 11 voluntary subjects, carefully chosen to screen out psychopathology, J. T. Shurley (1962), sought to explore the psychological effects of monotonous solitude (maximum tolerance exposure to an environment of minimal inputs of sensory stimuli), and found that *all* subjects were willing to repeat the experience. Most of the phenomena ensuing from the experiment were found to be surprising to the subjects and were experienced as either comforting or enjoyable. None caused panic. The visions included an Indian with golden earrings, fluorescent golden toadstools, orange and green apricot trees with vivid colors, and bright light.

In another carefully monitored experiment of sensory deprivation, J. H. Mendelson et al. (1965) compared two subjects and their reactions. These subjects were selected on the basis of the complete-

ness of their records prior to the experiment. They were exposed to the same external stress, which, realistically viewed, represented no stress at all, and in no way endangered their physical or psychological well-being. The subjects of the experiment were placed in a tank-type respirator, but were instructed to interrupt the test when they felt compelled to do so. This experiment yielded different results from the one described above.

One of the subjects was found to be extremely defensive, and to have withheld some information on his prior psychiatric interview. He was given to multiple fears, mostly involving the contraction of various diseases—cancer, TB, etc. In interpersonal relationships, he felt somehow superior. Under pressure, he was found to be lapsing into irrational thinking. This subject ended the experiment after three and a half hours. At that time he was found lying motionless, confused as to time and location, and entertaining delusions. He believed the sides of the tank were pressing on him and that, were a fire to break out, he would be trapped, despite a good knowledge on his part that he could at any time leave the experimental respirator. While entertaining these thoughts, he saw a dead insect and a gray curtain, which covered half of his vision field. On the day following the experiment he related that he feared the eggnog given to him as sustenance contained bacteria that would poison him. These experiences were very real to the subject, and at all times during their occurrence he was completely alert and conscious.

The second subject, described as a "professional school student," intellectual, and given to excessive fantasizing—which eventually became for him a major source of gratification—endured the experiment for almost six hours. At no time was there any evidence of delusional thinking or hallucinations, despite a high level of anxiety near the end of the experiment. He became panicky and involved in a vehement struggle with himself to terminate the test, which he finally did. The psychiatrists who had examined him before the experiment found this individual to be conveying a pervasive sense of failure.

Personality factors clearly affected the sensory deprivation experiences of both these subjects. When confronted with themSelves, both became unduly anguished. The first subject—who had shown deceptive tendencies and who dealt contemptuously with his fellow men, considering himself superior—suddenly felt threatened by poisonous bacteria and a dead insect, and his vision became impaired by the appearance of a gray curtain (of his deceptions). The second subject became engaged in a struggle very similar to that he was probably involved in all along: fighting his own weaknesses and sorrowing over his failures. Despite a rich fantasy life, this individual did not slip into "primary process thinking," nor did he experience visions of either Heaven or Hell. What he felt was but his own failure.

In another experiment, undertaken by S. J. Freedman et al. (1965), eight volunteers were subjected to continuous nonpatterned visual and auditory low-grade stimulation. Reduction of tactile and kinesthetic sensations was achieved through the wearing of gloves and immobility of the body. No one entered the room or spoke to the subjects during the experiment. All eight volunteers reported difficulties in concentration. Four felt as if dissociated from their bodies, which became rigid and unable to move. Four experienced auditory hallucinations: music, birds, buzzsaws, and undifferentiated human voices. Four subjects described fears of fire, abandonment, burning buildings; sensed as if a steel casket would drop from the ceiling; and thought that an infernal machine was advancing to destroy them. All these images appeared and disappeared spontaneously. They were not under the subjects' control. The character of the imagery, moreover, was described as quite different from that of dreams or daydreams. The images were felt as outside of the subjects; they were sensed as *given*. They were definitely not the experiencer's own creations and had nothing to do with past experiences.

Similar effects to those caused by sensory deprivation may be produced by "overstimulation" through excessive sensory input. Excessive input may actually produce a "jamming" of the circuits, with the appearance of hallucinations, deliria, and even psychotic excitement. The images perceived in such conditions were described as frighteningly vivid by L. J. West (1962).

With regard to the quality and content of the subject's experiences during sensory deprivation, little controversy exists among investigators; they all seem to agree that perception is selective, and that the content and quality of these experiences depend primarily on the subject's personality.

According to researchers L. Goldberger and R. R. Holt (1965), reactions to isolation depend, among other factors, on the ability of the individual to maintain "secondary process" thinking, on his resistance to regression to "primary process" thinking, and on his dealing with these, once they become evident in the stream of thought. They write:

To a person with an immature Ego, with unstable, fragile, or extremely rigid defensive structure, the invasion of conscious thought by the primary process phenomena provokes marked anxiety and guilt. Primary process manifestations are characteristically experienced as Ego-alien, unpleasant and highly disruptive.

Theories and explanations about the various experiences during sensory deprivation such as given by Goldberger and Holt, obviously lack accuracy as well as logic. First and foremost, they disregard the fact that for individuals devoid of prior psychopathology, experimentally induced sensory deprivation is a pleasant, enjoyable experience, that they even wish to repeat. That primary process imagery evokes anxiety is logically tenable, but guilt? How can one feel guilty for the involuntary intrusion into consciousness of threatening and disturbing visions? It may not be a fear of the Id that threatens the guilt-laden experiencer during sensory deprivation, but fears of retribution, graphically depicted by visions, misperceptions, and hallucinations.

Citing his own, as well as studies of other investigators on sensory deprivation, M. Zuckerman (1969, 1970) found that hallucinations—or as he preferred to call them, "Reported Visual Sensations"—correlated in their appearance and frequency with the degree of anxiety present in their subject. Not only visual, but other modality hallucinations made their appearance in states of fear, which may have ranged from mild anxiety to outright panic. At times, hallucinations formed part of delusions. Several cases of genuine psychotic reactions were observed to occur during conditions of sensory deprivation, and these had affected subjects who were not psychotic prior to the experiment.

It has long been recognized that retreat and isolation may be Ego-enhancing and conducive to Self-knowledge, as well as to spiritual truth. Isolation in the midst of nature often brings about a sense of clarity and harmony to those so attuned. An "oceanic" feeling and a peace-filled sense of unity with the universe may be experienced in such settings. For the beatific influence of such conditions, some religions have incorporated into their tradition periods of time to be spent in isolation and retreat from the world. The experience is blissful, however, only for those who put their trust in the Higher Power, in ascension and sublimation of desire.

For Huxley, the windows of the "unconscious" open to new, never seen vistas where, according to G. Russell, "images created by divine imagination" may become revealed. Conditions of sensory deprivation are frequently sought by writers, painters, and the religious, for during retreat from the world, a closer proximity to the Self may be attained. During such conditions, the windows of the soul may open wider and allow for glimpses of landscapes "created by divine imagination." The borders, if they existed at all, of the vistas revealed to the unconscious (or perhaps more accurately, the Superconscious), would tend to merge with infinity.

In subjective introspection we may see ourselves as we really are, and through the windows of the soul, perceive our existential position. The vistas thus offered would certainly extend far and beyond those of the theoretical framework constructed by modern behavioral scientists. When all external props which had served to divert our attention are being removed, as during hypnosis, sensory deprivation, meditation, or by the use of certain drugs, the primary realities of the soul become more evident. Joy and light might gush out from the wellspring of emotion and fluorescently color the multidimensional landscapes of Heaven. But fears and threats may also flood the meditators' "inscapes," and the various "circles" of Hell—personal as well as collective—shown to the condemned.

Drug-Induced Subjective Experiences

Certain plants and fungi as well as manmade chemical compounds can diminish sensory input through their action on specific centers of the brain. The study of drug-induced subjective phenomena convincingly demonstrates the primary position of the Self as spiritual center and regulator in the life of the "psyche." Through the dimming of external input by the use of certain chemicals, the primary reality of the Self, the soul, surges from the depths of the unconscious, as spiritual symbols address consciousness. The symbolic representations by which the Spirit imprints itself upon consciousness are experienced as "more powerful than ideas and they actually overshadow real experiences" (G. Bachelard 1943).

According to neuropsychiatrist A. S. Marazzi (1962), indole and indole-related substances—being chemical "cousins" to inhibitory neuro-humors, of which the neurotransmitter serotonin is believed most potent—exert their hallucinogenic action through synaptic inhibition in certain areas of the brain. Exogenous substances may be even more powerful than serotonin in producing synaptic inhibition. Bufotenine, for example, has been found to be the most potent synaptic-inhibiting substance known, and twice as active as serotonin. LSD-25, mescaline, cocaine, and other indole and indole-broken-ring substances exert their action, according to Marazzi, by impairing the normal afferent sensory transmission, while at the same time increasing the general level of arousal. Such substances are ideally psychotogenic because they reduce external inputs while increasing arousal, thus facilitating the emergence of material held below the level of consciousness and allowing for internal reality to assume dominance over other perceptions. Many other hallucinogens are sensory poisons and diencephalic stimulants at the same time. Whether these substances impair the transmission of sensory input or disturb its integration into conscious processes is an issue that has not been quite resolved.

Whatever the exact manner of their action, drug-induced visionary experiences begin in neutral position, just as the visions that occur in experimental sensory deprivation. With increased dosage of the drug employed, as with increments of time in isolation, the geometric forms initially perceived as cobwebs, spirals, lattices, vessels, tunnels, and so on, progressively acquire shape. Eventually they become three-dimensionally formed objects, whose nature and significance are largely unpredictable, nonetheless.

When the doors to outer perception become shut through the use of chemical compounds—not unlike conditions of sensory deprivation—the windows of the soul may open larger, and allow for revelatory experiences. The contents of these subjective phenomena, however, depend entirely upon the existential position of the visionary. The visions perceived by the soul may thus be lit up by the "Clear Light"—its objects rendered fluorescent and resplendent with heavenly beauty—or made dreadful by "the hateful glare of the land of lit-upness upon its horrifying inhabitants," as they were for Renée the schizophrenic.

The contents of drug-induced subjective phenomena do not seem to obey any law or follow pharmacological logic. Most abusers are aware of this fact and know that there is no surety as to the quality of their drug-induced experiences. They also seem aware that with continuous abuse, the landscape may suddenly change and become malignant, as illustrated by the following case described by S. Cohen and K. S. Ditman (1963):

> For three years a receptionist to a physician had used LSD and other drugs—which for a time had provided her with pleasurable experiences. She suddenly reported that her experiences had changed and that she had become dysphoric,

hallucinating now skulls of people she well knew, and other similar horrors.

It is of significance that the skulls this LSD user suddenly began to perceive presented to her the symbol of death, much as used by pharmacists to forewarn of the danger of drug poisoning. And as is true for every other delusional experience, hers contained the threat of punishment as well as its reason.

Comparing the hallucinatory phenomena produced by LSD and mescaline to those of schizophrenia, E. L. Bliss and L. D. Clark (1962) called attention to the fact that whereas schizophrenics experience hallucinations while their eyes are open, subjects under the influence of drugs see visions with their eyes closed. The hallucinations of schizophrenia moreover, were, according to these authors "highly symbolic and reflecting religious delusions." Nevertheless, drug-induced visions often contain spiritually meaningful symbols—whether or not coexisting with a schizophrenic illness. The lack of interest in the appearance of spiritually charged symbols and religious representations in schizophrenia and other psychiatric disorders, inclusive of drug abuse, clearly betrays the views held by the majority of mental health professionals, who consider religion to be delusional belief, and psychosis its derivative. Explaining auditory hallucinations on the same premise as suggested by Freud, namely as voicing the conscience's criticism, Bliss and Clark failed to account for the fact that hallucinations are not always accusatory, but may be commenting, commanding, ridiculing, or interfering, without obvious reason, in the thought processes of the schizophrenic. Were hallucinations but voicing the criticism of the conscience, they would not urge some individuals to repeat their sin or crime, as they frequently do. Moreover, many individuals suffering from the burdens of a guilty conscience do not have auditory hallucinations, nor are they schizophrenic.

Commenting on the visionary experiences induced by chemical substances, Huxley (1956) wrote as follows:

> The way to the Superconscious is through the subconscious, and the way, at least one of the ways, to the subconscious, is through the chemistry of individual cells . . . . In one way or another, *all* our experiences are chemically conditioned, and if we imagine that some of them are purely "spiritual," or purely "aesthetic" or purely "intellectual," it is merely because we have never troubled to investigate the internal chemical environment at the moment of their occurrence.

Whereas investigations intended to clarify the production of hallucinations by means of chemical substances can be left to psychopharmacologists, the *content* and quality of these phenomena ought to be of utmost concern to psychologists and psychiatrists, for, like every other subjective experience, they shed light on the functioning of the Self and its existential position.

A recent study on the effects of medicinal drugs on the quality, frequency, and intensity of hallucinations clarifies much of the confusion surrounding the issues mentioned above. In the investigation undertaken by C. G. Goetz et al. (1982), these researchers examined the effects of drugs used to relieve the symptoms of patients suffering from Parkinson's syndrome. The 20 patients investigated were all free from previous psychiatric illnesses and had no history of psychosis, but they all experienced hallucinations related to their treatment. All had suffered from Parkinson's disease at least five years prior to the study and were given accepted medications for their illness, namely specific dopaminergic drugs such as Levo-dopa, Carbi-dopa, Amantidine, Bromcriptine, Lergotrile, and anticholinergic agents such as trihexphenidyl, benztropine, and diphenidol. Possessing hallucinogenic properties, these compounds induced all varieties of hallucinations, including tactile, olfactory, auditory, and visual. The hallucinatory syndrome seen in Parkinsonism after long-term anti-Parkinsonian therapy was relatively consistent. One group of patients experienced hallucinations primarily involving formed images of animals and people, most commonly familiar to the patient and involving dead or absent friends or relatives. Not all hallucinations, however, involved formed images. Another group of patients suffered from formed hallucinations of a threatening character, and some from auditory hallucinations related to them. Of great interest ought to be the finding of this study, to the effect that threatening hallucinations were no more common than nonthreatening ones, although individual patients tended to suffer from *either one or the other type*, and did not report mixed patterns. Some patients experienced hallucinations regardless of the medication prescribed, whether anticholinergic or dopaminergic. Quality, intensity, and frequency of hallucinations appeared similar, whether or not an increase of dopaminergic or cholinergic medication had originally precipitated the hallucinations. From the patient's point of view and that of his family, the two hallucinatory states were indistinguishable. Some patients had threatening, and some nonthreatening hallucinations. When the dosage of medication was increased, if hallucinations were already present, they tended also to increase. *Yet, significantly, the characteristics of the hallucinations appeared to be constant for any given patient,* regardless of the anti-Parkinsonian drug and its dosage.

Describing his experiences with neurologically impaired patients, E. A. Weinstein (1970) found that 27 out of 30 patients experienced hallucinations while they were completely coherent and oriented. When their hallucinations were formed, they most commonly represented people, with animals being the next most frequently occurring category. Three patients with organic brain syndromes (post-traumatic, brain tumor, and Alzheimer's, respectively) impressed this writer by the benign character of their hallucinations, with representations of landscapes, people they knew, and domestic animals.

M. Zuckerman (1969) was struck by the fact that drug-induced hallucinations were similar to those that occurred in conditions of sensory deprivation. In both cases, the hallucinations progressed from simple geometric to more complicated forms of spirals, cobwebs, tunnels, and lattice-work, evolving eventually into fully formed panoramic vistas, people, and animals.

The most remarkable common characteristic of organically determined hallucinations is their content, which seems to derive solely from the subject's past experiences and stored memories. Neither the subject's personal unconscious nor the collective unconscious find representation in the hallucinations of organically impaired patients. It would appear thus that organic lesions of the brain give rise to signs and symptoms of deficit mostly in cognition, sensation, and motor function, and that when memory "flashes" images back into consciousness, they derive from the patient's past. Hence in organically determined lesions of the central nervous system, symbolic representations of the spiritual Self are conspicuously absent. Neurological damage does not bring forth hallucinations with spiritual symbolism and religious content, although some patients may suffer threatening hallucinations. Neurological damage does not produce insanity either. As master of the chariot, the soul retains its position of command, even as the charioteer, namely the brain (or mind), becomes disabled.

Immortality

Much has been spoken and written in recent years about "out-of-body" states and near-death experiences. According to G. O. Gabbard (1988), an out-of-body experience (OBE) occurs to anywhere from

14 to 34 percent of individuals in the general population. It may be a pleasant, even ecstatic experience (*ecstasy* derives from: *ex* = outside and *stasis* = staying), but for the schizophrenic an OBE may be associated with disturbing sensations, such as feeling oneself a machine, missing some body parts, or having a sense of identity dissolution. The majority of individuals who have had an OBE interpreted it as a religious-spiritual experience, even if they were not previously associated with any organized religion. The OBE imparted to them a belief in life after death, although only 10 percent occurred to individuals nearing death.

In a national study on OBE, which involved a large group of individuals, 83 percent of the respondents felt that their experiences caused them to develop a greater awareness of reality. A more detailed study of 339 individuals who had reported OBE, by S. T. Twemlov et al. (1982), revealed that all of them thought their consciousness had separated from their physical body. The majority of subjects described their experiences in superlatives and thought they represented spiritual-religious revelations. These experiences, generally described in terms of "great beauty," were reported as having had a dramatic impact and lasting effects on the lives of their subjects, even causing changes in their beliefs regarding life after death. Only 33 percent reported some fear, and 4 percent felt they were going to go "crazy" during the experience. The group as a whole proved, after additional testing, to be significantly healthier than a group of psychiatric patients (in- and out-patients) on the one hand, and a group of college students on the other. OBE appeared in a wide array of different conditions: to some, during the stress of awaiting surgery; to others it was associated with bereavement, loneliness, and nearness to death. OBE was also reported during relaxation, meditation, cardiac arrest, sexual orgasm, and childbirth. According to Twemlov et al., the experience imparted a sense of complete functioning of the Self located *outside of the brain*.

Data from other studies concur in validating the reports of individuals who had undergone OBE and seem to agree in defining them as religious-spiritual experiences that impart a sense of conviction about the existence of a Self or soul, which is not located in the brain and can separate from the body.

In his book *Life after Life*, R. A. Moody explores "clinical death" and "near-death experiences." The wider public has already become acquainted with much of what those "dead" and revived individuals had to tell about their experiences. Most commonly reported was the sense of detachment from the body, and the ability to see oneself, revived, operated upon, mourned, etc. But many subjects also reported that they had acquired a new, spiritual body, which they likened to a "vapor" (not consisting of any material substance), which travels fast and passes through walls and even mountains, without encountering resistance—just as described by Swedenborg (*Heaven and Hell* and *Arcana Celestia*). Ubiquitous was the experience of passage through a "dark tunnel," as "the shadow of the valley of death . . . " and of the sudden appearance afterward of a brilliant, radiant light attributed to a Being—"the Being of Light." This Being imparted to the "dead" a sense of warmth and love. The experience of having "passed on" also brought about a confrontation with one's past, which, miraculously, was all remembered. As the dead witnessed the display of all his deeds and misdeeds, the Being of Light seemed to emphasize the most important things in life: learning to love others and the acquisition of knowledge.

A personal account of a near-death experience is given by neurologist E. A. Rodin (1980) in the *American Journal for Nervous and Mental Diseases*. Dr. Rodin remembers his near-death experience vividly. While undergoing surgical exploration for a probable metastatic carcinoma of the lung, he remembers his last request to the Deity: "If it is metastasis, please, let me stay on the table," after which he immediately felt a tremendous bliss, accompanied by the knowledge that he was dead and free. He felt no sensory perception except the absolute certainty that "it is over and it's wonderful." Dr. Rodin remembers the experience as "the most intense and happiest moment of my entire life, which a quarter of a century has not erased nor diminished . . . ." Commenting further on his experience, he writes:

> Death is a gradual process. It can be assumed that what is important for the individual in his dying moments is the mental content of this anoxic psychosis, i.e., the visions that are being experienced and the beliefs about them. If the content of the final psychosis is pleasant, the individual who knows he is dying is likely to accept it as his version of Heaven. If it is terrifying and/or painful, one does not require medieval devils to realize that one has entered Hell. There is no way of knowing whether our individual brain in its last moments will send us to celestial shores or to the biblical bottomless pit. We know, however, from our epileptic patients that the mental content experienced during temporal lobe seizures is dependent upon the life experiences of the individual. It does not arise *de novo*, but is tied to the patient's fears, hopes, preoccupations.

> The dying individual acts as his own judge, jury, accuser, prosecutor, defense attorney and witness . . . . Inasmuch as the individual no longer is in voluntary control over his mental processes, the outcome of the verdict will be quite unpredictable.

Dr. Rodin goes on to say that "our limited sensory system will always provide us with a limited view of nature," and suggests the term "shared subjective reality" for experiences and opinions common to the majority of mankind.

Yet, after all is said and done, it matters little whether a subjective experience was determined principally by external or internal realities. Of major import is the power of certain experiences—appearing with unusual vividness and intensity—to dictate a *fundamental change in life's goals as well as its direction.* Even when very brief in duration, some of the conversion experiences described by William James (1902) in *The Varieties of Religious Experience* were so powerful as to induce a complete change within the individual, leading him to new shores and more blissful ways of existence.

When similar subjective experiences are shared by many, they cease to retain their subjectivity. The visions of Dante Alighieri, Emanuel Swedenborg, Antoine de Saint-Exupéry, Guy de Maupassant, and countless others, represent "shared subjective experiences" whose contents bear no resemblance to any childhood memory, and belie the possibility of these phenomena being but "regressions" to "primary modes of cognition."

Time has come perhaps for psychiatry to enlarge the scope of its interest and become engaged in the study of subjective phenomena, especially those shared by many. The systematization of shared subjective experiences might prove a most fruitful field for future investigators. The study of the "Superconscious" would certainly contribute to the expansion of accumulated knowledge and provide a clearer understanding of what may exist beyond.

Subjectively, the soul or Self is experienced as existing outside of the brain, and may be located just where it is felt to be—in the heart or in close proximity to it—where, with Swedenborg, the majority of us sense it to be. From the accounts given by those who were near death and revived, it would appear that the soul survives the physical body and continues to live after life. Yet in reflecting on the hereafter, we must remember the experiences of schizophrenic individuals: their perceptions of losses of parts of their body; their feelings of having become solid matter, robots, or machines; their sense of dissolution; and their dying while yet living.

All this is immensely important and concerns us all. While living our biological existence longitudinally in time and space, we can choose to repudiate hedonistic goals and set ourselves free from biologically determined inclinations. We might thus decide to leave behind the world of matter, and, propelled by the spiritual forces of our souls, ascend ever higher.

Chapter IX

Character Disorders and Border States of Sanity

There is no reality except in man's actions . . .
even feelings are formed by the deeds one does.
—Jean-Paul Sartre

The mental health profession must learn that what we do affects how we feel, just as much as how we feel affects what we do.
—George E. Vaillant

More than two hundred years ago, French psychiatrist Philippe Pinel (1745–1826), famous for liberating the insane from their fetters in the Paris Salpêtrière, was struck by the case of a peasant, who, after having pushed a woman down a well, felt neither remorse nor experienced a "delirium" afterward. The absence of a guilt-delirium, following an act as abhorrent as this, was described by Pinel as a case of *manie sans délire*—insanity without delusions.

The term "moral insanity" was applied in 1835 by J. Prichard to individuals who appeared blind to moral values, behaved in a way contrary to the laws of society, and manifested little capacity for experiencing guilt.

"Psychopathic inferiority," as many disturbances were then considered, and criminality were recognized to "run in families." B. A. Morel (1809–1873) observed and described these disorders in detail and was able to trace some to their origins in the family. A worsening of "psychopathic inferiority" was found to occur for three to four successive generations, the disorder coming then to a halt. Perceiving continuity as well as a progressive evolution of some mental disturbances, Morel described cases of *"démence précoce"* (dementia praecox), i.e., dementia affecting individuals of young age.

Whereas long-term studies spanning three to four generations are notably lacking from documents produced by modern research, existing data on the hereditary transmission of mental disorders in general tend to confirm a certain "clustering" of schizophrenia and schizophrenia-spectrum illnesses in families. Whether "psychopathic inferiority" worsens with succeeding generations cannot be answered by the currently available data.

The terms "psychopathic inferiority" and "moral insanity" became obsolete, however, with the advent of the Industrial Revolution, Humanism, and the movements for social justice. Psychiatric disorders came to be viewed from an entirely different perspective. Suddenly, man became but a "product" of his circumstances; and when deviant in behavior, he came to be regarded as a victim of adverse social conditions and various injustices. Accordingly, psychiatric disorders came to be understood as: 1. "reactions" to frustration, 2. products of faulty upbringing, 3. consequences of oppression, poverty, various "traumata," and 4. in the last few decades, as mishaps in biochemically or neuro-anatomically determined brain functioning.

Among existing trends of thought, the psychoanalytic movement came to assume a leading role in psychology as well as in psychiatry. Enormously convincing and containing many new insights, it can be said about psychoanalysis that it actually turned a page in the history of psychiatry. When appraised retrospectively, however, the doctrine appears less glamorous and its brilliant "discoveries" give rise to skepticism for their lack of scientific validation. Who can probe the experiences of preverbal children? How can hereditary trends be singled out? And why does one child and not another "react" to one and the same "traumatic" experience?

Yet the psychoanalytic movement can be understood, provided it is perceived as being a child of its time. Conceived during an era of rapid change and nurtured by the hopes of the Enlightenment, it is hardly surprising that psychoanalysis gained acceptance as a theory possessing scientific truth. On closer scrutiny, however, it shows itself merely reflecting the conflicts of the Victorian era—a time when Liberalism began to dissipate traditional and moral values, sweeping aside all the while, religious faith in its way. Thus it is hardly by chance that neurotic conflicts took a central position in the doctrine of psychoanalysis, and even less surprising that their majority revolved around matters of sexuality. In the eyes of psychoanalysis, it is repression that came to be regarded as the villain, not only of neurotic but of other mental illnesses as well. Freud was led thus to believe that with removal of the barriers erected by society, religion, and tradition against freedom in individual expression, and with the abolishment of moral constraints, neuroses—and for that matter, all psychiatric disorders—would tend to disappear. Even in his last publication, Freud (1940) persisted in regarding sexual inhibition as causative of later neurotic disorders:

> . . . we cannot escape the conclusion that neuroses could be avoided if the childish ego was spared this task [of repression], if, that is to say, the child's sexual life were allowed free play, as happens among primitive peoples.

He also wrote on the repression of aggressive urges in the same publication:

> Holding back aggression is in general unhealthy and leads to illness, to mortification.

And, indeed, so many years later, the prevalence of neurotic illnesses has steadily declined. Where are the conflicted neurotics of the Victorian era? In the permissive atmosphere currently prevailing in most of the Western world, authentic neurotics can rarely be found. Even the latest DSM-IV reflects the change of the times, for neurotic illnesses *as such* have been deleted from its list. Yet more individuals suffer now from "emotional disturbances" than ever before, and their "sicknesses" are far more serious than the various neurotic ailments prevailing in the not-so-distant past.

As for drugs and other pleasure-producing substances, Freud (1927) had this to say in *The Future of an Illusion*:

> That the effects of religious consolation may be likened to that of a narcotic is well illustrated by what is happening in America. There they are now trying—obviously under the influence of petticoat government—to deprive people of stimulants, intoxicants and other pleasure-producing substances, and instead, by way of compensation, are surfeiting them with piety. This is another experiment about whose outcome we need not feel curious.

There is little curiosity left, now that the "experiment" is over, done with, and its outcome all too evident. People are no longer deprived of the use of "pleasurable intoxicants," and they now suffer, not from an abundance of piety, but from a host of psychiatric disturbances and a multitude of substance-induced ills.

Although Freud claimed "neutrality" on matters of morality, he openly sided ,with those of his time who sought to abolish existing "bourgeois" mores, especially in matters of sexuality. And attempting to erase the borders between Good and Evil, psychoanalysis became by necessity rather relativistic concerning moral issues in general. Keenly perceiving that "without religion ethics preach in vain," it remains unclear why Freud (1930) set out to attack them both with all the powers of eloquence with which he was endowed. In *The Future of an Illusion*, Freud made a formidable effort to prove religion illusional, delusional, "nothing but narcotic for the masses," and, like Nietzsche, he denied the existence of God. Yet by so doing Freud (and psychoanalysis) severed the roots by which morality is meaningfully nurtured. One may rightfully question the role of psychoanalysis in "the great hundred-act horror play " predicted by Nietzsche:

> Morality from henceforth goes to pieces; this is the great hundred-act play reserved for the next two centuries in Europe, the most terrible, the most mysterious . . . . (*The Genealogy of Morals*)

Already commenced, the play has proven to be a horrendous tragedy. One may not want to pause for mention of the horrors perpetrated by the Nazis, whose "inspiration" has been attributed to Nietzsche and his philosophy.

In the narrative language of statistics, the script of the tragedy reads as follows: every fourth girl and one out of eleven boys are sexually molested or abused annually, according to statistics released by the New York State Department of Health in 1987; child neglect and abuse have steadily increased and affect 25.2 children per 1,000 (as of 1992); divorce breaks one out of two marriages—when marriages are contracted at all! Between 1980 and 1990 the rate of illegitimacy has steadily increased from 8 percent to the current 28 percent of live births (*National Center for Health Statistics*, August, 1993). And abortions, newborns thrown into garbage bins, and lust-murders, how many? Would not these ills alone suffice to pronounce themselves in condemnation of permissive attitudes toward sexual behavior? Violence has swept the land and is now considered an epidemic. From 2 to 4 million women are beaten by their husbands yearly. The rate of homicide, according to the *National Center for Health Statistics*, 1993, has increased by 23 percent (from 1985 to 1990), and the number of victims of violence exceeds 2 million annually. Yet these statistical computations hide many more abandoned, neglected, and abused children, brutalized parents and battered spouses, who are not always capable or willing to report these crimes to the appropriate authorities. Numbers would fail also to give adequate information about the havoc produced in society by pleasurable intoxicants, whereby millions of law-abiding citizens are sent "behind the bars" of their own homes, while drug-abusers and criminals are left free to roam the streets, to rob and kill. One half of all car accident fatalities is consequent to drunken drivers, according to statistics released by the *National Center for Health Statistics*, 1993. Mothers Against Drunk Drivers (MADD) report that during 1993 alone, 18,000 persons were killed and 350,000 were injured by intoxicated drivers. The crime rate has also shown a steep increase in recent years, and the state and federal prison population (according to statistics released by the Federal Bureau of Prisons, Justice Department, FBI, *USA Today*, March 24, 1994) has more than tripled since 1980—at a time when incarceration policies have actually slackened due to prison overcrowding. The 16 fatalities of the Amtrak tragedy in 1988; the *Exxon Valdez* oil spill in 1989; and the subway disaster of 1991 in New York City which claimed 6 lives and caused injury to many—all caused by intoxicated individuals—add additional horror to the possible consequences of pleasures indulged by a few— conductors, pilots, captains—the costs of which are disbursed by many. It is hardly surprising to find that, according to police statistics, drug use and abuse are implicated in a good majority of street crime, violence, and loss of life. Might it not be rather late to decry the indulgence in "pleasurable intoxicants?" After reviewing the results from the "experiment" alluded to by Freud, one can hardly avoid the conclusion that sexual freedom, the indulgence in pleasurable intoxicants, and the tolerance to expressed aggressive urges have contributed more to "psychopathic degeneration" and "inferiority" in our days than any other social calamity.

From crime to psychiatric disability. Is there a correlation between criminal behavior and mental illness? A parallel increase is noted in both. Whereas a decade ago the *National Institute of Mental Health Bulletin* (1985) released statistics showing that *one out of every five* Americans suffers from a mental disorder, and one out of every seven is so severely disturbed as to require the help of professionals, the latest statistics derived from research data reported by R. C. Kessler, (1994), reveal that now, *one out of every two* Americans have experienced a mental disorder at some point in their lives and *one out of every three* suffers from a mental disorder in any given year.

When one out of two Americans suffers from *at least* one mental disorder in his/her lifetime (48 percent lifetime prevalence), and 14 percent experience *three* or more psychiatric disturbances at one time (R. C. Kessler et al. 1994), one may no longer refer to the "mental health" of the current freedom-bred generation, but rather to its "sickness." The substantial increase in the number of psychiatric casualties can no longer be set aside with indifference. A decade ago, the lifetime prevalence of mental disorders was given as ranging between 29 percent and 38 percent (L. N. Robins et al. 1984); it is now 48 percent—an increase of close to 15 percent. The same increase is evident from a comparison of prevalence rates (i.e., the number of affected individuals in any given year): while a decade ago, between 17 percent and 23 percent of the adult population of the United States was reported as suffering from at least one psychiatric disorder in any one year (D. X. Freedman 1984), the prevalence rate reported in 1994 is given as 30 percent. As for "pleasurable intoxicants," the lifetime prevalence rate of alcohol abuse and dependence was found to range from 11 percent to 16 percent, and drug abuse from 5 percent to 6 percent of the population (L. N. Robins et al. 1984). The increase in suicide rates, given by the crude rate of 12.4 per 100,000 population, which shows an increase of 32 percent in the last decade for single older males and a rate of 15.1 for young people 20 to 24 years of age (*United States Department of Health and Human Services,* August, 1993), could serve as indicator of the rising tide of malaise and "sickness" which have overtaken our free society. The question whether freedom and permissiveness, divorced from moral constraints, have a deleterious effects on society in general and on the mental health of the individual in particular, needs the urgent attention of both policy-makers and mental health professionals.

It is of interest to note that while the lifetime prevalence of antisocial personality disorder was given a decade earlier as ranging from 2.1 percent to 3.3 percent (L. N. Robins et al. 1984), it has now reached a rate of 5.8 percent (R. C. Kessler, 1994). Does this increase have anything to do with the freedom granted to any one individual to act as he or she pleases? Does it measure society's increased tolerance to aberrant behavior? Although accurate statistics on the incidence and prevalence of schizophrenia are not available at this time (due to methodological difficulties in data collection), the life-prevalence (incidence of schizophrenia during one lifetime) has been given as 1.9 to 9.5 per 1,000 population for European countries and 2.1 to 3.8 per 1,000 for Asian countries (H. M. Babigian 1975). An increase in the prevalence of schizophrenia has been noted to occur in some of the most progressive and liberal countries of the world: Sweden, Germany, Denmark, Austria (A. Jablensky 1986) and the United States, among others. In a two-year pilot study on schizophrenia by the World Health Organization, N. Sartorius et al. (1977) found schizophrenic patients to fare better with respect to course and outcome on all variables in "developing" countries, as compared to those from "developed" nations. It is difficult to avoid interpreting these findings as indicating a correlation between the extent of permissiveness in "developed" countries and the incidence of chronic schizophrenia, on the one hand, and a more benign course and outcome in "developing" countries, where individual freedom is somehow curtailed and traditional moral values still abide strong, on the other.

In Western societies, at least, where "repressive" attitudes toward sexual behavior have been all but removed, the incidence of neurotic illnesses has shown a declining trend. The truly neurotic, struggling to overcome desire through the moral forces of his conscience, resembles now more an anachronistic Don Quixote than a hero in the strife. This does not mean that the consciences of modern men and women have ceased to warn and correct. The contrary seems actually to be happening. But now, instead of suffering from a conflict, an "illness," these individuals experience chronic anxiety, circumscribed phobias, and panic attacks when exposed to the tempting stimulus or its symbol, which they tend either to avoid or to erase by the use of anxiolytics. It would thus appear that with the abdication of parental authority, devaluation of educators, corruption in higher and lower places, and premarital and postmarital promiscuity, the individual who suffers from an authentic neurotic illness cuts a tragicomic figure on the scene of modern times.

Shy, sexually inhibited, and conflicted neurotics have now become displaced by proud, defiant, narcissistic, self-assertive, sociopathic, and borderline character-disordered individuals, who engage in indiscriminate sexual activities, avail themselves of the pleasures of intoxicants, act out their aggressive urges, and audaciously insist on various entitlements to boot. With the help of parents, educators, and mental health professionals, these disordered persons have now *learned how to sin and not feel guilty*. They deploy their defensive operations not as preventive measures against acting out their forbidden impulses in the future (as do neurotics), but in view of repressing, suppressing, and silencing the voice of their consciences. Even so, since it is not given to society to abolish spiritual-moral laws, those who transgress them suffer from a host of guilt-derived torments, experienced as depression, anxiety, paranoia, and nightmares, among others—not to mention an unusually intense dread of death and final decree of divine justice. And no one among mental health professionals could deny the fact that a set of psychiatric disturbances, more serious by far—termed "personality" or "character" disorders—have come to replace the neuroses. Yet, in the ever changing classifications of psychiatric disease-entities, personality or character disorders have proven themselves difficult to categorize, owing to the large overlap in psychopathology as well as similarity in their signs and symptoms of distress. Neither can deviant behaviors, ingrained into the personality as character traits, be relied upon to define and separate these disorders. The last DSM-IV, released in 1994, attempts to solve this problem by almost doubling the number of psychiatric disorders.

Deviancy can no longer be defined in terms of behaviors that run against the accepted norms established by society, either. This is particularly true for Western societies, where modernization has brought about a significant moral devaluation and considerably lower standards for tolerable behavior. Various eccentricities and "alternate lifestyles" are now accepted. A good number of individuals who would have been considered "psychopathic degenerates" just a few decades ago, function now as respectable members of society. Psychopathology, thus, can no longer be defined by deviant behaviors *per se*, because deviancy is currently defined by rather loose terms. When "morality goes to pieces"—as Nietzsche predicted it would—it is the craftiest who is admired and applauded. He may not necessarily be considered "sick"; he is often lauded as the "fittest" for survival.

The definition and classification of character disorders, be they categorized as "antisocial," "sociopathic," "borderline," "schizotypal," "dependent" or "mixed," have become the subject of much debate as well as challenging controversies. Personality or character disorders can be better understood, however, when deviant behaviors are examined separately from the symptoms of distress they tend to generate. The laws of logic certainly require that symptoms be compared to symptoms, and behaviors to behaviors. Moreover, a correlation of symptoms to behaviors—if existing—would need to be determined with regard to their sequential appearance: i.e., whether symptoms followed certain behaviors or else preceded them.

Certain character traits and some repetitive behaviors have been found associated with specific ways of experiencing life. The **Dependent Personality,** for instance—characterizing the individual who always leans on others for assistance—is by necessity bound to experience frequent depressions based on disappointment, for not many "others" will necessarily oblige. The dependent person, moreover, will eventually suffer the pain of rejection by others, who, at a certain point, are liable to refuse to abide by the dependent's persistent demands and expectations. As for the dysphorias generated by certain behaviors, these differ somewhat among individuals and are given to flux and change over time. Whereas criminals, socio-pathic and psychopathic persons may all be involved in very similar behaviors, their specific ways of dealing with the guilty dysphorias generated by their antisocial activities immediately separate them into different categories and distinct nosological entities. The criminal most commonly resorts to alcohol in order to dilute or drown his guilt; the sociopath denies his guilt altogether; the psychopath is guiltless by definition.

That society cannot determine the moral value of certain behaviors is borne out by studies with polygraph investigation. The polygraph shows itself to be color-blind with regard to lies and capable of detecting deception even when undertaken as part of an experiment. The polygraph is independent of public opinion, and its recordings are solely dependent upon the anxieties aroused by dysphorias pertaining to guilt. That society can in no way change certain moral laws, and influence thereby the subjective experience of guilt, is evidenced by the fact that individuals who engage in extramarital sexual activities, perversions, or excesses—now tolerated by society—still experience shame and guilt, and entertain ideas of being judged and condemned by others. Although the sensitivity of conscience may vary among individuals, it shows, nonetheless, certain universal and consistent trends, as, for example, its sensitivity to transgressions in the interpersonal realm. But the sensitivity of the conscience is also known to increase with maturity as well as with advanced spiritual development. Sensitivity to guilt, on the other hand, may decrease with the persistence of moral offenses, as the conscience may progressively "harden"; it may eventually be brought to silence altogether.

The Psychopathic Deviant
and Antisocial Personality

For a better understanding of the psychopathic personality, as distinct from the criminal and sociopath, i.e., the individual involved in antisocial activities, a closer examination of the psychopath's inner structure as well as a longitudinal evaluation of his life-adventures would need to be first undertaken.

According to polygrapher S. Abrams (1974) there exist two categories of "psychopathy": one, very rarely encountered, comprises individuals who appear unresponsive on the polygraph and produce a tracing "flat" for emotivity; the other comprises individuals who show rather accentuated, increased, and indiscriminate reactions. The findings produced by the research of Abrams lend confirmation to data originally reported by polygraph pioneers J. Reid and F. Inbau.

It is the true psychopath—guiltless by definition—who produces a tracing that appears "flat" on emotivity. Not every individual who engages in antisocial activities is a "psychopath," nevertheless, as some may experience guilt more inwardly, with rather increased reactivity when investigated by the polygraph. Experts in the field agree that true psychopaths are very rarely encountered. W. McCord and J. McCord (1964) describe the psychopath as a "rebel who has no goal, an unsocialized misfit who feels no guilt in breaking social mores." Extensive interest and research on the psychopathic condition have led the McCords to conclude that:

> Unless the individual exhibits the two critical psychopathic traits—guiltlessness and lovelessness—he should not be characterized as psychopathic.

This is a valuable definition. Not every criminal is psychopathic. According to H. Cleckley, author of the epoch-making *The Mask of Sanity* (1964), true "nuclear" psychopathy is a disorder "very central, far reaching and profound." Cleckley regards the motivations of the psychopath as already insane:

> The psychopathic individual is not only not dependable, but he, in more active ways, cheats, deserts, annoys, brawls, fails and lies with no apparent compunction. He will commit theft, adultery, fraud and other deeds for astonishingly small stakes and under much greater risks than any ordinary scoundrel. He will, in fact, commit such deeds in the absence of any goals at all!

Unlike the criminal, the psychopath seldom takes advantage of his spoil. He never works consistently and indulges in vice at a cost in punishment so great as to be considered insane. The psychopath, moreover, as distinct from the criminal, has little or no appreciation for the future, as if deep down he knows he has none. He commits the most abhorrent acts for the sake of thrills, power, or publicity. The murder committed by Loeb and Leopold, was, according to Cleckley, motivated mostly by a search for excitement. A young man who took out life insurance on his mother's plane, in which he deposited a bomb so that all aboard were killed, was motivated, according to Cleckley, less by the insurance money than by the sporting qualities of the exploit. For the psychopath, criminal acts committed with callousness and cynicism represent but casual, day-to-day activities. Cleckley believes the psychopathic individual to have an absolute incapacity for love and an erotic life that is trivial for the most part. But he also seems to have a penchant for the sordid and obscene, and is frequently confused with regard to amorous and excretory functions, as if intent on "smearing" his partner symbolically as well as literally. The psychopath, according to Cleckley, seeks to wallow in sordidness himself:

> Considering a longitudinal section of his life, his behavior gives the impression of gratuitous folly and nonsensical activity in such massive accumulation that it is hard to avoid the conclusion that here is true madness—madness in excelsis.

Cleckley considers the outbreak of psychosis, so frequently erupting on the life-journey of psychopathic individuals, as actually representing an "unmasking of the underlying disorder." He thus defines madness in different terms than most of his contemporaries, whose criteria rely on "departures from reality" and failures of the Ego-mind and reason. Such criteria of insanity would, by necessity, exclude the truly psychopathic, as his sense of reality may actually be "hypertrophied." He would not be able, otherwise, to assess so well new situations, circumvent conditions of danger, and so skillfully execute his often difficult aims. Because of his wit, charm and various ingratiating strategies, the psychopath may, in addition, win more in a social situation than is possible for the average person. He is endowed with many talents, of which the exploitation of others is not one of the least. On the psychopath's unusual endowment, Cleckley comments:

He directs his unblemished talents toward useless or highly undesirable goals and may carry out conscientiously and effectively the most disastrous antisocial acts.

Cleckley defines insanity thus by *the motivations of the individual*, which in the case of the psychopath comprise a wide array of evil choices, accepted by him without prior conflict, and executed with callousness, cynicism and little, if any, sense of guilt.

Cleckley perceives more similarities with the schizophrenic condition "in quality" than are generally recognized. He makes a point in emphasizing that schizophrenics are influenced by the same motives as are psychopaths:

After following for years obviously queer, distorted and socially restricted, but apparently not psychotic careers, a few commit without provocation murder or some other tragic misdeeds—for which they show little evidence of remorse.

According to Cleckley, psychopaths suffer from yet another central defect, which he termed "semantic dementia" or blindness to meaning. The precepts of morality are mostly understood by the psychopath on an intellectual level, but since they are not bound to any emotion, they remain to him devoid of meaning. Cleckley is in agreement with the McCords on the psychopath's lack of capacity for love, which is considered by him as absolute. Since the psychopath cannot be moved by emotion of any kind, he seeks forever new thrills and excitement.

Cleckley considers the psychopath emotionless and insane by motivation, whereas the McCords (1964) regard him as affectionless and guiltless by definition. If, indeed, the soul is qualified by its capacity for loving and ability for experiencing guilt; by its perception of meaning; and by its sense of the future—all of which the psychopath is lacking—can he be considered as one born without a soul?

The study of psychopathic deviance has been persistently fraught with difficulties, not only because true psychopaths are rarely encountered, but also because many individuals engaged in antisocial activities may, somewhere along their life-journey, be jolted spiritually and emotionally by an "explosion of conscience" in the form of a "mini" or major psychosis, which often evolves into a chronic schizophrenia. Many "sociopaths," moreover, persisting in their antisocial activities, may in time become truly psychopathic—that is to say, hardened, loveless, and guiltless individuals, whose spirit has ceased to strive and to correct. But regardless of their final destiny, all sociopaths suffer from paranoid ideas, fears, and ideas of persecution. Reflecting their antisocial activities and fears of retribution, they suffer from nightmares in which they become victims of bloody assaults, murderous attacks, and various tortures (A. Kales, C. Soldatos 1980).

L. N. Robins (1966) brought a valuable contribution to the understanding of sociopathy with her longitudinal investigation reported in *Deviant Children Grown Up*, in which she describes a follow-up of deviant children 30 years after their initial visit to a child guidance clinic. The early manifestations of psychopathy are sorted out, and the evolution of antisocial behaviors—branching out to produce various emotional disturbances in adult life—followed through. Only 19 percent of the children studied by Robins were symptom-free when examined 30 years after their initial evaluation. Of the 500 children originally examined (and 436 on the follow-up), 45 percent had become "antisocial" personalities. Of the 34 percent who had become "seriously emotionally disturbed," 11 percent were found to be suffering from schizophrenia.

According to Robins, antisocial personalities rarely originate *de novo* in adulthood and as a rule show signs of the disorder at an early age, even by age seven. Early antisocial behaviors were found to be significantly predictive of later antisocial behaviors, or, as Robins put it: "Bad children became bad adults." In some cases, antisocial behaviors anteceded later schizophrenia as well as other severely disabling emotional disturbances. Environment was found to have played a rather *insignificant* role in these developments. Robins (1978) wrote as follows:

> Severely antisocial children were found to be at risk—no matter how good or bad their environment; but moderately antisocial children with antisocial fathers were more likely to be more antisocial adults than were others.

Paradoxically, and contrary to the expectations of those who adhere to model-learning theories to explain psychopathology, children who were separated from their antisocial fathers early on, were more likely to develop later into sociopathic personalities than those who continued to live with them. That children whose sociopathic fathers were present in the home fared better than otherwise can be understood, however, in terms of yet another determinant—the factor of discipline:

> With good or strict discipline, only 21 percent of even the severely antisocial children become sociopathic as adults, compared with 48 percent of those where both parents are excessively lenient or disinterested. (L. N. Robins, 1966)

Several measures were found to be predictive of antisocial behavior in adulthood: the versatility of deviant behaviors, the number of episodes of such behaviors, and their seriousness. Neither family characteristics nor social status were found to be predictive of the outcome of childhood antisocial behaviors. Translated into existential terms, these findings may be interpreted as meaning that future psychopathology is largely predicated upon the accumulation of moral offenses early in life and their severity.

The disorder termed "psychopathy," as distinct from "sociopathy," gains clarity when deviant behavior is examined separately from antisocial activities, character traits, and dysphorias generated by antisocial behaviors. As has been said before, although the criminal, psychopath, antisocial, and schizophrenic individuals engage in quite similar behaviors (stealing, for example), the quality and outcome of such behaviors tend to be different. A longitudinal, lifelong existential analysis of individuals engaged in antisocial behaviors reveals an evolution that branches into several possibilities. When antisocial behavior is consistently repeated and the warnings of conscience ignored, an "explosion of conscience," might erupt at some point, and entail spiritual loss and an uncertain future. But repressed, suppressed, denied, and displaced guilty dysphorias may also produce—especially when cynically rationalized—a "hardening" of the conscience. Such an evolution may finally bring about a state of spiritlessness, not much different than that of the truly psychopathic, as he embarks on his life-journey. Antisocial activities, on the other hand, may be given up, renounced once and for all. Such a decision may follow a drastic life event, such as divorce, physical illness, or bereavement. Personal catastrophes have long been known to produce a jolt, an existential crisis, often resolved in favor of the renunciation of prior antisocial activities.

With the existence of a considerable overlap for the antisocial activities of criminals, antisocial persons, true psychopaths, and schizophrenic individuals, their symptoms of distress also tend to show more similarities than differences. Intended to impart awareness of wrongdoing and the need for remedial action, the various dysphorias of warning, on the one hand, and those pertaining to guilt, on the other, would need to be carefully sorted out.

Compiled from the writings of authors whose work is mentioned in this section, the following list makes visible the differences between the antisocial personality and the truly psychopathic—a difference mostly in degree. Behaviors, character traits, and symptoms of distress, specific for both of these diagnostic categories, are separately listed.

The Psychopathic and Antisocial Personalities

Behaviors	Character Traits	Symptoms of Distress
Refusal to help others	Defiance of parental authority	Anxiety
Refusal to work	Incorrigibility	Depression
Truancy	Shallowness of affect*	Somatic complaints
Poor school performance	Absence of guilt*	Paranoia
Impulsive, reckless	Absence of life-goals*	Concerns over body
Self-destructive acts	Trivial in sexuality*	Fear of death
Stealing	Absolute incapacity for love*	Obsessions and Compulsions
Pathological lying	Lack of loyalty	
Sexual perversions	Irresponsibility	
Wanderings	Pathological egocentricity	
Suicidal attempts	Manipulative, exploitive	
Accident prone	Ingratiating*	

* The underlined traits are most characteristic of true psychopathy.

Being absolutely incapable of loving and experiencing guilt, the true psychopath short-circuits all those dysphorias that, as a rule, torment the criminal, antisocial, and schizophrenic individuals. According to Cleckley, the psychopath aims directly at "protracted and elaborate social and spiritual suicide." Compared to the rate of suicide found among schizophrenics, the rate of suicide for psychopaths is higher. The death rate of psychopaths due to various causes, inclusive of "solicited accidents," is twice the national average, wrote

L. N. Robins (1966). S. Guze (1976) reported a 16 percent death rate from suicide among psychopathic individuals. "Through experience over some years in a general hospital where all attempted suicides are examined by a psychiatrist," wrote I. R. C. Batchelor (1954), "the largest majority of these 'birds of passage' were suffering from psychopathic states."

One month before his execution, convicted murderer Donald Evens, considered a psychopathic deviant, refused to ask for clemency on the grounds that he would lose his identity if sent to jail:

> It would be hypocritical of me to say that I am sorry, for I had fun and excitement. Now I want out—death. (*The New York Times*, March 13, 1979)

In a similar vein, murderer Gary Gilmore refused all appeals for clemency because, "My soul is on fire and is screaming to be released from this ugly house I've built around it" (*Newsweek*, November 29, 1976). Whether Evens and Gilmore were truly psychopathic or became so after their many crimes can only be guessed, pending a complete analysis of their life histories. But, as previously stressed, antisocial behaviors alone are neither predictive of the child's or adolescent's destiny nor can they place him in any one psychiatric diagnostic category. What seems to be decisive in such a determination has much to do with the content of one's dialogues with one's Self—with one's conscience—as well as with the outcome of these conversations. The youngster who repents and zealously attempts to make amends sets himself with his "reaction formation" on a higher spiritual plane, as he also brightens the outlook of his destiny.

Guilt, however, may become displaced onto minor, trivial moral misdemeanors; it may also be suppressed, repressed, or denied entry into consciousness altogether. The voice of conscience is not stilled by such defensive operations, nonetheless. It may address its subject by way of bodily dysfunctions, aches, and pains; it may also speak to him graphically, by way of nightmares, misperceptions, delusions, and hallucinations. Guilt may also become projected onto others, circumstances, and events, but the transgression causing it may be felt as if "broadcast aloud" and made known to others by so many "voices." Complexes of sin and guilt may also become dissociated and "split-off" from the subject, as frequently occurs in hysterical conditions, multiple personality disorder, fugue states, and schizophrenia.

Every intentionally committed moral violation, nevertheless, tends to weaken the conscience, the power of the will, and the capacity of the Ego to control its repetition. And, needless to say, the imbalance thus created tends to facilitate the commission of other, even unrelated antisocial acts. Such activities may become so habitual as to gain access into the inner chambers of the heart and become its "loves," its goals. Specific defensive operations against the pain of guilt, moreover, may become ingrained into the antisocial personality, cementing eventually its final structure. It is a dangerous state, nonetheless, when the conscience is consistently treated in this manner, for it may cease eventually to warn, correct, instruct, and condemn. Wrongdoing progressively strengthens its grip and becomes then true sin—a position. And since every unrepented sin represents added offense, a critical accumulation might eventually become that *unpardonable sin*, about which theologians have never ceased to debate. Even as they do, a good consensus seems to exist, which holds the opinion that as long as the Spirit strives with the individual, he has not committed the unpardonable sin.

As long as the conscience continues to admonish and warn, the patient's way to recovery remains open. Thus, individuals engaged in antisocial activities—who still experience anxieties, dread, nightmares, delusions, and hear "voices" that condemn them—may not despair of having committed the unpardonable sin, for their conscience is still actively striving to bring them to repentance and produce in them a "change of heart." Mowrer (1961) considered schizophrenics to be in a more favorable position than psychopaths. Having had at least the "common decency" to experience an "explosion of conscience," the schizophrenic has also a better chance for recovery than the sociopath, who no longer experiences guilt. According to G. O. Gabbard and L. Coyne's (1987) retrospective review of 33 patients with antisocial personality disorder or antisocial features, the presence of *psychosis or depression* was found to be conducive to a better response to treatment. Significant predictors of a negative response to treatment, on the other hand, were associated with felony arrests, unresolved legal situations, lying, conning, and aliases. The paradox that a more severe symptomatology, namely of psychosis or depression, presages a better prognosis in psychiatric disorders, may, nonetheless, be interpreted as meaning that *when not repressed*, the conscience has powerful forces at its disposal to reverse psychopathology and to cancel symptoms of distress.

An in-depth study of the antisocial personality begins with its separation from true psychopathy. The true psychopath is loveless and guiltless by definition; the person engaged in antisocial activities may eventually lose the capacity for loving and experiencing guilt: lose his soul or Self, in other words. The antisocial person may choose other life-paths, nonetheless, and these may bear upon his psychiatric diagnosis as well as ultimate life-destination. Psychopathy defines thus psychopathology, whereas sociopathy defines certain behaviors.

One half of the children who later became antisocial adults were described by L. N. Robins (1966) as "nervous"; they also had a profusion of somatic symptoms in addition to their antisocial behaviors. Not all persons engaged in antisocial activities could apparently accept their antisocial behaviors with equanimity, and their anxieties and various somatic symptoms betrayed their inner turmoil. A profusion of somatic symptoms is, indeed, characteristic of individuals engaged in antisocial activities, inclusive of criminals. Conversion disorders, hysteria, and Briquet's syndrome were most commonly encountered in men engaged in antisocial activities. C. R. Cloninger (1975) also found "sociopathy to be the most common disorder among men who report suicidal attempts or have unexplained conversion reactions."

A study on families of sociopaths led Cloninger to believe hysteria and sociopathy to be interdependent traits and to have also a common pathogenesis. Conversion reactions, hysteria, and Briquet's syndrome were found significantly more prevalent among felons than in the general population—a finding confirmed by several investigators. In a study of female felons, S. Guze (1976) found *conversion hysteria to be present in those who denied their guilt.* Complete innocence was claimed by 67 percent of the hysterics versus only 10 percent of the controls (p. 128). Hysterics were much more likely to attempt to mitigate their guilt, claim their arrest illegal, their trial unfair, and their treatment cruel. Guze interpreted the findings of his study as "supporting the hypothesis that hysteria and sociopathy are different but overlapping manifestations of the same underlying disorder." Both Cloninger and Guze failed, however, to search for the logical connections that relate these apparently distinct disorders: one defining a behavior, namely sociopathy, the other a distress, namely conversion symptoms. Could these two disorders be related by cause, i.e., sociopathic behavior, and effect, i.e., guilt converted into somatic symptoms? And if, indeed, the sociopath's anguish of guilt becomes converted into aches and pains arising from the body, the question as to *who* determines the transformation remains ever pertinent. Clinical observation tends to indicate that the forces at the disposal of the conscience are so powerful they can influence the emotions (by anxieties, panic attacks, and depression), physiological function (hyperacidity, bronchospasm), and even produce anatomical changes in an organ, i.e., psychosomatic illnesses such as duodenal ulcers and emphysema consequent to long-standing asthma. A denial of guilt is operative in hysteria as well as in other conversion syndromes (Chapter V). Often aware of his self-deceptive denial of guilt, the subject of a conversion syndrome deceives himself further by denying also the meaning of his symptoms.

Another possible evolution of persistent antisocial activities is a psychotic-schizophrenic development. Of the children studied by L. N. Robins (1966), 11 percent were later diagnosed as schizophrenic. Such an evolution, anteceded by antisocial activities, was also observed and described by S. Dunaif and P. Hoch (1955), who termed this category of schizophrenia "pseudo-sociopathic." Like every other schizophrenia, however, **Pseudo-Sociopathic Schizophrenia** gives rise to symptoms of "pan-anxiety, paranoid ideation, guilty feelings, and a sense of body disintegration" (quoted from Dunaif and Hoch) among its various manifestations. The author of these lines has witnessed several cases that presented initially as an antisocial personality disorder, but developed later into a clear-cut schizophrenia.

It would appear from the foregoing as if there were no other way to consider mental illnesses but on a longitudinal, lifelong existential-process basis, given their different evolution over time. Not all psychopathic deviants, observed Cleckley, belong to a class of legal criminals, for many among them are engaged in professions such as medicine, law, and politics. Not every criminal, on the other hand, belongs to the category of psychopathic deviation. The factor of recidivism, frequently used to identify the psychopath, might well be too arbitrary, for the "repetition compulsion" is operative for every moral violation that remains unrepented. Many "incarceration psychoses" may actually represent "explosions of conscience" erupting in jail, when all external storms have calmed down and the criminal is confronted with himself and his guilt.

Despite the various symptoms of dysphoria, be they depression, anxiety, panic attacks, phobias, or the horrors of psychosis, these "alarm" signals issued by the conscience need to be viewed with hope, nonetheless, for as long as the conscience continues to strive within an individual, there still seems to exist the possibility of a return.

When, on the other hand, there is a loss of emotivity, when nothing but anger is left, and the patient can no longer cry, he may have reached a state of no return. The criminal, sociopath, psychopath, and unrepentant schizophrenic all suffer from the consequences of their antisocial activities, and are progressively destroyed physi-cally, emotionally, and spiritually. The sociopath, "hardened" criminal, and unrepentant schizophrenic may thus reach in time a state of emptiness, with loss of vision for the future and a blindness to meaning, not dissimilar to the state of spiritlessness with which the truly psychopathic embarks on his life-journey. Cleckley's observa-tions and his conclusions on the psychopathic condition, as represent-ing insanity *in excelsis*, apply to the unrepentant sociopath as well as to the schizophrenic. They all become eventually what the psycho-pathic deviant *is*: affectless, guiltless, loveless, demented to meaning, and behaving in a manner mostly motivated by instinctual urges. But these individuals also tend to seek their own destruction, as noted by Cleckley, "Complexly organized functions being devoted to aimless or inconsistent rebellion against the positive goals of life," . . . and "wooing failure with elaborateness and subtlety."

After revising her earlier findings, Robins (1978) came to the conclusion that not every child who manifested antisocial behaviors became an antisocial adult, but as many as 41 percent of the children she studied did so become. Even those whose behaviors had improved over time still showed some undesirable character traits far into adulthood.

Several therapeutic strategies have been attempted in view of curing psychopathy. Cleckley, whose criteria have been considered rather narrow, has viewed all approaches as futile. Robins (1966) found that the children who were treated by psychotherapy improved *less often* than those untreated (22 percent vs. 57 percent). Milieu therapeutic approaches have been tried in various settings, such as in Hawthorne-Cedar-Knolls, Pioneer House (F. Redl and D. Wineman, *Children who Hate*), the Orthogenic School in Chicago, the Cam-bridge-Somerville project, and more. Results from these extensive and intensive treatment approaches have unfortunately yielded results that are equivocal at best. Of those children studied by Robins (1966) who gave up their antisocial behaviors, the majority did so through the influence of a loving parent, teacher, spouse, or minister; fear of punishment, prior prison sentences, physical illness, and religion reformed the rest. These findings may be interpreted to mean that lovelessness may be cured by the authentic love of a parent or spouse (much more impactful than the caring of a therapist), and that morality may be instilled through the influence of a devoted minister or a commitment to religion. Such realistic factors as a prison term, physical illness, and punishment may also be instrumental in deterring some of these individuals from continuing their antisocial activities.

All too soon, alas, the criminal, antisocial deviant, psychopath, and schizophrenic fall on the "discovery" of the bottle, which becomes, then, their staunchest ally and supporter. The most common diagnoses associated with crime were found to be alcoholism and drug abuse. Fostering disinhibition, alcohol use allows for a multiplicity of morally forbidden intentions to become enacted in reality. But alcohol obliges still further, by blotting out the memory of past transgressions and drowning guilty dysphorias later on. Alcohol and drugs, however, are not as faithful friends as they appear, for they tend to expedite quite efficiently those processes that lead to physical, emotional, social, and spiritual suicide. The following comments were gleaned from individuals engaged in antisocial activities on their way to becoming truly psychopathic:

1. I have learned to disregard feelings of guilt. Every time I feel guilty about something, I do something new, so as to forget my past misdeeds.

2. It becomes easier each time. I learned to disregard my guilt.

3. When I feel guilty, I take the bottle and drink . . . .

The Borderline State

In a recent review of the literature on **Borderline Personality Disorder,** J. C. Perry and G. K. Klerman (1978) proposed a moratorium on papers and psychoanalytic interpretations of the borderline state, urging the testing of existing hypotheses instead. This suggestion was advanced following their review of the major contributions made on the borderline condition by R. Knight (1953), O. Kernberg (1970), H. Kohut (1972), R. Grinker et al. (1968), and J. G. Gunderson and M. Singer (1975). A striking *lack* of overlap in diagnostic criteria was found to exist, producing such a long list of criteria as to preempt any possible definition of the borderline state. "It seems as if the whole range of personality pathology is represented in the combined aspect of the various negative characteristics of the borderline patient," wrote Perry and Klerman. But the list of psychopathological variables becomes even longer when behaviors are interchangeably added to symptoms of distress, and dysphoric are

Diagram # 8

Natural History of Antisocial Behavior, Acquired Psychopathy, Authentic Psychopathy, and Schizophrenia

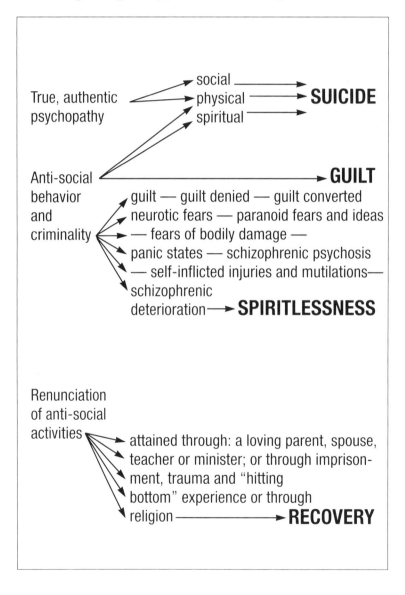

numbered along with various disturbances in interpersonal relationships which define the borderline condition. The composite picture of the borderline person becomes even more complicated by adding to it issues of etiology and ever new interpretations of his condition, as have been advanced by neo-psychoanalytical theorists.

Despite a great deal of confusion and endless diagnostic squabbles engendered by attempts to delineate more sharply the borderline patient, a consensus of opinion exists in positioning him between the neuroses and the psychoses. Controversies over terms and designations could be reconciled, nonetheless, by considering the borderline patient, whose internal structure lacks cohesion (O. Kernberg 1977), as closely related to the narcissistic, schizotypal, and antisocial personalities. All these individuals may be subject to pan-anxiety and pan-neurotic symptoms, as in the "pseudo-neurotic" class of schizophrenia described by P. Hoch and P. Polatin (1949). But their majority will also be found engaged in interpersonal abuses, "pansexual" activities, and the abuse of alcohol or drugs, or both. Almost all are subject to depression, so much so, that many patients are currently diagnosed as suffering from **Major Depression.** Borderlines are also known for their propensity to "fall apart" on the couch (R. Knight 1953), or experience otherwise a brief psychotic episode, through which an already existing "latent schizophrenia" (E. Bleuler 1911) may become unmasked.

Yet the views that recognize the borderline's negative character traits and undesirable behaviors as defining his "mental illness" carry important implications. Deviant behaviors produce distressing symptoms, and their aggregate may produce major disturbances, even full-blown psychoses. The term "borderline schizophrenia" to designate the borderline personality is justified in this sense. Genetic studies, moreover, have brought evidence to show that the borderline state stands close to schizophrenia. When the parents of adopted-away children who later became schizophrenic were investigated retrospectively, a significantly higher prevalence of severe character pathology, falling within the "schizophrenic spectrum"—where borderlines are positioned—was found among them (S. S. Kety et al. 1968, and P. H. Wender et al. 1976).

An inventory of the symptoms of distress reported by borderline patients reveals that they suffer from both the warning anxieties of the neurotic, such as fears, anxieties, phobias, and panic states, and from the dysphorias pertaining to guilt that torment the psychotic, such as conversion symptoms, paranoid fears and ideation, nightmares, delusions, and hallucinations. On the continuum of neurotic illnesses, the borderline may experience a "pan neurosis," and when closer to the pole of schizophrenia, he may become subject to perceptual aberrations, de-personalization, de-realization, anxieties, fears, phobic states, and panic. A "thought disorder" may also become manifest, especially in "unstructured situations" (O. Kernberg 1980). Among the patients treated by this writer, several borderline patients were observed to experience the eruption of a "mini" psychosis, which most commonly followed the commission of a crime in the interpersonal realm.

As has been previously emphasized, much can be gained—and this is especially applicable to the study of borderline pathology—by a separate listing of negative character traits and behaviors (Table # 3, p. 343) on the one hand, and the symptoms of distress these behaviors tend to engender on the other.

Here is an impressive list of negative characteristics, attitudes, and injurious, destructive behaviors. Yet it would be grossly inaccurate to attribute all of them to each and every borderline patient. The lack in overlap of clinical criteria that would identify the borderline condition may thus be justifiably interpreted as signifying that every patient has his own negative attitudes and ways of causing damage, hurt, and injury to others or to himself. The list serves also to demonstrate that the moral misdemeanors and felonies of the borderline hardly lack in versatility. But all these individuals have much in common with respect to their predicament (given in Table # 4, p. 352)—for borderlines suffer from what wrong they do and what right they do not.

The borderline condition may well serve to demonstrate the thesis this work has set to prove, namely, that undue accretion of moral transgressions brings those culpable near and over the borders of sanity. Whereas the conflicted and struggling neurotic spends most of his mental energies fending off and defending against acting out his sinful intentions, the borderline—less hampered by moral inhibitions (and this he shares with other character-disordered individuals)—acts out impulsively his inner inclinations and yields to the forces that induce him to sin. Like other character-disordered individuals, the borderline learns how to avoid guilt feelings by denial, evasion, suppression, and repression; and like the sociopathic deviant, the borderline may avoid his inner dysphoric state by frenzied hyperactivity or the use of drugs and alcohol. Both the sociopath and the borderline may dissociate themselves from their consciences and suffer, then, from various bodily dysfunctions, aches and pains, as guilt denied becomes guilt converted.

Table # 3
Negative Character Traits, Attitudes and
Behaviors of the Borderline Patient*
(compiled from the observations of researchers mentioned in this section)

1. Lack of impulse control
2. Lack of concern over predicament
3. Impaired integration of ideas
4. Unrealistic in planning
5. Suspicious   (R. Knight, 1953)
6. Lack of development of sublimatory channels
7. Corruptible morality
8. A repetitive pattern whereby a particular impulse, stealing or promiscuous sexual behavior, for example, erupt periodically
9. Project aggressive feelings onto external objects
10. Denies a whole sector of his life
11. Grandiose and omnipotent
12. Oral greediness
13. No real empathy for others
14. Emotionally shallow
15. Unreasonably demanding
16. Exploitative
17. Parasitic
18. Sexual feelings infiltrated with aggression
19. Intensely and chronically envious
20. Devalues others
21. Ruthless
22. Excessively aggressive   (O. Kernberg, 1970, 1975)
23. Angry in all facets of life
24. Hostile
25. Acts out his rage
26. Dependent, clinging
27. Puts himself first in all relationships
28. Negativistic
29. Argumentative
30. Acts entitled
31. Sarcastic   (R. Grinker et al. 1968)
32. Delinquent activities
33. Pathological lying
34. Frightfully revengeful   (H. Kohut, 1972)

* Each characteristic behavior is mentioned only once.

Both the sociopath and the borderline engage in behaviors injurious to others, and it would appear as if no substantial difference existed that would separate the two. It is the nature of their crimes that is dissimilar: whereas the sociopathic deviant inflicts somewhat indirectly his damaging activities on society-at-large, the scope of the borderline is narrower, for he hurts mostly those to whom he directly relates. And while the sociopath is liable to land in jail for breaking the law, the borderline becomes a "patient" in the emergency facilities of mental institutions. The borderline's deceptions, exploitations, manipulations, and devaluation of others naturally provoke rejection by the injured other/others. Yet, rejection is experienced by the borderline as utterly unbearable. Rejection may cause him to erupt in angry, violent behavior, or else to attack himself in a suicidal gesture. But from an overall view of his negative characteristics and persistently injurious behaviors, which may be termed "moral misdemeanors," the borderline individual emerges as nothing more than *a glorified* (by psychiatrists) *sociopath,* who makes victims mostly of those who revolve in his orbit: family, relatives, friends, colleagues, and others belonging to his social circle. Compared to the schizophrenic—penalized by his conscience with various guilty dysphorias—the borderline seems to exist in a perpetual state of probation for repeated misdemeanors, but he also stands precariously close to the borders of the schizophrenic pit. The borderline suffers whenever he sins, and small increments in added offenses frequently cause him to experience a "mini-psychosis." When he commits moral felonies, however, these often lead him across the borders of sanity and into a full-blown psychosis.

Not unlike the schizophrenic, the borderline resorts to various deceptive operations, but does so in a more ingenious manner, by making use of some half truths. The thought disturbances of the borderline, if and whenever present, contain, as a rule, a good number of justificatory-delusional statements—some so adeptly constructed they are almost convincing. Projections and denials are used by both the schizophrenic and the borderline—defenses against their failure to honor their contracts with family and society. Keenly perceiving the defects and weaknesses of others, the borderline knows how to make use of them for his own justification.

Being positioned close to the pole of evil, due to his many negative characteristics and behaviors, the borderline perceives others as either evil like himself, or idealizes them as totally "good," by a mechanism termed "splitting." In the mutually contradictory Self and object-representations, considered typical of the borderline's apperceptions—and not unlike the ambivalence of the obsessive-compulsive neurotic and frankly schizophrenic—he vacillates between Good and Evil.

Attempts have frequently been made to separate the borderline condition from its narcissistic core, otherwise known as selfishness and egotism—not always contingent on infantile narcissism or a "regression" to it. Notwithstanding, **Narcissism** stands to the borderline condition as autism to schizophrenia—centrally. How far the narcissist is willing to veer from the laws of society and morality may best measure the distance between him and the borderlines of sanity. Whereas the autistic, and to some degree the schizoid, tend to shun the company of others due to their almost exclusive self-absorption, the narcissistic and borderline persons demand the attention of others, and seek to extract from them the maximum possible of acclaim and admiration. Both the narcissistic and the borderline individuals "have no use" for others, except insofar as they can abuse and exercise power over them. Kernberg considers the narcissism of such individuals to be pathologic, compared to the normal narcissism of children. He disputes the opinion of H. Kohut, who believes these disorders to originate from an arrest in the oral stage of development. Describing the difference between infantile and adult narcissism, Kernberg (1974) unwittingly exposes an essential attribute of sin:

> Normal infantile narcissism is expressed by the child's demandingness related to real needs—the demandingness of pathological narcissism is excessive, cannot be fulfilled, and is secondary to a process of internal destruction of the supplies received.

Sin bears no relation to need. Both Kernberg and Kohut seek to explain the coexistence in the narcissistic and borderline persons of grandiosity, omnipotence, and the need to devalue others, on the one hand, and their shyness and excessive vulnerability to injuries to self-esteem, on the other, as seemingly contradictory trends. Yet these contradictory trends originate from one and the same sinful attitude, that of *hubris*, or arrogant pride, manifested by its two facets. Kernberg (1970) perceives how these persons "mercilessly mistreat and exploit" those from whom "they have extracted all the admiration they can get." Both Kernberg and Kohut, nevertheless, tenaciously adhere to the psychoanalytic model of developmental psychopathology.

Pathological interpersonal transactions and excesses in aggressive trends—as observed in the narcissistic and borderline persons—are attributed principally to "injuries to the child's primary narcissism" by "inevitable maternal shortcomings" (H. Kohut 1972). This presumed narcissistic injury compels the narcissist and borderline to seek revenge in the hope of:

> . . . undoing the hurt by whatever means—and compulsion in this pursuit, with utter disregard for reasonable limitations. The irrationality of this vengeful attitude is frightening because reasoning is not only intact, but sharpened.

Kohut thus assigns blame to a chronically unempathic mother for the child's "oral rage," which is presumably projected onto the parents who are perceived as more sadistic than in reality. The sharpened reasoning of the borderline with his twists and rationalizations, so glaringly evident in his verbal behavior, immediately argues against a possible weakening of the Ego-mind-reason in this disorder, such as has been frequently invoked to explain the eruption of a psychotic illness. But the heightened reasoning capacity of the borderline—used by him for the execution of various deceptive and manipulative operations—is experienced by others as outrageous. Such is the sensitivity of humans to any voluntary adulteration of truth that even minor distortions or half truths immediately engender feelings of anger, resentment, and scorn.

A sharper delineation of the narcissistic personality and its separation from the borderline have been recently attempted. The narcissistic individual has been considered to be in possession of a more cohesive Self, which may have allowed him to succeed in achieving his ambitions in position and career. Achievement in various areas of life has been considered a major determinant in preventing him from decompensating into psychosis, as frequently occurs with the borderline. The disturbance termed **Narcissistic Personality Disorder** has been positioned on a continuum of psychopathology with borderline disorder, but closer to the pole of the neuroses, for its more favorable prognostic outlook.

Some theorists tend to side with Kohut when he considers narcissism to be antithetic to "object love." Object love needs to be differentiated from "object relations," however, the latter being much easier to maintain and requiring a lesser commitment and little, if any, expenditure of Self. Kohut (1966) wrote as follows:

> In certain psychological states the Self may expand beyond
> the borders of the individual, or it may shrink and become
> identified with a single one of his actions and aims.

Kohut goes somewhat further when he considers the narcissistic
individual as one driven by ambition, and failing, for this reason, to
look up to the light shining from his Ego-ideal. He wrote also:

> I am tempted to say that the Ego experiences the influence
> of the Ego-ideal as coming from above and that of the narcis-
> sistic Self as coming from below.

When Kohut speaks about expansion of the Self, he takes leave
of the psychological model of man as biological unit and explores
regions more sublime. He traces a vertical, spiritual axis to human
existence. In attempting to follow the movements of the soul in the
clear light of transcendence, we observe how in self-detachment,
renunciation, and sacrificial love it expands and ascends toward the
Sublime.

Existentially considered, narcissistic and borderline persons appear
to be spiritually dwarfed. They are incapable of self-detachment even
in humor, adventure, or otherwise. They commit themselves mostly
to self-serving goals and are driven by ambition, but it is principally
a "blind" and self-defeating ambition which oftentimes crushes the
interests of others. They do not love but in a clinging, dependent, and
demanding way, and their affection may entail the use, abuse, and
exploitation of the objects of their "love." They are pulled from below
and steadfastly hold to the "pleasure principle" while letting go of the
principles of morality. More than the narcissist, the borderline is
angry without apparent reason and demands without a definite need.
He delights in, and will go to amazing lengths for the sole purpose
of humiliating another. The borderline goes further than the narcissist
when he not only uses others for his own glorification, but abuses
them also through various deceptions, manipulations, and exploitations. In "fits" of "oral rage" (i.e., rage corresponding to the oral
stage of development) he may even physically injure or destroy
another. The borderline has been considered capable of murder; not
infrequently he "succeeds" in completing suicide.

In terms of dysphorias, both the narcissist and the borderline suffer
from what they have done or failed in doing. The following list of
dysphoric states (compiled from the work of authors mentioned in this
section and arranged according to degree of severity) describes the

various symptoms characteristic of the narcissistic and borderline conditions:

1. Chronic free-floating anxiety
2. Polysymptomatic neuroses (pan-neuroses)
3. Depressions of the vacuous type
4. Pervasive sense of futility
5. Low self-worth
6. Inability to tolerate aloneness
7. Deficient self-identity
8. Self-destructive compulsions
9. Disturbances of consciousness, de-personalization, dissociation
10. Repetitive patterns of "regressions" to "mini" psychoses
11. *Perception of themselves as crooks*
12. Pre-psychotic perceptual distortive experiences

Situated as it is between the neuroses and the psychoses, the borderline state offers a good opportunity for the study of mental illnesses in general, as well as for the understanding of the etiology of insanity, to which it stands close.

The immediate reason for the eruption of a "mini" psychosis may be investigated and the psychological stimuli that cause the borderline to "fall apart on the couch" subjected to analysis. As for the perceptual aberrations experienced by borderline patients and considered to be "prepsychotic," these phenomena are not as rare as has been believed. In a study on a large college population, L. J. Chapman et al. (1980) found a greater than expected prevalence of such phenomena. Fifteen percent had experienced "voices" at some time; six percent felt thought-transmission; three percent experienced states of passivity; and this in a control group, not in the group of anhedonic or psychotic-prone individuals studied. Experiences of thought-withdrawal, out-of-the-body, and being cut off from others were also reported more frequently than would be expected from a regular student population. A closer scrutiny of the contents of these experiences showed a striking preponderance of spiritually charged "revelatory" phenomena, with the presence of God, angels, spirits, and the devil most frequently encountered. The perception of hearing the voice of one's conscience was extremely common. All these experiences were interpreted by the authors of the study as indicating psychosis-proneness. And so they are. But instead of discarding them as "regressive" in nature—nothing but "primary process" phenomena intruding into consciousness—these experiences need to be further explored and their essentially spiritual messages decoded. The warnings, moreover, contained in many of these experiences need to become incorporated into the process of psychotherapy. Yet regardless of intervention, many subjects of perceptual aberrations, visions, and hallucinations well grasp their experiences as revelatory in nature, and quite a few understand the message as a warning. They also seem to understand these experiences as representing danger signals, and as carrying a threat of impending loss of soul, outbreak of madness, insanity, and descent into the underworlds of Hell.

*   *   *

Quite distinct from the currently prevailing biological interpretations of the "psychic" life, existential psychiatry presents a view of psychopathological phenomena much in accord with the mainstream of philosophical thought and religious tradition. From Homer to Sartre, the consensus of opinion has persistently charged man with the responsibility for forging his character. But how much is one the captain of one's soul? And how much the master of one's destiny? Sartre (1957) took a very definite position by asserting that:

> Man is nothing else than what he makes of himself, but man is also responsible for what he is. In making his choices and decisions, which determine what he is, man cannot consult his feelings as guides, for "feelings are formed by the deeds one does." (*Existentialism and Human Emotions*)

Sartre's opinion may represent an extreme position. It does not disqualify the truth it contains, nonetheless, nor diminish its relevance to psychiatry. In existential terms, man suffers from the wrong he does and from the right he does not; and more clearly than individuals with other mental disorders, the borderline writes the script of his life-destiny. In possession of a rather sharpened capacity for reasoning, and of excessive willfulness, the borderline can hardly claim "confusion" and weakness of volition.

A deeper analysis of the symptoms presented by the borderline frequently reveals their true source. Symptoms of somatization, for example, may need to be examined for the possibility of representing guilt that has been denied and converted into organ dysfunction, discomfort, or pain. Such is frequently the meaning of premenstrual pain or dysfunction, the source of which is found in sexual excesses or perversions. The delusional sensation of "pins and needles" in the rectum or genitals may be indicative of homosexual practices.

Hysterical paralyses may serve to alert consciousness of past misdeeds as well as to prevent intended transgressions:

> A youngster who suddenly became paralyzed in his right arm was prevented in this manner from stealing money from his mother. (From author's caseload)

Both borderline and narcissistic persons suffer from depressions that have frequently become responsible for placing these personality disorders into the "affective" category, or that of "bipolar depression" (recently interpreted in biochemical terms). Suffering from a sense of futility, alienation, boredom, and vacuous depressions, borderlines quite frequently resort to rather "alloplastic" chemical solutions in order to attenuate their painful life-experience. And more than others, borderline and narcissistic individuals reflect in their souls the general malaise of our times, so well described in Samuel Beckett's *Waiting for Godot*, Albert Camus' *The Stranger*, and Sartre's *Nausea*. The central theme of these works concerns the loneliness (or lovelessness) of modern man and the futility of a life devoid of faith. The dirge is one of existential despair for the nothingness that overtakes those who have lost the capacity for loving their neighbor, and who refuse to seek the order, truth, and love of the divine Thou.

Both narcissistic and borderline individuals feel impaired in identity. They may have failed, as perhaps their healers have also, to appreciate the fact that identity and self-esteem are contingent upon merit. The self-esteem of narcissistic and borderline individuals is fully attuned to reality. Identity cannot be given from outside, for its sense derives from the positive impact one succeeds in making on the welfare of another, others, or the Common Good. Praise and applause never suffice in establishing anyone's identity. The borderline's use of others, his deceptive ways, demandingness, manipulations, and exploitations cause him to be avoided and rejected by those "others" who do not consider him worthwhile. And for being denied by others, the borderline frequently seeks to establish for himself a "negative" identity, which he feels is better than none. Yet this choice of himself as evil brings him closer to decisions in favor of such actions—and to the borders of schizophrenia.

When the borderline perceives himself as being a crook, this self-estimation may not be a "misperception" after all. Directly related to his ways of being-in-the-world, his self-appraisal may best serve to underscore the faithfulness with which the Self-assessing system imparts its existential truth. Even when not overtly in conflict with society or engaged in criminal activities, the borderline knows well, deep within himself, that he deals dishonestly in interpersonal matters and fails, as a rule, to honor his social contracts, be they with family, friends, or in business. And if the Self-system is indeed faithful to reality and disregards the opinions of the crowds, it becomes clearer why narcissistic and borderline persons complain of being worthless. Even if the narcissist has had the good fortune of achieving success and of attaining much-craved status or position, extracting perhaps even some shallow tokens of admiration from the amorphous crowds, a sense of worth he has not gained. The masses, apparently, are powerless in establishing anyone's identity. Sensing the narcissist's contempt, and his "no-use-for-others" attitude, (except to exercise power over them and extract much-craved acclaim), those "others" readily dispense of the narcissistic and borderline persons' oppressive ways. In existential terms, the narcissistic and borderline individuals' appraisal of themselves reflects their essential nature, but it is confirmed in nothingness. According to Kohut (1966), feelings of worthlessness represent their most troublesome dysphoria. And this may well be their punishment—the just decree of their consciences for humiliating and *devaluing* others.

In addition to the various dysphorias that torment the narcissistic and borderline persons, an existential analysis of their life-histories reveals with amazing logic how their pathological ways of being were instrumental in forging their destinies.

If we correlate the inner attitudes, intentions, and overt behaviors of the narcissistic and borderline individuals with their dysphorias and predicament, in general, we can come to a better understanding of the nature of "craziness," antecedents and all. The borderline does not depart from any painful reality when he falls apart on the psychoanalytic couch, or when he flares up in an outburst of aggressive rage, as has become tradition to regard. By way of nightmares, hallucinations, visions of angels and devils, he has been given to understand his rather precarious existential condition and nearness to the bottomless pit. He has also been forewarned of the possibility of losing his soul by way of "annihilation anxiety," out-of-the-body experiences, and has felt the world as unreal. Yet he has made the choice to disregard these warnings.

Whenever the borderline increases his burden of guilt by adding more to accumulated offenses, he comes nearer to the experience of a true schizophrenia. He may also "decompensate" when confronted with a view of his true Self. The psychotic episodes that punctuate the course of his existence are not the results of any conflict with "reality," as conjectured by psychoanalysts, nor do they represent a sudden weakening of his Ego-mind-reason. Like the inferno of the schizophrenic, the psychosis of the borderline, if and when occurring, contains all his complexes of sin and guilt, spiritual degradation, and visions of Hell. Whether remaining close to his narcissistic confines or proceeding further on a path of self-seeking satisfactions to the detriment of others, the borderline may not be able to avoid the same state of meaninglessness that overtakes the unrepentant sociopath and schizophrenic anywhere on their life-journey.

Table # 4
Predicament of the Borderline and Narcissistic Personality

Lack of achievement over time (applies mostly to the borderline)
Faces stark loneliness in middle life
Hypochondriacal preoccupations
Self-destructive behaviors and mutilations (more in borderline states)
Alcohol and drug abuse
Alienation
Periods of "mini" psychoses (for borderlines)
May decompensate into schizophrenia (for borderlines)
Suicidal attempts either manipulative or completed
Brief psychoses in situations lacking in structure
Brief psychoses following outbursts of rage
Meaninglessness

With this rather tragic view of their predicament, the following question immediately surges and begs for an answer: How and when can narcissistic and borderline persons begin to love? To which the answer, simply stated, is: *When they choose to do so.* Love is first and foremost, a decision—a decision to *act* lovingly—it is not just sentimentality. If indeed man's main task on his earthly pilgrimage consists in simply loving his neighbor, as attested by the subjects of religious-mystical experiences, it becomes somewhat clearer why the narcissist and borderline feel themselves so empty and consider their existence meaningless.

It is unfortunate that modern psychological theories have come to consider object relations as a function of the Ego-mind; and no less distressing that in these theories object love is frequently confounded with erotic love, from which it may differ considerably, nonetheless. Whereas object relations—subject to the Ego's wisdom—may be useful to the individual, and erotic love satisfy his biological needs, object *love* implies almost the opposite. Authentic love transcends the bounds of Self, renounces self-serving narcissistic goals, and is directed upward along the axis of spiritual ascendance. Authentic love expands the bounds of Self, the soul. It qualifies man's spirit; in no way does it qualify the "mind."

Narcissistic and borderline patients need, therefore, to be advised to begin to love by sacrifice, renunciation, and humility. It may be the outcome of a decision, but it always needs to be put into action. Love is an attitude. Loving actions create loving feelings. Only after caring for and watering his particular rose does the Little Prince of Saint-Exupéry begin to love her.

Concerning the etiology of narcissism and the borderline condition, there appears to exist a consensus among the adherents of psychoanalytically oriented theorists that regards these conditions as being the results of presumed failures in gratification of dependency needs during the oral stage of development (roughly corresponding to the first year of life). An absent, cold, ungiving, and generally frustrating mother has frequently been invoked to explain the rage and aggression of the borderline, "who continues through life to seek an all-out revenge, for alleged injuries to self-esteem sustained early in life" (H. Kohut 1966). O. Kernberg (1974) tends to view the pathological relatedness of the borderline as due to "constitutional" factors. The shallowness of the borderline's emotional reactions, according to Kernberg, is "more directly connected with the incapacity to experience guilt, concern and related deeper awareness of interest in others." With this statement, Kernberg actually describes in somewhat attenuated terms the essential guiltlessness and lovelessness that characterize the truly psychopathic. But going even further, Kernberg (1975) invokes the factor of *morality*: "Patients with at least a limited or minimal morality have a much better prognosis." Kohut sees *honesty* in their daily lives as a favorable prognostic indicator, yet fails to mention dishonesty as pathogenic.

According to M. Mahler (1971), the borderline condition stems from an "unresolved conflict in the rapprochement phase of development"—a conflict engendered by an overprotective or domineering mother, who prevents individuation in her offspring.

One of the early pioneers of the psychoanalytic movement, A. A. Brill (1924), investigated 400 "only and favorite children in adult life." His description strikingly depicts the borderline's psychopathological ways of being:

> It is due to the undivided attention and abnormal love which
> the only and favored child gets from his parents, that he

develops into a confirmed egoist. He is never neglected in favor
of sisters and brothers. He is the sole ruler of his household,
and his praise is constantly sung. No wonder he is vain, one-
sided, and develops an exaggerated opinion of himself in later
life. He is extremely conceited, jealous and envious. He is
spoiled and coddled, because the parents gratify all his whims
and do not have the heart to be severe with him and punish him
when necessary. The slightest depreciation in adult life, hardly
noticeable by the average person, is enough to throw him into
a fit of depression and rage, lasting for days, even weeks.

Brill's description casts a different light on borderline and
narcissistic disorders and, with respect to their etiological background,
creates a negative of the image developed by psychoanalytic theorists.
The dynamic forces motivating individuals with these disorders thus
emerge as: pride, conceit, willfulness, inordinate egotism, and a
tendency to tyrannize others. As for the derivation of these forces,
they might well originate from a "constitutional" predisposition to
which environmental factors are added later. A need for the child's
affection and excessive love for him may certainly predispose the
parents to adopt submissive and permissive attitudes toward the
child's willfulness, whimsical demands, and temper tantrums.
Needless to say, such attitudes create for the child *an environment
that is actually deprived of deprivation.*

Fearing the possible "traumatization" of children tender in age
(presumably predisposing them in this manner to neurotic disorders
later in life), modern Western societies have tended to adopt permissive attitudes in child-rearing practices as well as in education. This
method, which "spares the rod," spoils the child, nonetheless. When
the only demand usually made upon children, namely *respectful
obedience* to parents and those caring for them, becomes overruled
in view of enhancing the child's free "self-expression and individuality," it only serves to undermine parental authority, as it weakens the
child's will. Whereas it is the parents' duty to be fair and just to their
children, as much as this is possible, it is the child's obligation to
submit to parental demands. Harmonious family living, self-discipline,
and charity begin at home. The need for obedience thus supersedes
the right to individuation, at least in the early stages of development.
Mature and loving parents know, as a rule, how much they can
deprive their children without unduly traumatizing them. A strong will
is that which can renounce its own. Character is built precisely upon
the renunciation of some of one's particular wishes and desires—a

process that might be painful and require sacrifice. Strength of will is directly but inversely proportional to willfulness.

The currently prevailing permissive attitudes can be held responsible, to a large extent, for the weakening of society's moral fiber. "What is good for the individual is not necessarily beneficial to society," was the best argument provided by the preachers of social reform. It is the essence of morality. When the family nears collapse; when gender roles are reversed; when parents vie for their children's affection, approval, and company; when lies are given survival value; when premium is given to achievement and success instead of personal integrity; when every human depravity finds a psychiatric justification, then, borderline, sociopathic, narcissistic, drug addicted, and alcoholic individuals will naturally tend to thrive. It is thus hardly surprising that when all becomes permitted and morality goes to pieces, neurotic illnesses become replaced by "character disorders." The numerical increase of persons with a borderline psychopathology has been confirmed by R. Grinker (1968), as well as other experts in the field. An inordinately high percentage of antisocial personalities has also been reported by L. N. Robins et al. (1984). The lifetime prevalence of antisocial personality disorder, fluctuating between 2.1 percent and 3.3. percent in 1984, has now risen to 5.8 percent (R. C. Kessler, 1994). With such an incredible increase in the number of individuals with sociopathic character disorder, one is tempted to muse pessimistically about the prospect of further "psychopathic degeneration," to affect the descendants of these individuals for the generations to come.

With respect to prevention, the studies of Robins have revealed the importance of discipline and the presence of the father in the home in averting the development of antisocial deviancy. As for the narcissistic, borderline, and allied disorders, their prevention seems to be contingent on early limit-setting, denial of the child's whimsical demands, taming his aggressive urges, and breaking his indomitable will. The narcissistic as well as the borderline persons need to *experience deprivation*, for this alone can teach them to renounce gratification of some wishes, especially when these clash with moral principles. Permissive attitudes in the management of the borderline, which allow the outward "expression" of anger, hate, jealousy, revenge, and similar emotions, may actually increase existing guilt and bring these persons closer to the borders of sanity and beyond. Confrontations with their negative character traits and injurious behaviors are essential ingredients of psychotherapy with borderline and narcissistic individuals (and are also recommended for sociopaths), but need to be undertaken with a good measure of tact commingled with authentic caring. The borderline, moreover, needs to be urged to follow the dictates of the code of ethics: *this is the structure* he sorely needs for rebuilding himSelf, his soul. In the treatment of the borderline, obedience and submission also need to be emphasized: obedience to the voice of conscience and submission to the laws of men, with little ambiguity left. Morality, however, cannot just be "instilled" by a loving, caring therapist. The promotion of his "mental health" would hardly suffice to convince a patient to give up some pleasurable satisfactions, even if they clash with moral principles and laws established by society. Morality, doubtless, "preaches in vain" when divorced from religion, and Dostoyevsky's warning that, " . . . if God is dead, all would be permitted . . . " resonates today with relevance and poignancy.

Although character-disordered individuals, inclusive of narcissists, borderlines, antisocial deviants, and drug and alcohol abusers, would not be so easily dissuaded from continuing their offensive antisocial behaviors, their own out-of-the-body experiences, nightmares, visions, delusions, and hallucinations may impart to them the dreadful reality of their existential position. Interpreted in the light of their spiritual meaning, their *own experiences* may well prove to be the strongest lever to lift them out of their precarious condition. It becomes incumbent on the therapist, for this reason, to seek out the meaning of the patient's experiences, but always in following the patient's, not the therapist's, associations. These interpretations need to become incorporated in the process of psychotherapy. As for the depressions that frequently visit character-disordered persons, these affect-laden disturbances need not be set apart as yet another psychiatric disease or regarded as undesirable manifestations. Depression might signify that the individual so affected is capable of sorrowing over his failures, and instead of allowing him to use projections and denials— which always distance him from the prospect of recovery—he needs to be encouraged to admit his guilt, even if it entails pain, contrition, and depression.

Sin's Best Ally

The most perfect and palatable of transgressions, **Alcohol Abuse** or **Alcoholism,** may seem to affect no one but the drinker. Bringing gratification at a relatively low cost and minimal investment of effort, alcohol appears to offer a solution to a multitude of problems and difficulties. It drowns the sorrow of the bereaved; eases the pain of the rejected; lifts the spirits of the dejected; and tranquilizes even the guilt-ridden sinner. Alcohol can make the cowardly brave and the audacious shy. Subtle and enticing, alcoholic beverages have the capacity of insinuating themselves into every crack and defect of the personality. Often alcohol will fill the vacuous depressions of the borderline and narcissistic persons. Alcohol is sin's best friend as well as its promoter. It has the capacity of smoothing the edges of painful sin-guilt complexes, of lubricating the various incongruities within the personality, and of allowing wishes from an "underworldly" Id to surface into consciousness. And by weakening the reasoning powers of the Ego-mind and lowering the barriers of moral inhibition, excesses in alcohol intake may permit the enactment of morally forbidden inner inclinations and intentions long held in check. Thus during **Pathological Intoxication,** sexual and aggressive urges may become enacted. Yet even during intoxication, no one can act otherwise than in conformity with one's inner wishes, inclinations, and intentions. As sin's ally, it is hardly surprising that alcoholism is so frequently associated with other mental disorders and criminality, as well as with recidivism. Alcohol may oblige further by providing a cloud of amnesia, and by preventing sin and guilt complexes from entering awareness in this manner, alcohol promotes sin's repetition.

Sharing an important attribute with other "pleasurable intoxicants," alcohol permits a trip to unreality, and initially, at least, it is a pleasant traveling experience. Unlike other, "harder" substances, alcohol dispenses its pleasures at a relatively low cost and long-term credit margin. This means that alcoholism waits longer to settle its accounts with the abuser than LSD or cocaine, for example. But when the time arrives, alcohol addiction presents a bill enormously costly to physical, psychological, and spiritual well-being. Alcohol enslaves more subtly, insidiously, and gradually than other addictive substances. "First man takes a drink, then drink takes a drink, then drink takes a man," claims a Chinese proverb. Once drink has taken a man, however, it will not release him before subjecting him to a round of terrors, visions, and tremors, universally known as "delirium tremens."

The second most common disorder (after depression), according to investigations by R. C. Kessler (1994), is alcohol dependence, with 7 percent having the problem during a given year and 14 percent at some point in life (lifetime prevalence). This number represents a considerable percentage of the U.S. population and immediately brings forth the question as to why people drink. Freud believed that people resort to alcohol in order to escape from painful realities. Self-destructive urges were invoked by K. Menninger, who thought that such aggressive urges are actually directed at rejecting parents. M. E. Chafetz (1975) attributed drinking to certain childhood deprivations, whereas Alfred Adler pointed an accusing finger at the parents for their overindulgence. Fixations and arrests at the "oral stage" of development have also been offered as explanation and an "oral" personality described. In their book *Twelve Steps, Twelve Traditions*, the founders of Alcoholics Anonymous cite studies by eminent psychologists and psychiatrists who refer to the alcoholic as being "childish, emotionally sensitive and grandiose."

All research efforts notwithstanding, the quest for a specific personality or character trait that would mark the later alcoholic seems doomed to futility. The essence of sin is such that it does not necessarily need a cause, and alcohol is frequently taken solely for its capacity for providing a "high." That 28 million Americans have fallen prey to the vice of alcoholism argues against the existence of any particular personality or trait, since such a large proportion of the population is affected. The fact that so many Americans have become "problem drinkers" attests to the popularity of this vice, more than it identifies any particular type of "sickness" or psychological need as its cause. The association of alcoholism with crime, recidivism, and other mental illnesses merely exposes the affinity of alcohol to evil in general.

A variety of alcohol-induced mental illnesses have come to be recognized and categorized. **Alcoholic Paranoia, Alcoholic Hallucinosis, Alcoholic Deterioration, and Korsakoff's Psychosis** stand for clearly defined clinical syndromes. Chronic, heavy alcohol abuse causes damage to body, mind, and soul, and frequently it is irreversible. Duodenal ulceration, polyneuritis, avitaminosis, hypoglycemia, cirrhosis of the liver, cardiomyopathy, and seizure disorder are known sequelae to prolonged alcohol abuse. The brain may suffer from losses of neuronal cells as well as damage of their tracts—the net result of which may be cerebral softening at certain sites with specific neurological deficits such as ataxia and blindness, for example. Various cognitive capacities may also suffer permanent loss, such as memory, learning, and orientation, as well as the ability for feeling.

It has been thought that psychoses associated with chronic alcohol abuse represent but "release phenomena," unmasking latent schizophrenic illnesses. Were this to be true, however, such illnesses would tend to make their appearance much earlier in the drinking career of the alcoholic and not become evident, as they do, after protracted use for years and even decades. Psychotic illnesses, moreover, by no means afflict all "heavy" drinkers. The fact that alcohol-related schizophrenias develop gradually, as a rule, over a prolonged period of time with **Chronic Habitual Drinking,** tends to suggest that causes other than the direct toxicity of alcohol on the nervous system are here in operation.

In his description of **Alcoholic Hallucinosis,** P. Hoch (1972) makes a point in stressing that these phenomena occur in a clear setting—that is, in the absence of obtundation, such as takes place with toxic levels of alcohol in the fluids of the body. In alcoholic hallucinosis the personality remains unchanged and the patient may continue to perform his daily functions, preserving contact with his environment and other aspects of reality. The hallucinations experienced by these patients are mostly auditory, and their contents have a definite meaning. Alcoholic hallucinosis resembles certain "hysterical psychoses" which also engraft themselves on otherwise premorbidly well-adjusted individuals, and manifest themselves by hallucinations and delusions only, without disturbances in thinking. As is true for all other psychotic illnesses, in alcohol-induced psychoses, delusions, and hallucinations most faithfully mirror those offenses that gave them cause, and contain also threats of appropriate penalties. It is of interest to note that in alcohol-induced psychoses, the "voices" mockingly allude to the alcoholic's drinking habit and his inability to control it. Frequently, the "voices" comment on the patient as a third person, with statements that are mostly accusing and disparaging. The dreams (more accurately, nightmares) of alcoholics frequently contain experiences of drowning.

Korsakoff's Psychosis has been considered as one carrying a rather ominous prognosis, and often presaging the beginning of a progressive deterioration and dementia. P. Hoch (1972) comments on the observation that Korsakoff's psychosis may develop quite insidiously and in a gradual manner, without necessarily being preceded by delirium tremens or a toxic psychosis. It would thus appear that in Korsakoff's psychosis organic lesions of the brain, nutritional deficiencies, and avitaminosis conspire with the psychological damage incurred from the various moral offenses that drinking entails—sins of omission as well as commission—to produce and aggravate this serious disorder. Experiences of impending doom, hallucinations, visions of wild beasts and threatening animals, and a general atmosphere of dread render these psychoses almost indistinguishable from true schizophrenias.

"The most prevalent feeling in these states," writes Hoch (1972), "is anxiety." These patients are extremely fearful, and paranoid delusions serve to further aggravate their anxiety. Commenting on the interrelatedness of emotions and physiological factors in the living organism, and citing aberrations in carbohydrate metabolism, which are also present in neuroses and schizophrenia as well as in alcohol-induced psychotic illnesses, Hoch concludes that "emotion works as an organic force, as does a toxin."

The same affect that pervades the inner domain of the emotions in every case of schizophrenia—namely guilt as a fear of the unknown—also lurks behind psychoses induced by chronic alcohol abuse. As with every other sin and vice, drunkenness leads to losses in self-esteem, feelings of failure, and dysphorias pertaining to guilt. More often than not, drunkenness becomes compounded by other transgressions and vice. In the best of cases, the alcoholic is bound to neglect or reject the significant Other(s) in his life, and by necessity he becomes guilty for causing them pain. But the alcoholic is also frequently incapable of working with consistency, and may become a financial drain on family or society, if not an outright parasite. Needless to say, the alcoholic fails primarily himself, and some believe that he engages in a protracted act of suicide, which would explain his restless self-destructive tendencies.

In a follow-up study of alcoholics 10 to 15 years from their admission to four hospitals in London, P. Nicholls et al. (1974) found the death rate of alcoholics to be 15 times that expected for other patients; 85 percent of these deaths were caused by accidents, poisoning, and other acts of violence. The suicide rate of alcoholics was found to be *25 times* higher than the expected average.

While the search for pathogenic factors in childhood, deprivations, and various "stressors" continues to engage researchers intent on identifying a specific "sickness" or defect in the alcoholic's personality, most sobering ought to be the fact that many *heavy* chronic drinkers attain permanent abstinence, whereas "light drinkers may go on to progress in the direction of chronic alcoholism and deterioration," according to G. Vaillant and E. Milofsky (1982). "Paradoxically, alcoholics who were *most severely afflicted* often achieved the most stable abstinences." These conclusions were drawn from a study of 110 alcohol abusers followed from adolescence until age 47. Among the heavy drinkers, who also rated high on the Robins scale for sociopathy, 48 percent achieved a stable abstinence, whereas only 28 percent of alcoholics with no other antisocial behavior than their drinking were able to achieve abstinence. From the "medical model" vantage point, the findings of Vaillant and Milofsky appear indeed paradoxical, considering that severe psychopathology and alcohol-related symptoms do not necessarily lead to deterioration, but may lead to a more favorable outcome than otherwise. Neither childhood nor premorbid factors were found predictive of the long-term outcome of alcoholism, which, according to Vaillant and Milofsky, is not only a disease, but a habit as well. These authors also report that increased religious involvement and participation in Alcoholics Anonymous together accounted for 67 percent of secure abstinences. While medical illnesses consequent to alcohol abuse provided sufficient aversive clout to deter a good number of alcoholics from drinking, behavior modification methods and court supervision did not succeed in bringing back to sobriety even *one* alcoholic.

Of great interest and relevance ought to be the finding produced by Vaillant and Milofsky to the effect that secure abstinence was also associated with social-psychological recovery. At their last examination, the 21 patients who were securely abstinent were found "nearly as free from psychopathology as men for whom alcohol abuse had never been a problem."

Abstinence, needless to say, does not simply happen, but follows a conscious decision as an act of the will. The translation of this decision into action, as well as its maintenance, require an enormous emotional effort on the part of the alcoholic. Support from recovered alcoholics, personal commitment such as is provided by the "sponsor," and faith in a Higher Power all contribute to the success of Alcoholics Anonymous. Lack of interest, perhaps, insufficient supplies of caring, and a refusal to accept spiritual-moral principles as instrumental to recovery may well explain the failure of most routine therapeutic approaches—offered privately or in mental health facilities—to assist the drinker in his battle against the bottle. But, then, most therapies and therapists deny also the beneficial influence of the Higher Powers.

In one of its editorials, the *Journal of the American Medical Association* (1967) issued a report stating that membership in Alcoholics Anonymous remains the most effective means for the treatment of alcoholics. The recovery rate of A.A. was given as approaching 75 percent. The treatment strategies of Alcoholics Anonymous are highly instructive and can be applied to other intractable disorders contingent on involvement with sin and vice as well. When compared to conventional medical and psychological treatments, often based on rather abstract theories and involving costly long-term therapies, the framework of reference and practical approaches of A.A. prove themselves superior by far. Similar programs have already been successfully applied to the treatment of such disparate disorders as overeaters, overspenders, gamblers, and even to homosexuals. A.A. can boast, moreover, that it has been instrumental not only in loosening millions from the grip of alcoholism, but in influencing a reconstruction of their lives as well. Most recovered alcoholics readily attest that their participation in A.A. has reshaped their personalities and brought an overall improvement in the quality of their lives.

Alcoholics Anonymous is a self-help group of equals—a congregation of individuals enslaved by vice, whose activities proceed without recourse to a leader. Acceptance, support, understanding, and help are offered to every alcoholic, provided he is ready to admit "I am an alcoholic" and desires to give up drinking. A.A. requires that its members follow their twelve steps and twelve traditions. The healing process begins with the alcoholic making a complete and honest *moral inventory* of his past. Long known as confession, the alcoholic is required to share with at least *one* other person what he considers his moral offenses and shameful deeds. Wherever possible, he is also required to make amends for injuries he has caused to others. Discouraging projections of blame and denials of all sorts, A.A. does not accept psychiatric "alibis," either. Unlike the therapist in individual psychotherapy settings, the "sponsor" provided to the new member by A.A. is an abstinent alcoholic who does not treat other alcoholics as inferior, and makes himself always available. The whole organization is carried on the shoulders of recovered alcoholics. Their voluntary services, dedication, and commitment to the task of reforming other alcoholics is considered by them to be that "precious gift of sobriety which can be kept only when given away." (*Twelve Steps and Twelve Traditions*)

The therapeutic approach of Alcoholics Anonymous is essentially grounded in faith in a Higher Power, but it is a faith that requires obedience to spiritual principles and observance of the moral law. A.A. promotes self-detachment as well as commitment to others. There is no place in A.A. for games of pride and power struggles, as it organizes humbly and anonymously. In addition to help and support, A.A. provides its members with a most worthwhile cause— that of salvaging other alcoholics.

Substance Abuse, Crime, and Insanity

Alcoholism and the abuse of "pleasurable intoxicants" most poignantly expose the true nature of sin as a "bypath preferred by people"—a luxury (because it is not dictated by need) that all can ill afford. When the abuser of substances indulges in this vice, the costs of his pleasure are disbursed not only by himself, but by others as well as the larger community. More damaged than the alcoholic, the drug abuser soon loses the capacity for work and becomes a social burden if not a financial parasite. But more costly even than his parasitism is the damage caused to society at large. Manslaughter on the highways alone tolls nearly 40,000 deaths annually, and more than 50 percent of these have been attributed to alcohol or drug intoxication. When the pleasures of a few cause pain and suffering to many others, those few become guilty of breaking the laws of morality. Past consultant to the Manhattan House of Detention, E. S. Petursson (1972), wrote on the relationship between drug abuse and crime:

> A teenager or adult with a teenage mentality is ten times more likely to commit a crime or get into other kind of trouble if addicted to an intoxicating substance.

Petursson reports further that of the ten newly arrested murderers each week, three were alcoholic, three were drug dependent, and the rest had lesser involvement with intoxicating substances. From a study on the population of 4,000 U.S. jails, it was found that 21 percent of state prison inmates had a history of drug addiction and 61 percent of drug abuse (*Newsletter, American Journal of Orthopsychiatry,* Winter 1982). But these statistics are no longer valid, as it has been estimated that whereas in 1980 drug offenders comprised 25 percent of the federal prison population, in 1992 their number climbed to 61 percent (*USA Today,* March 24, 1994) and nearly 75 percent of all prison inmates have had some involvement with alcohol and drugs. But the prison population has increased to a record high, with one and a half million prisoners currently in Federal and local prisons (*The New York Times* October 28, 1994).

As is true for alcohol, certain drugs have the capacity to produce a "pathological intoxication" during which a variety of violent acts and sexual indiscretions may be committed. Some drugs more than others have the capacity for whipping up aggressive urges, while at the same time releasing the restraints of reason. Substances belonging to the class of mood elevators or stimulants—generally referred to as "uppers"—are most frequently implicated in acted out aggressive or sexual urges. The recently popular modified cocaine, known by the street name "crack," has become a favorite among drug abusers for the unusual arousal it tends to produce. But this drug has also earned a reputation for inspiring the most vicious acts of violence and sexual abuse, and has distinguished itself for the potency and rapidity with which it creates craving—and addiction. "Marijuana, no less than alcohol, can be held responsible for the recent increase in violent crime" wrote Petursson (1972). But other substances, such as PCP (angel dust), amphetamines, and LSD have made themselves a similar reputation. Hashish is five to eight times more potent than marijuana and has been used, for this reason, for the preparation of killers before their engagement in battle (the word "assassin" is said to derive from "hashashin"). Inevitably, alcoholism and the abuse of drugs become intertwined within a specific "lifestyle," and it matters little whether the abuser resorts to drugs because of loneliness, lack of achievement, emptiness, rejection or other reason, or attempts to quench dysphorias of guilt resulting from deviant behaviors—for he is bound to become an antisocial person just the same. As with other sinful attitudes and acts, substance abusers are subject to the laws of the "repetition compulsion," but the corrupting forces of their drug habit, reinforced by biological dependency and craving, go far and beyond, for they dictate a wide array of unrelated sins and crimes, contingent on the drug-abuser's lifestyle.

It is now well recognized that certain substances more than others, when used for some time, may lead the abuser to the borderlands of sanity and over. The process is considerably accelerated by the use of stimulants and hallucinogens. In a study designed to verify whether drugs contribute to the precipitation of schizophrenia, W. R. Breakey et al. (1974) found that in at least 26 out of the 46 schizophrenic patients they examined, authentic schizophrenia was precipitated by preceding drug abuse. The onset of schizophrenia was found to occur, on the average, four years earlier when drugs had been abused. The average age for drug abusers who suffered a schizophrenic psychosis was 19, whereas the average age for nonabusers was 23. According to Breakey et al., the "taking of amphetamines, marijuana, hashish, LSD or mescaline might play some precipitating role in the onset of schizophrenia, bringing on the disorder more quickly and to patients who seemed less constitutionally vulnerable." When the duration of the psychosis outlasts the duration of the toxic effects of the drug abused, other causative factors need to be sought as responsible. M. Tsuang et al. (1982) wrote as follows:

Compared with drug abusers suffering from short-duration psychoses, in whom this illness lasted less than six months, drug abusers with psychoses of longer than six months duration had more symptoms, more premorbid personality disorders and greater familial risk of schizophrenia and affective disorders.

In an exhaustive review of the subject, M. Stone (1973) takes cognizance of genetic, psychological, and constitutional factors in assessing the role of drugs in precipitating psychoses. Stone makes a distinction between drug-induced psychoses, consequent to the toxic effects of the drug on otherwise "normal" premorbidly functioning individuals, and the aggravation of preexisting latent states that are brought to the surface by the use of drugs. Drugs with a stimulating effect, i.e. "uppers," have a greater tendency to produce psychoses. Among chemical substances, the stimulants marijuana and hashish (both possessing "mind-expanding" capacities) were found by Tsuang et al. (1982) to be implicated in 93 percent of their cases of short-term psychoses and in 82 percent of long-duration psychoses.

Not all abused chemical substances have a psychotogenic effect, however; nor do all affect a preexisting psychotic illness. Some substances, known on the street as "downers"—barbiturates, Placidyl, Quaaludes, heroin, and methadone, among others—actually tend to reduce central nervous system excitation, providing thus for a sense of relative peace and tranquility. Yet because of the prohibitive cost of most of these substances and their powerful addictive properties, their users often find themselves compelled to resort to crime in order to satisfy their craving. Sooner or later, the personalities of the abusers of "downers" will be transformed and become indistinguishable from those belonging to other categories of antisocial deviancy and 22 percent of them will develop a psychosis. Objectively regarded and subjectively experienced, their lives turn into a nightmare. Nirvana, it would appear, can be neither bought nor sold in the marketplace of drugs.

* * *

The thesis assuming the etiology of insanity to be contingent on an undue accumulation of sin and guilt complexes is substantially solidified by research findings that concern the effects of certain drugs on psychological well-being. According to S. H. Snyder (1976), the best-known drugs to model schizophrenia are the amphetamines. Amphetamine-psychoses so well mimic schizophrenia of the paranoid variety as to deceive even experienced psychiatrists (S. Snyder 1970,

1973). The emergence of these psychoses has been found related to amphetamine dosage as well as to duration of abuse over time. In lower animals, chronic amphetamine intoxication produces characteristic behaviors related to fear and suspicion: side-glancing, peeking, head-turning, self-examination, grooming, and sometimes excoriative activities. Chronic amphetamine abusers have reported being aware of similar behaviors, namely, furtive side-and-back glancing and the experience of a subjective, overwhelming sense of *fear*. Compulsive self-picking and excoriation have also been reported (E. H. Ellinwood, Jr., 1972).* During amphetamine intoxication, time seems to pass slowly, but thoughts are sensed as "speeding." Experimentally, amphetamine intoxication produces an emotional enhancement, which appears to be the major reason for the abuse of these substances. Amphetamines create a state of "clear-mindedness" and intense curiosity, as new cognitive and perceptual constellations come into being.** Characteristically, amphetamines increase arousal and perceptual acuity. A compelling search for meaning, even in the most insignificant of objects or event, is also frequently experienced by the use these substances.

E. H. Ellinwood (1972) wrote as follows:

> More paranoid patients tend to search intensely for minute signs and meanings. Their "speed" art is replete with complicated syntheses and often depicts universal themes and signs of the mandala. The content of their subjective experiences strikingly resembles that of authentic schizophrenia.

Amphetamines seem to be mostly sought by those incapable of achievement or reciprocal loving relationships—the sources of inner rewards and satisfaction for the majority of "normal" people. Chemical "felicitogens," however, are not capable of producing much more than an artificial excitement that is quite distinct from true, inwardly originating feelings of happiness. During amphetamine-induced excitement, curiosity, a sense of well-being, appetite, and sexuality become greatly enhanced, whereas withdrawal of these substances is experienced as a "crash" into depression.

---

* The "affect-toxin" of Jung may well be the biological equivalent of fear, guilt, hostility, and other negative emotions transmitted through dopamine-coded messages.

** Emotional enhancement is known to induce creativity.

Amphetamine reactivity has been recognized to depend, among other factors, on individual susceptibility, tolerance of the nervous system, dosage, and frequency of abuse. Of utmost import to all concerned is the finding that the margin between amphetamine-induced excitement states and amphetamine psychoses is extremely narrow. A comparison of amphetamine-induced psychoses with paranoid schizophrenia reveals a common and central characteristic affective state, from which all else emanates—a state of fear. Arousal, hyperacuity, hypervigilance, paranoid fears and ideation, self-mutilative activities, and attempts at penetrating the mysteries of the cosmos can all be regarded as manifestations of a central affect, namely dread, which gains sovereignty in consciousness and determines the symptomatology of both of these disorders.

How do amphetamines—exogenous chemical compounds—produce disorders that can be distinguished only with greatest difficulty from authentic, endogenous paranoid schizophrenias? Sufficient evidence has now accumulated to implicate amphetamines in the alteration of neurotransmission involving the catacholamines, most notably dopamine and norepinephrine. Whatever the manner of this alteration—still under investigation—its net effect is an increase in dopaminergic activity:

> Although it is difficult to make a clear-cut distinction, the action of amphetamines in exacerbating schizophrenic symptoms and eliciting amphetamine-psychoses probably involves brain dopamine, more than norepinephrine. (S. H. Snyder 1976)

The most interesting aspect of amphetamine-induced psychoses may still be their confirmation of both the dopamine theory of schizophrenia and the major role played by norepinephrine—by its relative absence, that is—in these disorders. Evidence suggests that whereas normally dopamine is converted to norepinephrine through the activity of the enzyme dopamine-beta-hydroxylase, the presence of the amphetamine molecule (similar to that of norepinephrine) prevents, through a feedback mechanism, the conversion of dopamine into norepinephrine—substance of felicity and inner rewards—while dopamine begins to accumulate. In schizophrenia, dopamine has been held responsible for producing hallucinations, delusions, fears, aggressive behaviors, and more, whereas emotional shallowness, apathy, and anhedonia have been attributed to a relative decrease in dopamine and noradrenergic activity.

If, indeed, norepinephrine is the substance associated with the system of inner rewards, as postulated in the theory of Stein and Wise (1971), an impairment in its transmission would produce anhedonia, affectlessness, and even depression, such as are characteristic of schizophrenia. According to Stein and Wise, the "noradrenergic system, which is a system mediating reward behavior, would provide feedback to ongoing behavior . . . . " Amphetamines may not do so. The theory of Stein and Wise would apply to amphetamine-induced excitement, nonetheless, provided the dosage and duration of amphetamine abuse have not exceeded a certain level. Beyond that level, emotional enhancement becomes irrational fear, and fear may assume psychotic proportions.

In schizophrenia, increased dopaminergic reactivity is *generated* by fear; in amphetamine psychoses, increased dopaminergic reactivity is *experienced* as fear. A lack of norepinephrine and its diminished transmission are correlated with states of emotionlessness and depression, whereas an increase in norepinephrine and its transmission are associated with states of felicity through activation of the system of inner rewards. In lower animals, an increase in noradrenergic activity is associated with exploratory behavior, enhanced appetite, and sexual interest. With respect to the role of amphetamines and similar compounds in inducing psychosis, Snyder (1976) wrote as follows:

> If amphetamines exacerbate schizophrenic symptoms by increasing synaptic dopamine, other pharmacological maneuvers that produce the same biochemical end-product should also worsen schizophrenic symptoms. In the studies in which L-Dopa has been administered to schizophrenics, it does cause marked exacerbation of behavioral abnormalities, much like that elicited by amphetamines.

Whether amphetamines act as "false transmitters," enzyme inhibitors, or otherwise, their net effect is an increase in dopamine transmission, with a production of symptoms closely simulating authentic schizophrenia. The experience of overwhelming fear produced by amphetamine-induced dopaminergic hyperactivity on the one hand, and the guilt-related affect of fear, impending retribution and doom manifested in schizophrenia on the other, lend support to the dopamine theory and tend to validate Jung's hypothesis regarding the existence in this state of an "affect" (fear) which acts as a "toxin" (dopamine and/or its metabolites).

Whereas amphetamines tend to increase arousal and open wider the doors to outer perception, the substances known as hallucinogens exert their influence in a somewhat different manner. Endowed with the capacity to expand the borders of consciousness—in this case by "shutting the doors to outer perception" (A. Huxley 1956)—the compounds known as psychedelics facilitate a journey whose direction leads inward. It is mostly a spiritual journey, nonetheless, which imparts a deeper knowledge of oneself as well as of one's destiny. During a psychedelic "trip," external stimuli may become attenuated, distorted, or completely shut off in favor of inner realities.

From time immemorial, man has sought to fathom the beyond. He has always striven to understand the meaning of his life and the order of the Universe. Relentlessly, he has sought to substantiate his hopes for an eternally blissful life after life, and cannot resist the temptation to divine the future—turning even to the stars for counsel. While the ancient Greeks resolved some of these mysteries through the logical methods of philosophy, modern man hopes to acquire such knowledge by means of scientific exploration. For the believer, his faith grants him a key to the mysteries of life as well as the beyond.

Since an ageless past and till today, men have also tried to satisfy their curiosity by making use of certain naturally growing plants, roots, mushrooms, cactuses, and weeds that allegedly endow their users with extraordinary intuitive knowledge and visions. For their capacity to expand the conscious mind and grant spiritual insight, some substances derived from nature's wealth of vegetation are still employed to this day, especially by peoples deemed "primitive." "Hallucinogenic substances," wrote R. Schultes (1972), "represent holy mediators between man and the pantheon." The poisonous mushroom *Amanita muscaria*, for example, was used in India as a narcotic. It was held to be sacred and even deified. It is still revered among Finno-Ugrian tribes in Siberia for its capacity to carry one into the dwelling places of the dead, and for its ability to provide protection against the evils encountered on terrestrial paths. The Koryaks believe that Soma—the liquid of the milkweed *Asclepias acida*—has been left on earth by the god of existence, in order to instruct man in the mysteries of nature. Various puffballs, mushrooms, cacti, and seeds are still in use among contemporary tribes. Some plants, such as the Mexican puffball *Lycoperdon,* for example, are taken with the purpose of communion with the spirits; others are used because of the belief that they enhance the powers of witchcraft, introspection, and divination. Best known in the Western world, and also widely abused, is the Mexican cactus peyote (*Lophophora*

Williamsii), from which mescaline is derived. This substance has gained for itself the reputation of having the capacity to help its users "to find their lives." According to R. Schultes (1972), hallucinogens are not taken for the pleasure they afford. As a matter of fact, some afford no pleasurable sensations at all, but on the contrary, are "most definitely a trial to take." Taken mostly by the curious in view of attaining another state of consciousness—euphoria perhaps—the psychedelic "trip" may indeed release one from the bonds of reality and carry him away to some heavenly pastures. Unfortunately, one cannot exactly order oneself a "chartered trip," by way of psychedelics, and a "bad trip" remains an ever present hazard from such an undertaking. Some "bad trips" have even shown the psychedelic traveler the underworlds of Hell by way of a psychotic decompensation.

Derived from the fungus ergot, lysergic-acid-diethylamide, or LSD, is a semisynthetic substance with hallucinogenic properties whose mind-expanding effects have been the subject of extensive study. At one time, LSD was utilized for its capacity to expand awareness in the process of psychoanalytic psychotherapy. Like many other hallucinogens, or "illusionogens," as S. Cohen (1963) prefers to call them, LSD is used for both its euphoriant effects and for its capacity to expand awareness. By being capable to "shut the doors of perception," as Aldous Huxley (1954) succinctly put it, LSD directs attention inwardly, allowing thus for introspection. And as was previously emphasized, the trip directed inwardly may lead into some hidden recesses of the Self and even reach the spiritual Me, center of the personality. "It exposes one," claims the LSD abuser. "The journey can lead to disaster," warns the chronic LSD abuser and "latent" schizophrenic. "It causes dissolution of the Ego and its defensive operations," explains the psychoanalyst. Overwhelmingly distressing material may be released during an LSD analytic session. A deluge of guilty dysphorias and guilt-laden insights (complexes of sin and guilt) may suddenly invade the conscious mind.

But LSD can also produce deep spiritual-religious experiences. Mexican shamans take peyote before religious events of import for precisely this reason. S. Cohen (1963) describes such experiences:

> Without impairment of mental capacity, LSD produces intense feelings of unity, death, rebirth, salvation and redemption experiences.

Although LSD is the perfect agent to sponsor a spiritual journey, it cannot guarantee its destination. On the inward LSD journey, one may encounter complexes of sin and guilt of such number and magnitude as to overwhelm awareness. Intense anxiety, fears, panic, a sense of judgment and condemnation, as well as a premonition of an eternity in Hell, may thus be imparted. The following case, described by S. Cohen (1960), confirms much that has filled the preceding pages:

> The patient was given progressively larger doses of LSD by an experienced psychotherapist. He was a 31-year-old male who suffered from multiple fears, phobias, intolerance to noise and to threatening political events. He feared elevators, heights, and entertained paranoid ideas and delusions. After a dose of 125 mcgs. of LSD had been attained, he confessed that when he was a child *he had smothered his baby brother* in order to keep him from crying . . . a secret he had kept all of his life. The confession brought about a "psychotic decompensation" which required hospitalization. Eventually, this patient was able to recover. [emphasis added]

This case history may also serve as an example to clarify the nature of a potentially psychotogenic childhood "traumatic" experience.

An LSD trip may unleash hidden aggressive inclinations, which, when acted out, may generate the eruption of a catatonic state with uncontrollable destructive behavior. Most observations on the LSD experience converge in agreement that the worse the premorbid psychopathology, the higher the risk of a bad trip (M. Stone 1973).

In more than one way, the LSD experience parallels that of the dream. When darkness and silence of the night subdue stimuli arising from the world outside and the Ego-mind suspends its vigilance, we turn inwardly, toward the center of our being. This inward journey may bring us some important insight by way of a dream; it may also bring to consciousness the horrors of Hell by way of a nightmare. Both the dream and the nightmare, when correctly interpreted, lead to a deeper knowledge of one's Self, nonetheless. It is that precious "know thyself"—sought from the time of Socrates to the present era of psychoanalysis.

It remains questionable, nevertheless, whether the dread experienced during a bad LSD trip has anything to do with the fear of losing control, as psychoanalysts have suggested. When S. Cohen (1960) gave LSD to terminal cancer patients, facing the ultimate loss of control, namely their extinction, he found that even those patients who had difficulties in accepting the prospect of their death experienced no untoward effect from their LSD-induced "trip." Whatever the meaning of this experiment, the burden of its interpretation falls on psychoanalysts and psychopharmacologists, who would need to explain how a chemical compound, instead of producing confusion, leads to Self-knowledge and even brings into experience something so outstanding as religious consciousness, which supersedes, then, other realities.

From a study on drug-induced psychoses, M. Bowers (1977) found that of the 15 patients who had used psychotomimetics—primarily LSD—and whose course was followed up from 1.9 to 5.8 years later, two had committed suicide, approximately one half of the remainder continued to be psychotic, and the rest recovered. The extent of drug use prior to the psychosis was not found correlated with either dosage or duration of abuse. Bowers distinguishes drug-precipitated psychoses from toxic drug reactions:

> Prolonged psychotic reactions are triggered by some mechanism which the drug sets in motion—a behavior pattern that runs its own course beyond the period of drug effect.

Evidence has now accumulated to show that the indole-amine-structured endogenously manufactured neurotransmitter serotonin acts as a modulator of emotions in the central nervous system. When the neurotransmission of serotonin is interrupted or interfered with through chemical manipulation, emotions are liable to go "haywire." This occurs with the use of LSD, bufotenine, psilocybin, harmine, and the synthetic compound DMT (dimethyl-tryptamine), all of which become "false transmitters" because of the resemblance of their molecule to that of serotonin. These substances have disastrous effects on the emotions and can lead to unwanted "trips" leading inward to the recesses of the Self.

Symbol of rebellion, independence, and a way of hedonism, marijuana-smoking has become almost a status symbol among the younger generation. All the more spicy because it is forbidden, the vice of marijuana-abuse has invaded schools, college campuses, business enterprises, and, of course, the streets. And as is true for drugs and alcohol, marijuana is abused for many psychological as well as social reasons. The active ingredient of *Cannabis sativa*—delta-9-tetrahydro-cannabinol—is believed to exert its action through its high solubility in fat, concentrating in the tissues of the brain for this reason. Cleared from the fatty tissues of the brain at a relatively slow rate, it has been estimated that cannabinols can remain up to 30 days in the organism. It becomes, therefore, difficult to assess the toxicity of marijuana in quantitative terms, for a marijuana smoker who indulges once or twice weekly in this vice continues to add toxic cannabinol to already present quantities. By measuring cerebral mass through the method of pneumo-encephalography, A. M. Campbell et al. (1971) were able to demonstrate cerebral atrophy in adolescent cannabis smokers. Diminished cerebral mass would explain the cognitive and emotional deficits found by these authors in long-term cannabis smokers. "Pot" is usually sought for its stimulating propensities and ability to expand the borders of perception. But marijuana may also induce a sense of "relaxation" from the bonds of reality as well as from the demands of conscience; it may even "stone" one into torpor. Delusions and hallucinations are frequently experienced, and, as has been previously stressed, these subjective phenomena of primary importance contain, more often than not, spiritually charged symbolic representations as well as reminders of some complex(es) of sin and guilt. Derived from *Cannabis indica*, hashish is five to eight times more potent than marijuana and can be considered both euphoriant and hallucinogen. Even without preexisting psychopathology, the long-term use of cannabis-derived stimulants that provide artificial excitement may eventually produce a severe "amotivational syndrome" with depression, loss of interest, will, and zest for life. Along with the excitement that cannabis use affords, it may whip up aggressive intentions, unleash totally unprovoked violent behavior, and—through sexual disinhibition—compel the abuser to engage in acts that are frequently regretted later.

The effects of marijuana may be further enhanced by sprinkling it with PCP (phencyclidine), popularly known as "angel dust." Alone or in conjunction with marijuana, angel dust has made for itself a name rivalled only by "crack." Acute intoxication with PCP or crack may produce a state of combativeness, catatonic excitement, and even *cannibalistic acting out*. Convulsive seizures and death have also occurred following the use of these dangerous intoxicants. As stimulants, they enhance perceptual acuity and general arousal. Subjectively, at certain levels, marijuana, hashish, PCP, cocaine and its derivative may give rise to dread, fears, and paranoid delusions. Both marijuana and hashish have long been recognized for their capacity to induce schizophrenic reactions, delusions of grandeur, ideas of reference, and incongruity of affect. Experiences of depersonalization, "loss of soul," and de-realization have also been reported.

Most noteworthy is the finding that after cessation of stimulant abuse, chronic users are left with a flattened affect in addition to a "vestigial thought disorder," which, according to Stone (1973), persisted after a six-month follow-up. Marijuana abuse causes short-term attentive amnesia and interferes, for this reason, with the process of learning. Chronic marijuana abusers show a tendency toward a speedy "burn-out" process, and if these are school-aged adolescents, they may waste precious years of basic education. After many marijuana-induced "highs," abusers fall eventually into a deep depression. If not engaged in other antisocial activities, the chronic marijuana abuser—due to his loss of affect, interest, will, and motivation—may follow the ways of the "simple" schizophrenic, who drifts aimlessly on the paths of life, victim of his destiny, instead of being its master.

The debate as to whether stimulants such as marijuana, PCP, cocaine, and hashish produce or tend to facilitate the outbreak of psychosis is gradually dying out, for the evidence implicating these substances as psychotogenic has become overwhelming.

Substances belonging to the class of "downers," such as the alkaloids extracted from the poppy plant *Papaver somniferum* and their derivatives (meperidine, codeine, morphine, and papaverine, among others), have not been found directly conducive to psychotic illnesses, although the long-term effects of their abuse may not differ much from those of stimulants. But the reason for their psycho-togenicity is not so much related to any of their psychopharmaco-logical properties as it is to the addict's lifestyle: "The opioid addict has two addictions," wrote E. S. Petursson (1972), "drug dependency and a way of life which is criminal." Prostitution, robberies, assaults, and murder flourish in the subculture of the drug-addicted. "The lifestyle of the opioid addict and the substance itself potentiate each other; their action is synergistic," wrote Petursson further. And as every other criminal comes eventually to the borders of sanity and beyond, the opiate addict frequently passes through states of paranoia, incarceration psychosis, and frank schizophrenia before deteriorating into the same spiritlessness which is the lot of the true psychopath, unrepentant sociopath, and schizophrenic patient.

Opiate addiction holds its victims in an unusually powerful biological grip, from which it releases them only rarely, and this at the price of agonizing physical pain and incredible mental anguish. Indirectly, the crimes committed because of drug addiction represent one of the most serious social as well as psychological calamities of our time. It has been estimated that New York City alone harbors from 150,000 to 300,000 narcotic addicts, which includes those attending methadone programs. Can such a large segment of the population be considered "sick" and "suffering" from the psychiatric disorder termed antisocial personality? That one-third to two-thirds of a population of 157 opiate addicts was found to suffer from depression (B. J. Rounsaville et al. 1982) is hardly surprising. And the problem is not whether opiate addicts fit into this or that depression research category, but whether the depression descends upon them as a sudden unheralded calamity that needs to be "treated," or represents the consequence of a chronic failure of achievement in the real tasks of life, and an *unwillingness* to measure up to the challenge.

The problem of drug addiction may be regarded from another angle as well: were the drugs unavailable, they could not be abused. In his comments on alcohol and drug abuse, Petursson (1972) attempts to convince that when stringent legal measures are vigorously undertaken, the problem ceases to exist. He mentions Iceland as an example of successful law enforcement, which rid the country of the vice of alcoholism, and where the empty jails became converted into apartment houses. Petursson cites also the Japanese experience with amphetamines—abused after World War II—as an example of vigorous law enforcement, which effectively cleared an epidemic involving nearly one million individuals. The epidemic of opium addiction in China, which according to Petursson involved 100 million people, was ended after the extreme measure of "chopping off" several heads was taken by the newly established Communist regime.

No chemical compound, especially such as is aimed at altering psycho-neural physiology, can be taken without the risk of habituation, side effects, withdrawal symptoms, and various "rebound" phenomena. No substance, moreover, is known to be exquisitely cell or tissue-specific. Chemical compounds, in other words, cannot be sent to any specific location in the human body, although some substances more than others may concentrate in certain areas and have an affinity for certain tissues: i.e., alcohol and marijuana to the fatty tissue of the brain. In one way or another, chemical substances affect all the cells and fluids of the body. Moreover, they cannot be programmed to act always in the same manner. Neuroleptic medication, for example, prescribed in view of extinguishing acute psychotic illnesses, may actually precipitate a **Toxic Psychosis** in some predisposed individuals in certain circumstances.

The question then arises as to the manner by which certain chemical substances alter psychological and cognitive function and exert their psychotogenic effects. The answer to this question is provided by the concept of "affect-toxin." It assumes that changes in affect can be produced by altering neurotransmission at certain specific locations, through substances which either block or increase neurotransmission. Hence, by causing alterations in neurotransmission, exogenous substances can produce changes in affectivity as well. The term "psychotoxicity" describes changes in affect produced by certain substances through their interference with physiological neurotransmission. An increase in the amount of certain neurotransmitters or the rate of neurotransmission may, however, be toxic to the tissues of the nervous system and produce either temporary or permanent damage to the brain.

Alcoholism and drug addiction cover a rather large territory of psychiatric disturbances. All addictions are associated with a profusion of dysphoric symptoms inclusive of rage, anxiety, and depression—the latter especially pronounced during stages of withdrawal. Depression is the most common dysphoria associated with alcoholism as well as with the abuse of drugs. This depression, however, is vacuous, empty, and mostly tearless—devoid of true sadness—although all varieties might be experienced. In an investigation of opiate addicts by B. J. Rounsaville et al. (1982), 86.9 percent met the criteria for at least one psychiatric diagnosis other than drug abuse. The most common diagnoses were: a heterogenous group of chronic or episodic depressive disorders, antisocial personality disorder, and alcoholism. Psychopathological theorists may try to explain the abuse of alcohol and drugs on the basis of the abuser's depression; they may also blame the substances abused for transforming these individuals into sociopaths and criminals.

Existentialists would refute assumptions such as these. The common denominator to substance abuse, they would insist, is not depression, but a chronic failure to measure up to the tasks of life and a refusal to extend caring affection to others. The painful "boredom," common to the schizoid, sociopathic deviant, narcissistic, and borderline persons, is created by the vacuum that results from these individuals' lack in affective interest in others, as well as from their failure to invest an effort in causes other than such as gratify their immediate selfish interests and appetites. Instead of the rewards obtained by achievement and thrills experienced from goodness and love reciprocated, these individuals soon discover a by-path—in this case a short-cut—to some elusive excitement, effervescent "high" or "kicks," which chemical substances are capable of providing.

Substance abuse needs to be regarded as sinful, nonetheless, because of its destructive potential to the body, mind, and soul of the abuser. It also promotes many other sins, vices, and crimes. What do alcoholism, drug abuse, recidivism, and homosexuality, for example, have in common? Yet, statistically they have been found correlated. According to the studies of C. R. Cloninger et al. (1973), 93 percent of reconvictions were associated with sociopathy. Recidivism rates were also found positively correlated with alcoholism, drug dependency, and homosexuality. The diagnosis of sociopathy and a history of homosexuality "were each associated with recidivism and with each other . . . . " But serious crimes and recidivism were also found associated with alcohol and drug abuse. Logically, not only statistically, these psychiatric disorders are all interconnected, and alcoholism binds them all.

Chapter X

Healing

One ought to feel compassion for so great a disaster to the human mind . . . .

—Juan Luis Vives (*On Insanity*, 1524)

Before even attempting to broach the subject of treatment, thought would need to be given to the possibility of preventing the occurrence of psychiatric disturbances in general. At least with respect to schizophrenia, epidemiological data[*] may be read as indicating a higher prevalence and increased morbidity in those societies in which a greater latitude of tolerance is accorded to the individual's behavior. Permissive attitudes, in other words, would allow for the development of more sociopathic, borderline, schizophrenic, and similar conditions, since the limits to acceptable behavior would be stretched wider. In an atmosphere of stringent social and moral constraints, on the other hand, one would expect less serious, mostly neurotic illnesses to flourish. Many other factors enter into the climate of any society, and it goes without saying that the individual has an impact on society also. And while it might be impossible to manipulate given genetic constituents and so prevent the hereditary transmission of undesirable traits, and difficult to change certain anatomical-neurological substrata, it is given to each and every individual to effect changes

---

[*] cf. p. 325 for the prevalence of schizophrenia.

within himself for his own psychological well-being, as well as for the promotion of such conditions as will enhance the well-being of his community.

If, indeed, psychiatric disorders tend to spread in climates of permissive attitudes and moral decay, it is incumbent upon policy-makers to take appropriate measures. Undue repression, coercive and punitive measures in family and society are to be avoided, however, for these may give occasion for rebellion. It would also require of each and every individual to conform his behavior to the laws promulgated by his society and abstain from transgressing the laws of morality. Injustices are to be minimized, as much as possible, for they are liable to create resentment and breed cynicism. Evil begets evil.

*   *   *

It is of interest to note that throughout recorded history, the treatment approaches applied to the mentally disturbed have consistently tended to follow empirical rather than scientifically based guidelines. Yet the multiplicity and diversity of methods of treatment—then and now—best serve to demonstrate the limited usefulness of any single one of them. Similarities between past and present-day methods of treatment allow, nonetheless, for parallels to be drawn.

The psychodrama staged by the ancient Greeks in Epidaurus, for example, differs but little from that played in our modern therapeutic settings. Shocking the patients with the reality of their finiteness has also quite a long history. But while in Epidaurus the insane were hurled into real pits of living snakes, so as to "scare them to death," and not long ago in Europe, they were immersed in the icy waters of the sea with a stone hanging from their necks, the inmates of our modern wards and institutions—subjected to various "shock" treatments such as insulin-coma and electro-shock (ECT)—are brought to experience a nearness to death and fear of death not much different than those afflicted by insanity before them.

Not only diversity, but a marked nonspecificity has also character-ized the treatments applied to the mentally diseased. ECT, for example, is now used for such diverse conditions as endogenous depression, obsessive-compulsive neuroses, and schizophrenia, among others. Antidepressants are currently dispensed to panic-stricken neurotics as well as borderline patients; lithium carbonate—become panacea for almost every mental illness—makes part of many medical "cocktails"; and neuroleptics are prescribed for every case of agitation, irrespective of the underlying condition, whether manic, neurotic, borderline, or schizophrenic.

Not so long ago, and not so much by chance, the care of the mentally deranged was delegated to the clergy, shamans, and religious institutions. Understood as being the consequence of sin and guilt, insanity was considered a spiritual disease, whose cure was sought by spiritual means. "More needs she the Divine than a physician . . ." remarked Lady Macbeth's physician. In the first mental hospital, established by Father Joffré of Valencia, monastic serenity, prayer and contemplation, music, and the gifts of nature were the means employed for lifting the insane from their spiritual fall. The moral approach, or "*méthode morale,*" now credited to Jean-Baptiste Pussin (D. B. Weiner 1979), included the abolition of all violent measures of restraint, while the mentally deranged were persuaded with kindness and gentleness to work, for it was considered pivotal to their recovery. Pussin wrote:

> The greatest service one could render these men is to give them work to do . . . . I have noticed that when the mentally ill works as servant, his mental illness improves every month, and may sometimes later, be completely cured.

The moral method seeks to bring the offender of the laws of morality to change himself by way of action, not mere intention. This method had its counterparts in England as well as in the United States. In England, it became associated with the names of William Tuke (1732–1819) and his son Samuel. At the York retreat, established in 1796 by W. Tuke, kindness and sympathy were dispensed to the mentally ill in an atmosphere of serenity, with the assistance of the religious order of the Quakers. The whole scheme of the moral treatment may be condensed in a few words—those of Horace Mann, who founded the Worcester State Hospital in 1933: "An approach of love and sympathy by which the suffering of another is relieved." Self-restraint, discipline, and moral responsibility were, nonetheless, demanded from the inmates of the asylums where the moral treatment was implemented.

With its emphasis on work, the moral treatment approach has its parallel in the Morita method practiced in modern-day Japan. This is a method that leads the patient to self-detachment, contemplation, and productive work. It advocates the practice of self-denial instead of promoting self-expression. A similar treatment modality, also practiced in modern Japan, is the Naikan method, which stresses the here and now, gratefulness to others, and the fulfillment of duty. Naikan produces guilt, "but it is a guilt which propels to useful action, self-sacrifice and gratitude that expresses itself in service" (D. Reynolds 1989). In more than one way, Morita and Naikan come close to the existential approach of treatment, stressing as they do the need for self-detachment, personal responsibility, and the pursuit of goals that intend the welfare of others and the larger community.

The moral treatment approaches just described stand in sharp contrast to those employed in our Western modern mental institutions—methods based more on speculative theories and regard for expediency than on any solidly established and validated treatment strategy. Braced in their "chemical straitjackets"—instead of chained in fetters—psychiatric patients are now kept on the acute wards of mental hospitals for relatively short stretches of time. Their great majority are treated with chemical compounds, group encounters, occupational and art therapies, and some are subjected to ECT. Very few among the "acutely psychotic" are eventually transferred to long-term care institutions, and even then, they are released sooner or later "back to the community." Within a span of weeks, or perhaps months, these patients are taught some "basic social skills" which would enable them to survive among their fellow men, combat their paranoia, and cancel even their alienation. In this process, however, little attention is given to the murderous hostilities these patients harbor in their breasts, and even less to possible measures that would attenuate or cancel their pervasive, global hatefulness. The inmates of mental institutions are now occupied with the manufacture of pot holders or similar trinkets—of doubtful utility to others or benefit to their producers. In view of the avoidance of sexual repression—considered the villain of a great number of psychiatric disturbances—men and women are now lodged in rather close proximity, and, despite rules to the contrary, sexual encounters frequently take place in service rooms, often in full view of other mental patients. Instead of art, dance, music, and the gifts of nature, these patients are now exposed to the horrors and violence shown on television screens, while their ears are relentlessly struck by the beats of modern "rock" music. Considered proof of their "craziness," the spiritual visions of these patients are "treated" with increased doses of "reality" as well as hikes in neuroleptic medication. Regarded etiologically and causally related to their psychotic state, religious preoccupations are either derided or diffused away, for fear of aggravating these patients' condition. Visions of the devil are aggressively combatted through changes of neuroleptic medication, or else by increments in dosage—

often endangering the life of the visionary—without having effect on the vision, nonetheless. As a rule, the families of patients are also dragged in for treatment, but less in view of securing authentic care than as a solution to the hospital's problem of "disposition."

It thus becomes apparent that the hasty treatments dispensed on the wards of modern psychiatric institutions offer little by way of inducing serenity, and even less in effecting a change in the patients' morbid personalities. Hospitalization is of value, nonetheless, and a good majority of patients do, indeed, respond in some way to the benevolent attitudes of the staff as well as to the presence of other patients as afflicted as themselves. Divested here of their pride, many patients begin to share with others their burdens, distresses, and sad predicament. Occurring mostly during the various hospital-sponsored group-therapy sessions and to some extent through interpersonal communications, sharing may well be the single most important factor responsible for these patients' improvement. With the aid of medication and the opportunity for—if even only superficial—socialization in far-from-ideal circumstances, the hostilities of these patients may become submerged somewhere below the surface, as the "florid" symptoms of psychosis become progressively attenuated.

The return of these patients to their communities is another matter altogether. Presumably "improved" or "cured," released mental patients only serve to swell the ranks of the homeless. Not only did de-institutionalization—this seemingly modern and "progressive" method of treating the insane—fail in producing the expected advantage to the coffers of the state, it has also proven to be grossly harmful to patients, family, and community alike—exacting an enormous toll in terms of anguish, suffering, and even loss of life.

"More mental patients will be freed to kill," noted Robert Weddle in the *New York Post* (January 27, 1982). Citing the prosecutor of wife-killer "ex-mental patient" Adam Berwid,[*] Weddle joins in to bemoan the fact that "psychiatrists recklessly release patients and never wonder about the innocent victims who die because the patients are released 'prematurely.'" In another report, Guy Hawtin put it quite succinctly when he wrote:

> Bernadette Noel is the latest victim of a state-imposed Catch-22 system which abandons highly dangerously ill people—

---

[*] This case became pivotal in changing the laws of discharge from mental hospitals. It stirred an enormous outrage, especially after it became the subject of a film and was shown to millions on television.

leaving them free to prowl the streets of New York. This victim
was hacked to death by her crazed husband Paul Wilner . . . .
It is impossible to get dangerous, homicidal patients admitted
to a state hospital for long-term treatment; they have to be first
diagnosed as "acutely dangerous." People who are chronically
dangerous can be out . . . . (*New York Post*, April 29, 1982)

But if the community-at-large suffers from the consequences of a
prematurely released mental patient, the brunt of the disaster is borne
by the family. For the family, a schizophrenic member means tragedy
"far greater than death," wrote A. T. Boisen (1936). Not only does
the presence of a schizophrenic in the family cause multiple disrup-
tions in its harmonious functioning, it poses also a threat to the very
life of its members—for it is they that most frequently become the
victims of assault and murder. In reviewing 30 years of his involvement with the care of psychotic patients, H. Lehman (1975) remembers more than 30 healthy persons who were killed by mentally
deranged patients—a figure he considers "frighteningly" high. The
most significant single triggering factor of the homicide was found
to be the factor of *rejection*.

Mental patients themselves fare no better under the present system
of "care." According to E. Ringel (12th International Symposium on
the Psychotherapy of Schizophrenia, 1978), mental patients frequently
commit suicide following discharge from the hospital; their arrest rate
is *three times* that of the adult population as a whole; and one ex-
mental patient out of every ten is arrested within 19 months of
discharge.

It thus becomes incumbent upon every discharging psychiatrist to
alert the family that they expose themselves to danger by living close
to an ex-mental patient. And it may be also ethically untenable to
impose the care of the insane on the family, for no one ought to
burden another with a load he himself is not ready to shoulder. The
difficulties inherent in caring for and of supervising a mentally
deranged psychiatric patient are enormous, and this is especially true
for large urban settings, where people tend to live crammed closely
together. From the data just presented, it becomes quite obvious that
the current system of mental health care delivery in the United States
is nearing a breakdown and crying out for reform.

Outside the wards of mental hospitals, the truly mentally disabled
are mostly left to fend for themselves. Many prefer the structureless
environment of the street and hold on to their homeless status. On the
streets, these patients feel less lonely. Outdoors, moreover, extraneous

noises dampen somewhat the loud and intrusive sound of the "voices" that incessantly torment them. By and large, discharged mental patients tend to shun the various mental health clinics provided for their after-care. They seem to well appreciate the sad reality that they can rarely obtain more than pills and sympathy in these mental health centers. Verbal psychotherapy for schizophrenic patients has now been largely abandoned as "useless." And so it is, when the central problem of these unfortunates—their sense of sin and overwhelming guilt—remain for their healers but peripheral issues.

* * *

Ideally, some patients ought to be removed from crowded urban settings and sent to country farms under guard and supervision, so as to prevent their hurting others or themselves. In such farming communities—a good example of which is the *Greenways* farm for horticulture in Canada and the *Rose City* in the United States— patients can work productively, free from pressures and undue stress. Their work should be commensurate to their abilities and willingness to work. They could be given some routine assignment which would not tax unduly their poor capacity for concentration. But, *by no means should these patients be exploited* in any way or manner, as has happened in the past. Exposed to fresh air and beauty of the country-side, to the scent of woods and song of birds, these unfortunates might, perhaps through meditation, come somewhat closer to themSelves—to their souls. Contemplation amid the wonders of nature might lead some among them to appreciate the order and harmony of Creation, and perhaps even the Creator. Removed from the objects of their envy, hatefulness, anger, and revengeful inten-tions—and with the help of the *lowest effective dose* of medication— these patients may well be able to achieve a higher level of function-ing, better mental health, and a more peaceful existence.

The Psychotherapies

a. Psychoanalysis

Most influential among modern trends, psychoanalysis has established itself as a doctrine as well as a method of treatment for psychiatric illnesses.* Yet while the doctrinal structure of psycho-

---

* The doctrine is briefly outlined on p. 18.

analysis is progressively crumbling—mostly from the weight of evidence in favor of the genetic transmission of psychological and personality factors, as well as from data provided by neuro-scientists—its method will, hopefully, enjoy a larger measure of permanence. The "talking cure," which depends on verbal communication, has proven itself to be, indeed, the most basic and efficacious tool to benefit a substantial majority of individuals beset by one or another psychiatric disturbance. While orthodox psychoanalysis is taught mostly in academic circles and practiced among the wealthy, a good number of current psychotherapies have come to adopt rather "eclectic" approaches, which along with psychoanalysis, integrate various other systems in their treatment strategies.

Fundamental to the psychoanalytical method of psychotherapy is its reliance on the evocation of "childhood traumata" and past memories of painful events. Dreams, resistances, and transference issues are also analyzed. The method relies heavily on a process whereby the patient "free associates," which means that he communicates to the therapist all that comes to heart and mind. Most eclectic psychotherapies, however, do not content themselves with analyzing the patient's childhood, his past, and his foibles, but strive to bring about a "synthesis" in the patient's "psyche" through resolution of conflict by way of a dialogue. The neutral stance required of the psychoanalyst is no longer taken seriously by the majority of psychotherapists, and when the "I" of the patient encounters the "You" of the therapist and his empathic understanding, a spark of love may become ignited. It may find its way into the recesses of the patient's soul and initiate there process that is healing. Indeed, much authentic healing does take place within the closed chambers of psychotherapy sessions—irrespective of the therapist's theoretical orientation.

The question then arises as to how verbal psychotherapy enhances the healing of the human soul. Not one, but several factors seem to be operative:

a. self-expression has an invigorating effect
b. the patient is validated by the therapist
c. an opportunity is afforded for the ventilation of negative thoughts and emotions
d. the patient's suffering is shared by the therapist
e. introspection is encouraged and may reveal some hidden attitudes and intentions, often leading to emotional insight

f.   and last and first: the flow of truthful communication has a healing effect of its own. It may also bring about the unburdening of conscience through the confession of some shameful or morally forbidden attitudes or misdeeds.

Confession may then lead to sorrowing over one's failings—to depression. Yet such a depression may bring about repentance, i.e., a resolve by which the patient decides to will a change within himself, and this in itself is conducive to healing. Every effort spent in this direction seems to be of enormous import to the process of recovery.

All religions around the world contain a ritual of confession—according to their manner—as prerequisite to spiritual healing. And worthy of consideration is the possibility that psychoanalysis has harvested most of its brilliant successes precisely due to the *healing power of truthful communications and confession*. Yet, faithful to its doctrine, psychoanalysis has tended to extol the merits of self-expression and catharsis as major therapeutic factors, rather than acknowledge the *healing effects of confession*. Psychoanalysis, for that matter, has refused to recognize *truth as being also a reality*. It has denied, in addition, the fact that it is truth that sets one free. Neither can psychoanalysis be credited for its interest in dreams and their interpretation, for this practice dates all the way back to antiquity. So seriously were dreams regarded in times past, that they often dictated drastic actions in the visible world, leading even to wars, as was the case of Gideon's battle which was undertaken following a dream and its interpretation by one of his armed men; or Pharaoh's storage of provisions for the seven years of envisaged famine. The message conveyed by the symbols of the dream needs thus to be decoded, not only in biological terms (as psychoanalysis has attempted to do), but with consideration given to matters of realistic, psychological, as well as of spiritual import.

Final evaluation of the merits of psychoanalysis remains pending, nonetheless. J. Malcolm (1980) quotes a psychoanalyst as saying that "psychoanalysis is for the healthy—the healthier the patient, the better the treatment." In reality, psychoanalysis is not only for the healthy; it can be afforded only by the wealthy. As for the "not-so-healthy," the poor, the masses of alcoholics, drug addicts, gamblers, anorexics, and sexual perverts, their lot seems to fall far and away from the domain of psychoanalysis. For criminals and psychopaths psychoanalysis has been found counterproductive.

b. Cognitive Therapy

Cognitive approaches are based on the associative connections operative in the human "mind." Certain thoughts can thus evoke emotions and influence their quality and intensity, and vice versa: certain emotions have the capacity to initiate specific thought processes. The notion of "pessimism" may serve to illustrate how gloom can becloud one's perceptions. According to A. Beck (1972), who has been influential in developing and applying cognitive strategies for depression, these patients characteristically interpret their experience by the triad of depression: "I am worthless, the world is hostile, and the future hopeless." In their treatment, therefore, depressed patients are encouraged, by way of provocative questions, to change certain "schemata," such as: "I will be rejected, why try?" Positive thinking, however, has been found insufficient in changing certain perceptions that need to be worked through. Many strategies have been employed in view of inducing a more positive outlook in depressed patients, such as confrontations, clarifications, and guided imagery. "Homework" assignments are also frequently given to these patients, as for example, to monitor certain of their thoughts and the reactions these evoke. Patients are also asked to review the thought or thoughts that preceded a sudden depressive mood, which they learn then to modify. Counter-measures for the pain of rejection may also be undertaken, requiring for example that the patient place himself in a situation in which rejection is bound to occur. This is actually what behavioral strategies—which have much in common with cognitive therapy—try to achieve, when they advocate "exposure" to the depression- or anxiety-provoking situation. Cognitive approaches are part and parcel of a good variety of other therapies, inclusive of existential psychotherapy. This relatively new treatment strategy has much to recommend it; demonstrating also that we are not just "driven" by emotions, but have some control over them, and even the capacity to modify their nature.

c. Group Therapy

The group is one of the most relevant and appropriate settings for the treatment of psychiatric disabilities of every kind. It may well be regarded as a tiny world—a microcosmos—where sooner or later the patient will reveal his ways of being-in-the-world, as he will also be brought to experience the impact he makes on others. The participant will invariably demand from the group and its members that which he expects from the world; and conversely, his contributions to the group will be commensurate with his willingness to give to others, to the world. Imbalances are brought into focus. Even when admixed with criticism, the support of a group is liable to be much stronger than that of any one individual therapist, and it often surpasses the influence of the family. Suffering and pain, moreover, are likely to become alleviated by reason of their being shared with others in the group. To schizophrenic patients, group therapy sessions provide another—maybe their last—chance for socialization and opportunity for sharing and caring. When encouraged to discuss their fears, their past misdeeds, their guilt, hallucinations, and delusional experiences, patients frequently acquire a new understanding about themselves, their sad predicament and tormenting symptoms. Many among them are freed thereby.

The healing effects of group therapy for regressed schizophrenics can hardly be described. It is a noetic, exhilarating experience which does not lend itself to measure or statistical validation. As for self-revelation and confession—which frequently take place during group therapy sessions—their healing effects are greatly enhanced in such settings. Not infrequently, the group becomes "family"—a nucleus for the establishment of a new brotherhood among its participants. And similar to what occurs in groups of Alcoholics Anonymous, the beneficial influence of groups frequently reaches far and above the improvement of the participants' mental well-being.

d. Behavioral and Other Therapies

Behavioral therapy is based upon the premise that when thoughts are bound to emotions (and vice versa), their impact is greater than that of emotions or thoughts alone. Developed by J. Wolpe (1982), behavioral therapeutic strategies include exposure to the anxiety-producing situation (a counter-phobic measure); repetition of a given dysphoria-producing stimulus (attenuating its impact thereby); coupling the feared situation with an aversion-provoking stimulus (by way of guided imagery or video techniques); and more. Repeated behaviors do indeed have an impact, and, by becoming habit, may modify certain character traits. For obsessive-compulsive neuroses and anxiety disorders, the exposure technique has been found highly effective.

In times not so long past, natural affections, family life, the joys and satisfactions of duty carried out, work well done, and sweetness of friendship were the principal natural stimulants to ordinary living. But since much loving and useful activities have departed from the life of modern man, antidepressant substances have become substitutes for natural satisfactions, and Valium reigns now supreme in the inner domain of the emotions as antidote to existential *Angst* and despair.

Various other means to make one "feel good" have also found their place in the diversified market of "psychotherapies." Since sexual repression came to be regarded as the villain of most neurotic states, it is sexual "expression" that is now promoted and offered in various settings as "sex therapy." Considered to derive from unexpressed aggression, which then turns against the Self, depressive states are currently treated by providing the patient with various opportunities for self-assertion that frequently involve the outward expression of anger. Based on Freud's original theories, which hold repression of aggression to be "morbid" and leading to "mortification" (p. 321), the expression of aggression is frequently encouraged, and may be achieved by the "dummy-punching" maneuver, as example. Encounter groups are also now available, where one may indulge in "primal scream" or be offered an opportunity for "touching." Hypnotic and other means of mind-manipulation are becoming ever more popular. With the "bio-feedback" technique, one attempts to reach one's mind through relaxation of the body. With Transcendental Meditation (TM) one is asked to consciously attempt to "empty" one's mind, and this may be aided by certain postures and repetitive chanting. However, due to the partial sensory deprivation so created, some meditators bring forth to the surface of awareness more psychopathological manifestations than were present before the meditation.

According to D. H. Shapiro (1982), who reviewed several studies on the effects of various self-control strategies, the emergence of negative feelings during meditation are far from infrequent. He mentions the studies of L. S. Otis, whose data reveal that a considerable number of meditators became aware of an intensification of negative feelings such as anxiety, boredom, confusion, depression, and dissociation. Psychotic manifestations have also been reported in subjects so predisposed (R. Walsh 1979).

One may be exalted, humiliated, made omnipotent, aggressive, assertive, guilty, and also "mentally healthy"—all at the discretion of the leader of an Erhard Seminar Training (EST) workshop. Yet several participants in these seminars have become frankly psychotic as a consequence of EST, and of these, some have remained permanently disabled *(vide infra)*. In a report by L. I. Glass et al. (1977) on five EST trainees who became psychotic, only one gave a history of a prior psychiatric disturbance. One became psychotic through the induction of feelings of omnipotence that led him to dive nude into a swimming pool, as he sought to prove he could survive under water. *Another became extremely guilt-ridden and lapsed into a psychotic state from which he failed to fully recover.* EST may be regarded as a highly instructive phenomenon, nonetheless, for it demonstrates that psychosis is induced by psychological, not biological or biochemical challenges. Here as elsewhere, when psychotic decompensation occurred, it was consistent with the preexisting character traits and inner motivations of the personality. Individuals who tended to view themselves high above the level of their fellow men—proud, aloof, defiant, and grandiose—became psychotic during their EST experiences after they were pushed further along the path of their omnipotent aspirations. Adding more guilt to individuals already so burdened, gave rise to a psychosis from which some subjects emerged with a loss of Self and scarring of their personality.

e. Family Therapy

Persisting in the belief that mental illnesses are caused by externally determined precipitants or "stressors," modern-day researchers have tirelessly sought to identify sources for psychopathology within the patient's family and social environment. Twenty years of focused attention on the families of schizophrenics has produced little evidence, however, to implicate the family environment, and even less to suggest that treatment of the family would help to cure their insane. Inspired perhaps by the notion of a "schizophrenogenic mother," or for lack of other anchors, "family therapy" is still employed in various therapy settings, in spite of rather nebulous objectives. Assessing the usefulness of these treatment interventions, L. R. Mosher and S. J. Keith (1980) candidly admitted, nevertheless, that "A remarkable gap exists between research on families, on the one hand, and the translation of research findings into treatment principles, on the other." As for the benefits to be derived from family therapy for schizophrenic patients, no more than a "lack of clearly negative results" was reported by these authors. Some recently adopted theories, such as the highly fashionable Systems theory, for example, have proven even more misleading. That the families of the insane have a vested interest in keeping their sick member disabled—serving them as a "scapegoat"—tends to reach the borders of the absurd, for there is nothing more disruptive, anxiety- and anger-provoking than the presence of a schizophrenic in the midst of a family. A study by the University of Southampton in England found that among primary supporters and families of a schizophrenic patient, 72 percent reported symptoms of emotional and physical ill-health. Financial problems, reduced performance at work, and physical ill-health affected 80 percent of the caretakers of a schizophrenic patient (S. Guze, *Psychiatric Capsule & Comment*, June 1984).

Much can be learned, nonetheless, from encounters with the relatives of schizophrenic patients. Above all else, one may obtain a more objective story about the past of these patients from family members, and one may glean also clues regarding the reasons for their illness. Meeting with the parents of a schizophrenic patient offers also a good opportunity for comparing the character traits and life-histories of both generations. The parents' failures and negative characteristics (the sins of the fathers) are frequently evident in their offspring, but one is always struck by finding the "crazy" son or daughter to have gone far and beyond. In a meeting with the whole family, inclusive of siblings and, as applicable, with cousins, grandparents, aunts, and uncles, one may also be able to observe their way of relating to each other. Needless to say, the offenses of any individual affect other family members in one way or another, and may create family imbalances and deformities in its structure.

Thus far, no one particular attitude or deviance in behavior could be clearly identified as characteristic for the family containing a schizophrenic member. It is this diversity of pathological attitudes—specific for each family—that has rendered family studies so difficult to replicate and has often produced contradictory results. J. H. Liem (1980), for example, finds that contrary to the reports on deviance in communication on the side of the parents—as reported by M. Singer and L. Wynne (1965):

> . . . there is "no evidence found that communication from parents had an adverse effect on normal sons in the respondent role. On the other hand, there was considerable evidence that communications from schizophrenic sons had handicapped the performance of normal as well as schizophrenic parents."

Schismatic divisions and skewed family relationships in families of schizophrenic patients have been described by T. Lidz et al. (1965). Egocentric and domineering fathers who compete with their sons have been invoked by C. M. Wild et al. (1977). Symbiotic mother-child relationships, emotional aloofness or its opposite: excessive intrusiveness on the part of the mother, have also been given as explanations for the development of schizophrenia. But in the list of possibilities for deviant attitudes and behaviors, eroticized relationships, frank incest, overt abuse, and violent attacks would also need to be included, and not only "pseudo-hostility." Eventually, it is the parents who are bound to suffer from their failure in commanding obedience and their inability to instill moral values in their children. Much could have been achieved through personal example, nonetheless.

Family therapy can be immensely profitable to the little world of the family, where imbalances and disharmony unavoidably tend to occur. As a preventive measure, intended to forestall the accentuation of markedly undesirable traits and behaviors in a member of the family, such therapy might be of value. Family interventions, however, ought to avoid crossing generational boundaries, undermining parental authority, or exposing "the sins of the fathers" to their children. Being an individual matter, sin needs to be discussed in circumstances of privacy. No member of the family should be shamed or humiliated before an Other or others of significance. Neither tolerance nor intolerance for certain family patterns ought to be fostered or condemned by the family therapist, as he would not be the one to have to endure them. In family therapy, it is reconciliation through forgiveness and tolerance—with a willingness to sacrifice—that needs to be fostered as a means toward strengthening the family unit and bonding of its members.

Once a schizophrenic illness becomes established in a member of the family, this event revolutionizes its world. The family of the schizophrenic patient is anguished and in pain. The relatives suffer to see their loved one sliding down a dangerous path; they suffer for loving one that hates them; but they also live in fear due to the constant threat of violence his proximity imposes. The family of a schizophrenic thus needs consolation, advice, and massive supplies of sympathy and understanding. Yet any intervention with the family that relies on the cooperation of the schizophrenic member is doomed to failure in advance, for the proud, willful, and defiant schizophrenic will refuse to abide by the rules of any set agreement. A study by G. Brown et al. (1972), which investigated family influences on the relapse of schizophrenic illnesses, produced findings almost identical to those of other investigators (i.e., those of C. E. Vaughn et al. 1976). The advice given by these researchers is to avoid becoming excessively involved emotionally with the schizophrenic family member, and to abstain from criticism and accusations.

These suggestions seem logically sound and may be interpreted as meaning that excessive love or caring on the part of the family may serve to increase feelings of guilt in the individual who hates. Undue intrusiveness, attempts at correction, and hostility on the part of the family may, on the other hand, intensify the malevolence of the schizophrenic member. As to accusations and criticism, the advice given by Brown and Vaughn actually echoes that of the Anonymous psychologist (1958), whose theory of schizophrenia has been mentioned earlier: accusations and exposure only serve to drive the schizophrenic further away and "underground."

Psychopharmacotherapy

The insane were reliberated in 1952, but this time by a chemical compound, namely chlorpromazine (Largactil, Thorazine). So effective has been this phenothiazine in the treatment of psychotic illnesses that it allowed acutely as well as chronically ill mental patients to be released from the wards of mental institutions. The early successes of chlorpromazine were instrumental in the development and use of other "neuroleptic" agents, eventually replacing most of the existing somatic therapies and, unfortunately, psychotherapy as well. Although more than 30 varieties of neuroleptics are currently available on the market, none has fulfilled the expectation of producing a cure for schizophrenia. "It is fairly evident now that the phenothiazines have not solved the schizophrenic problem," wrote L. R. Mosher et al. (1975), following their reassessment of modern therapeutic trends. S. C. Goldberg et al. (1977) put it even more succinctly:

> Despite acknowledged efficacy of drugs, almost half of drug-treated patients relapsed within two years, and a small, but not unsubstantial number of patients treated by placebo did not relapse . . . . Clearly, there are limits to the effectiveness of any treatment, including drugs.

According to H. E. Lehman (1975), the number of patients *who have fully recovered has not significantly changed,* despite the introduction of neuroleptics in the treatment of schizophrenia. Recent reassessments of the effectiveness of neuroleptics—their benefits weighed against damaging consequences following prolonged use—have lessened the enthusiasm with which they were first introduced. After evaluating 30 years of use of neuroleptic agents, J. R. Baldessarini (*Psychiatric Times*, January 1988) came to the conclusion that these compounds are "neither curative nor prophylactic." Essentially, they represent a symptom-ameliorating or palliative treatment, but it is far from curative. Even the recently introduced drug Clozapine—its use fraught with the danger of a lethal blood dyscrasia—has been found "most effective" when *combined with psychotherapy.*

What can neuroleptics do and what are they incapable of doing? Three decades of clinical experience have consistently brought evidence to show neuroleptics to be highly efficacious in the *symptomatic treatment* of schizophrenia, psychotic depressions, mania, and **Organic Brain Syndrome with Psychosis** (J. M. Davis et al. 1980). Davis makes a point in stating, however, that neuroleptics are not necessarily sedating, as they may arouse the retarded and calm the agitated. Improvement in specific schizophrenic symptoms parallels, as a rule, improvement in all areas of cognition as well as psycho-physiological functioning and behavior. By reducing over-arousal through the administration of chlorpromazine, H. E. Spohn et al. (1977) found their patients significantly improved in attention, concentration, and perceptual judgment. But also worthy of mention is their finding that 25 percent of schizophrenics improved while on placebo.

Neuroleptics need to be judiciously used, as has been demonstrated by J. M. Davis (1980). Hikes in dosage do not necessarily produce increments in benefit, and the curve that plots dosage against therapeutic response becomes asymptotic at a certain level. Investigating the effects of dosage on clinical improvement, R. F. Prien et al. (1969) were able to demonstrate that a dose of 15 mg. trifluoperazine was just as effective as 80 mg.—five times the optimal dose. After a certain dose, just where the curve begins to swing, benefits were found to be infinitesimal, whereas the risk of side-effects tended to increase. Paradoxically, high doses of neuroleptics have also been known to produce a rather intensified psychotic symptomatology in certain cases, with aggravation of hostility, excitement, assaultiveness, general dysphoria, and catatonic posturing. According to Prien, a daily dose of 535 mg. chlorpromazine or its equivalent nears the optimal dose. For Baldessarini, the ED-50 (half-maximally effective dose) of haloperidol (Haldol) ranges between 5 and 7.5 mg. a day.

The addition of lithium carbonate to a combination of other drugs in so-called "drug cocktails" has been found to be fraught with danger. Used rather broadly for the treatment of disorders in which agitation has been translated as meaning manic behavior and depression regarded separately from its schizophrenic nexus, the addition of lithium to other chemical compounds has been found responsible for a wide array of serious complications: memory deficit, renal insufficiency, megaloblastic anemia, thyroid dysfunction, colitis, skin rashes, aggravation of tardive dyskinesia, and sudden death due to hyperkalemia (F. C. Goggans 1980).

With respect to their mode of action, the beneficial effects of neuroleptics are believed to be contingent upon their ability to produce a "dopamine blockade." As demonstrated by histochemical and other techniques, the locus of their action seems to be along crucial neuronal centers and pathways, where dopamine-coded messages become "blocked," i.e., their transmission is inhibited by the presence of neuroleptics. A cursory glance at the map of dopamine centers, tracts, and relay stations may explain how inhibition of dopamine-coded messages can block reactions of anger, combativeness, and similar urges; how feelings of guilt may be prevented from reaching higher centers of integration associated with consciousness; and how fear, aggression, and hate may become attenuated. It is also quite possible that neuroleptics block the formation of some newly developed psychological reflexes such as obsessions-compulsions and complexes of sin and guilt.

Neuroleptics cause a general slow-down of all mental processes, which may allow time for the impulsive to consider his actions, as well as for the aggressive to abstain from resorting to violence. Nevertheless, the emotional blockade effected by neuroleptics, while blunting the passions of revenge, anger, hate, and aggression, dulls enthusiasm also, and cancels the motivation to self-reform. The chemically induced blunted affect may thus prevent the patient from engaging in useful activities such as would enhance recovery, especially socialization and work. And as has been hypothesized before (Chapter III), it may well be that, by blocking dopamine transmission, neuroleptics also prevent the release of norepinephrine— substance of felicity and inner rewards.

In a two-year follow-up investigation, S. C. Goldberg et al. (1977) found that 80 percent of placebo-treated patients had relapsed, while 45 percent relapsed in spite of treatment with neuroleptics. The clue to this enigmatic statistical result may be found perhaps in the small but "not unsubstantial number of placebo-treated patients who did recover without the aid of chemotherapy" (20 percent according to this study), and the 45 percent who relapsed in spite of treatment with neuroleptics. An exploration of heredity, life-history, significant events, premorbid personality, as well as a study of these patients' opinions on the factors responsible for their recovery, would be of immense significance and might also prove less costly than large-scale controlled investigations. Relevant to this suggestion is a study by M. J. Goldstein (1970), whose results showed that there was no difference in outcome of acute schizophrenic illnesses between drug- and placebo-treated patients whose past histories revealed "good premorbidity." Drug effects would depend thus more on personality factors than on presumed biochemical aberrations or catastrophes involving the dopaminergic system of neuro-transmission. Several investigators concur in observing that good premorbid and nonparanoid patients do well on placebos, whereas the contrary is true for poor and paranoid premorbids.

As the abrupt cessation of any chemical compound, if used over time, is liable to bring about a "rebound," the sudden withdrawal from neuroleptics may cause a reemergence of symptoms, if not a full-blown psychosis. Unfortunately, such "rebounds" have been understood as meaning that, similar to the diabetic, the once-schizophrenic would need neuroleptics for the rest of his life. Assumptions such as these have been, however, seriously challenged in the recent psychiatric literature. The "unmasking" of tardive dyskinesia, *(vide infra)* as well as the reemergence of psychotic symptoms with discontinuation of neuroleptics do, indeed, represent serious disadvantages; they may even discourage some prescribers from attempting a necessary withdrawal. The dangers fraught with cessation of medication may be minimized, however, by a *very gradual* decrease in dosage, while the patient is carefully monitored. In order to avoid complications from neuroleptic treatment, A. Ortiz and S. Gershon (1986) have suggested the use of a "minimal effective dose" and the addition, in some cases, of anxiolytics such as diazepam (Valium) or other benzodiazepine. More recently, carbamezapine (Tegretol), a drug initially used for temporal-lobe epilepsy, has been found to be useful as an adjunct to neuroleptic medication. Considering that carbamezapine acts specifically on the temporal lobes—loci of aggression and violent behaviors—it is hardly surprising that this drug was found useful in decreasing violent behaviors in all the patients studied by P. A. Hakola and U. A. Laulumaa (1982). Carbamezapine has also been introduced in recent years as a treatment option for resistant cases of schizophrenia.

In addition to occasional complications ensuing from the short-term use of neuroleptic medication, such as life-threatening dystonic reactions, the **Malignant Neuroleptic Syndrome** (with fatal hyperkalemia and hyperpyrexia), and allergic reactions, among others, the long-term use of these drugs may bring about **Tardive Dyskinesia**—a disorder of movement which is often irreversible. Ugly deviations of the body, mask facies, wiggling movements, drooling, lip-smacking, teeth-grinding, grimacing, etc., usually become "unmasked" upon cessation of treatment. A "supersensitivity psychosis" may also become then evident. Worthy of attention is a study of 50 long-stay patients, 17 with tardive dyskinesia and 33 without. The tardive dyskinesia group showed more deficits in cognitive functions, and on CAT-scan examination demonstrated more anomalies in ventricular indices (O. O. Famuyiwa et al. 1979). The possibility that neuroleptics facilitate the development of dementia in patients already suffering from *dementia praecox* cannot be lightly dismissed in view of these findings.

Unfortunately, the general public has considerably trailed behind in recognizing the sad reality that neuroleptics do not have the capacity to effect a cure, neither for schizophrenia nor for related disorders. In vain have many families sent their relatives to costly mental institutions, and so many criminals and sex offenders been remanded by the courts to mental hospitals and centers in view of "treatment" and cure. For psychiatric disabilities, medicines can only act as *psychoactive aspirins* and nothing more. Obviously, molecules cannot effect changes in these patients' personalities, still less influence their will to reform. Being an attribute of the will—and in the case of the schizophrenic, a will that wills excessively—defiance is not cancelable by chemical compounds. The same applies to malevolence. Being determined by psychological and spiritual factors, schizophrenia is curable by psychological and spiritual means.

The use of neuroleptics as well as other psychoactive drugs requires selectivity as well as caution. Tailored to individual need, the minimal effective dose should be sought, and the patient instructed to increase it during times of stress, as in family crises, job interviews, and anger-provoking situations. Such a flexible regimen may be applied only when the prescriber is available and the patient cooperative. With certain patients, dosage may be negotiated. Eventually, the patient is weaned from all medications.

Notwithstanding their effectiveness, the use of neuroleptics by no means exempts the caring mental health professional from engaging in a meaningful psychotherapeutic process with the patient, during which attempts are made to decode the meaning of nightmares, delusions, and hallucinations. More effective by far than neuroleptics, this method has driven away a surprisingly large number of ghosts, shadows, monsters, and their likes from the patient's chaotic world.

Shocking Treatments

Psychological and physical "shock" procedures, employed in view of healing the mentally deranged, have a surprisingly long history. The consistency with which this treatment modality has been applied throughout the centuries may best serve to recommend its efficacy. Before insulin-coma and electro-convulsive treatments came into use, the insane were subjected to various procedures that would induce convulsions (camphor, for example, used by L. von Meduna, 1896–1964) or produce states of extreme fright (the snake pits of Epidaurus). Not long ago, patients were first twirled into unconsciousness and then submerged into the icy waters of the sea, with or without stones bound around their necks. Such methods of treatment were practiced as late as the time of J. E. Esquirol (1782–1840). Among psychiatrists, some believe that shock treatments owe their effectiveness to their ability to create states of fear; others think that shock is experienced as a punishment that assuages feelings of guilt.

Designed to induce convulsions, which were observed to have some kind of antagonistic effect on mental illnesses in general (perhaps inhibiting aggression, which becomes converted, then, into a seizure or its equivalent), insulin "shock" was introduced by Manfred Sakel in 1933 as an effective treatment modality for a variety of psychiatric disorders. It was found to be especially beneficial for schizophrenia, and more effective when instead of shock, "insulin coma" was induced.

Following its introduction in 1938 by Bini and Cerletti, electro-convulsive shock (ECT) soon replaced the dangerous and "messy" insulin treatments. But in spite of newly modified techniques (unilateral application to the nondominant hemisphere), some workers in the field believe the beneficial effects of ECT are related to the organic changes (actually damage) that these treatments produce. According to L. B. Kalinowski, the response to ECT of patients with endogenous depression is "one of the most spectacular in medicine." Used as treatment for a variety of psychiatric illnesses, ECT has been found effective for schizophrenia only when applied in its initial stages, and most effective during the first year of the illness (L. B. Kalinowski 1975).

The wide array of psychiatric disorders responsive to insulin shock, coma, and ECT immediately raises questions regarding the mode of their action. If these treatments would affect neurotransmitters, they could do so only indirectly—by producing conditions untenable to the organism. During insulin-shock, the brain is deprived of its major fuel, namely glucose. Vital processes may be interrupted through the passage of an electric current as in ECT—creating in this manner conditions of extreme stress, with an outpour of catecholamines. Both insulin and ECT may produce convulsions. Understood as being contingent on the organic damage in the brain these treatments produce, their effectiveness may also be explained by their possible *destructive action* on newly acquired thought-patterns and/or psychological reflexes. Obsessional thoughts, depressive constellations, complexes of sin and guilt, compulsions for deviant sexual activities, etc., may well be the connections severed during the passage of an electric current, or during the temporary interruption of the brain's metabolic processes by glucose deprivation. The neuronal connections, however, must apparently be recently established in order to be susceptible to the damage induced.

On a psychological level, the common denominator to the various "shock" treatment modalities—inclusive of the immersion in icy waters, metrazole shock, ECT, etc.—is their creating experiences of impending death. This final and most dreaded of life-events is brought to awareness and so experienced by these patients. Similar to the "life-and-death" possibilities—hanging in the balance during an epileptic seizure—the convulsions induced by shock treatment carry with them a foreboding of impending death, or perhaps, an *experience of death*. Considered a "most vexing psychological phenomenon," a residual irrational and unexplainable fear remains to trouble most of the recipients of ECT. This phenomenon was found to occur even when patients were shocked while under general anesthesia. Being on the verge of death, or "dead" for a brief moment, seems to impart a message to these patients that is read by them as a warning— something of an *existential ultimatum*. Not infrequently, when this message is so understood and also heeded, it becomes instrumental in inducing permanent recovery.

As previously mentioned, it is not only artificially produced threats to existence that have such an effect on psychiatric disorders; other life-events and physical illnesses may act in a similar manner (pp. 207, 210, 401). As far back as the era of Hippocrates (377 B.C.), serious physical illnesses, fever, malaria, and convulsive disorders were noted to improve and even cure coexisting psychiatric illnesses. Similar observations were made and described by Galen (A.D. 130–200), Sydenham (1624–1689), P. Pinel (1745–1826), and many others. The subject is extensively elaborated in the work of S. Lipper and D. S. Werman (1977), as they describe remissions from schizophrenia following surgery, life-threatening illnesses, and similar circumstances. Carrying different diagnoses, 100 psychiatric patients were studied by H. E. Clow and C. T. Prout (1946). These investigators found that among their 29 dementia praecox patients, intercurrent physical illness, surgery, or accidents caused improvement in 14 and marked improvement in 2; no changes were noted in 11, and 2 actually became worse. Similar to the effects of ECT on schizophrenia, intercurrent illnesses were found most beneficial within a year's duration from the schizophrenic breakdown. Intercurrent illnesses were found to produce a more pronounced salutary effect on depressives than on patients with a persecutory symptomatology.

Various interpretations, (none of which quite satisfactory), have been advanced to explain the seeming antagonism between mind and body. Most hypotheses that attempt to explain the improvement of psychiatric disorders by intercurrent illnesses, accidents, shocks, convulsions, and other threats to existence would, nonetheless, merge into one, were the substantial reality of the living soul, the Self, to be acknowledged. Sin and guilt would need then to be recognized as powerful psychological forces that can come to assert themselves during crises and threats to the biological existence. Since depressed is the patient who repents and sorrows over his failures, it is hardly surprising that shocking him with the realization of the finiteness of his earthly existence brings him closer to recovery than the patient who denies his guilt and persists in defending himself by way of paranoid projections and delusional justifications.

The Existential Approach

Faithful to existential principles, we begin the healing process by giving due respect to the free will of those who suffer from a mental illness. With humility we acknowledge that with the best of intentions and serious efforts, we cannot *force* into recovery those who have become "psychiatric patients." We renounce *a priori our need* to triumph over their illness and abstain from blasting them with shocking treatments and coercive measures by way of chemical "warfare." As for schizophrenia—most resistant to cure—we can induce, nonetheless, a process that is healing. With due consideration being given to the appropriate diagnostic category to which the specific psychiatric disorder belongs (necessary for exchange of information), for the central task of healing, this determination ought to remain but a peripheral issue.

The tormented world of the insane needs to be approached with compassion, patience, and optimism. A bridge of nonjudgmental understanding needs to be built toward the healthy islands of their personality—as many as are still left. Instead of positing our "omniscient" superiority against the defiant and omnipotent kings of Egypt, Hitlers, and Stalins (be they manic or schizophrenic), we invest all of our creativity, and in humility and sincerity we assume the challenging task of restoring to integrity a human soul—of salvaging, as it were, "a world entire."

Facing the individual in need of care, our first concern is the determination whether he is *victim*, i.e., traumatized by the impact of external circumstances, or suffering from abuse, humiliation, or torments by others, or else, *perpetrator* of damage and hurt—inflicting sorrow, pain, and harm on others. He may be both. Nevertheless, the victims of others, or of external blows of fate and various calamities, may be reassured as to the outcome of their plight, for their majority recovers. With the passage of time, their suffering tends to abate, and most of them will be healed without recourse to treatment. Quite the contrary for the perpetrators of damage, hurt, and destruction: they are the ones liable to become psychiatric patients, suffering then both from the repercussions of their actions in reality—divorce, abandonment, imprisonment, etc.—as well as from the various dysphorias associated with guilt: defensiveness, paranoia, and depression among others. These are the truly needy, and psychiatry as an art and a science is called to respond. Yet, with these patients, psychotherapy ceases to be just "supportive"—becoming a creative effort instead. Benevolence and kindness need to be combined with confrontations and admonitions. The aim of this kind of psychotherapy is to induce in the patient a sincere desire to reform.

Unfortunately, psychotherapy has come to mean different things to different psychotherapists, and a considerable number among them have remained undecided as to *what* exactly they *want* to achieve. Some therapists seldom go beyond sympathetic nods and offers of paper tissues when their patients break down in tears. Years on end of "supportive" and even "insight-oriented" psychotherapies have seldom been successful in inducing real change, and this applies to most sexual perverts, gamblers, borderlines, and antisocial persons, as well as to schizophrenics. Can a trusting relationship alone, such as may become established between patient and therapist, be of sufficient clout as to induce healing and reform? But looming larger is the question of whether a therapist devoid of a sense of morality, or blinded to it, can serve as *moral* guide and role-model to a morally failing patient.

*   *   *

A debt of gratitude is due to Victor E. Frankl for bringing back to recognition man's essentially spiritual quest. The Logotherapy that Frankl initiated is not just a method of treatment, but a frame of reference as well—and quite distinct from psychoanalysis, at that. With Frankl we leave the stuffy world of "objects" and enter the spheres of transcendence, where love is not just a biological attachment, but a process of self-giving, frequently entailing sacrifice. We search for meaning and read the signs of our predicament. As Frankl put it: "There is only one meaning to each situation, and this is its true meaning . . . ." (*The Will to Meaning*, 1970). The moral conscience ceases, here, to be related to parental introjects, resolution of the Oedipus complex, culture and tradition—becoming an attribute of the soul, instead. For Frankl, the conscience is not just a "punishing agency" of the mind, as it is for psychoanalysts. It is a compelling force that issues not only "do not's," but "ought's" as well, and that searches out the true meaning of every experience. Along with other Existentialists, Frankl emphasizes man's responsibility and capacity for choosing. Yet, he asks, responsible to what? To whom? (*The Unconscious God*, 1975). Along with Kant, Frankl finds an irreducible quality to the conscience. He perceives it as rooted in transcendence, which he dares to call by name—God. In Frankl's Logotherapy, the "unconscious" is not decoded along biological determinants, as it is in psychoanalysis, but interpreted by way of conveyed meanings—often spiritual and religious in nature. Instead of guiding the patient toward self-serving goals, as does psychoanalysis, Logotherapy fosters self-detachment and actions beneficial to others. As for the method of Logotherapy, Frankl remarked in *Psychotherapy and Existentialism* (1967) that whereas during psychoanalysis the patient lies on the couch and expresses whatever he wishes while free-associating, the patient in Logotherapy (*logos*, standing for meaning as well as for spirit) sits facing the therapist and frequently hears what he does not want to hear.

Within the existential context, psychotherapy becomes a dialogue between an I and a You, during which certain important truths concerning the distressed, soul-sick individual become disclosed. The searchlight of truth, however, moves not only longitudinally—into the patient's heredity, childhood, and past experiences—but vertically also, seeking to reveal his major transcendental aspirations. In existential analysis, the patient's relationships are explored: to himself, to the Yous he encounters in the world, as well as to the divine Thou—to transcendence. The Existential approach finds unity in body, mind, and spirit.

And as is true for all verbal psychotherapies, whatever their orientation, the most substantial benefits of existentially oriented psychotherapy are contingent on the *flow of truth* brought forth by the patient. The highest point of psychotherapy is usually reached when the patient *confesses*. Whether induced by the patient-therapist dialogue or as a spontaneous occurrence, the acknowledgment of certain truths about oneself does have the power to set one free.

a. Neurotic Disorders

Neurotic conflicts and allied disturbances have traditionally been responsive to psychoanalysis, due to the exposure of conflictual motivational forces to the light of reason. Neurotic illnesses, however, can be *permanently* cured only following a decision on the part of the patient: the decision to renounce, once and for all, the tempting but morally forbidden wish/desire responsible for the disorder. When signalling anxieties, panic states, and phobias begin to assail the neurotic, they do not flash a message of danger on account of the unresolved conflict, but serve rather as warning measures issued by the conscience, the purpose of which is to forestall the enactment of a tempting yet morally forbidden possibility. Characteristically, and so perceived by Freud, in the dream of the neurotic the morally forbidden wish becomes fulfilled, but it is fraught with punishment. The neurotic is always the *acting party* of his dream, and from the dream alone one can decide whether he *intends* to act in a certain manner. The punishments appearing in the dream can also be useful for the separation of neurotic from psychotic disorders. Whereas the neurotic acts in a certain way and is punished for it, the psychotic is the recipient of threats and punishments for acts already accomplished (the latter may not necessarily appear in his dream). Existentially and spiritually, in the punishment dream of the neurotic, there is a message, and it needs to be heeded. "Covering" neurotic disorders with anxiolytic drugs such as Valium, treating phobias with imipramine, alprazolam, etc., and using various desensitization strategies may well be effective in providing some measure of symptomatic relief. Yet the therapist must take into account that by merely eliminating signaling anxieties and facilitating the enactment of a forbidden wish/desire, *neurotic disorders might become converted into psychotic illnesses.*

The fears of the neurotic of insanity, of loss of soul or Self, and spiritual death are fully justified, nonetheless. When the hate-obsessed neurotic patient converts malicious intention into an action of this kind, he may suddenly experience the onslaught of a catatonic psychosis. Homosexual panic, preceding such an encounter, may explode into a psychosis, which usually follows the act (p. 245). The thought-stimulus and circumstances precipitating the patient's attacks need always to be carefully investigated, for they can provide the crucial insight needed for resolution of the problem. The name of the phobia, however, is insufficient in describing the feared temptation, since its symbolism is rather overinclusive.

Agoraphobia—the fear of open spaces—for example, commonly affecting married women under 35 years of age, frequently symbolizes the fear of finding a desired lover in the open places of the world.

Social phobias may represent preventive measures, undertaken by the conscience in view of forestalling the enactment of a sought-out quarrel, for example; but they may also be related to fears of persecution and condemnation by others for some secret intention or past misdeed.

Neurotic anxieties have little to do with the fear of castration—as Freud conjectured—and even less with the Oedipus complex, unless the forbidden wish is incestual desire. The fear of castration or of impotence, as previously stressed, appears in every case of sexual misconduct, and is not specific to incest.

In treating neurotic patients, the therapist should in no wise (and for no fee) "ally" himself with those of the patient's feelings that carry him toward the feared temptation, especially when such feelings run against reason and morality. It is also inappropriate to provide the patient with cheap therapeutic absolutions, and very dangerous to attempt the "demolition" of his conscience. Quite to the contrary, it is incumbent upon every therapist to strengthen the patient's moral forces, for they are crucial in determining and maintaining his mental well-being.

b. Character Disorders

Due to their long duration and tendency of psychopathological trends to become ingrained within the personality structure, character disorders have long been recognized as resistant to treatment. The most loving concern of the most caring therapist may still be insufficient in providing the necessary leverage to lift these patients from their entrenched position. The character-disordered individual is usually past neurotic conflicts and turmoil, for certain of his choices have already been made in favor of the enactment of forbidden wishes and desires. He has learned how to act them out in spite of warning anxieties, and has conditioned himself to sin without directly experiencing guilt. He is usually engaged in a variety of antisocial or personally abusive behaviors. He may be breaking the laws established by society: stealing, embezzling, falsifying, abusing drugs or selling them to others; he may be committing crimes in the interpersonal realm: deceiving, exploiting, manipulating, even causing physical harm, injury, and destruction. He may be breaking natural-spiritual laws by deviant sexual practices. But, irrespective of the offense, character-disordered individuals learn to avoid their feelings of guilt and resort, as a rule, to repression, suppression, denials, and projections. They may drown their guilt feelings in alcohol, use chemical substances, or seek the excitement of danger. But it goes without saying that, while clearing away the signals of danger arising from within, all of these activities only serve to propel these individuals farther along the paths of self-destruction. For these reasons, the treatment of character-disordered individuals—not unlike that of sociopaths—calls for the *arousal of guilt*, by way of gentle, nonjudgmental confrontations. No less important in the psychotherapy of these individuals is the moral integrity of the therapist, for his benevolent criticism would certainly be better accepted and carry more weight than it would otherwise.

The various dysphorias of these patients need to be carefully analyzed and traced back to their sources. Somatic distresses, fears, anxieties, and depression may well represent converted guilt—addressing consciousness in this manner. Every symptom needs to be decoded, but always following the patient's (not the therapist's) associations, for the symbolism of nightmares, visions, delusions, and similar phenomena, is best understood by the patient himself—derived as it is from his wealth of knowledge and fund of past experience.

Notwithstanding, endless intensive, extensive, and expensive therapies may not resolve the borderline's mistrust, dissolve the hate of the obsessional-neurotic, or uncover the deceptive and manipulative operations of the white-collar criminal. "Transference cures" can hardly be expected in the treatment of deviant personalities. The basic anger of the borderline, contempt of the narcissist, hostility of the passive-aggressive, and manipulativeness of the sociopath may, however, yield to a decision, but it is *a decision only these individuals themselves can make*. It would consist in a resolve to replace their injurious ways of being with loving and caring attitudes, produced in action. A spirit of forgiveness may, to a great extent, dissolve existing anger and hostilities. Loving actions generate love of their own accord. Love, after all, extends far and above cheap sentimentality, and one does not need to wait for loving feelings before acting in a way that is advantageous to another, to others. Loving actions may be costly, nonetheless, and entail self-sacrifice. Yet in a paradoxical and mysterious way, acts of charity—where no self-interest is involved—instead of creating a sense of loss, are experienced as acquisition, as spiritual gain.

The innermost longings and life-goals of character-disordered individuals, as well as their transcendental strivings, need to be exposed during psychotherapy, and the absurdity of greed, consuming ambition, revenge, and jealousy brought into relief. Eventually, the patient may replace his life-goals with such strivings as are of benefit to others, to the Common Good. He may discover then that self-detachment, sacrifice, and activities that enhance the well-being of others reward the giver with feelings of hope, peace, and self-satisfaction.

c. *Schizophrenia*

Similar to the autonomous, destructive potential of a cancerous growth, the undue accretion of unrepented sin leads toward death—death of the soul. There may not exist a better proof of the corruptive powers of sin than provided by the manifestations of a schizophrenic illness. Here we can observe how the potentiation of whatever is evil and deceptive in an individual progresses in a perfect parallel with losses in cognitive and emotional faculties. And not unlike the malignancy of cancerous growths, the insanities have shown themselves remarkably resistant to a wide array of treatment approaches. But for schizophrenia, this is hardly by chance. Being rooted in willfulness, defiance fueled by pride, and a malevolence that confers power, madness is not so easily eradicated.

Yet these serious psychiatric disturbances are treatable as well as curable, and, this being the case, all available approaches need to be attempted and all resources mobilized in view of reaching this goal. To each and every one of these unfortunates, a fair chance needs to be given.

It is now just about fifty years since I became convinced
through practical experience, that schizophrenic disturbances
could be treated and cured by psychological means.

The testimony of Carl G. Jung (1957) is binding upon all those
engaged in the care of the mentally diseased. It urges them to
mobilize all their good will, creativity, and resources, as well as to
apply such psychological approaches that would reach the soul—the
spiritual center of the personality. For in spite of sustained losses in
mental faculties and undue accumulation of complexes of sin and
guilt, schizophrenic states are reversible conditions. Their psychotherapy requires, nonetheless, that it be conducted in such a way as
to induce: *confession, repentance, restitution to the injured, a turning
away from past ways of being, and a self-transformation that would
dictate a whole new life-orientation and transcendental strivings.*
These psychological events may follow one another, with various
intervals of time in between; they may also occur spontaneously, all
at once. Recovery, especially following a first schizophrenic "explosion of conscience," with its visions of Heaven and Hell, often takes
place during the patient's silent withdrawal, as he meditates on the
meaning of his horrendous ordeal. The confession of wrongdoing, to
anyone—be this priest, relative, friend, or psychotherapist—
immediately lifts a weight from the burdened conscience. Confession
also opens the way to meaningful psychotherapy, since the patient no
longer needs to hide and pretend. The Holy Scriptures' recommenda-
tion, to confess one's sins to another, is psychologically sound, for
when put into effect, it produces benefits that are dramatically
evident. Not in vain has confession become incorporated as a ritual
of the Catholic church. True confession, however, cannot be forced
on any one, and if it could, it would be of little healing value. Many
non–thought-disordered schizophrenics—open with regard to their
past misdeeds—continue to suffer from the same distresses as others
so afflicted, although their truthfulness brightens their prognosis
considerably.

The crucial moment of confession may occur quite suddenly, in
some cases when least expected, and after years of intensive psychotherapy. It is a dramatic event, nonetheless. The pressure generated
by the schizophrenic complex(es); the confidence the therapist may
have inspired; and exhaustion from the mental efforts spent to shield
past offenses, may all have been contributory in forcing the walled-off
complex(es) to burst open. The therapist may expedite the process,
nevertheless. And since the schizophrenic patient betrays himself in

everything he says and does, it is not difficult for the therapist to reach at least a workable formulation about the contents of his patient's schizophrenic complex(es). The therapist comes even closer to understanding the individual in case by bringing to scrutiny his visions, fears, nightmares, delusions, and hallucinations. The interpretation of these subjective experiences is significantly facilitated by the use of the following formula:

> The threat experienced by the patient reveals the punishment expected for an unrepented transgression, committed in the past, and which the patient may still be repeating.

As a general rule, the threats of the nightmare, delusion, or hallucination follow the laws of talion: "An eye for an eye, a tooth for a tooth." But the variety of possibilities being so numerous, the burden of their interpretation falls heavily on the therapist. The following commonly experienced nightmares and delusions may serve as examples as well as guidelines:

1. The nightmare of falling and fear of falling warn of a possible moral fall, which is most commonly observed in adolescents and in patients subject to neurotic conflicts. Similarly, but more explicit, dreams and fears of crashing with a plane, elevator, etc., represent warnings of an impending psychological "breakdown."

2. Fears, delusions, and nightmares of castration, venereal disease, AIDS, and impotence are commonly observed in individuals given to sexual excesses or perverse sexual activities, incest, and excessive masturbation, among others.

3. Delusions of dirt and of emitting odors are commonly experienced by those who hate.

4. Delusions of bodily damage, injuries, and attacks by wild beasts are commonly experienced by individuals who have been or still are engaged in violent behaviors.

5. Fears, delusions, and hallucinations of transparency, criticism, judgment, persecution, condemnation, and punishment—all inclusively subsumed as paranoia—are encountered in all serious mental illnesses, predicated as these are on complexes

of sin and guilt. There is *no schizophrenia without paranoia.*
The severity of the crucial transgression and the secrecy with
which it is maintained, parallel, as a rule, the intensity of the
paranoia.

For all practical purposes, one can be guided by the observation
that whatever the therapist suspects from the patient's symptomatology, he has, in all probability, been guilty of committing. But the
therapist should never rely on his suspicions alone, the variations and
multiplicity of possible transgressions being so numerous. The
therapist has to keep in mind, nonetheless, that fantasies and intentions give rise to a milder symptomatology—a good example being
the hand-washing rituals performed as atonement for hating. Being
predicated on sinful fantasies and intentions already translated into
actions, schizophrenia and related disorders give rise to signs and
symptoms more severe by far.

Bearing in mind the connection between the patient's symptoms
and his verbal communications, the psychotherapist may facilitate
confession by offering his own interpretations in a gentle, nonjudgmental manner. When these interpretations are faithful to their
meaning, the patient will be observed to react. Some patients respond
with laughter—laughing at the truth as it is—but this inappropriate
response augurs for them a rather ominous prognosis. Surprised by
the similarities of their and the therapist's interpretations, many
patients are startled. Some begin to cry. A correct interpretation of the
patient's subjective experiences immediately opens the channels of
communication between patient and therapist, and the healing process
is enhanced by the trust thus generated. Interpretations of delusions
and hallucinations, moreover—when true to their meaning—have the
power to liberate the patient from the painful grip of these symptoms
(M. Niv 1981).

Pursuing the meaning of subjective experiences such as visions,
nightmares, and hallucinations often speeds up an imminent confession. Yet in spite of the enormous relief that ensues from the
admission of guilt, the patient is by no means cured. Unless he
grieves over his failures and repents, which entails the renunciation
of past attitudes and misdeeds and a resolve to change, he cannot be
expected to achieve a cure. The road from confession to cure may
stretch long, and begin with *depression.* Varying in degrees of
severity, depression is experienced not only as a loss of Self, but also
as a failure. The feelings of guilt that become interwoven with the
symptomatology of depression do not represent a neurotic manifesta-

tion to be rid of, as modern psychiatry regards them, but on the contrary, an opportunity to grieve in humility, and to seek the forgiveness of others, as well as of the divine Thou the patient has offended. Grief may be the most powerful force to motivate the patient to reform. When a patient confesses in a nonchalant manner some or even all of his misdeeds, such a confession does not lead to healing. It is not the "emotional insight" psychoanalysts have rightly insisted upon. True repentance is a decision, but it has to be put into action. The patient needs to attempt with utmost sincerity to give up his hostility, malevolence, deceptions, sexual perversions, or other such attitudes and activities. Several patients who did relapse after relatively long remissions admitted to this writer that they were *unwilling* to renounce their hate and malevolence because these endowed them with a *sense of power*. Instead of making use of "aversive techniques"—such as have been devised by psychologists for the purpose of inducing change, and used mostly for smokers, gamblers, overeaters, drug abusers, etc.—the schizophrenic can simply be reminded of his own subjective experiences: nightmares, visions, delusions, and hallucinations. To him, these frightening experiences would certainly speak more eloquently than images projected on a screen or derived from guided imagination. It thus becomes incumbent upon the therapist to make the patient aware of the meaning of his terrifying experiences and to associate them with their source, namely his complex(es) of sin and guilt.

The effects of a spontaneous confession are always striking and dramatic. The whole of the patient's countenance is changed overnight. The characteristic stare and bulge of the left eye are gone. The facial expression of the patient is now peaceful, harmonious, and even beautiful!

For some proud, defiant, and negativistic patients, confession is no easy matter. It requires an admission of their failings and wrongdoing. In cases such as these, along with interpretations of their symptoms, a good therapeutic strategy is to give these patients the following assurance: *"You may be forgiven!"* Even when given completely out of context, this assurance immediately engages the attention and interest of such patients; it has been effective in reaching the most regressed, anxious, and agitated schizophrenic. So obvious and consistently beneficial is this assurance, that it may well be compared with the effects of an intravenously administered major tranquilizer—but it is much more.

Assaultive, catatonic, and confused patients have dramatically responded to this call.

- A young woman, held three days in seclusion, was freed by this assurance almost immediately and returned to the ward.

- A catatonic patient finally released his terrible grip on another after hearing this assurance.

An accepting, benevolent attitude conveying to the patient that we are all sinners and in need of repentance may, by avoiding the patient's humiliation, open a slit in the closed chambers of his heart. Nevertheless, a number of proud, defiant, and cynical individuals, who will refuse to respond and even laugh off the suggestion, will always be encountered. Not much can be done in cases such as these.

Repentance cannot take place in the presence of excessive hostility and similar feelings. When the patient complains that he cannot cry, this means he is blocked by some negative emotion such as anger, rage, contempt, or bitterness. Whenever applicable, the patient is asked to make an effort to forgive those whom he may have provoked to anger, envy, hate, etc. This may involve the patient's parents, siblings, teachers, spouse, and others of significance. The patient who has truly repented is also advised to seek forgiveness from all those he has injured, and as applicable, attempt to make amends.

Whenever unexplained hostilities persist in blocking the way to repentance, these feelings need to be further investigated with respect to their roots. Hostilities may have been implanted by the patient's heredity. They may have been provoked by parental cruelty and injustice. They may also have sprung from certain defects in the patient's physical or mental makeup, for which he now accuses Divine Providence. Hostilities may simply draw their substance from the patient's greed, covetousness, jealousy, envy, and similar sources. Cain murdered his brother for the positive attributes that he himself was lacking.

What can one do in the face of hostility? That love is the best antidote to neutralize hatred has long been recognized. Yet love can neither be administered to the patient like a medicine, nor forced upon his will—for he is the one that needs to will it. In order to neutralize their hostilities, these patients are advised *to act in a loving manner* by way of works of charity, service to others, or involvement in benevolent causes. They are also advised to seek someone, something, a cause, an occupation—a pet maybe—they would be capable of loving. Meaningful work distracts the mind from inner hell and produces increments in self-esteem. And it goes without saying that work confers also financial benefits, and with them a sense of freedom. Patients are also advised to take in the free gifts provided by Mother Nature: her lakes and woods; her shores and seas; her singing birds and fragrant flowers; her richly colored dawns and sunsets. Being a potent "mood elevator," music can stir the heart and elicit sweet tears from the wellspring of emotion. Music has induced true repentance on several occasions in this writer's experience. Other arts are also endowed with certain healing powers. Achievement in any area of endeavor is beneficial. And when love—instead of finding expression in sentimental effusions—becomes translated into action, it has the capacity of imparting significant increments in self-esteem as well as to solidify the sense of identity.

Sooner or later in the process of psychotherapy with schizophrenic patients—while transferential feelings begin to crystallize—the patient will develop hateful feelings toward the therapist. This is truly a hate "without a cause," for it has little to do with the process of psychotherapy or the person of the therapist. The schizophrenic individual simply relates with hostility to the world, to others, and the therapist cannot claim exemption. If the therapist can bear it, therapy continues as before. Resolution of this particular "transference," however, in no way produces healing, and its interpretation serves no purpose whatsoever. The patient is a *hater* and will always find good reasons for despising the therapist. Whenever murderous fantasies begin to float up in the therapeutic session, both patient and therapist become aware of having reached an impasse. This may be the moment for the therapist to accept failure and for the patient to quit. Simply terminating or closing the patient's case ought to be avoided at all costs, however, for by so doing, the therapist exposes himself to danger. Feeling rejected, the patient may seek revenge. The best way to resolve the impasse is to pressure the patient to follow at least some of the given advice. If the patient is ready to heed some of the therapist's suggestions, he is bound to improve and therapy will naturally resume. If he persists, however, with his murderous hostility and refuses to follow the therapist's recommendations, he will eventually leave therapy of his own accord.

The existential approach to depression—whether contingent on a schizophrenic illness or not—diverges somewhat from the cognitive strategies devised by A. T. Beck (1972). And while, indeed, affect and behavior may be largely determined by the way an individual constructs his world, the question whether the powers of the intellect can be sufficient to modify these constructs remains ever pertinent. Existential psychotherapy directs the patient *toward self-improvement first*, for in the Self—the soul—reside the sources of emotional outflow that color the perceptions of the world outside. But the wellspring of emotion is also closely related to the system of self-esteem. Achievement of any kind, self-mastery, self-detachment, acts of renunciation, love, and self-sacrifice, all tend to enhance the sense of one's worth and produce feelings of elation. Failures, on the other hand, as well as frank violations of what one knows to be good and true, tend to lower self-esteem and produce anxiety and depression. What is so remarkable about the system of self-esteem is its exquisite sensitivity to breaches in interpersonal contracts and relationships, as if, indeed, our self-worth as well as our felicity were contingent upon fulfillment of the spiritual-moral law that requires that we love our neighbor. But even more remarkable is the accuracy with which the system of self-esteem is attuned to reality and truth. The self-esteem of the schizophrenic as well as the sadness of the depressed are thus not given to change through various "supportive" measures and false praise. No one can esteem oneself highly when aware of one's deceptions, parasitism, exploitations, embezzlements, hostilities, or murderous intentions. Yet one can better oneself and so alter one's self-perceptions. And while one may have little control over certain painful externally determined circumstances, one can, to a large extent, attenuate feelings of distress through working on one's Self— by the expansion of one's soul, be this by action or else by patient endurance.

Existential therapy, nevertheless, is not a behavior therapy, as would appear on the surface. It is an action-oriented therapy, for it fosters the induction of positive feelings through positive actions. But further than that, existential psychotherapy demands a change in the patient's life-goals and orientation. As graphically represented on Diagram # 7 (p. 274), small changes in the center of intention, namely in the heart's "affections," create substantial differentials in the structure of the personality. Thirst for power, for example, when transformed into a search for love, creates a whole new personality. Pride transformed into humility changes all of the individual's ways of being, and by rendering him more acceptable to others, enriches and transforms his world as well.

A good frame of reference for treatment, and applicable for schizophrenic disorders, has been provided by the Twelve Steps and Twelve Traditions of Alcoholics Anonymous. This nonprofit organization can proudly boast of a very high rate of recovery for its participants. The treatment program of A.A. demands as prerequisite that the participant make a thorough moral inventory of his past and confess to at least one other. A.A. also stresses reliance on the Higher

Power, and requires that its participants adhere to the moral law and commit themselves to the demands of their religion. To its bedazzling statistics for recovery from alcoholism (nearing 75 percent), Alcoholics Anonymous may add many nameless criminals, sexual deviants, antisocial and borderline persons, as well as a substantial number of schizophrenics to whom this organization has made a difference.

* * *

After the patient has confessed and come to repentance—striving to renounce old ways of being and replacing them with new, more benevolent ones—his threatening world begins to change also. Instead of darkness, he begins to perceive flashes of light, and instead of wild beasts, finds himself surrounded by flowers, trees, and singing birds. Golden landscapes and sparkling jewels begin to shine in his consciousness. He is on the road to recovery.

Religion

To those remote from Western culture and the intricacies of modern psychological trends, it would appear paradoxical that psychiatry has built its entire superstructure upon one human frailty, namely Oedipal desire, while it has ignored religious faith as one of the deepest and most fundamental of human strivings. That the various cultures and traditions around the world imprint their own specific ways on the practice of religion, in no way detracts from the universality of the spiritual quest. And by reason of the belief of the majority of mankind in a Higher Power, religion needs to be respected and regarded as a primary reality in the life of the "psyche."

Although a fundamental principle of all the major world religions has been the furtherance of human brotherhood, religion has been frequently profaned, used, and abused. In the name of Christianity, men and women were tortured and burned at the stake. "Holy" wars are still proclaimed to this day with the aim of destroying "infidels." Taken out of context, certain religious precepts have even been used to create new pseudo-religious movements and various cults. That political and even religious leaders may take upon themselves to abuse religion in order to advance their own selfish interests, only serves to demonstrate that profanation of the most sacred can find justification, can be rationalized.

Among the merits of Existentialism, one of the most important may be considered its emphasis on the immediacy of man's relationship to the divine Thou, without necessary recourse to organized religion. This relationship, however, cannot otherwise be maintained but through a worship that is "in spirit and in truth." Existentialists have been frequently assailed for producing a "Kierkegaard's neurosis" by their stress on the need for scrupulous honesty in all of one's dealings: with oneself, with one's fellow men, and the divine Thou. Existentialists have also insisted upon man's need to live authentically by assuming responsibility not only for himself and his own destiny, but for the welfare of others as well. Instead of siding with any particular religious doctrine, common to all Existentialists is their emphasis on matters of the spirit, as opposed to the letter of any particular religion. Existentialists have, in a way, contributed to interfaith communication, and have also been instrumental in bridging the various religions as well as the philosophical systems of the modern world. And while, indeed, religious worship and ritual may markedly differ from culture to culture, the precepts of all major religions around the world are strikingly similar. All religions insist on the observance of the moral law, imparted to the individual through the voice of his conscience as divine counsel. All insist also on the need for obedience to the will of The Most High. This is the meaning of Islam—obedience, submission. But most basic to all true religions, according to R. O. Ballou (1972), who has studied them all, is the commandment requiring that one love one's neighbor as oneself.

For the majority of psychiatrists, raised on the knees of psychoanalytic doctrine, religious faith is regarded as a delusion of the insane; a crutch for the weak and helpless; a socio-culturally–induced tradition, at best. Yet the fact that religious faith has inspired the noblest acts of self-sacrifice and highest feats of courage and transcendence of the human spirit, finds no representation in the modern, mostly biologically based psychological systems and theories. Religion is here to stay, notwithstanding. It is the central life-force for billions who believe. In the city of Chicago alone stand 2,500 churches, cathedrals, and synagogues in which thousands gather to worship. Montreal, a city of similar size, has a number of houses of worship no smaller than that of Chicago. Political-cultural systems such as Communism and Fascism, for example, were powerless in their efforts to extinguish religious faith. In Thailand, instead of military service, every male, inclusive of the king, must serve as a Buddhist monk upon reaching maturity. Remarkably, many among the citizens of that country choose to serve as monks for more than the required three-month service.

An enormous disparity seems to exist between mental patients and their healers with respect to religious faith, however, and it has becomes focal to misunderstanding on more than one level. According to the latest poll on religion commissioned by the City University of New York (conducted between 1989 and 1990), 9 out of 10 Americans were found identified with one or another religious denomination: 86.4 percent with a Christian and 3.7 percent with a non-Christian religion; 2.3 percent refused to answer; and 7.5 percent professed no religion at all. Among psychologists, according to a Gallup poll taken in 1981 (p. 224), only 5 percent were found to entertain a religious belief, and the highest rate of apostasy, namely 40 percent, was found among psychoanalysts, as compared to 26 percent among psychiatrists.

The disparity between the religious beliefs of mental patients and those of their healers has been responsible for gross errors in interpretation. That the delusional experiences of the insane are interwoven with spiritually meaningful phenomena does not by necessity identify religious faith as causative of madness, nor does it imply that to believe means to be delusional-psychotic. Yet religion has frequently been blamed for *causing* psychiatric disturbances. A closer look into the contents of delusions and hallucinations and a scrutiny of the reasons the insane obsess with religion and philosophy, immediately reveals these patients' condemned state of existence. Relentlessly perturbed by their schizophrenic complex(es) of sin, guilt, and spiritual degradation, they search for a solution to ease their torment. Their heavy burden of guilt motivates many among them to engage in acts of atonement and various rituals in view of redemption and salvation. And it appears on the surface as if schizophrenics are "overly religious." But this is in appearance only, for more frequently than not, schizophrenics actually abuse religion and many acts of arson, murder, torture, and crime committed by these patients are rationalized by them as intended to stamp out some evil. A sadistic mother, for example, claiming to follow the scriptural injunction "Whoso spares the rod, hates the child," when correcting her children, abuses actually this religious precept in order to vent on them her malevolent inclinations.

We are all sinners and fall short in loving our neighbor as we really should. But those who have succumbed to madness can well demonstrate to us all what defiantly undertaken acts of malevolence, which break basic moral-spiritual laws, may bring about as a consequence.

*   *   *

While it is given to various treatments and psychological approaches to reach the sin-sick soul, and even to induce healing, religious conversion can accomplish cure at once. Conversion means a turning away from past ways of being and a rededication to new life-goals and strivings. Conversion may follow a first psychotic decompensation—after the message of its threatening visions has been grasped and heeded. About one-third of patients who recover do so following their first psychotic episode.

Religious faith, nevertheless, implies that the I becomes bound (religion derives from the word *ligare,* "to bind") to the divine Thou by a covenant that demands from the believer to *live by faith.* This living by faith encompasses all of life, and when the believer is required to worship "in spirit and in truth," it means that he is to follow inwardly as well as outwardly that which is good and true.

Nevertheless, mental patients are known to frequently bypass these requirements. The distance between their profession of faith and its actual application in daily living measures the degree of inauthenticity in their existence. Often, mental patients are heard complaining their faith to be vain, yet refuse to perceive their failure in fulfilling the requirements of their religion. But as every other sign, symptom, and experience of the schizophrenic deserves attention and needs to be interpreted, religious beliefs and their actualization in daily living are also to be scrutinized. The way of return may, indeed, remain open to even regressed schizophrenics, but they need to seek it in humility, reverence, and intention to submit to the demands of their religion. All hostilities, anger, revengeful passion, jealousy, lustings, perversions, etc., are to be forsaken—renounced once and for all. Sincere attempts must also be made to love the neighbor in action and readiness for sacrifice. A renewal of loving relationships through bridges of forgiveness, built from all sides, has revived many vegetating chronic schizophrenic patients, some after decades of institutionalization.

Conversion can turn morbid trends around, engender healthy attitudes, and, needless to say, infuse the convert with renewed hope for the future. The participants in Alcoholics Anonymous bear witness to the power of spiritual-religious renewal, not only for maintaining their abstinence, but for the transformation of their personality as well. Even sexual deviations, presumed "incurable" for their allegedly inborn origins, have been shown to respond favorably to religious conversion. Such a change in sexual orientation following religious conversion was reported by E. M. and M. L. Pattison (1980).

*   *   *

With all the variety of treatments in existence, statistics show the rate of recovery from schizophrenia to be relatively low. In sheer numbers, the treatment of schizophrenia appears to be unprofitable. With so much effort and financial drain on family, hospital, social agencies, medical personnel, etc.—not to mention all the love, devotion, care, and sacrifice invested—it would seem as if the treatment of the insane represents a poor investment. But in terms of the individual who improves and later recovers as a result of treatment, to him it is pure gain.

Unless based on long-term studies comprising the entire life-span of the schizophrenic patient, statistical evaluations will fail to tell the whole story with respect to treatment and recovery. Statistics, usually, do not take into account the fact that although schizophrenia is a process that may take several decades, it can also be arrested at any given moment. In a 30-year follow-up study (the "Vermont study"), the subjects of which were drawn from a population of 269 patients from the Vermont State Hospital and placed in a rehabilitation program, C. M. Harding, its chief investigator, reported to the American Psychiatric Association Convention of 1985 in Dallas that one-half to two-thirds of her subjects had recovered or significantly improved (*Psychiatric News,* June 21, 1985). Some of these patients had been hospitalized for up to 25 years and had suffered an average of 16 years from their illness. Their condition was considered so hopeless that their families were told to mourn them as if they were dead. Of the 82 patients interviewed 25 years after their discharge to a rehabilitation program, two-thirds functioned well enough, and 68 percent showed no sign of schizophrenia. Dr. Harding corrected the old adage by saying, "Once schizophrenic, not always schizophrenic." Only half of these patients took their prescribed medication, and some kept them stored away, using them whenever they felt the need.

That the world of the individual schizophrenic shrinks with every new psychotic episode has long been recognized and is in no need of further documentation. But how can emotional scarring, defects in personality, losses in the capacity for joy, and spontaneous expression be measured and compared?

A substantial number of chronic, deteriorated schizophrenic patients have come to the attention of this writer. Of them, a small number has recovered as a consequence of psychotherapy, and many more have improved so that life became possible for them again. The knowledge that the help extended to them had been instrumental in their improvement or cure, that it did make a difference, largely compensates for the substantial number of cases that have failed to respond at that given moment—for whom the treatment appeared of little or no consequence. With schizophrenia, the therapist must be prepared for defeat.

To those who care for the mentally disturbed the following words spoken by Lao Tzu may be relevant:

> Those who are good, I treat as good. Those who are not good, I also treat as good. In so doing, I gain in goodness. Those who are of good faith, I have faith in. Those who are lacking in good faith, I also have faith in. In so doing, I gain in good faith.

—Lao Tzu, *Tao Te Ching*

Bibliography

Abel G. G., Becker J. V., et al. *Multiple Paraphiliac Diagnosis Among Sex Offenders*. Bulletin of the American Academy of Psychiatry and the Law, 16:153, 1988.

Abrams S. *The Validity of the Polygraph with Schizophrenics*. Polygraph, 3:328, 1974.

Allport G. *Becoming*: *Basic Considerations for a Psychology of Personality*. Yale University Press, 1955.

Allport G. *Pattern and Growth in Personality*. Holt, Rhinehart & Winston, New York, 1961.

Andreasen N. C. *Thought, Language and Communication Disorders*. Arch Gen Psychiatry. 36:1315, 1979.

Andreasen N. C., Smith M. R., et al. *Ventricular Enlargement in Schizophrenia: Definition and Prevalence*. Am J Psychiatry, 139:292, 1982.

Andreasen N. C., Olsen S. A., et al. *Ventricular Enlargement in Schizophrenia: Relationship to Positive and Negative Symptoms*. Am J Psychiatry, 139:297, 1982.

Angyal A. *Disturbances of Thinking in Schizophrenia*. In: Language and Thought in Schizophrenia. JS Kasanin (ed.). W.W. Norton & Co, New York, 1964.

Anonymous. *A New Theory of Schizophrenia*. Jl Abn Soc Psychology, 57:226, 1958.

Arieti S. *Interpretation of Schizophrenia*. Basic Books, New York, 1974.

Arieti S. *Parents of the Schizophrenic Patient: A Reconsideration*. Jl Am Academy of Psychoanalysis, 5(3):347, 1977.

Arthur A. Z. *Theories and Explanations of Delusions*: *A Review*. Am J Psychiatry, 121:105, 1964.

Astrup C., Noreik K. *Functional Psychoses: Diagnostic and Prognostic Models*. Charles C. Thomas, Springfield, Ill. 1966.

Atkinson J. H. Jr., Grant I., et al. *Prevalence of Psychiatric Disorders among Men Infected with Human Immunodeficiency Virus*. Arch Gen Psychiatry, 45:859, 1988.

Babigian H. M. *Schizophrenia: Epidemiology*. In Comprehensive Psychiatry, A.M. Friedman, et al. (eds.). The Williams & Wilkins Co., Baltimore, 1975.

Bachelard G. *L'Air et les Songes*. Librairies José Corti, Paris, 1943.

Bachelard G. *La Terre et les Rêves de Repos*. Librairie José Corti, Paris, 1948.

Bachelard G. *La Psychanalyse du Feu*. Editions Gallimard, Paris, 1949.

Ballou R. O. *The Portable World Bible*. The Viking Press, 1972.

Ban T. A. *Perspectives in Biological Psychiatry—Schizophrenia and Organic Brain Syndrome*. Psychosomatics, October 1977.

Barnitz H. W. *Existentialism and the New Christianity,* Philosophical Library, New York, 1969.

Baruk H. *Des Hommes Comme Nous.* Editions Robert Laffont, Paris, 1976.

Batchelor I. R. C. *Psychopathic States and Attempted Suicide.* Br Med J 1:1342, 1954.

Bateson G., Jackson D. D., et al. *Toward a Theory of Schizophrenia.* Brunner/Mazel, New York, 1956.

Beck A. T. *Depression: Causes and Treatment.* University of Pennsylvania Press, Philadelphia, 1972.

Becker E. *The Denial of Death.* The Free Press, McMillan Publishing Co., New York, 1973.

Berrios G. E. *Musical Hallucinations: A Historical and Clinical Study.* Br Jl Psychiatry,156:188, 1990.

Betz B. J. *Some Neurophysiological Aspects of Individual Behaviour.* Am J Psychiatry, 136:1251, 1979.

Bleuler E. *Dementia Praecox or the Group of Schizophrenias.* (1911). J. Zinkin (trans.) International Universities Press, 1950.

Bleuler M. *A Longitudinal Study of 208 Schizophrenics and Impressions in Regard to the Nature of Schizophrenia.* J Psych Res, Vol: Supply 1968.

Bleuler M. *Die schizophrene Geistesstoerungen im Lichte langjaehriger Kranken und Familiengeschichten.* Georg Thieme, Stuttgart, 1972.

Bleuler M. *On Schizophrenic Psychoses.* Am J Psychiatry, 136:1403, 1979.

Bliss E. L., Clark L. D. *Visual Hallucinations.* In Hallucinations, LJ. West (ed.). Grune & Stratton, New York, 1962.

Bogerts B., Meertz E., et al. *Basal Ganglia and Limbic System Pathology in Schizophrenia.* Arch Gen Psychiatry. 42:784, 1985.

Boisen A. T. *Exploration of the Inner World.* Harper & Brothers, New York, 1936.

Bok S. *Lying: Moral Choice in Public and Private Life.* Vintage Books, Random House, New York, 1979.

Borland B. L., Heckman H. K. *Hyperactive Boys and their Brothers. A 25 year Follow-up Study.* Arch Gen Psychiatry, 33:669, 1976.

Boss M. *Psychoanalysis and Daseinanalysis.* Basic Books, New York, 1963.

Bowers M. B. *Psychoses Precipitated by Psychotomimetic Drugs.* Arch Gen Psychiatry, 34: 832, 1977.

Brain W. R. *Brain's Clinical Neurology.* Revised by Roger Bannister. Oxford University Press, London, 1975.

Breakey W. R., Goddell H., et al. *Hallucinogenic Drugs as Precipitants of Schizophrenia.* Psychol Medicine, 4:255, 1974.

Brenner C. *An Elementary Textbook of Psychoanalysis.* Doubleday, New York, 1974.

Breslau N., Davis, G. C. *Chronic Stress and Major Depression.* Arch Gn Psychiatry, 43:309, 1986.

Brill A. A. *Only and Favourite Children in Adult Life.* In Outline of Psychoanalysis, JS. Van Telsaar, Modern Library, New York, 1924.

Brown G. W., Birley J. L. T., et al. *Influence of Family Life on the Course of Schizophrenic Disorders: A Replication.* Brit Jl Psychiatry, 121:241, 1972.

Buber M. *Good and Evil.* Charles Scribner's & Sons, New York, 1953.

Buber M. *I and Thou.* Charles Scribner's Sons, New York, 1970.

Campbell A. M., Evans M., et al. *Cerebral Atrophy in Young Cannabis Smokers.* Lancet, 2: 1219, 1971.

Carlsson A., Linquist M. *Effects of Chlorpromazine or Haloperidol on Formation of 3-Methoxytyramine and Normetanphrine in Mouse Brain.* Acta Pharmacol Toxicol 20:140, 1963.

Chafetz M. E. *Alcoholism and Alcohol Psychoses.* In Comprehensive Psychiatry, AM Friedman, et al. (eds.). The Williams & Wilkins Co, Baltimore, 1975.

Chapman L. J., Edell W. S., et al. *Physical Anhedonia, Perceptual Aberration and Psychosis-Proneness.* Schizophrenia Bullet, 6:639, 1980.

Ciompi L. *Catamnestic Long-Term Study on the Course of Life and Aging of Schizophrenics.* Schizophrenia Bull, 6:606, 1980.

Cleckley H. *The Mask of Sanity.* The C.V. Mosby Co, St. Louis, 1964.

Cloninger C. R. *Recognizing and Treating Sociopathy.* Medical World News, October, 1975.

Cloninger C. R, Guze S. B. *Psychiatric Disorders and Criminal Recidivism: A Follow-up Study of Female Criminals.* Arch Gen Psychiatry, 29:266, 1973.

Clow H. E, Prout C. T. *A Study of the Modification of Mental Illness by Intercurrent Physical Disorders in One Hundred Patients.* Am Jl Psychiatry, 103:179, 1946.

Cohen S., Ditman K. S. *Prolonged Adverse Reactions to Lysergic Acid Diethylamide.* Arch Gen Psychiatry, 8:475, 1963.

Cohen S. *LSD: Side Effects and Complications.* J Nerv Ment Dis, 130:30, 1960.

Crow T. J. *Discussion: Positive and Negative Schizophrenic Symptoms and the Role of Dopamine.* Br J Psychiatry, 137: 383, 1980.

Daco P. *Les Prodigieuses Victoires de la Psychologie Moderne.* Gerard & Co, Verviers, Belgique, 1973.

Dasberg H. *Psychological Distress of Holocaust Survivors and Offspring Forty Years Later: A Review.* Israel J Psychiatry & Rel Sciences, 24:243, 1987.

Davis J. M., Schaffer C. B., et al. *Important Issues in the Drug Treatment of Schizophrenia.* Schizophrenia Bullet, Spec Report, 109, 1980.

De Grazia S. *Neuroses as a Moral Disorder.* In Morality and Mental Health. O. H. Mowrer (ed.). Rand McNally, Chicago, 1967.

Delgado-Escueta A. V. *The Nature of Aggression During Epileptic Seizures.* New Engl J Med, 305:711, 1981.

Dimsdale J. E., Moss J. *Plasma Catecholamines in Stress and Exercise.* Jl Am Med Assn, 243:340, 1980.

Dunaif S., Hoch P. *Pseudoneurotic Schizophrenia.* In Psychiatry and the Law. Hoch P & J Zubin (eds.). Grune, New York, 1955.

Eitinger L. *Schizophrenia Among Concentration Camp Survivors.* Intl Jl Psychiatry, 3:403, 1967.

Eitinger L., Stroem A. *Mortality and Morbidity after Excessive Stress.* Humanities Press, New York, 1973.

Ellinwood E.H., Jr. *Amphetamine Psychoses: Systems and Subjects.* In Drug Abuse, W. Keup, (ed.). Charles C. Thomas, Springfield, Ill., 1972.

Ellinwood E. H., Jr. *Amphetamine Psychoses: Description of the Individual and Process.* J Nerv Ment Dis, 144:273, 1967.

Famuyiwa O. O., Eccleston D., et al. *Tardive Dyskinesia and Dementia.* Brit Jl Psychiatry, 135:500, 1979.

Farkas T., Wolf A. *PETT Scans May Provide Psychiatric Diagnosis.* Psych News, November, 1980.

Feighner J. P., Robins E., et al. *Diagnostic Criteria for Use in Psychiatric Research.* Arch Gen Psychiatry, 26:57, 1972.

Fingarette H. *On the Relation between Moral Guilt and Guilt in Neurosis.* In Morality and Mental Health, O. H. Mowrer (ed.). Rand McNally, Chicago, 1967.

Fish B. *Neurobiologic Antecedents of Schizophrenia in Children.* Arch Gen Psychiatry, 34:1297, 1977.

Foucault M. *Madness and Civilization.* Vintage Books, New York, 1973.

Frankl V. *Man's Search for Meaning.* Beacon Press, Simon & Schuster, New York, 1963.

Frankl V. *Psychotherapy and Existentialism.* Washington Square Press, New York, 1967.

Frankl V. *The Unconscious God.* Simon & Schuster, New York, 1975.

Frankl V. *The Will to Meaning.* New American Library, New York, 1970.

Freedman D.X. *Psychiatric Epidemiology Counts.* Arch Gen Psychiatry, 41:931, 1984.

Freedman S. J., Grunebaum H. U., et al. *Perceptual and Cognitive Changes.* In Sensory Deprivation, P. Solomon, et al. (eds.). Harvard Universities Press, Cambridge, Mass, 1965.

Freud A. *The Ego and Mechanisms of Defense.* The Writings of Anna Freud. International Universities Press, New York, 1966.

Freud S. *An Outline of Psychoanalysis*, (1940). W.W. Norton & Co, New York, 1969.

Freud S. *Neurosis and Psychosis* (1924). Complete works of S. Freud, Vol XIX, The Hogarth Press, London, 1961.

Freud S. *The Psychopathology of Everyday Life* (1905). The Standard Ed. of Compl. Psych. works of S. Freud, J Strachey, (ed.). Vol VII, The Hogarth Press, London, 1957.

Freud S. *Three Case Histories: Psychoanalytic Notes on an Autobiographical Account of a Case of Paranoia* (Dementia Paranoides) (1911). P. Rieff (ed.). McMillan Publishing Co, New York, 1963.

Freud S. *Analysis of a Phobia in a Five-Year-Old Boy* (1909). In Collected Papers, Vol X, 3, The Hogarth Press, London, 1957.

Freud S. *Beyond the Pleasure Principle* (1920). In Collected Papers, Vol XVII, The Hogarth Press, London, 1957.

Freud S. *Civilization and its Discontents* (1930). W.W. Norton & Co, New York, 1961.

Freud S. *Construction in Analysis* (1937). In Collected Papers Vol XXIII, The Hogarth Press, London, 1964.

Freud S. *New Introductory Lectures on Psychoanalysis* (1933), W.W. Norton & Co, New York, 1964.

Freud S. *On Transformation of Instinct as Exemplified in Anal Erotism* (1917). Standard Edition, J. Strachey, (ed.). Vol XVII, The Hogarth Press, London, 1957.

Freud S. *The Economic Problem of Masochism* (1924). In Collected Papers, Vol II, The Hogarth Press, Toronto, 1949.

Freud S. *The Future of an Illusion*, (1927). W.W. Norton & Co, New York, 1961.

Freud S. *Totem and Taboo* (1913). Standard Edition, J. Strachey (ed.). Vol XIII, The Hogarth Press, London, 1957.

Gabbard G. O., Coyne L. *Predictors of Response of Antisocial Patients to Hospital Treatment*. Hospital & Community Psychiatry, 38:1181, 1987.

Gabbard G. O. *Out-of-Body States*. Psychiatric News, January, 1988.

Galanter M., Westermeyer J. *Charismatic Religious Experience and Large Group Psychology.* Am J Psychiatry, 137:12, 1980.

Galin D. *Implications for Psychiatry of Left and Right Cerebral Specialization.* Arch Gen Psychiatry, 31:572, 1974.

Glass L. L., Kirsh M. A., et al. *Psychiatric Disturbances Associated with Erhard Seminar Training: Report of Cases.* Am Jl Psychiatry, 134:245, 1977.

Goetz C. G., Tanner C. M., et al. *Pharmacology of Hallucinations Induced by Long-term Drug Therapy.* Am J Psychiatry, 139:494, 1982.

Goggans F. C. *Acute Hyperkalemia During Lithium Treatment of Manic Illness.* Am Jl Psychiatry, 137:860, 1980.

Goldberg S. C., Schooler N., et al. *Prediction of Relapse in Schizophrenic Outpatients Treated by Drug and Sociotherapy.* Arch Gen Psychiatry, 34: 171, 1977.

Goldberger L., Holt R. R. *Experimental Interference with Reality Contact: Individual Differences.* In Sensory Deprivation, P. Solomon et al. (eds.). Harvard Universities Press, Cambridge, Mass, 1965.

Goldstein K. *The Effects of Brain Damage on the Personality.* Psychiatry, 15-245, 1952.

Goldstein, M. J. *Premorbid Adjustment, Paranoid Status, and Patterns of Response to Phenothiazines in Acute Schizophrenia.* Schizophrenia Bullet, 3:24, 1970.

Greeley A. M., McCready W. C. *Are we a Nation of Mystics?* The New York Times Magazine, Jan. 26, 1975.

Grinker R. R., Werble B., et al. *The Borderline Syndrome: A Behavioral Study of Ego Functions.* Basic Books, New York, 1968.

Gruhle H. W. *Denkstoerungen und Sprache bei Schizophrenen.* Zeit Ges Neurol Psychiatrie. 103:185, 1926.

Gunderson J. G., Singer M. T. *Defining Borderline Patients: An Overview.* Am J Psychiatry, 132:1, 1975.

Guze S. B. *Criminality and Psychiatric Disorders.* Oxford University Press, New York, 1976.

Guze S.B. *Suicide in Cancer Patients.* Psychiatric Capsule & Comment, 4:6, 1982.

Hakola H. P., Laulumaa V. A. *Carbamezapine in Treatment of Violent Schizophrenics.* Lancet, 1:1358, 1982.

Halleck S. A. *Psychodynamic Aspects of Violence.* Bull Am Acad Psychiatry and the Law, Vol IV:328, 1976.

Harrow M., Prosen M. *Intermingling and Disordered Logic as Influences on Schizophrenic "Thought Disorders."* Arch Gen Psychiatry, 35:1213, 1978.

Harrow M. *Cognitive Markers: Signs of Nuclear Schizophrenia.* 134th Annual Meeting of the APA, New Orleans, Louisiana, 1981.

Heinroth J. C. *Textbook of Disturbances of Mental Life*, or *Disturbances of the Soul an
d their Treatment* (1818). The John Hopkins University Press, Baltimore, 1975.

Heston L. L. *Psychiatric Disorders in Foster Home Reared Children of Schizophrenic Mothers.* Br J Psychiatry, 112:819, 1966.

Heston L. L. *The Genetics of Schizophrenia and Schizoid Disease*, In The Schizophrenic Syndrome, R. Cancro (ed.). Brunner Mazel, New York, 1971.

Hoch P. H. *Differential Diagnosis in Clinical Psychiatry.* M.O. Strahl & N.D.C. Lewis (eds.). Science House, 1972.

Hoch P., Polatin P. *Pseudoneurotic Forms of Schizophrenia.* Psychiatric Quarterly, 23:248, 1949.

Hollander E., Liebowitz M. R., et al. *Cortisol and Sodium Lactate-Induced Panic*. Arch Gen Psychiatry, 46:135, 1989.

Huber G., Gross G., et al. *Longitudinal Studies of Schizophrenic Patients*. Schizophrenia Bull, Vol 6: 592, 1980.

Huxley A. *The Doors of Perception* (1954) and *Heaven and Hell* (1956). Granada Publishing, London, 1979.

Jablensky A. *Multicultural Studies and the Nature of Schizophrenia: A Review*. J Royal Soc Medicine, Vol 80, February, 1987.

Jablensky A. *Epidemiology of Schizophrenia: A European Perspective*. Schizophrenia Bull, Vol 12:52, 1986.

James W. *Psychology* (1892). Fine Editions Press, Cleveland, Ohio, 1948.

James W. *The Varieties of Religious Experience* (1902). The Penguin American Library, 1982.

Jaspers K. *General Psychopathology*. The University of Chicago Press, 1963.

Jeffress J. E. *Genes and the Psyche*. Jl Am Med Women Association, 30:15, 1975.

Jung C. G. *Memories, Dreams, Reflections* (1957). Aniela Jaffe (ed.). Random House, New York, 1973.

Jung C. G. *The Psychology of Dementia Praecox* (1907). Bollingen Series XX, Vol 8, The Collected Works of C.G. Jung, Princeton University Press, Princeton, 1968.

Jung C. G. *The Psychogenesis of Mental Disease* (1907–1957). Bollingen Series XX, Vol 3, The Collected Works of C. G. Jung, Princeton University Press, Princeton, 1973.

Kales C. R., Soldatos C. D., et al. *Nightmares: Clinical Characteristics and Personality Patterns*. Am J Psychiatry, 137:10, 1980.

Kalinowski L. B. *The Convulsive Therapies*. In Comprehensive Textbook of Psychiatry, A. Freedman et al. (eds.). The Williams & Wilkins Co, Baltimore, 1975.

Kallmann F. J. *The Genetics of Schizophrenia*. Augustin, New York, 1938.

Kallmann F. J. *Heredity in Health and Mental Disorder*. W.W.Norton & Co. New York, 1953.

Kaplan H. I., Sadok B. J., et al. *The Brain in Psychiatry*, In Comprehensive Textbook of Psychiatry, A.M. Freedman, et al. (eds.). The Williams and Wilkins Co., Baltimore, 1975.

Kasanin J. S. *Language and Thought in Schizophrenia*. W.W. Norton & Co, New York, 1964.

Kazantzakis N. *Report to Greco*. Simon and Schuster, New York, 1961.

Kelly D., Richardson A., et al. *Stereotactic Limbic Leucotomy*. Br J Psychiatry, 123:141, 1973.

Kelsoe J. R., Cadet J. L., et al. *Quantitative NeuroAnatomy in Schizophrenia*. Arch Gen Psychiatry, 45:533, 1988.

Kernberg O. *Borderline Conditions and Pathological Narcissism*. Jason Aronson, New York, 1975.

Kernberg O. *A Psychoanalytic Classification of Character Pathology*. J Am Psychoanal Assn, 18:800, 1970.

Kernberg O. *Contrasting Viewpoints Regarding the Nature and Psychoanalytical Treatment of Narcissistic Personalities: A Preliminary Communication*. J Am Psychoanalytic Assn, 22:255, 1974.

Kernberg O. *The Structural Diagnosis of Borderline Personality Organization*. In Borderline Personality Disorders, P. Hartocollis, (ed.). International Universities Press, 1977.

Kernberg O. *Two Reviews of the Literature on Borderlines: An Assessment.* Schizophrenia Bullet, Vol.5: 53, 1979.

Kessler S. *The Genetics of Schizophrenia: A Review.* Special Report, Schizophrenia Bullet, 14, 1980.

Kessler R. C., McGonagle, K. A., et al. *Lifetime and 12-month Prevalence of DSM-III-R Psychiatric Disorders in the United States: Results from the National Comorbidity Survey.* Arch Gen Psychiatry, 51:8, 1994.

Kety S. S., Rosenthal D., et al. *The Types and Prevalence of Mental Illness in the Biological and Adoptive Families of Adopted Schizophrenics.* In The Transmission of Schizophrenia, D. Rosenthal and S.S. Kety (eds.). Pergamon Press, Oxford, 1968.

Kidd K. K., Cavalli-Sforza L. L. *An Analysis of the Genetics of Schizophrenia.* Social Biology, 20:254, 1973.

Kierkegaard S. *The Concept of Dread* (1844). Princeton University Press, Princeton, New Jersey, 1957.

Kierkegaard S. *Christian Discourses* (1848). W. Lowrie (ed.). Princeton University Press, Princeton, New Jersey, 1971.

Kierkegaard S. *Fear and Trembling* (1843) and *The Sickness unto Death* (1849). Princeton University Press, Princeton, New Jersey, 1954.

Knight R. *Borderline States.* Bullet. Menninger Clinic, 17:1, 1953.

Kohut H. *Forms and Transformations of Narcissism.* J Am Psychoanal Assn, Vol 14:243, 1966.

Kohut H. *Thoughts on Narcissism and Narcissistic Rage.* Psychoanal Study of the Child. 27:360, 1972.

Kolb L. C. *Modern Clinical Psychiatry.* W. B. Saunders Co, Philadelphia, 1973.

Kraepelin E. *Lectures on Clinical Psychiatry*. Bailliere, Tindall and Cox, London, 1904.

Kramer M. *Psychiatric Services and the Changing Institutional Scene, 1950–1985*. National Institute of Mental Health, Series B, #12, 1976.

Kramer M. *The Increasing Prevalence of Mental Disorders: A Pandemic Threat*, Psychiatric Qtly, 55:115, 1983.

Kramer M., Baldridge B., et al. 8th Annual Convention for the Psychophysiogical Study of Sleep. Denver, Colorado, Psychophysiology, 5:221, September, 1968.

Kringlen E., Cramer G. *Offspring of Monozygotic Twins Discordant for Schizophrenia*. Arch Gen Psychiatry, *46:873, 1989.*

Lagos J. M., Perlmutter K., et al. *Fears of the Mentally Ill, Empirical Support for the Common Man's Response*. Am J Psychiatry, 134: 1134, 1977.

Langfeldt G. *The Schizophreniform States: A Catamnestic Study Based on Individual Re-examination*. Copenhagen, Munksgaard, 1939.

Larson J. A. *Lying and its Detection*. Preface by Paul Schielder, p. XX, Patterson Smith, Montclair, New Jersey, 1969.

Lehman H. *Schizophrenia: Clinical Features*. In Comprehensive Textbook of Clinical Psychiatry, A. Freedman, et al. (eds.). The William & Wilkins Co. Baltimore, 1975.

Lewis H. B. *Shame and Guilt in Neurosis*. International Universities Press, New York, 1971.

Lidz T., Fleck S., et al. *Schizophrenia and the Family*. International Universities Press, New York, 1965.

Liem J. H. *Family Studies of Schizophrenia: An Update and Commentary*. Schizophrenia Bullet, 82, 1980.

Lipper S., Werman D. S. *Schizophrenia and Intercurrent Physical Illness: A Critical Review of the Literature.* Comprehensive Psychia try, Vol18:17, 1977.

Liskow B. I., Clayton P., et al. *Briquet's Syndrome, Hysterical Personality and the MMPI.* Am J Psychiatry, 134: 1137, 1977.

Luchins D. J., Sherwood P. M., et al. *Filicide during Psychotropic-induced Somnambulism: A case report.* Am J Psychiatry, 135:1404, 1978.

Luria A. R. *The Working Brain.* Basic Books, New York, 1973.

Mahler M. S. *A Study of the Separation-Individuation Process and its Possible Application to Borderline Phenomena in the Psychoanalytic Situation.* Psychoanal Study of the Child, 26:403, 1971.

Malcolm J. *The Impossible Profession.* The New Yorker, December 1980.

Marazzi A. S. *Pharmacodynamics of Hallucinations.* In Hallucinations, L.J. West (ed.). Gruene and Stratton, New York, 1962.

Marcel G. *The Philosophy of Existentialism* (1946). Citadel Press, Secaucus, New Jersey, 1956.

Mascaro, J. *The Bhagavad Gita*, (transl. from the Sanskrit), Penguin Books, New York, 1978.

McCord W., McCord J. *The Psychopath.* Van Nostrand, Princeton, New Jersey, 1964.

McGlashan T. H., Carpenter W. *Post Psychotic Depression in Schizophrenia.* Arch Gen Psychiatry, 33: 231, 1976.

McKay A. V. P., Iversen L. L., et al. *Increased Brain Dopamine and Dopamine Receptors in Schizophrenia.* Arch Gen Psychiatry, 39:991, 1982.

McKenna P. J., Kane J. M., et al. *Psychotic Syndromes in Epilepsy.* Am Jl Psychiatry, 142:895, 1985.

McKinnon B. L. *Post-psychotic Depression and the Need for Personal Significance.* Am J Psychiatry, 134:427, 1977.

McLean P. *Hypothalamus and Emotional Behaviour.* In The Hypothalamus, W. Haymaker & E. Anderson & E. Nauta, (eds.). Charles C. Thomas, Springfield, Ill. 1969.

Mendelson J. H., Kubzansky P. E., et al. *Physiological and Psychological Aspects of Sensory Deprivation: A Case Analysis.* In Sensory Deprivation, P. Solomon, et al. (eds.). Harvard Universities Press, Cambridge, Mass. 1965.

Menkes M., Rowe J., et al. *A 25-year Follow up Study on the Hyperkinetic Child with Minimal Brain Dysfunction.* Pediatrics, 39:393, 1967.

Menninger K., Mayman, et al. *The Vital Balance.* The Viking Press, New York, 1963.

Mora G. *History and Theoretical Trends in Psychiatry.* In Comprehensive Textbook of Psychiatry, A.M. Freedman et al. (eds.). Williams & Wilkins Co, 1975.

Morrison H. L. *Neuropsychiatry and the Forensic Psychiatrist.* The 13th Annual Meeting of the American Academy of Psychiatry and the Law, October 21, 1982.

Mosher L. R., Keith S. J. *Psychosocial Treatment: Individual, Group, Family and Community Support Approaches*, Schizophrenia Bullet, 127, 1980.

Mosher L. R. *Schizophrenia: Recent Trends.* In Comprehensive Textbook of Psychiatry, A. Freedman et al. (eds.). The Williams & Wilkins Co, Baltimore, 1975.

Mowrer O. H. *The Crisis in Psychiatry and Religion.* Van Nostrand, Princeton, New Jersey, 1961.

Mowrer O. H. *Abnormal Reactions or Actions?* Wm. C. Brown, Dubuque, Iowa, 1974.

Nasrallah H. A., Bigelow L. B., et al. *Corpus Callosum Thickness in Schizophrenia.* APA 132 Annual Meeting, Chicago, 1979.

Nestoros J. N. *Diazepam Shown to Reduce Many Schizophrenic Symptoms.* Psychiatric News, August 20, 1982.

Nicholls P., Edwards G., et al. *Alcoholics Admitted to Four Hospitals.* Quarterly Jl for the Study of Alcoholism in England, 35: 841, 1974.

Niv M. *Schizophrenia: An Existential Approach.* Am Jl Psychoanalysis, 40:43, 1980.

Niv M. *Symbols, Symptoms and Delusions: An Existential Analysis,* Am J Psychoanalysis, 41:239, 1981.

O'Connor W. A., *Some Notes on Suicide.* British Jl Med Psychology, 21:222, 1948.

O'Neal P., Robins L. N. *The Relation of Childhood Behaviour Problems to Adult Psychiatric Status: A 30 year Follow up Study of 150 Subjects.* Am J Psychiatry, 114:961, 1957.

O'Neal P., Robins L. N. *Childhood Patterns Predictive of Adult Schizophrenia: A 30 year Follow up Study.* Am J Psychiatry, 115:385, 1958.

Ortiz A., Gershon S. *The Future of Neuroleptic Pharmacology.* Jl Clin Psychiatry, 47:5 (suppl.) 3, 1986.

Paravati M. P., Wasser J., et al. *Suicide Prevention in Correctional Facilities.* 13th Annual Convention, Psychiatry and the Law, October, 1982.

Pattison E. M., Pattison M. L. *Ex-Gays: Religiously-Mediated Change in Homosexuals.* Am Jl Psychiatry, 137:12, 1980.

Pauls D. L., Towbin K. E., et al. *Gilles de La Tourette Syndrome and Obsessive-Compulsive Disorder.* Arch Gen Psychiatry, 43:1180, 1986.

Perls F. *Gestalt Therapy Verbatim.* Real People Press, Moab, Utah, 1959.

Perry J. C., Klerman G. L. *The Borderline Patient.* Arch Gen Psychiatry, 35:141, 1978.

Petursson E. S. *Comparative Addiction.* In Drug Abuse, W. Keup, (ed.). Charles C. Thomas, Springfield, Ill. 1972.

Piaget J. *Will and Action.* Bullet. Menninger Clinic, 26:138, 1962.

Piran N., Bigler E. D., et al. *Motor Laterality and Eye Dominance Suggest Unique Pattern of Cerebral Organization in Schizophrenia.* Arch Gen Psychiatry, 39:1006, 1982.

Plomin R. *Nature and Nurture*: *An Introduction to Human Behavioral Genetics.* Brooks-Cole, 1990.

Pollin W. *A Possible Genetic Factor Related to Psychosis.* Am Jl Psychiatry, 128:91, 1971.

Prien R. F., Levine J., et al. *High Dose Trifluoperazine Therapy in Chronic Schizophrenia.* Am Jl Psychiatry, 126:305, 1969.

Procci W. R. *Schizo-Affective Psychosis: Fact or Fiction? A Survey of the Literature.* Arch Gen Psychiatry, 33:1167, 1976.

Prosen M., Clark D. C., et al. *Guilt and Conscience in Major Depressive Disorders.* Am J Psychiatry, 140:7, 1983.

Rada R. T., James W. *Urethral Insertion of Foreign Bodies.* Arch Gen Psychiatry, 39:423, 1982.

Reid J. E., Inbau F. E. *Truth and Deception: The Polygraph Technique.* The Williams & Wilkins Co, Baltimore, 1977.

Ressler R. K., Burgess A. W., et al. *Rape and Rape-Murder: One Offender and Twelve Victims.* Am J Psychiatry,140:1, 1983.

Reynolds D. K. *Flowing Bridges—Quiet Waters: Japanese Psychotherapies Morita and Naikan.* State University of New York Press, New York, 1989.

Reynolds G. P. *Increased Concentrations and Lateral Assymmetry of Amygdala Dopamine in Schizophrenia.* Nature, 305:527, 1983.

Robins L. N. *Deviant Children Grown Up.* The Williams & Wilkins Co, Baltimore, 1966.

Robins L. N., Helzer J. E., et al. *Lifetime Prevalence of Specific Psychiatric Disorders in Three Sites.* Arch Gen Psychiatry, 41: 949, 1984.

Robins L. N. *Sturdy Childhood Predictors of Adult Anti-Social Behaviour.* Psychological Medicine, 8:611, 1978.

Rodin E. A. *The Reality of Death Experiences: A Personal Perspective.* J Nerv Ment Dis, 168:259, 1980.

Rogler L. L, Hollingshead A. B. *Trapped Families and Schizophrenia.* John Wiley and Sons, New York, 1965.

Rosenberg S. T., Tucker G. *Verbal Behavior and Schizophrenia.* Arch Gen Psychiatry, 36:1331, 1979.

Rosenheck R. *Malignant Post-Vietnam Stress Syndrome.* Am J Orthopsychiatry, 55:166, 1985.

Rosenthal D., Wender P., et al. *Parent-Child Relationships and Psychopathological Disorder in the Child.* Arch Gen Psychiatry, 32: 466, 1975.

Rosenthal D., Wender P., et al. *Schizophrenics' Offspring Reared in Adoptive Homes.* In The Transmission of Schizophrenia, Pergamon Press, Oxford, 1968.

Rosenthal D., Wender P., et al. *The Adopted-away Offspring of Schizophrenics.* Am J Psychiatry, 128:307, 1971.

Roth S. *The Seemingly Ubiquitous Depression Following Acute Schizophrenic Episodes: A Neglected Area Of Clinical Discussion.* Am J Psychiatry, 127:51, 1970.

Rounsaville B. J., Goodell H., et al. *Heterogeneity of Psychiatric Diagnosis in Treated Opiate Addicts.* Arch Gen Psychiatry, 39: 161, 1982.

Rounsaville B. J., Weissman M. M., et al. *Diagnosis and Symptoms of Depression in Opiate Addicts.* Arch Gen Psychiatry, 39:151, 1982.

Rozanski A., Bairey C. N., et al. *Mental Stress and the Induction of Silent Cardiac Ischemia in Patients with Coronary Heart Disease.* New Eng J Medicine, 318: 1005, 1988.

Saltzman L., Thaler F. H. *Obsessive-Compulsive Disorders: A Review of the Literature.* Am J Psychiatry, 138:286, 1981.

Sartorius N., Jablensky A., et al. *Two-Year Follow-Up of the Patients Included in the WHO International Pilot Study of Schizophrenia.* Psychological Medicine, 7:529, 1977.

Sartre J.-P. *L'Existentialisme est un Humanisme.* Nagel, Paris, 1946.

Sartre J.-P. *Existentialism and Human Emotions.* Philosophical Library, New York, 1957.

Sartre J.-P. *Self-deception,* In Existentialism from Dostoyevsky to Sartre, W. Kaufman (ed.). The World Publishing Co. Cleveland, Ohio, 1969.

Sathananthan G., Angrist B. M., et al. *Response Threshold to L-Dopa in Psychiatric Patients.* Biological Psychiatry, 7:2-139, 1973.

Satterfield J. H., Hoppe C. M., et al. *A Prospective Study of Delinquency in 110 Adolescent Boys with Attention Deficit Disorder and 88 Normal Adolescent Boys.* Am J Psychiatry, 139:795, 1982.

Scheibel M. E., and Scheibel A. B. *Hallucinations and the Brain Stem Reticular Core.* In Hallucinations, L.J. West (ed.). Grune and Stratton, New York, 1962.

Schneider K. *Clinical Psychopathology.* Grune and Stratton, New York, 1959.

Schultes R. E. *The Utilization of Hallucinogens in Primitive Societies—Use, Misuse or Abuse?* In Drug Abuse, W. Keup, (ed.). Charles C. Thomas, Springfield, Ill. 1972.

Séchehaye M. A. *Journal of a Schizophrenic*, International Universities Press, New York, 1952 (and Paris, 1950).

Semrad E. V., Zaslow S. L. *Assisting Psychotic Patients to Recompensate.* Ment Hosp, 15 (7): 361, 1964.

Shapiro D. H. *Overview: Physiological Comparison of Meditation with other Self-Control Strategies.* Am J Psychiatry, 139:267, 1982.

Shlien J. M. *A Case History with Commentary.* In Morality and Mental Health, O.H. Mowrer (ed.). Rand McNally, Chicago, 1967.

Shoeps H. *The Religions of Mankind.* Doubleday & Co, Garden City, New York, 1968.

Shurley J. T. *Hallucinations in Sensory Deprivation and Sleep Deprivation.* In Hallucinations, L.J. West (ed.). Grune and Stratton, New York, 1962.

Singer M. T, and Wynne L. C. *Thought Disorder and Family Relations of Schizophrenics.* Arch Gen Psychiatry, 12:187, 1965.

Slater E., Cowie V. *The Genetics of Mental Disorders.* Oxford University Press, London, 1971.

Snyder S. H. *Amphetamine Psychosis—A Model Schizophrenia Mediated by Catecholamines.* Am J Psychiatry, 130:61, 1973.

Snyder S. H., Taylor K. M., et al. *The Role of Dopamine in Behavioural Regulation and the Action of Psychotropic Drugs.* Am J Psychiatry, 127:117, 1970.

Snyder S. H. *Dopamine and Schizophrenia.* Psychiatric Annals, 6:53, 1976.

Snyder S. H. *The Dopamine Hypothesis of Schizophrenia: Focus on the Dopamine Receptor.* Am Jl Psychiatry, 133:197, 1976.

Socarides C. W., Bieber I., et al. *Homosexuality in the Male: A Report of a Psychiatric Study Group*. Int Jl Psychiatry, 460, December, 1973.

Spitz R. A. *Hospitalism: A Follow-up Report*. The Psychoanalytic Study of the Child. 2:113, 1946.

Spohn H. E., Lacoursiere R. B., et al. *Phenothiazine Effects on Psychological and Psychophysiological Dysfunction in Chronic Schizophrenics*. Arch Gen Psychiatry, 34:633, 1977.

Stein L., Wise, C. D. *Possible Etiology of Schizophrenia: Progressive Damage to Noradrenergic Reward System by 6-hydroxy-dopamine*. Science, 171:1032, 1971.

Stekel W. *Disorders of the Instincts and the Emotions*. Liveright, U.S.A., 1929.

Stern M. *Office Management of Organic Mental Syndromes*. Psychiatric Annals, 12:618, 1982.

Sternberg D. E., Van Kammen D. P., et al. *CSF Dopamine beta-Hydroxylase in Schizophrenia*. Arch Gen Psychiatry, 1983.

Stevens J. R. *Neuropathology of Schizophrenia*. Arch Gen Psychiatry, 39: 1131, 1982.

Stevens J. R. *Psychiatric Aspects of Epilepsy*. Jl Clin Psychiatry, 49:4,(Suppl), 1988.

Stoller R. J., Herdt G. H. *Theories of Origins of Male Homosexuality*. Arch Gen Psychiatry, 42: 399, 1985.

Stone M. H. *Drug-related Schizophrenic Syndromes*. International Jl Psychiatry 11: 391, 1973.

Sullivan H. S. *Schizophrenia as a Human Process*. W.W. Norton & Co., New York, 1962.

Sullivan H.S. *The Interpersonal Theory of Schizophrenia*. W.W. Norton & Co., New York, 1963.

Terzian H., Dulle-Ore G. *Syndrome of Kluver and Bucy Reproduced in Man by Bilateral Removal of the Temporal Lobes.* Neurology, 5-373, 1955.

Thomas A., Chess S., et al. *Temperament and Behavior Disorders in Children.* New York University Press, New York, 1968.

Tournier P. *Guilt and Grace.* Harper & Row, New York, 1962.

Tsuang M. T., Simpson J. C., et al. *Subtypes of Drug Abuse with Psychosis.* Arch Gen Psychiatry, 39: 141, 1982.

Twemlov S. W., Gabbard G. O., et al. *The Out-of-the-Body Experience: A Phenomenological Typology Based on Questionnaire Responses.* Am J Psychiatry, 139:450, 1982.

Vaillant G. *Prospective Prediction of Schizophrenic Remission.* Arch Gen Psychiatry, 11:509, 1964.

Vaillant G. *The Prediction of Recovery in Schizophrenia.* J Nerv Ment Dis 135:534, 1962.

Vaillant G. S., Milofsky E. S. *Natural History of Male Alcoholism.* Arch Gen Psychiatry, 39:127, 1982.

Van Dusen W. *The Presence of Other Worlds.* Harper & Row, New York, 1974.

Vaughn C. E., Leff J. P. *The Influences of Family and Social Factors on the Course of Psychiatric Illness.* Brit Jl Psychiatry, 129: 125, 1976.

Von Knorring A-L., Bohman M., et al. *Early Life Experience and Psychiatric Disorders: An Adoptee Study.* Acta Psych Scand, 65:283, 1982.

Walsh R. *Precipitation of Acute Psychotic Episodes by Intensive Meditation in Individuals with a History of Schizophrenia.* Am Jl Psychiatry, 136: 8, 1979.

Watt N. F. *Patterns of Childhood Social Development in Adult Schizophrenics.* Arch Gen Psychiatry, 35:160, 1978.

Watt N. F., Storolow R. D., et al. *School Adjustment and Behavior of Children Hospitalized for Schizophrenia as Adults.* Am Jl Orthopsychiatry, 40: 637, 1970.

Weinberger D. R. *Structural Brain Abnormalities in Schizophrenia.* 132 APA Annual meeting, Chicago, 1979.

Weiner D. B. *The Apprenticeship of Philip Pinel: A New Document. Observations of Citizen Pussin on the Insane.* Am Jl Psychiatry, 136:9, 1979.

Weinstein E. A. *Relationship Between Delusions and Hallucinations in Brain Disease,* In Origins and Mechanisms of Hallucinations, W. Keup (ed.). Plenum Press, New York–London, 1970.

Wender P., Rosenthal D., et al. *Schizophrenics' Adopting Parents: Psychiatric Status,* Arch Gen Psychiatry, 34:777, 1977.

Wender P. H. *Borderline Schizophrenia.* Medical World News, 17:23, 1976.

Wender P. H., Rosenthal D., et al. *Crossfostering, A Research Strategy for Clarifying the Role of Genetic and Experiential Factors in the Etiology of Schizophrenia.* Arch Gen Psychiatry, 30:121, 1974.

West L. J. *A General Theory of Hallucinations and Dreams.* In Hallucinations, L. J. West, (ed.). Grune and Stratton, New York, 1962

Westermeyer J., Wintrob R. *"Folk" Criteria for the Diagnosis of Mental Illness in Rural Laos: On Being Insane in Sane Places.* Am J Psychiatry, 136:755, 1979.

Wild C. M., Shapiro L. N., et al. *Communication Patterns and Role Structure in Families of Male Schizophrenics.* Arch Gen Psychiatry, 34:58, 1977.

Wise C. D., Stein L. *Dopamine beta-Hydroxylase Deficits in the Brains of Schizophrenic Patients.* Science, 181:344, 1973.

Wolpe J. *The Practice of Behavior Therapy.* Pergamon Press, New York, 1982.

Woodruff R. A., Clayton P. J., et al. *Hysteria: Studies of Diagnosis, Outcome and Prevalence.* J Am Med Assn, 215:425, 1971.

Woods B. T., Wolf J. *A Reconsideration of the Relation of Ventricular Enlargement to Duration of Illness in Schizophrenia.* Am Jl Psychiatry, 140:12, 1983.

Yalom I. D. *The Theory and Practice of Group Psychotherapy.* Basic Books, New York, 1965.

Zitrin A., Hardesty, A. S., et al. *Crime and Violence among Mental Patients.* Am J Psychiatry, 133:2, 1976.

Zuckerman M. *Hallucinations, Reported Sensations and Images.* In Sensory Deprivation: Fifteen Years of Research, J. P. Zubek (ed.). Appleton Century Crafts, New York, 1969.

Zuckerman M. *Reported Sensations and Hallucinations in Sensory Deprivation.* In Origins and Mechanisms of Hallucinations, W. Keup (ed.). Plenum Press, New York–London, 1970.

Subject Index

A

Abulia (apathetic withdrawal), 287

achievement, 38, 89, 156, 188, 413; lack in, 346, 375, 376

Acrophobia, 152

actions, 35, 36; and emotions, 42; instead of words, 27, 28; more powerful in determining feeling states 166-7; consequences of, 263

acute confusional psychoses, 285

acute-onset psychoses, 262

acute schizophrenic deliria, 284-5

acute turmoil schizophrenias, 285

addict's lifestyle, 374

addictions, 149-50, 188

adrenaline (epinephrine), 71, 77, 240

adverse reality, 111-2

affect, 125, 287; affective state of schizophrenics, 176

affect-toxin, 201, 242, 248, 281, 376

agape, 214

Agitated Depression, 155

Agoraphobia, 152, 405

AIDS, 183, 409

aimless wandering, 249, 271

"alarm" signals, 337

Alcohol Abuse, **Alcoholism**, 356-62; and crime, recidivism and other mental illnesses, 357, 358, 377; damage to body soul, and mind, 358; prevalence of, 357-8

alcoholic amnesia, 357

Alcoholic Deterioration, 358

Alcoholic Hallucinosis, 358, 359

istics, 323; and substance abuse, 363-4, 365, 374-5, 377

Crime and Punishment, example of a paranoid schizophrenia, 26; 169-70

criminality and mental illness, 323

criminals, 126, 215-6, 251-2, 265, 336, 338

cross-cultural: psychoses, 265; similarity in the experience of Hell, 225

"cross fostering" method, 104

CT (Computerized Tomography) 67-9, 79

cults, 244-5

cynicism, 167-8

D

dangerous potential of the mentally ill, 275-6

Daseinanalyse, 38-9

DBH (dopamine-beta-hydroxylase), 76-77

death: concern with, 42, 236, 287; gradual, 316

deception, 2-3, 36, 123, 171-4; consequences of, 51; and double vision, 135; parental deception and hypocrisy, 108; intention to deceive, 3; persistent lying, 102; in schizophrenia, 55; stressful, 174

defiance, 89, 101, 103; family reaction to defiant child, 103-5

delusional ideas, 226; serve as justification, 225, 233; versus delusions proper, 225-6; justificatory, 126;

delusions, 27, 133-6; interpretation guidelines, 409-10; contents of, 4, 133; in denial of guilt, 129-30; function of, 133; proper, 226-7; persecutory, 267; reversible, 134; reveal source of guilt, 114

Dementia praecox, 70, 211; antecedents of, 191

denial of feelings, 176

Dependent Personality Disorder, 156-7, 327

depression: anaclitic, 107; after confession, 410-11; and subjective dread, 122; and norepinephrine, 76; in schizophrenia augurs a better prognosis, 286-9; in narcissism and borderline states, 350; and opiate addicts, 375; prevalence of, 357

Depression, Endogenous, 157-8, 399 *See* **Involutional Melancholia**, *See also* **Major Depression** and **Reactive Neurotic Depression**

derailing, 259

despair, 288-9

destiny, forged by character, 263; reading the "signs" of one's, 41

destructive rage, 161

devaluing others, 351

deviancy, 326

devil, in schizophrenia, 16-7; 222-3

discipline, 331-2, 355

Name Index

A

Adler A. 160, 358
Angrist B. 73
Aristotle 218, 250, 257

B

Baldessarini RJ. 23, 395
Beauvoir, S. de 36
Becker E. 161
Beckett S. 350
Beethoven L. van. 297
Bertalanffy L. von 9
Bini L. 399
Binswanger L. 37-38
Blake W. 8
Boffey PM. ix
Bradburn N. 298
Brentano F. 21, 39
Bucy P.C. 58

C

Camus A. 32, 37, 350
Carlyle T. 221, 222

C

Cerletti U. 399
Charcot, J-M. 127
Chiarugi V. 14

D

Dante A. 317
Dostoyevsky FM. 9, 28, 29, 36, 37, 66, 118, 157, 169, 190, 213, 222, 231, 236, 251, 278, 356

E

Eliot TS. ix
Erasmus 158
Erikson E. 20
Ey H. 15, 267
Esquirol J-E. 187, 399

F

Ferenczi S. 128, 182
Fromm E. 20

G

Galen 400
Gall FG. 14

Give this Intriguing Book to Your Friends and Colleagues

ORDER FORM

YES, I want ____ copies of *Reason in Madness* at $19.95 each, plus $3 shipping per book (New York residents please add $1.65 state sales tax per book). Canadian orders must be accompanied by a postal money order in U.S. funds. Allow 15 days for delivery.

My check or money order for $_____ is enclosed.

Name _____ Phone _____

Organization _____

Address _____

City/State/Zip _____

Please make your check or money order payable and return to:

EVER Publishing
900 West 190th Street
New York, NY 10040

14 BOSCH A Pastredes
FANTASTIC gogeL Lif